TEEN SEY CHHEY

Rewinding Bollywood

Bobby Ghatak

Become
Shakespeare
.com

ISBN - 978-81-947726-8-2

In Memory

To my late parents, Dilip 'Bishu' Ghatak & Pratima Ghatak.

Dedication

I thank my Lord 'Bajrangbali. He has given me more than I deserve.

Through His blessings, I dedicate this book to all movie buffs, cinephiles, movie maniacs and those multitudes whose footprints decide the fate of a Friday.

Especially, to all those travelling salesmen like me who battle market forces during the day and spend their lonely nights in the comforting bosom of a cinema-hall.

About Author

Bobby Ghatak is a hyperbole movie freak and this is his first book on Bollywood. He works for the 'Delta Group', lives in Bangalore with his family and eagerly awaits your comments at: bobbyghatak@hotmail.com

Contents

Contents

Contents

Prologue

Circa 1948:

A feel of happiness enveloped the young resurgent country. Even though the aftermath was bloodied by riots, the nation had indeed achieved freedom through non-violence. The national flag had the symbol of Truth emblazoned on it. People of this free country wanted to cast away those memories of blood and hatred which happened not in a distant past. Just a couple of years back after Jinnah's hard cuts in the form of 'Direct Action' culminated in to hopelessness where, despair raised it's ugly forms through riots, rape and loot. The country was dismembered and was barely picking up torn threads when she had to grapple with twin shocks inflicted in quick succession: The assassination of the Mahatma and the shock of a military conflict over Kashmir. While Sardar Patel set about resolving the issue of borders with menacing neighbours and warding off avaricious designs of the Princely states, on the other side, the task of nation building was taken up earnestly by Jawaharlal Nehru. Slavery, a bitter memory, was consigned to the past. India was free and Pandit Nehru and his team set about in fulfilling their dream of making India self reliant. Her rich resources would be put to good use to make her prosperous.The commissioning of the huge Bhakra Nangal dam was a big step in feeding her teeming millions. The path to regain confidence was taken up by her young leaders to set up a self reliant India and thus began an era of hope.

Fields were ploughed with renewed vigour, mills hummed at a frenetic pace and the makers of cinema set about caressing the minds of the wounded through films based on legends and myths; like the excitement in watching Lord Ram symbolizing victory of truth in 'Maryada Ram'; the power of obedience and subservience in 'Jai Hanuman' where Hanuman is shown squatting triumphantly on miles of his own tail coiled to rise like a tower, dwarfing the arrogant Ravana. Grieving socio stories based on untouchability, like 'Achut Kanya', the power of persistence in 'Savitri' or the upholding of truth in 'Raja Harishchandra' not only entertained but also kept their hopes soaring.

Those days equal space was shared by the likes of Bharat Bhushan, Bhagwan Dada, Prem Adib, Mahipal, Trilok Kapoor & Sohrab Modi. Many came and many went, few flourished while most fell. Ashok Kumar Ganguly, an aspirant who came to Bombay in the early 40's became a known name with 'Achut Kanya'. Two years later he became a big star with 'Kismet', a film bankrolled by 'Bombay Talkies' which was owned by a man with deep pockets called Himanshu Rai & his actress-wife Devika Rani. From the aftermath of partition emerged the three Anand brothers: Chetan, Dev and Vijay. From that same fissure also appeared Prithviraj Kapoor and his famous progeny of Raj, Shammi & Shashi. Blessed with a broad frame, deep voice and distinct Aryan features, Prithviraj became a natural choice to essay roles of mythical conquerors and fabled lovers. Social and historical dramas like 'Rustom-Sohrab' 'Sikandar' and 'Alam Ara' made him a natural choice. Cinema acquired a sense of more relevance and interest with the advent of three young men; Dilip Kumar who was introduced by Devika Rani, Dev Anand brought in by a group of film makers who owned 'Prabhat Studios' & Raj Kapoor, who got his break with film maker Kidar Sharma. The three men swiftly scaled up and came to be known as 'The Big Three'.

This triumvirate held sway from 1950's until the rollicking 60's. They were the ones whom the nation looked up to. The serious Dilip Kumar whose acting reached legendary proportions compelling writers to pen scripts befitting his grasp on the medium. Dev Anand, the handsome lover who easily made beautiful women fall in love with him, while Raj Kapoor endeared himself to the old and young alike with his touching performances as an underdog or a destitute…

The joy of watching films was greatly enhanced by the presence of these three. Foremost being Dilip Kumar. Unknown to many, Dilip's origins were rooted in Peshawar and his original name was Yusuf Khan. He not only knew Urdu but was also educated in the English medium. Belonging to a family of fruit merchants and he himself having done a short stint as a canteen contractor, his career was chequered from the beginning itself. Destiny led him to the doors of 'Bombay Talkies' and a chance encounter with the owner's wife and actress, Devika Rani. She made him give a screen test and also gave him a 'hindoo' name- Dilip. That is how, from a studio hand he graduated into bagging the leading man's role in 'Bombay Talkies' production 'Jwar Bhata'. This was a mediocre success but Dilip was noticed. The handsome Dilip wasted no time and soon followed up his noticeable appearance with two hits. They were 'Jugnu' where Noorjehan, the reigning songstress, played the protagonist's role and 'Shaheed' where he essayed the title role and was paired with Kamini Kaushal. Both were successful. Both were different.

'Jugnu' was a love story where rich and poor are pitted against each other leading to heartbreak & sacrifices. Released just two months before independence it became the biggest hit that year. 'Shaheed' was based on an unknown revolutionary whose story line resembled the life of Bhagat Singh. The film struck a chord and was a huge success.

However, Noor Jahan and her producer husband went off to Pakistan. She was quickly replaced by the upcoming Lata Mangeshkar.

Dev Anand came in just a year before independence in a film 'Hum Ek Hain'produced by a banner called 'Prabhat Pictures. Soon Raj Kapoor too came in the same year in 'Neel Kamal' opposite Madhubala. While Dilip and Dev Anand were rank outsiders, Raj Kapoor had a shade of pedigree by being the son of Prithviraj Kapoor. Dev Anand by now a small time hero impressed Ashok Kumar (Ashok was not only a big star but also one of the owner's of 'Filmistan' studios which was a breakaway mould of 'Bombay Talkies') to cast him in a film called 'Ziddi. This was the film that elevated Dev Anand to a new level promptly placing him alongside Dilip Kumar. In due course Dev 'the Debonair' turned a film producer and set up his own banner along with his brothers Chetan and Vijay.

They called it 'Navketan'. His first film was 'Afsar' directed by his older brother Chetan Anand but the second was directed by a friend from his struggling days whose name was Guru Dutt. The film was 'Baazi'. Its success fortified his chances to face the juggernaut of Dilip Kumar.

Raj Kapoor, the prodigious young lad of twenty three had his eyes set towards a higher plane. He learnt the ropes of film making under the tutelage of director Amiya Chakravarty and in a year's time he started his own production house called 'R.K.Films'. While his colleagues merely opened a banner which in reality was a business offshoot to help them earn more money, Raj Kapoor went many steps further to set up a brick-mortar factory, where he wove his dreams, and called it 'R.K.Studios'.That same year he turned director wih a film called 'Aag' where he was paired with Nargis. 'Aag'also had his real life brother- in- law Premnath in the role of his friend. It would turn out to be the cusp in the blooming of Raj-Nargis as a 'star pair'. 'Aag' was an average performer but this did not dampen his passion. In fact, his maiden attempt helped him hone his skills to come out with his next. This was called 'Barsaat' and he was paired, again, with Nargis, Prem Nath and new actress, Nimmi. This film turned out to be his first success as a film maker.

Dilip Kumar's 'Jogan' and 'Babul' though successful still had him playing meek roles but that year it was Raj Kapoor and his R.K.Productions that towered with his magnum opus 'Awara'(The Vagabond)

Blue Eyed Vagabond

A story of a destitute boy born of an aristocratic family, destined to live life in a slum and gradually trained to be a thief. 'Awara' was built on the background of a pertinent topic: Does lineage & worthiness of a father decide the fate of his child? It puts to doubt one of society's commandment that a "worthy man begets a worthy son" and vindicates the reality of 'circumstances determining a man's destiny'.

Raghunath (Prithviraj Kapoor) is a lawyer of repute with immense social stature. He dotes on his wife (Leela Chitnis), lives in a large house and loves his work. He also rigidly believes that a man is known by his parental lineage. One day his contentment as a family man is shattered by the revenge wreaked by a bandit, Jagga (actor K.N.Singh). Earlier Jagga was sent to prison for a crime but claims that he being born and bred in a family of dacoits greatly influenced the Judge in being biased towards him. The bandit retaliates by abducting the lawyer's wife to make him feel slighted. Upon knowing that the wife is pregnant he sends her back with a long term plan of tormenting his prey. Tongues wag, questioning the fatherhood of the impending pregnancy. Finally, Raghunath blinded by the taunts of his relatives and his own mind pierced with doubt, mercilessly throws out his wife on the streets to fend for herself. She gives birth to a boy who grows up to be the young Raju. The boy bears the brunt of being ridiculed due to unknown whereabouts of his father for which, is generally ostracized by all whom he meets in society. His only moments of being loved are with his heartbroken mother and his bubbly classmate Rita. But poverty forces Raju to leave school and find work as a shoe shine boy. Jagga who by now has metamorphosed into the local goon takes him under his wing and under his influence the innocent son of a meritorious judge grows up to be a thief-par-excellence. Raju is now trapped under Jagga's influence and is gradually in awe of him.

The Lawyer meanwhile has moved away from his ancestral house. Determined to leave behind his past with bitter memories he comes to the city of Bombay. The Judge, lives in an opulent mansion and is now the guardian of his friend's daughter, the little Rita who has grown in to a beautiful lawyer (Nargis).

Raju and Rita meet again, fall in love and towards the end he learns the truth of Jagga being the main perpetrator of the misery brought upon his mother. He kills Jagga and in a fit of rage tries to kill his father and is sent to stand trial. Rita fights out the case on his behalf while Raju vindicates himself in a long,lengthy sermon.

Scenes & Songs:

- Rolling of credits: a boy under a lamp post, playing with a mongrel.

- Farmers singing aloud to the boatmen across *"Naiyaan teri Majhdaar...hoshiyaar...hoshiyaar.."*.A sense of foreboding to the lawyer's wife that this is a lull before a storm........

- Raju (Raj Kapoor), flush with his earnings from thievery and having got a pat from Jagga, enters the night club 'James Dean' style to the crooning of *'Ek do teen aaja mausam hai rangeen'* by Cuckoo, an actress who in those times, excelled in dancing roles. There is a special effect too by sound recordist Rajoo Katrak, where in between the music, one stanza sounds low and the din of the laughing men in the bar is increased.

- Raju playing with street urchins reliving his child hood: lifting a naked child in his arms, looking into his eyes and singing *'duniya main teri teer ya takdeer ka maara hoon....awaara hoon.'*

- The mesmeric nine minute dream sequence song *'Ghar Aaya mera pardesi'*-the song and dance is more of a ballet. The effort and labor is seen in its grandeur.

- Radhu Karmarkar's hold of his medium by capturing of a life- like moon on the sets of a film studio in the song *'dum bhar jo udhar mooh ...."*

- Rita calls Raju a 'junglee' and Raju in reply strikes a slap across her face only to be begged for an encore by being called a 'junglee' again ....a faint hint of sado-masochism!

'Awara' translated means a vagabond. A term loosely used to depict a person who is a wastrel, a failure. 'Awara' taken philosophically could also mean a person in search of truth. Many parallels can be drawn. Like from the Ramayana; Justice Raghunath's wife & Ram's consort Sita meet a similar fate. Another curious similarity is from Charles Dickens 'Oliver Twist', where the orphaned boy is being taught the art of stealing by the crafty Fagin, played here by K.N.Singh. But such inspirations are excusable.

This movie was in a way the arch of Hindi cinema. It saw the rise of a very young prodigy named Raj Kapoor. Besides pumping in equity he also infused his soul into his movies. He looked up to woman as strong characters and loved to give them rivettingly definitive roles. His extremely handsome looks, light-eyes (actually ultra blue as realized in color films later) make it difficult to believe that such a man could be poor, a thief, a rustic, anything but 'awara'. The character of 'Raju' became an iconic symbol and 'Awaara' had the distinction of being truly the first bollywood film to be an equally big hit away from the country. Unfortunately, at the time of its release, 'Filmfare,' the only leading film magazine of those times had not conceived its platform for awarding excellence.

Historicals and mythologicals still could make their presence felt. Films like 'Jai Shanker', 'Sri Ram Avatar' all by- products of Dadasaheb Phalke's 'Krishna Leela' led to many similarly styled; but this cult was now down to a trickle. Mythologcals faded away but historicals continued to blossom. Prominent in that year was 'Anarkali' made by the Ashok Kumar-

Shashadhar Mukherjee owned 'Filmistan 'studios in 1953. Pradip Kumar & Bina Rai played the doomed lovers. Pradip Kumar, an accomplished actor who had gradually begun to acquire a regal bearing in his demeanour making him the natural choice in playing roles of prince and kings. 'Anarkali' was more focused on the love between the prince and the courtesan and was a far cry from its gigantic cousin who was to emerge seven years later. Even though 'Anarkali' was a success, another veteran film maker Sohrab Mody, whose forte lay in making historicals failed with his Magnum opus 'Jhansi Ki Rani'.

The same year,Dilip Kumar marched yet ahead with 'Shikast'. As Raj Kapoor was still savouring the success of 'Awara' which rippled away in to distant Russia, his younger sibling Shammi Kapoor was reeling from yet another failure. His third release called 'Laila Majnu' with Nutan had just flopped. Based on the legendary love ballad, Nutan played the role of 'Laila'. She was an excellent actress though casting her as the ethereal beauty was stretching her too far! But Shammi's moment would come in just a few years.

The stock of Dilip Kumar and Dev Anand rose further with two releases called 'Amar' & 'Taxi driver'. 'Amar' had the beautiful Madhubala while 'Taxi Driver' had the petite Kalpana Kartik. The daily interactions of romancing beautiful women certainly took their toll on leading men sparing not even the Big3. While Dev Anand had shrugged off his failed romance with the voluptuous Suraiya by marrying Kalpana Kartik, both Dilip and Madhubala remained muted about their visible attraction for each other. But it was Raj Kapoor who threw caution to the winds and remained unabashadely linked to Nargis. They were confirmed as a couple by the magazines of their times. He also immortalised their relationship by basing the emblem of his production house with a classic love lorn pose from 'Barsaat'.

Amongst the Three, while Dev Anand had acquired the image of a debonair lover boy, and Raj Kapoor the eternal 'underdog, it was Dilip Kumar who could not be ensnared within the shackles of any image. His 'Kohinoor', a period film set in distant lands where a kingdom is ruled by a young prince,surrounded by ministers with their evil eye on the throne and a haughty princess turned damsel in distress, were all pleasant departures from his tragically inclined films. Films like 'Azaad' and 'Uran Khatola' further established his versatility.

As a rich and successful producer-director with his glory reverberating across to Russia, Raj Kapoor had indeed cemented himself as being a part of the triumvirate. His empathy for the underdogs in society took the form of two large hearted films which he produced and these endeared themselves to the people by their simplicity. Those films were 'Boot Polish' and 'Jagte Raho'.

JAGTE RAHO

An unknown peasant, uprooted by a failing agrarian system in his village, meanders towards a city. Loitering aimlessly, the hungry and thirsty man stumbles inside an apartment complex to quench his thirst from a leaking tap. This innocuous act triggers an alarm by the watchman and then his ordeal begins. The panic stricken man starts scampering away to save himself. Darkness helps him to hide in some unlit corner but the scared man has to keep moving and remain unseen for which out of sheer fright he has to sneak in to several flats and in each, he watches all sort of sordid happenings. Every house is a stage for committing dark deeds. In one, a man hopes to win a fortune from betting at races by pawning his wife's jewels. In another, a rich man (actor Motilal) shuns home so as to spend time at the'kotha'; in fact he had just crossed his path a couple of hours ago, a few streets away, where the rich man, drunk, is condoning his drunken antics in *'zindagi khwab hain khwab mein jhooth kya aur bhala sach hain kya"*. In one of the larger flats resides a respected businessman who is slyly printing counterfeit notes in one of his many rooms. Some more, where a priest is out to swindle gullible devotes with a pack of lies.Unaware of the many misdeeds taking place in their own world, the residents cobble up an in-house patrol regiment where each one takes it upon himself to nab this invisible 'chor'. The peasant has to hide inside apartments, under beds and even wriggle inside an empty drum. Tying a cloth around his head he tries blending into a group of sanguine Sikhs who roll up a classic 'bhangra' whose lyrics spell out the bountiful injustice abounding all around:

"haq dooje da maar maar key baney log amir log kehndey rabdi maya mein kehnda anyaay tey ki mein jooth boleya!"

(people trample the rights of each other and gain wealth. You may say its fate but I call it oppression)

The grim events end with the counterfeit maker to be nabbed and all wake up to the futility of their thoughts. As dawn breaks and the innocent peasant(also nameless) is let off, his thirst still unquenched, he timidly approaches a woman (Nargis) washing the steps of a nearby temple. As he bends low, she smilingly tilts her pot letting the cool water quench away his thirst. As the background bursts forth with the eloquent song *'Jago re jago re jag duniya jaage'* the woman walks away. Figuratively, after this shot, Nargis walked out of the 'Showman's life forever.

Landless

Zameen to apni maa hoti hain' -Shambhu Mahato

Both 'Jagte Raho' and' Boot Polish', were telling representations of the potholes accruing on the social fabric.

But a man whose forte lay in potraying social issues was an immigrant by the name of Bimal Roy. He migrated from Calcutta where he was in the rolls of New Theatres, a prosperous film company of the nineteen-fifties. He had begun his career as a cameraman on the sets of P.C.Barua's 'Devdas' which starred K.L.Saigal: An actor known more for his singing!

After the decline of New Theatres he had to search for greener pastures and this led him to Bombay, where he set up a core team comprising of Hrishikesh Mukerjee, a qualified film editor, Asit Sen, who was an assistant director and musician Salil Chaudhary. No sooner after setting up office in Bombay the man along with his team crafted the much feted 'Do Bigha Zamin'.

Much before the advent of smugglers, terrorists & corrupt politicians, the nation had following factors as 'villain': they were 'zamindars' or the land owners; money lenders; natural elements in the form of a failed monsoon or a ravaging flood; malaise of the caste system; evil designs of family members.

'Do Bigha Zameen' had two of the above; a failed monsoon and a merciless zamindar.

The film's detailed insight touchingly portrayed the poverty prevailing in India's villages and how a failed weather and man's greed can destroy families. This fact is relevant even in today's times.The misery upon Shambhu Mahato (Balraj Sahni) is cast by a wily zamindar(played by actor Murad) who is eyeing his small piece of land. He offers him a price which Shambhu refuses so in order to evict him he rakes up some old mortgage loan. Badly hit by the occurrence of two consecutive famines, Shambhu the peasant, his family and their small piece of land are now at the mercy of this 'Zamindar'. To repay this doctored mortgage, the peasant migrates to the city of Calcutta. No home, no hearth, the man and his son loiter as destitutes in a city teeming with people. Finally, finding a place to dwell and some work by plying a hand-pulled rickshaw,Shambhu takes in many hardships. He works hard,pulls his rickshaw for long hours but can barely arrange enough food to fill their bellies. Soon his son falls sick. Money is hard to come by, and one day, while being egged on to a race by a pair of sparring lovers who promise him extra fare, he ends up crashing his rickshaw. Very soon his wife Paro (Nirupa Roy) suffers an accident which eats away his savings he has been collecting to save his land. When they return back to their village, they find a factory standing on it! The three stare at the gigantic structure with its chimney sending out black smoke; which is a metaphor of their aspirations blowing away. They turn back and start walking, whether to slog under a landlord or do they go back to the city of hand-pulled rickshaws is not clear. Bimal Roy, dissected the two masterfully; a nondescript village in pan India and a city which was the epitome of wealth and infamously known for its inhabitants co existing in a web of inequalities; one of the scene begins with the camera panning neon-lighted hoardings of 'Polar' fans, 'Players'cigarettes, and 'K.C.Das'sweet-meats, which are an obvious reference to symbols of the privileged, and then moves on to a migrant worker huddled with his fellow buddies beside a shanty, regaling them with a song that addresses God with a long questionnaire: *'Ajab tori duniya kadam kadam dekhi bhool bhulaiya.'*(O lord, your world is strange, seems to be an unending labyrinth)

Bimal Roy's technique impressed not only the audience of the fifties but even film makers of later generations. In fact, the song *"matwala sawan'* is a direct influence on the inhabitants of the famine affected village of 'Bhuvan' the peasant in Aamir Khan's 'Lagaan' made five decades later ! They too burst forth in to a song praising the "shortlived promise of a few dark clouds".

The surge of industrialization manifesting with greed waiting on the sidewalks to uproot the poor peasant, was merely a result of seeds sown a long time ago by the British. A decade ago, in his seminal book 'Discovery of India', Jawaharlal Nehru had elucidated "due to policies implemented by the British the burden of agricultural debt grew and ownership of the land often passed to moneylenders. The number of landless labourers increased by the million; India became a passive agent of modern industrial capitalism, suffering all its ills and with hardly any of its advantage". The misery of

Shambhu, the uprooted peasant, was symptomatic of those very conditions created by our former masters.

Bimal Roy seemed to be a man in a hurry. In a quick span of seven years he directed about ten classics out of which eight were super hits and path breaking. His films like 'Do Bhigha Zameen'—Inspired from a poem by Rabindranath Tagore which was based on zamindar tyranny and famine; 'Biraj Bahu'—a stormy husband-wife relationship written by Sarat Chandra; 'Sujatha'---on the stigma of untouchability; 'Madhumati'—the theme of reincarnation used as a retribution; 'Parineeta'- based on a story by Sarat Chandra Chatterjee about love trying to survive in face of parental opposition; 'Devdas'—based, again, on the same author's classic tale of caste barriers that leads to a self inflicted life of despair in deriving succour from alcohol.

Roy's 'Parineeta'was a love story based on class and caste barriers. It was based on Sarat Chandra Chatterjee's novel of the same name. Produced by Ashok Kumar and starring himself as the lead 'Shekhar' and Meena Kumari as 'Lalita' with support from others like Nazir Hussain and Manorama. The treatement by Bimal Roy was in sync with the book. Meena Kumari played the young Lalita who in a moment of playful prattle places a garland on Shekhar. This coincided with the exact moment when the kid sister of Lalita is conducting a playful matrimonial alliance between her clay dolls. The act of exchanging garlands at that moment was seen by them as a metaphor of their feelings for each other. Lalita now considers him as her husband, but familial differences, mainly because of money matters between their parents, force them apart. Through many twists and turns, Lalita and her beloved unite in the end. 'Parineeta' was a success and Meena Kumari's performance as 'Lalita' turned out to be the highlight. It was again attempted about two decades later in a Jeetendra film called 'Sankoch' which was a flop. Five decades later it was remade, as a success, by film maker Vidhu Vinod Chopra where the roles were played by Saif Ali Khan, Vidya Balan and Sunjay Dutt.

A Broken Heart

In 'Devdas' the caste system as a factor, played the main villain, dwarfing the incessant consuming of alcohol by Devdas (Dilip Kumar). Bimal Roy showed the feudal zamindari system which beside Bengal had definitely prevailed in many parts of the country. Perhaps only Bengal found a Sarat Chandra to base his tragic love parable interweaving this factor as its back drop. The zamindar resides with his family in a huge mansion at some mofussil town far away from the then cultural capital of India: Calcutta. The era is of those times when the 'Brahmo Samaj' was grappling with a society dead against its cause; bridging caste barriers; widow remarriage and prevention of child brides. Intermingling between a high and low caste was frowned upon and marriage between them was not only taboo, it was almost a cause for getting excommunicated. In such a world, Devdas & Paro (short for Parvathi) are little kids who live as neighbours. Their childhood antics are dismissed as harmless prattle by their parents. The two kids not only play, fight and tease, they also care for each other. Realizing this, Paro's mother utters the cardinal sin of broaching 'marriage between the two in a near future'. The zamindar father (actor Murad and father of today's actor Raza Murad) is furious and to nip it in the bud he sends his son away to Calcutta to study. Paro is left alone and suffers the pangs of remembering Devdas silently. In her sorrow she finds some empathy from wandering 'Bauls' (travelling singers of Bengal who seek alms while singing the legends of Lord Krishna and his companion Radha). 'Baul singers' (played here by Nana Palsikar and Dulari) usually play on a short one-stringed musical instrument and are distinctly spotted with a long dab of sandalwood paste on their foreheads.The duet *'Aan milo aan milo aan savaraey'* narrates Radha imploring Krishna to come back from lands afar and see for himself the agony that she is going through. Owing to their separation, it alludes to the same torment felt by Paro. Sung by Geeta Dutt & Manna Dey it was aptly composed by Sachin Dev Burman.

Dilip Kumar excelled as the indecisive lover who finds solace in a bottle of hooch, expanded his list of iconic roles making him more of a 'Tragedian'. Suchitra Sen, a versatile actress from Bengali cinema played 'Paro' and Vyjayanthimala, an immigrant from South Indian cinema, played the role of the courtesan. According to an interview with writer Nabendu Ghosh, their preferred choice was Meena Kumari to play 'Paro' and Nargis for the courtesan however things didn't fit in place and they had to settle for Suchitra and Vyjayanti..

Scenes worth mentioning:

- The little 'paro' dipping her pot in a pond with the water rippling away towards a fully bloomed lotus and the camera pans back to reveal 'Paro' in the beautiful Suchitra Sen.

- When Devdas returns back from his 'exile' the childhood lovers,now grown up, still feel shy to revel in the moment.

- Devdas explaining to the courtesan 'Chandramukhi' on why he has willed his body to drink so he can be allowed to 'breathe' *"main to isliye peeta hoon kay saans le sakoon"*.

- A moth trapped inside a lamp attached to the ceiling of a train desperately buzzing its wings, which is a metaphor of Devdas's will to live, slowly ebbing away.

- The bullock cart ambling away with Devdas lying restless where he keeps on beseeching the cart driver *"aur kitna door'*; The short distance is weighing upon him like an eternity of pain whose eyes are in search of a last glimpse of his beloved 'Paro.'

The success of 'Devdas' was enormous. The appeal of this character finds place in every generation. Five decades later, film maker Sanjay Leela Bhansali, literally colour xeroxed this film by garnishing it with humongously sized sets, garish costumes and some cinematic liberties.

Bimal Roy's list of hit films would have grown further if not for cancer which abruptly cut short the life of this genius.

His record of garnering 7 Filmfare trophies in the 'best director' category remain unbroken. However, when Raj Kapoor made 'Awara' the Filmfare award was not yet instituted. From that view it remains awkwardly difficult to pass judgement and declare, who was the greatest of the three; Raj Kapoor, or Guru Dutt or Bimal Roy ? The death of Bimal Roy ended the reign of 'Bimal Pictures' but his protégés, well oiled by the skill and tutelage of their late master greatly prospered; prominently Salil Chaudhury, Asit Sen & Hrishikesh Mukherjee.

Around that time Balraj Dutt, a radio jockey with AIR decided to try his luck in films. In 1955 he got his break in 'Railway Platform'. As there was already a 'Balraj'in the form of the veteran Balraj Sahni present, Balraj Dutt rechristened himself as 'Sunil Dutt'. A dedicated actor, Sunil Dutt, like his peers, starred in mainly socially relevant films which were decent successes. However, Sunil Dutt mostly thrived where the main protagonist was usually played by the heroine; as the doctor who rejects untouchability in Bimal Roy's 'Sujata', the rebel son in Mehboob Khan's 'Mother India', as the loyal help who is drawn towards his 'malkin' in 'Milan' and the dashing lawyer in B.R.Chopra's 'Waqt'. He also shone as the bumbling, goofy hero in Mehmood's classic comedy 'Padosan'. But he mostly drew fame in the role of a bandit in the award winning 'Mujhe Jeene Do'.

With the coming of colour the joy of watching cinema turned exquisite. Mehboob Khan's 'Aan' which was the first, had Dilip Kumar and a Jewish girl called, Nadira. 'Aan' was inspired from Shakespeare's 'Taming of the Shrew'. Mehboob Khan, the owner of 'Mehboob Productions' had earlier made few films among them an ordinary historical based on the life of the Mughal prince 'Humayun'. While Nargis played a princess, Ashok Kumar played an unconvincing prince! All failed to impress, but very soon Mehboob Khan and Nargis gained immortality through his 1958 classic: 'Mother India'.

"Mere roop mein aaneki laaj nahin aayi"-Radha.('You never felt ashamed to 'look' like me?')

Radha (Nargis) the wife of a poor farmer lives in a village which epitomizes Mahatma Gandhi's vision of a progressive India where equality and brotherhood are deemed to reside. But these factors get turned on their head when a failed monsoon ravages it. Crops fail, hay withers away, livestock perish, and people begin to die of starvation. The song *"dukh bhare din bêete re bhaiya ab sukh aayo re'* where little green sprouts change in an instant to lush crops swaying in the breeze, soon turns out to be a symbol of temporary relief when nature again batters this village with a ferocious flood leaving behind an aftermath of starvation and abject poverty. The film was all about the pain of suffering terrible blows by fate: in the form of the vicious 'Sukhilala'(actor Kanhaiyalal), a brahmin moneylender, a failing crop, coupled by the desertion by her husband, who vanishes in to thin air as he is unable to shoulder the brunt of life and his lifeless arms. The 'Lala', who has been waiting for an opportune moment to play out his lust, moves in for the kill. Radha faces all fearlessly and survives-her honour and spirit intact.

But Radha's greatest challenge arrives years later from her youngest son 'Birju' (Sunil Dutt) who is still nursing a deep desire to exact revenge from his mother's tormentor. He abducts the lala's young daughter but faces the wrath of his mother. The mother pleads and screams at her son to release her. When the son stubbornly refuses, in an act of supreme justice,she guns him down.

Radha's suffering swept 'Mother India' from the gigantic sea of tears shed by the weeping millions, to the highest realms of cinematic glory.Mehboob Khan reached his pinnacle. Awards and lots of adulation came his way, temporarily casting a shadow on his peers. However, his very next,'Son of India' awaited with much bated breath was an appalling failure, ending the legacy of 'Mehboob Khan Productions'.While Mehboob Khan was fading away, Dev Anand was bringing up his 'Navketan' steadily towards a bigger success. His friend from his struggling days, a man called Guru Dutt, had formed a mutual admiration society between them. Dev Anand found that his friend's expertise on the medium of film making was far reaching. He offered his friend to wield the directorial baton for his film 'Baazi'. It was a hit and its rippling affect not only pushed up Dev Anand's stature but also established his friend and his banner. In a short time Guru Dutt himself became an actor in entertaining films like 'Aar Paar' and soon enough a film maker of repute with names like 'Mr & Mrs 55', 'Jaal', 'Sahib Bibi Ghulam' and of course, the immortals 'Pyaasa' & 'Kaagaz ke phool'.

'Sahib Bibi aur Ghulam' narrated the decadence of the zamindari system of Bengal which was once brimming with prosperity. One such is the 'Chaudhury' family headed by two siblings: Elder brother known as 'Bade Sarkar' (Sapru) and younger brother 'Chottey Sarkar' (Rehman). These two drink wine, puff on hookahs and frequent the 'kotha's' to be entertained by dancing 'Baaiji's (nautch girls). Of the two, the older one has other pastimes like burning cash on the marriage of his pets, or setting up pigeon wars with rival zamindars. The younger one is in the habit of spending his entire days and nights at the feet of the 'Baaiji'. In the fragrance of the white jasmines entwined around his wrist, sipping the expensive 'Vat69' whiskey he is drowned in the jingling from the musical trinkets of the nautch girls. He is completely oblivious of his responsibilities towards his young wife 'Choti Bahu' (Meena Kumari). Even though the other women in this feudal family have accepted such delinquency of their husbands as their fate, it is 'Choti Bahu' who remains obstinate. When her husband jokingly asks her if she can drink alcohol with him? She says "yes" and seriously starts mulling on this prospect.

She confides in 'Bhootnath' (Guru Dutt) an employee, who is the only person outside the household whom she can trust. Bhootnath is appalled on hearing his 'Malkin' put forth an impossible request for arranging alcohol. And boy, does she drink!! Her single minded motivation helps her in polishing off several glasses and as a quid-pro-quo she also gets her husband's love in return. Dressing herself up in all finery the 'Chotti bahu' sips whiskey in the arms of her husband and croons *'Na jaon saiyaan chudake baiyaan, kasam tumhari mein ro padoongi…'* simply translated it means 'O beloved do not go and leave me in tears'. But the song per se was not so simple. Composed by Hemant Kumar and sung by Geeta Dutt where her voice was slightly modulated to quiver which transformed this simple song in to a captivating narrative.

With her face resting on her nonchalant husband's lap, hair set loose on one side to partially cover her forehead bedecked with an undisturbed red bindi; that eternal sign of married womanhood which here, seems as a beacon to recall her disinterested husband.

But for fulfilling her quest she pays a heavy price by becoming enslaved to it. As time passes, the film shows the gradual decay of the Chaudhury haveli due to wrong business prospects. Unscruplous partners swindle them hastening their downfall leading to penury, with the 'Sahib' (Chote Sarkar) becoming sick and the 'Bibi' (Choti Bahu) becoming an alcoholic. The riches of the haveli start disappearing to feed the rich lifestyles of the family making them reach a tragic dead end. The' Ghulam' (Bhootnath) is a mute witness to this riches-to-rags story being played out. Bhootnath by now who has moved out of the haveli and become an apprentice to an architect is heart broken, seeing his 'malkin' trying to nurse her sick husband and grappling with her alcoholic needs. The Lady of the house, who once adorned in gold ornaments living in the opulence of unmatched luxury, is now reduced to selling her gold bangles to buy medicines and feed her need for alcohol. In the end, he discovers that the 'Bibi' was done to death by her own brother-in-law as he suspected her of having an affair with Bhootnath. The story is a telling commentary on the churning of an affluent society; men's pursuit of hedonistic pleasures; the rise of the Brahmo Samaj and the precarious stature of women.

Teen Sey Chhey

Scenes:

1.   A buggy driven by a pair of horses enters the haveli in the dead of night. In the back seat a man is lying sprawled drunk. As the camera pans, it focuses on the silhouette of a woman looking down below. As the drunken man is helped on his feet the silhouette recedes back in to the dark interiors.

2.   Two rival zamindars wage a proxy war setting a bunch of pigeons from their aviary on a collision course with each other. The match winner is decided by the number of pigeons felled.

3.   The invite by 'Chhoti Bahu' (Meena Kumari) to 'Bhootnath' in to her inner chambers. He is too awed and is unable to speak due to the 'rasgolla'(a kind of sweet) popped inside his mouth. Through his lowered eyes he can only see the gold adorned feet of his 'Malkin'. As the camera moves upwards it pans on the radiant face of 'Choti Bahu' who is majestically adorned with ornaments and looks extremely resplendent.

4.   The songs, *'Bhaura Bada Nadaan hai'* and *'Na jaon saiyaan'* voiced a rare kind of oomph and seduction in Geeta Dutt's voice.

'Sahib Bibi aur Ghulam' though rumoured to have been a luke-warm success vindicated Guru Dutt's authority over the medium. Though directed by his pupil Abrar Alvi, the unseen hand of Guru Dutt and the influence of his Calcutta days are evident. Unlike the 'Big Three' and other peers, Guru Dutt lacked a handsome persona of say, Dilip Kumar, the rosy looks of Raj Kapoor or the charming demeanour of Dev Anand. He looked ordinary because of his wheatish appearance, a hairdo that seemed oily and a girth which appeared well-fed. But he more than made it up with his infinite talent in films which was way ahead of his times. Tragically, failed whispers of an unwanted romance broke his heart and he chose death.

The untimely death of Bimal Roy and Guru Dutt slowed down the lights of renaissance in film making. Films based on literature and socially relevant topics became scarce.

As the country stood up, her matinee idols had now turned into a new 'Avatar'. He was mostly fair, handsome and clean shaven. This epitome of goodness was usually close to his mother, God fearing, sincere and studious. His grades in college were always "first- class- first' indicating his total dominance over his college mates. While in college he won all the debates, elocutions and his favorite sport was Badminton. Naturally, all the pretties and charming girls in his college, neighbour hood, and office had to but naturally fall in love with him. He preferred vegetarian dishes and his favourite 'Gaajar Ka Halwa' usually cooked by his sister or 'Kheer' prepared by his mother. Above all, this hero was a thorough gentleman and a teetotaller.

Most of them essayed such roles; Joy Mukherjee, Sunil Dutt, Manoj Kumar, and Biswajeet but this pack was usually led by Rajendra Kumar. From being the flutist 'Gopal' in V.Shantaram's 'Toofan Aur Diya the name 'Gopal' stuck on to him. Rajendra Kumar or Kumar Tuli which was his real name came to Bombay to push his luck. He not only did well but went on to become a safe mascot earning himself the tag of 'Jubilee Kumar'; There was never a flop starring Rajendra Kumar. The roles he played were seemingly based on tales from travelling sages and their memoirs. Truth and innocence seemed to become his forte. In a role that brimmed with mischief he appeared to be a miscast. But there came a time when he did transcend and break new grounds in the swashbuckling 'palace-politics' film called 'Gora aur Kaala'. Another good looking man who had just landed from Phagwara, a town in Punjab was Dharam Singh Deol, who altered this immensely long name to 'Dharmendra'. He starred in socially relevant films like 'Anpadh', 'Shola Aur Shabnam', 'Bandini', 'Anupama'. In all of these the female lead played the author backed roles.

Nonetheless, Dharmendra endeared himself by his macho looks blended with a tint of boyishness. He played the empathetic suitor in 'Anupama', the foil for the rebel comrade in 'Bandini', both by Bimal Roy, the husband in 'Anpadh' who is appalled on knowing his wife to be an illiterate and the self-righteous honest-to-a-fault in becoming a social outcast in Bimal Roy's protégé Hrishikesh Mukherjee's 'Satyakam. Those were the black and white days where Dharmendra just about managed to maintain a steady presence.

The partition also threw up another talented family: Baldev Raj Chopra and his brothers, Yash & Dharam. Baldev, popularly known as 'B.R.Chopra' proved to be a good storyteller and his stories were based on social messages. He was a serious film maker who had started following his passion even before the Partition. But his maiden attempt was scuttled as he alongwith his family that fateful night had to flee Lahore. He found peace in the city of Bombay and there, well ensconced, gave him an opportunity to relaunch himself in little known films which he made like 'Afsana' and 'Chandni chowk'. But it was the 1957 film 'Naya Daur' which underscored his contribution and made his banner 'B.R.Films' a dominant power.

'Naya Daur' had the biggest from the triumvirate: Dilip Kumar as it's hero.The heroine was Vyjayantimala, an actress who had already established a name for herself in films like 'Nagin' and 'Devdas'.The story was topical yet contradictory with new found themes on modernism.

'Naya Daur' starts as a simple tale in a non-descript village which could be located anywhere pan-india. It was perhaps the first and only film that brought man in direct conflict with the emerging industrial revolution spreading its tentacles; starting from cities and affecting villages. This village where several families live in their own houses made out of bamboo reeds and courtyards plastered neatly with cowdung, has a railway station and few miles ahead a large temple dedicated to the Lord Shiva. Some of the menfolk work in the nearby forest where they chop at logs and the others ply horse drawn 'tongas' to ferry passengers arriving at the railway station. Shanker (Dilip Kumar) is one such 'tonga wallah' and his bosom friend is Krishna (actor Ajit). Life goes on well for these villagers where basic necessities of food, clothing and shelter are duly met by their meagre earnings and this fulfillment is enough cause to celebrate. All of them own hearts that speak of love and carry loads of empathy for all ills.

The timber layout where men chop on wood is owned by a benevolent owner, reverently addressed as 'sethji' (actor Nazir Hussain). One day 'sethji' decides to go off on a pilgrimage so to look after the business in his absence he calls over his son Kundan (actor Jeevan). A city bred educated aristocrat, Kundan decides to modernize his father's business by putting up machines in his father's saw mill leading to a large scale retrenchment of workers. His next step is in buying a bus and posting it right at the railway station where the tonga wallahs ferry passengers. These twin shocks of modernism deprive the men of their livelihood shattering the very survival of the villagers. The villagers led by Shanker plead with Kundan to strike a balance where efficiency can be achieved but not at the cost of large scale retrenchment. Kundan refuses and as a way out, to shake the villagers off his back challenges Shanker to a race to be had between his bus and Shankar's tonga- the bet being the loser will withdraw from the village. The village backs Shanker and in a valiant attempt Shanker wins the race. The race is the climax because immediately it resolves every issue plaguing all; Shanker's tiff with his friend gets resolved; the sethji returns back from the Himalayas and the village gets back to normal times. However, the pertinent issue of 'Bus versus tonga' is not further delved in to nor the case of mechanized saws doing the work of twenty hands, remains unspoken. What stands out is Dilip Kumar's role as the belligerent but logical Shanker, the impishness of his better-half to be Vyjayantimala and the rest of the Star cast. A new facet what we see in Dilip Kumar is as Shanker he is shown alone, speaking his mind aloud to 'Shanker' the huge Shiva idol in the temple where he seeks His blessings and courage to win the race and free the villagers from unemployment and imminent starvation. This scene years later is cleverly modified by Yash Chopra to be used in one of his future films called 'Deewar', where 'Vijay' , an atheist, gives a 'piece of his mind' to the 'Lord'.

The film starkly laid bare the battle between modernity versus an empty belly and was honest in all that it portrayed. The genuine happiness of the villagers leading their simple lives where food clothing shelter was all they wanted, the faith and belief of temple goers, and the fear in waging a race against machines.

The plaudits showered on 'Naya Daur' had barely quietened, when Dilip Kumar strode again with his biggest film: K.Asif's Epic 'Mughal-E-Azam'

Doomed Love

"Bakhuda hum mohabbat ke dushmun nahin, apne usoolon ke gulam hai,ek ghulam ki bebasi par gaur karogi to shayad tum humein maaf kar sako" –Emperor Akbar

'I am not against love but am a slave shackled by my principles. Hope you will empathise with the helplessness of this shackled slave'- Emperor Akbar.

It was a dream unbelievably pursued by its maker K.Asif for 17 years. The tale of a Mughal, declared as the 'Greatest' and the 'Just'; who united his subjects, married a Hindu princess, fought and won many great battles but in this glorious legend, came close to disaster lurking in the form of a scalding love brewing between Anarkali a nautch girl and his tempestuous son, Prince Salim. The movie opens up with an un-partitioned India narrating an introductory footnote on Emperor Akbar. Prithviraj Kapoor the real life patriarch of the famous Kapoor clan essayed the role of the reel life Emperor with rare élan. His tall and broad frame, imposing walk with slightly halting foot falls and a booming voice added greatly to the persona of 'Akbar the Great'. For him, the Throne of Hindustan was not a thing to be bequeathed to a faulty heir. In early scenes of the film he is shown as banishing his beloved son, born from the blessings of a Sufi saint Khwaja Chisti, after having discovered that 'Shaikhoo baba' (a nickname for the prince) was hopelessly addicted to opium and the harem.

Dilip Kumar played the only Muslim role of his career. As Prince Salim he lent a subdued silence to an otherwise tempestuous role sparking his resilient romanticist leanings even though he was expected to toe the line of princely protocol. Though Salim was born a prince, his banishment as a child made him grow up to be weathered mostly in battlefields. He does not lose his poetic streak but finds himself being sucked into an abyss of romantic despair.

Madhu Bala, as the sensuous dancing girl of the royal court, fiercely attracted to the crown prince, but a reluctant protagonist drawn into a love story doomed by the king, his kin, his subjects, and perhaps, God himself.

Naushad's music & R.Mathur's camerawork helped in adding more repeat value to this fabled tale. The film's basic premise was of a father- son rift over the issue of choosing one's wife. Whether medieval India or today's modern India, echoes are felt even today where most families usually prefer to choose their child's spouse. 'Mughal-E-Azam' too explores this issue by choosing to narrate this tale from a Royal perspective. The Emperor and his son are torn between the love of their hearts. Akbar perhaps would look away if Salim agreed to keep Anarkali concealed in his Harem; she never aspired to be an Empress. She was resigned to her fate as a nautch girl and being a part of Salim's harem would have been the next logical step. It was Salim who thought otherwise. The Father –Son rift arose out of the fact that Akbar, saw the Throne as a sacred altar and Anarkali a vandal defiling the altar.

Teen Sey Chhey

Epoch making scenes:

- The opening scene of a pre-partitioned map of Hindustan speaking aloud, extolling virtues of Akbar and his love showered on her.

- A Muslim emperor (Akbar) swinging the cradle carrying an idol of 'bal krishna' and his hindoo wife Jodha (actress Durga Khote) applying sandalwood paste on his fore head.

- Prince Salim, treating his military victories as mundane. He would rather speak about the romantic prose etched with a quill on his blood stained sword with Durjan, his 'man Friday' (actor Ajit).

- A philosophical sculptor (Santraaksh) who conveys his line of thinking through his art. When asked to describe one of his works, he replies " Victory bestowed on one after shedding the blood of the innumerable".

- *'Ek bereham Shahenshah aur kar bhi kya sakta hain'*! A prince's retort to his mother that a merciless emperor cannot do more harm than killing his beloved.

- Anarkali swooning on Salim's chest with the shock of having been discovered by the Emperor in the prince's chambers.

- Durjan urging his heavily wounded body to rise and battle for the sake of a 'rajput's oath"

- *"Rajputon ki soormaon ki beti, tere haath kyon kaap rahe hain"*? Akbar chiding his wife Jodha, by casting doubt on her noble Rajput lineage on seeing her hands quiver when handing him his sword, ostensibly meant for slaying her rebel son.

- Battle scenes between the fledgling army of the rebel prince and the mighty Emperor; a thrusting sea of armed men on cavalry, plunging head on with spears and swords. Observe the emperor's side with cannons blowing & elephants trumpeting, stamping hordes of foot soldiers of the prince; The scenes are almost on par with any Cecil D. Mille production devoid of color.

- With color effects coming of age to India around that time, K.Asif thought it fit to showcase a song & dance. To get maximum mileage and repeat value from the audience the shrewd maker put the entire main players under a set made of glass aptly titled "Sheesh Mahal" and made Madhu Bala dance to his 'piece-de-resistance *"pyar kiya to darna kya"* (when in love why fear). It was more than a song. It was a battle cry announced by a nautch girl on Akbar's face which added fuel to a raging fire. The livid Akbar stomps out, determined to weed out Anarkali from his son's life.

The film's princely budget and collections remained unsurpassed for a good many decades. Produced by construction tycoon Shapoorji Pallonji, the film defied all the naysayers to emerge triumphant. However, in later years it was not financially viable for other banners to bring alive pages from history, hence history remained largely untouched. Plots eventually stuck to family dramas studded with melodious music and locales of Kashmir. These starred Rajendra Kumar, Biswajeet (an actor from Bengal), Joy Mukherjee (son of Shashadhar Mukherjee), Shashi Kapoor (youngest in the Kapoor Clan), and the lower runged Ravi Kapoor who operated under his screen name 'Jeetendra'. But the biggest of them all was Shammi Kapoor

Yahoo !

" Hasney sey log chichore ban jaate hain"--Rajmata

Shammi Kapoor was the second son of the patriarch, Prithviraj Kapoor. The 'Kapoor Gharana' as they came to be known came to India from the NorthWestFrontierProvince. Prithviraj had found his place in historical mountings like 'Rustom-E-Hind', 'Sikandar aur Porus' and many more. His broad, tall physique made him a natural choice for playing such characters where physical largeness conveyed dominance. But amongst his sons, the real genius lay within his eldest, Ranbir Raj Kapoor. When Raj was unlocking his streak of genius in various Chaplinesque inspired characters, Shammi Kapoor made a quiet entry via sloppy films like 'Laila Majnu' opposite actress Nutan. But it was his later on transformation as the yodeling, dancing character modeled on western Icons like, the 'Beatles' and Elvis Presley that made him a darling of the masses. What followed were trailblazing films starting from the breezy 'Junglee' right up to late sixties master thriller 'Teesri Manzil'. He was perhaps the first whose roles advocated that life needs to be spent with gusto and being chilled out, was not a crime.Where shedding tears and reflecting tearfully had become a way of life, Shammi Kapoor pierced this haven with just one shriek: 'Yahoo" ! 'Junglee' became a trailblazer flipping the young and the old. If the elder bro was the epitome of a 'tramp' the younger one symbolized one who was devoid of worries; never battled any emotional scars nor had any qualms of preferring dazzle over simplicity.

The biggest factors instrumental in Shammi Kapoor's success were the films made by 'Filmistan' which was jointly owned by Shashadhar Mukherjee along with brother in law Ashok Kumar. Their 'Tumsa Nahin Dekha' was a breezy musical which made Shammi Kapoor discard his old weepie look and wear an image laterally upturned for a script written by young writer Nasir Hussain. This group folded to re-emerge as 'Filmalaya' with Ashok Kumar exiting and what remained was the Mukherjee clan as its owners. Shammi followed up with his next 'Dil Deke Dekho', this time directed by Nasir Hussain. Nasir soon left Filmalaya to start off on his own with 'Nasir Hussain Productions'. But the film that made Shammi the 'sensation' of the 60s was Filmalaya's 'Junglee'directed by Shashadhar Mukerjee's brother Subodh, where he introduced actress Naseem Banu's pretty daughter Saira who, like her mother was tall and fair with Persian features. After the hit 'Dil Deke Dekho' Shammi Kapoor needed more breezy musicals to soar higher so 'Junglee' was a perfect fit. The story was about a former royal family now spending an opulent life as rich, honest industrialists.The scion of this family Shekhar (Shammi) is normal except for one imperfection; he has a perennial frown and carries a negative attitude. For him happiness is a form of 'laziness'. Not his fault though, he has merely followed his haughty mother's (Lalita Pawar as Rajmata) diktat of wearing a strict look for his office employees, his servants and with life in general. But one fine day, in the snowy vales of Kashmir, destiny pushes Shekhar with the pretty Rajkumari(Saira) to get stuck in a fierce blizzard where they find shelter in a log cabin. With no respite from the storm outside, and the cold threatening to engulf the log cabin a small fire is lit inside. This heady mix of snow, blistering cold, a crackling fire and the warmth and beauty of the bold girl, melts Shekhar. The result is an engulfing deluge of love expressed loudly, echoing all around the vale as "Yahoo".

Shammi Kapoor dived in to the snow and with him the audience. The music rendered by Shankar-Jaikishan aided in unraveling transformation of the stone-hearted man into a lover non-parallel in numbers such as:

*"Ehsaan tera hoga mujh par"*a confession of a man just opening up to the rigors of love.
"ai ai ya suku Suku':Mainly thrusted for Shekhar's distaste for his past bland life.

After this, Shammi Kapoor the actor never looked back. In spite of the 'Big3' occupying a larger space, Shammi had just carved a niche of his own.

Manoj Goswami, or Manoj Kumar as the country knew him was a poor old soul who also had felt the pain of partition. He too formed a part of the long chain of leading men who wooed heroines in Kashmir and green valleys of Himachal. He was backed by considerable success notably from the thriller (Woh Kaun Thi), socio changing 'Himalay Ki Godh Mein' and the weepy (Do Badan). One fine day he gained his moment of epiphany.

The Chinese aggression of 1962 broke Nehru's dream of peace and tranquility with our slit-eyed neighbor. The war was sudden and India's defeat swift. None of the powers to be gave any assistance except for a token, one line condemnation.

While the 1948 border skirmish with West Pakistan was quickly repulsed, the Chinese fracas was a different ball game. The revelation of an ill-equiped Indian army came to the fore and the stigma hastened Nehru's demise.Not surprisingly, the 1962 debacle found only one film based on it. This was 'Haqeeqat' made by Chetan Anand. Though the battle was a lost cause, he certainly hit bull's eye with his touching and convincing take on this debacle through 'Haqeekat. A song, though not from the film, but based on the backdrop of the Chinese conflict written by the poet Pradeep and rendered by the 'nightingale' Lata Mangeshkar '*Ae Mere watan ke logo*' had famously moved Nehru to tears.

Just as the country was gathering itself, to pick up broken pieces from a lost war, Pakistan again launched its second attempt to wrest Kashmir. But this time our treacherous neighbour's timing was wrong. The debacle of 1962 may have been a witness to India's defeat against China but the lessons learnt certainly helped her in repulsing Pakistan's second illogical attempt in the 1965 war. This is where Manoj Kumar made hay. His foray to direction could not have been better timed. The Indian army backed strongly by the airforce defeated her neighbour's evil designs and this time Manoj Kumar, (under the prodding of prime minister Lal Bahadur Shastri) based his film 'Upkar' on Shastri's tag line of 'Jai Jawan Jai Kisan'.

'Upkar' stamped Manoj Kumar's authority as a director. His films celebrated the thought of 'being Indian'. Upkar also, for the first time, brought to the fore ace villain Pran in a positive role.

Until then, through his strictly negative roles Pran had become a towering force as the eternal malefactor. As 'the villain' he had become emblematic and the very thought of giving him positive shades was perhaps never thought of by any maker. The swell of pent-up talent within him required a natural aperture. It came in 1971 from Manoj Kumar. To avoid the spectre of two decades of villainy looming over him, Manoj Kumar knew that the character of 'Malang Chacha' had to be radically different; he not only made him a soft-spoken 'fakir' but also a cripple! Yet, as a lame man, he stood the tallest in 'Upkar. 'Malang' has grown watching the two brothers,Bharat(Manoj Kumar) and Puran(Prem Chopra) growing up in the midst of love and affection. When their love grows sour, due to property disputes, it breaks this 'Mussalman's'heart; limping away in the fields the heart broken man sings in dismay *"Kasme vaade pyaar wafa sab baatein hain baton ka kya"* (oaths and promises being nothing but a mirage full of lies and decit). The audience was so impressed with this 'Villain's about-turn, that it paved the way for him to bag his first Filmfare trophy. The role of 'Malang Chacha' extended Pran's career by several decades.

Manoj Kumar's next 'Purab Paschim', portrayed an Indian by the name of 'Bharat' who arrives in England for his studies and finds a sense of rot, embedded deeply in the Indian diaspora living there. Manoj Kumar's films as a director celebrated the spirit of patriotism never surpassed by any one. The name 'Bharat' stuck to him like a second skin!

Raj Kapoor and his split with muse Nargis was further cemented when he cast Padmini, a heroine from Madras in his 'Jis Desh Mein Ganga Behti hain'. Even though this dacoit drama was directed by his team member Radhu Karmakar, it actually added to Raj's glory. But as a dacoit, it was Dilip Kumar who stood tall.

Bandit

"Humko to kouno maaf nahin kiya babuji"--Ganga

After enacting many roles such as a pining lover, a martyr, a 'tonga wala', a rebel prince taking up cause of his fellow compatriots, a suffering suitor, prince of a fabled kingdom and then a Royal prince from a page of medieval India, he wore another crown.

That crown was the role of a bandit in the film 'Ganga Jamuna'. The film had several firsts;

It was produced by Dilip Kumar; The language spoken was entirely in the Bhojpuri dialect which is spoken extensively in Uttar Pradesh and had Dilip in the role of a 'daku' for the first and only time. It also introduced his younger brother Nasir Khan in the role of Jamuna. The story had the classic clash between law & outlaw; a rebel with a cause who suffers for no fault of his so feels no wrong in deviating from the path of remaining a law abiding citizen. Ganga the local village boy, who works at the zamindar Haribabu's warehouse, is wrongly accused of pilfering food grain. As a young child, the churning in Ganga's life was ushered by the same Haribabu (actor Anwar Husaain) an alcoholic and womanizing zamindar. But Ganga knows this cooked up charge is a malicious way of revenge by Haribabu because he had foiled his plans of raping his beloved Dhanno (Vyjayantimala). Ganga is tried in court and has to serve a nine month sentence which in turn leads to his brother Jamuna's misery in a far off city where he has been sent to complete his studies. As the money-orders disappear Jamuna totters between starvation & survival. As hopes recede he finds relief from a benevolent Commissioner of Police (Nasir Hussain). He is impressed by Jamuna's honesty who in the face of starvation had handed over an expensive necklace at a police station which was stolen by a band of thieves. He takes Jamuna under his wing who soon lands a job as a police inspector. Jamuna is now standing on his feet, which was his brother's dream, but Ganga is now the hunted one. In the interim period, unknown to Jamuna, when Ganga had learnt about Jamuna's incarceration he had looted the zamindar's 'tijori' (money-chest). Chased by the villagers and the zamindar's men, Ganga had to take refuge in the mountains and align with bandits where he gets a gun and food for survival. As events unfold the chasm between Ganga & Jamuna widen to a point of no return. In the end Jamuna shoots down the escaping Ganga.

Ganga epitomized those parts of India where young illiterate men find subsistence in tilling land, have simple needs and see happiness in the simple errands and chores of daily life. Jamuna epitomized those literates who become restless and gain a serious demeanour. For people like him they know that the path to self-reliance and a society free of corruption and violence is never going to be easy. Haribabu the typical villain who sees alcohol and fornicating as a way of life, represents those in society for whom, power & wealth are a means to continue their vice riddled life.'Ganga-Jamuna' won Dilip Kumar his 7th filmfare trophy and there was no stopping him.

Scenes worth a rewind:

The boy Ganga deprived of education due to poverty works as a domestic help in Haribabu's mansion gets slapped by his drunk master. The next scene cuts to a sermonizing song *"Insaaf key dagar mein bachon dikhaon chalke yeh desh hain tumhara neta tumhi ho kal ke'* where a school teacher is fondly singing it to his students.

"(Oh Children, in the quest for justice be sure to walk in to that world for this country is yours, you're the leaders of tomorrow.)

The song seemed to convey that the leadership was tired; the task taken up earnestly, after more than a decade, remained incomplete.

- The friendly prattle between Ganga and his immediate boss- the Munimji (actor Kanhaiyalal)

- The song *"nain lad jayi hain'*….which is a victory celebration by Ganga and his 'kabaddi' team. From the Big3 he was the only one who could dance remarkably well in a rustic way.

- The starving 'Jamuna' struggling to make ends meet. Starvation takes its toll on the young man who can barely stand when questioned by the Commissioner.

- Ganga and his wife Dhanno (Vyjayanthimala) walking away from the ravines towards their village bidding goodbye to a life of dacoity and confident that Jamuna, the new cop in town, will help them in returning back to a life of yore. The couple oblivious to what is in store joyfully walk away humming a song by Mohamad Rafi which unfortunately is missing in the album:

"Chal chal ri goriya peekey nagariya, nadiya kinarey mora gaon…."

Let us go girl, to our place, where the river and village both find their space.

- An attack on a moving train launched by Ganga and his horse borne gang of 'dakus'. This scene is slickly shot and perhaps an inspiration for Sippy's long train sequence in'Sholay.'

- Ganga's revenge on Haribabu. The man pleads to 'forgive him let him go, not to touch him as he is covered in sin". Ganga cocks his gun and retorts in his classic thoughtful style with a pause in between:

" haath nahin laghayenge babuji, sirf do goli tohri paapi badan mein gaad denge""I will not touch just bury few bullets in side you"

- The climax where Jamuna shoots down his brother: In his last moments and throes of pain he reaches that spot in their old home where pictures of Gods are kept revered. In a blood soaked condition he cries out in relief *"main ghar aagya re munna"* (we have finally come home brother)

- The last scene where Jamuna pours a few drops of "gangajal' down his brother's throat and all present uttering a hymn which was dear to Mahatma Gandhi: *"Raghupathi Raghava Raja Ram.."*

The killing of Ganga never eliminated the ills. They still remain alive in all the Haribabu's of this land.

Raj Kapoor lived up to being feted as batting for the underdogs of life. 'Shree420' and 'Anari' were films that showcased this trait in him with outstanding success.

In most of his roles Raj Kapoor excelled in crying aloud at the pile of lies and inequalities surrounding him, while his younger brother played roles where swinging music, expensive wines and hour-glass women enwrapped him!

Soon came a day in 1965 when even Raj Kapoor ejected out of the 'poor man' mode. He flew fighter planes and watched operas in Paris. This deflection though was in his own: R.K's fifth film 'Sangam'.As a film maker the man was now being known as 'The Showman'and he stamped his authority all over. 'Sangam', with reigning actress Vyjayanthimala and 'jubilee star' Rajendra Kumar, was one of his biggest in both terms: budget and success. A film infinitely long (it had two intervals) had three main characters; Radha, Sunder & Gopal gasping within their own emotional battles to find their real place in this triangle; as a lover, as a friend as a martyr. It was a confluence of all the good things which makes life worth living: 'love-friendship-sacrifice'. The film saw Raj Kapoor in a new light: the poverty stricken look which had become so repetitive in'Shree 420','Anari', 'Chalia' was discarded.

'Sangam' showed him as 'Sundar, a stylish pilot, focused on friendship and love that he finds in Radha and Gopal.

Unlike his earlier films, 'Sangam' had no place for poverty, in fact all the characters are educated, follow decent professions and generally lead a privileged life. By shooting a great deal of it in Europe, Raj Kapoor took 'Sangam' to a new level. The film gracefully attempts to explore the deepest core of a woman's heart and examine her feelings.

Sunder (Raj) loves Radha (Vyjayanthimala) who actually loves Gopal (Rajendra Kumar). Radha is the only child of a retired and wealthy army captain. Gopal is the only child of parents who claim lineage to blue blooded Judges while Sundar is a fighter pilot but, an orphan brought up by foster parents. In this unequal level playing field, Sundar persists in wooing Radha, totally oblivious of her fondness for his dear friend Gopal. Circumstances curve to carve a dramatic cul-de-sac when the Airforce pilot Sundar is declared "dead' in a wartime zone. Gopal now confesses his love for Radha but the 'dead man' soon returns and Gopal promptly ditches Radha. She is shattered and very soon marries Sundar who whisks her away on a month long honeymoon to Europe. The idyllic paradise of their marital life is thrown upside down when Sundar to his shock discovers that Radha indeed was in love with another man, whose identity is not known to him. This torments all the three involved and the saga tragically ends in the form of Gopal's mortal ashes to be immersed in the confluence of 'Sangam': that sanctamonious point where the rivers Ganga & Jamuna converge.

Scenes worth a mention:

- The little 'Radha' smirking at Sunder's attempt to play with her.

- Sunder swearing that one day he would sweep Radha away and show her the world.

- Radha in a really futile attempt screaming or rather confesssing loudly to Sunder that she never loved him, even while he is wrapped in his jumpsuit, head in a helmet and strapping his headgears to manouvere his fighter plane.

- The news of Sunder being alive after being declared 'dead' and the immediate fallout act by Gopal advising Radha to forget their love. This convinces her that Gopal is a spineless man. The song-'*Dost dost na raha pyar pyar na raha zindagi humein tera aitbaar na raha*' became an anthem for brokenhearted castaways.

- Radha now married to Sundar, begins life as a devoted wife who has obliterated all memories of Gopal. Her new life with Sundar and their love for each other, their conjugal bliss and argumentative chats is very believable and beautifully complemented by the exotic locales of Europe

- Gopal finally revealing to Sundar that he was madly in love with Radha but his attempts to lay bare his feelings remained futile because of of his inability to thwart away the concern and empathy for his friend.

- In the final climax, Radha analyzing justfully that she was in love with Gopal but her marriage with Sundar had indeed, completely erased whatever feelings she had earlier for Gopal.

'Sangam' indeed was a memorable product from R.K.Films. But Raj Kapoor was being weighed down by age and a pronounced inability to remain slim and fit like his colleagues. Soon he would be consigning himself to remain behind the Camera. He now began work on a subject close to his heart. A film which he immensely believed in and carved it as an Ode to his act of being the underdog.. Impoverished, in search of that twinkle in the eyes of the ones he loved... unconditionally....The dream took form as 'Mera Nam Joker'...

The late 60's also saw the advent of two new entrants. One was a handsome Punjabi called Vinod Khanna while the other was a Bihari and an FTII graduate. With minor scars on his cheek and face embossed with a Raj Kapoor styled pencil -cut -moustache. His name was Shatrughan Sinha.

They came in as villains; those bad guys who covet the rights of the heroes of their wealth; their fame; their power and the heroine. Strangely, their villainy overshadowed the heroes. For example: the heroine of 'Aan Milo Sajna' had Asha Parekh trying to ward off, rather unconvincingly, the overtures of a dashing Vinod Khanna. In some cases Shatrughan Sinha overshadowed the heroes with his dialogue delivery. Even the audience rooted for him. Because of their ability to garner loud claps from the audience their transition from villains to heroes was imminent.

With Raj Kapoor remaining busy at the drawing board chalking out plans for 'Mera Naam Joker', Dev Anand and his banner 'Navketan' collaborated with younger brother Vijay 'Goldie' Anand to bring alive a book by R.K.Narayan. The film was 'Guide.'

"Dukh woh amrit hain jisse paap dhulte hain": Raju the guide.

A young man Raju (Dev Anand) earns his living as a tourist guide. One day his life collides with a lady called Rosy (Waheeda Rehman). She is beautiful but emotionally distressed. A proficient dancer stuck in a marriage that is loveless and asphyxiating. Exacerbated by convenient conditions such as an out-of-town husband, Rosy befriends Raju and with his unconditional help gains her life quotient of becoming a celebrated dancer. The neglectful husband is tossed aside- not that he cares. Soon there is fame with lots of money. Raju succumbs to their charm and he soon turns in to a squanderer living off the earnings of Rosy. The unspoken, the unconfessed, and a love which was anything but platonic, succumb to the charm of ready cash which has an instant power to buy scotch, swine and succour!

Soon enough, the unspoken love between Raju & Rosy turns bitter. The 'Guide' is accused of embezzlement and soon finds himself in prison.

After his release a year later, he refuses to align with his past and instead chooses to live incognito in a distant village where he again entraps himself in to being sucked into pitfalls of faith and spiritualism. In the climax he finds himself in the midst of an awakening where he gains salvation posthumously. A kind of redemption for his grey-shaded past.

Tears of the Guide

- Sachin Dev Burman's ballad *"wahan Kaun hain tera musafir jayega Kahan'* (who is there Oh traveller, where will you go ?) a heavily loaded song written by Shailendra which spells out Raju's lost cause as he is let off from prison to enter again the same world which reminds of his maligned past and a yet to be mended heart.

- Rosy breathing in deeply a fresh sense of freedom. The act is brought out by bursting in to the rapturous *"Aaj phir jeene ki tamanna hai aaj phir marne ka iraada hai"* (once again is the desire to live and so is the plan to die) spelling independence from a suffocating ritual called "marriage'.

- Raju, the man who lived on humble earnings, is now drunk with the finest wines and for whom losing cash on a game of cards has become a daily ritual. He tries to find solace with Rosy who is in no mood to hear his mind.The song *"Din Dhal Jaaye hai Raat na Jaaye'* (the day passes off not the night) is in effect Raju's conscience, chiding 'Raju the hedonist'- in a soothing way.

The Third Floor

"My my my, too many things for a little girl"- Somu alias 'Rocky', a drummer.

After the hit "Guide" Vijay Anand gave another thriller with his bro, a fast paced suspense drama based on a heist aptly called 'Jewel Thief'. Vijay or "Goldie' as he was called was certainly hitting purple patch and very soon he crafted another master thriller: A murder mystery called 'Teesri Manzil'.

The film was produced by Nasir Hussein who had few years back broken off from the 'Filmalaya' group after making for them the immensely successful 'Dil Deke Dekho', and 'Phir Wahi Dil Laya Hoon' - The last one gave a footing to actor Joy Mukherjee (son of his former employers 'The Mukherjee' clan). All these films had the typical Nasir Husain template embossed; childhood suitors-parents separated-rich girl-poor son-meet at picturesque hill station; funny clashes; queer situations; filled up with five or even six superlative songs. Ah yes! Songs! The only factor which Nasir mostly focused upon. 'Teesri Manzil' had his invisible hand in styling the songs greatly aided by maestro Rahul Dev Burman's music that encapsulated the shadow of singer Elvis Presley and the refined influence of his father Sachin Dev Burman. When all factors matched the template of Nasir Hussain why did he not direct this film beats me. So what was this film about?

A local beauty is flung from the third floor of a hotel. The death is viewed as a suicide but the locals whisper that 'Rocky'(Shammi Kapoor) a local drummer who plays at the hotel was the abettor. The police led by their detective (Iftekhar) believes it to be a case of 'cold blooded murder'.

Director Vijay Anand who directed this 'who-dun-it' garnished it on the top of a hill station with precipitous cliffs where screeching tyres are chasing each other down a 'ghat' (steep hill roads); where hat wearing detectives in black trenchcoats chew upon cigars and belch out smoke rings in solitary lobbys that lead to domed ampitheatres styled in Broadway fashion; where 'Rocky' is swinging around with the sexy 'Ruby'(Helen) prancing and playing around with a claronet.

Scenes to hold your Breath:

- The opening credits where the camera carries you inside a speeding car on a down-hill spin with R. D. Burman's entire orchestra belting out a background score making you clutch your seat ...drums, claronet, trumpets, organ- you name it.

- Rocky serenading to '*O Haseena Zulfon Wali...*' with wonder girl Helen. The set, the dancers, the costumes is something that has glued three generations

- The number '*Aaja Aaaja mein hoon pyar teraa...*' a song preceded by a long symphony which sounded like the blooming of a hundred guitars; a new lesson for all dating couples on how to let out a lover's war cry. Taboo or 'tehzeeb' be damned so 'Long Live being coquettish'; shake your hip vigorously and bat your eyelashes -that is how Shammi Kapoor & Asha Parekh danced their hearts out.

- When a big clue (actor Prem Chopra) turns out a cold trail and a non-starter (actor Premnath) turns out to be a bigger game.

Indeed, this third floor murder mystery turned out a first grade thriller!

B.R.Films after the success of 'Naya Daur' had emerged as a respected brand. Their next was also notable in many ways and the most momentous was the handing over of the director's baton to his younger brother Yash. It was also one of the first multistarrers where more than two bankable leading actors are cast together and all are given equal footage. The story was perhaps, the first of a new template in filmdom, a start of the 'lost-found' formula..

The film called "Waqt" was way ahead of its times. More than the story the grandeur was in the star cast: Balraj Sahni, Raj Kumar, Sunil Dutt, Shashi Kapoor, Rehman, Jeevan and Madan Puri. Each of them had a distinct resume of their own. Balraj Sahni was a veteran who had gained hallowed status after Bimal Roy's 'Do Bigha Zameen'; Raj Kumar after his 'limbless' role in 'Mother India' had made his presence felt in the 'tear-duct-filled' 'Dil Ek Mandir'; Sunil Dutt had by then already become a fixture in B.R.films vide their earlier

'Gumraah'; while Shashi Kapoor who had a fair pedigree of the 'Kapoor' membership and bright spots like 'Mehndi Lage Mere Haath' had yet not marked his presence in filmdom; Rehman had acted in remarkable classics like 'Sahib Bibi Ghulam', 'Chaudvin Ka Chand' and now well past his middle age, rightly suited the role of 'Chinoy Seth; Actor Jeevan who played 'Kundan', the villain in BR's earlier 'Naya Daur'. Also Madan Puri who had gained recognition through V.Shantaram's 'Jhanak Jhanak Payal Baaje' and of course those pretty lasses -Sadhana and Sharmila.

A "time" In brief:

Lala Kedarnath a wealthy shop owner loses everything: his wife, three sons, and his wealth in a devastating act of nature: an earthquake.

The family survives in different parts of Bombay where one son is picked up by a Judge, another is picked up by a thief while the third manages to cling to his mother.The judge's foster son grows up to be a Lawyer, the one picked by a thief becomes an even bigger one while the third left clinging to his mother's bosom becomes a driver to a rich heiress.

All the brothers collide with each other in remarkably well made situations until one day, when the thief brother is entangled in a murder.

Actor Raaj Kumar overshadowed all by his trademark raspy voice in dialogues which explained his mastery of thievery thru conversations that backed his claims: " *Jinke Ghar shishe ke hon woh doosro par patthar nahin phekte"* (those who stay in Glass houses do not pelt stones at others)

"yeh bacchon ke khelne ki cheez nahin. Haath cut jaaye to khoon nikal aata hain'
(this knife is not a toy for kids. If you cut yourself you will bleed).

Besides making us glimpse in to the livin styles of the rich: their sea facing mansions, those topless cars, their neat suits, perfect furniture, Yash Chopra also inserted the elements of foreboding in a perfectly laid out party where love, treachery and murder can roost at the same spot:

" Aage bhi jaane na tu peeche bhi jaane na tu jo b hi hain bas yahi ek pal hain" showcased it aptly

The grand finale is where all are present in the courtroom for their involvement or a connection in their own little way with the scene of murder leading to an unbelievable reunion of Lala Kedarnath's family.

'Waqt' was a success and brought to the fore a sharp director called Yash Chopra

A few months later, the industry was knocked out of its breath when Raj Kapoor's quasi autobiographical 'Mera Naam Joker' sank.

Some more shocks followed in the form of a lukewarm response to the patriotism laced 'Leader'starring Dilip Kumar and then his ambitious 'Gopi collapsed. Followed by successive failures like 'Bairaag' and 'Sagina' the lionized icon dejectedly withdrew from the scene. Prior to 'Mera Naam Joker'Raj Kapoor had started putting on weight and as a consequence offers of leading roles naturally had come to a halt. Even though, Dilip Kumar had gone in to complete retirement, the other two, Raj and Dev had their first love intact; that of being behind the camera as a master crafter aka Director. The reign of the Big3 in leading roles seemed to be coming to an end 'Showman' Raj Kapoor through his classics had the R.K. banner flying high though as an actor Dev Anand still had a longer run. He too kept his fire intact by flying high the 'Navketan' banner. He also received a fillip when at the age of fifty one he entered the 70's era with a swagger that immortalized his styles; classic nodding and the same swift speaking dialogues. Ironically, while his colleague was mourning a loss called 'Mera Naam Joker' he extended his run in a super smash hit called 'Johnny Mera Naam', directed by Vijay Anand and produced by Bombay midas Gulshan Rai who owned a banner called 'Trimurti Films'.

Rewinding 'Johnny':

Two brothers, Sohan & Mohan(Dev & Pran) are separated due to their father's (a cop) relentless fight against criminals and who gets killed by a smuggler called 'Bhishamber' (actor Premnath).

One is left to be brought up by his mother while the other is reared by the same man who had orchestrated the cop's murder. Bhishamber Singh's forte lies in sneaking off rare artefacts and expensive jewels in to his domain located in the princely state of Nepal.

Mohan grows up under the smuggler's wing that distinguishes him with rare loyalty that delights his foster mentor who recognizes his expertise in bringing in large caches of smuggled goods with ease.

Sohan grows up to be an undercover cop with the Bombay police who infiltrates Mohan's gang under the alias 'Johnny'. If Mohan is loyal, sharp and incisive, Johnny(Sohan) is honest, cool and several steps ahead. He wins over Mohan easily who is already impressed with Sohan's skills that have brought in swift results for him but in the process, Johnny the 'crook' (actually a Cop), falls head over heels for the beautiful Rekha (Hema Malini) who too has infiltrated this gang in search of her father.

A classic razzmatazz, it was a story that travelled through oscillating twists and turns, into situations that see-saw and interspersed with some of the best songs by Kalyanji-Anandji; But the narration was scandalizingly topped by a cabaret number that bordered on a shocking strip-tease and classic villainy which remain unapologetic till the end.

Dev Anand as 'Johnny' gloriously commenced his sunset in a role that was the best loved and unforgettable in his career; A role for which any peer of his times would forfeit their right arm. Equally memorable were the others: Pran as 'Moti' or Mohan, the incisive lieutenant of Bhishambar; Hema Malini as 'Rekha' who was akin to a dainty jasmine fresh out of a bouquet: made the males swoon and the women envious- She showed the stuff what 'Dream Girls' are made of !

There was actor Jeevan as the diamond-carrier 'Heeralal' who was at his snarling best, & Iftekhar the 'smooth-as –unruffled feathers' top cop who is Sohan's boss.

And finally, there was Premnath as 'Bhishamber Singh', the ruthless villain who remains immersed in whiskey and debauchery; who will stop at nothing to get his jewels: be they by imprisoning his brother or punishing a traitor by seducing his mate !

Scenes to rewind & sit back:

- Heera & Johnny locked up in a cell; whispering sweet nothings and helping each other melt the ice by lighting up their fags in striking a 'quid-pro-quo' deal.

- Johnny meeting Rekha for the first time. Awe struck by her beauty Johnny delves in to reciting a long dialogue in his trade marked rapid chatting way.

- Mohan impressed initially by Sohan's skills but one day finds this judgement clouded. In a taunt to Sohan he says " *apni teesri aankh ka istmaal karo. Yeh kuch zyaada hi dekhtey hain*" (trust your third eye, it seems to be watching more than required)

- Raja Bhishamber (Premnath) and dancer Padma Khanna's daringly picturised strip tease performed naughtily to the song '*Husn Ke Laakho rang*' it was an ode to an orgy. With her hair let loose, pieces of outerwear falling off at every stanza sung by Asha Bhosle and the proceedings being watched by embarrassed palace guards. Padma Khanna and

Asha Bhosle both seemed to effortlessly ensnare his uncontrollable lust!

- Raja Bhishamber revealing to his brother that 'his goodness always pushed him to a corner'. " *jawaani woh behtareen mauka hai jisey acchaiyon par nahin aiyaashiyon par* chadaya *jaata hain* " –youth is that period in every man's life which should be consumed for debauchery and not to be spilt on goodness.

- The climactic scene where 'loyalties' and intentions of all the characters start see-sawing driving the villain up the wall to distinguish between friend and foe.

Tectonic Shifts

Lymphosarcoma of the intestine. Wah! kya bimari hain, bimari ho to aisi ho varna na ho.--Anand Sehgal

The very next year under his own banner'Navketan', Dev Anand amazed the young Indian with his hippie cult 'Hare Rama Hare Krishna'. It was all about a disjointed family, divorced parents, runaway sister and a searching brother. On one side was the 'Hare Krishna ' movement gaining swiftly and on the sidelines, besotted devotees from the western world began adopting its slogan as an emblem for their vagabond lifestyles; the connection with this lifestyle is adapted, when, the sister 'Jassi' takes off with a hippie gang incognito. 'Hare Rama Hare Krishna' brought forth basically the worrisome issue of partying parents more engrossed in the machinations of their adulterous liasions; where raising kids was a neglected matter to be shoved under the carpet. It starred Dev as the older brother 'Prashanth' and the sister's role was played by Zeenat Aman who had just bagged the 'Miss India' crown. Though the 'heroine' in the film was actress Mumtaz, it was Zeenat Aman as 'Jassi'- the gone-astray 'chillum' puffing girl belting *Dum-Maro-Dum*', walking away with awards and accolades.

Just as the success of this film raised expectations, Dev Anand faltered--from the ordinary 'Gambler' to inane ones like 'Yeh

Gulistan Hamara', Shareef Badmash'and his own productions 'Bullet' and 'Heera- Panna' -leaving Dev Anand the actor, with nothing much to write about.

With the 'Big3' now on their wane, the throne of the youth was lying vacant. For reasons mentioned, the Big 3 had stepped aside, but the ones in power like Dharmendra, Shammi Kapoor, Rajendra Kumar, Manoj Kumar had their own distinct styles, but largely all fished in the same lake; a whistling hero prancing around trees in hilly Simla or icy Kashmir; music by a Naushad or an S.D.Burman ensured a film could manage a decent opening and celebrate at least 100 days (15 weeks) all depended on dates available or how wide the producer's purse could open to sign them up. There was no dearth of films rolling out every Friday. Few hit Bull's eye, many fell of on the way side while most kept whizzing over the target. When Dharmendra gave a super hit in 'Jeevan Mrityu'' then he ought to have maintained the momentum; in the case of all, if one Friday was a blockbuster, the next arrivals few weeks later pulled them down. For example, If 'Jeevan Mrityu' was a hit then it was followed by average ones like 'Man Ki Aankhen', 'Sharafat', 'Kab Kyon Aur Kahan'. In such a world where expectations were meeting a dead-end, walked in a young rookie.

In 1966, a talent hunt organized by FilmFare magazine brought young Jatin Khanna. He won the contest where he was one of the chosen eight from the 16000 participants!

Jatin Khanna was christened as 'Rajesh Khanna' and chosen to star in a love story shot in black and white called 'Aakhri

Khat'. This film was directed by Chetan Anand. 'Aakhri Khat' came in quietly and went away pretty much the same way but Rajesh Khanna the 'new hero' was noticed. Next came 'Raaz' and 'Ittefaq' that brought him fame but in dribbles. Few months later Shakti Samanta, maker of films like Howrah Bridge(with Ashok Kumar), China Town (with Shammi Kapoor), Kashmir Ki Kali(also Shammi Kapoor) and the foreign localed 'Evening in Paris' (Shammi Kapoor yet again) was planning his next.

'Evening in Paris' was not the kind of hit envisaged by its maker. It did celebrate a Silver jubilee which meant a run of twenty-five weeks, but not at as many centers which would have delighted the maker. Shakti Samanta was now in search of a script which he got from Sachin Bhowmick but because Shammi Kapoor was past middle age and putting on bulk- Shakti preferred a new hero and Rajesh Khanna caught his eye. Casting Sharmila Tagore with Rajesh and teaming up with S.D.Burman for composing music, the result was 'Aradhana'.

A young airforce officer falls in love with a pretty girl and impregnates her. But before he can marry her, he dies in an unfortunate plane crash. Few months later, the unwed mother is sentenced to jail for killing her molester. The little son grows up to not only look like his late father but also get in to the same profession, that of a pilot. The story had Rajesh Khanna playing double roles,as the father and son while Sharmila Tagore too, in a sense, played dual roles: as the young beloved of the pilot and aged mother of the son. The freshness and lilting songs sent the nation in to ecstasy. If *'Mere Sapnon Ki Rani'* was a new style in popping the question, the other song *'Roop tera Mastana'* went a step ahead by enwrapping sensuousness in warm fire. 'Aradhana' went on to celebrate diamond jubilees (75 weeks) at many centres. People seemed to have found their next Icon after the Big Three. Devyani Chaubhal, a reputed journalist of the seventies gave him the appellation of a 'SuperStar'-This title was uttered for the first time in filmdom. In the same year, came 'Do Raaste' which was directed by Raj Khosla. Maker of earlier hits such as 'CID'(with Dev Anand) 'Woh Kaun Thi'(with Manoj Kumar), 'Mera Saaya'(Sunil Dutt) all in the thriller genre, now attempted a family social but this time produced by himself. Raj Khosla was not too sure about the look to be given to his hero. 'Do Raaste' was a family social where Rajesh Khanna for most of its proceedings played an unemployed youth. To give him that harangued look of a jobless man a stubble would be apt but yet, he was in two minds. However, the success of 'Ittefaq' where his role was of a patient on the run from a mental hospital and for most part of this film Rajesh Khanna is shown with a stubble, solved his dilemma. Therefore in 'Do Raste' he sports both: a stubble and a clean shave, said to be influenced by the twin success of 'Ittefaq' & 'Aradhana'!

'Do Raaste' followed the path of 'Aradhana' and soon ascended a long string of successes: 'Amar Prem', 'Anand', 'Safar' (a bland 'Anand'), Haathi Mere Saathi, Doli, 'Bandhan', The Train, 'Sachaa Jhuthaa', 'Kati Patang', 'Aan milo Sajna', 'Andaz', 'Maryada', 'Apna Desh', 'Dushmun'. Each of them a convincing hit!

In 'Amar Prem', Rajesh Khanna delivered a powerful author backed role. Based on a Bengali novel written by Bibhuti Bhushan, the film moistened the eyes of all. In 'Anand' whose story was of a lateral kind where a cancer stricken man named Anand thumbs his nose in a rivetting "i-give-a-damn' attitude that grows taller than the disease. He whittles away his serious doctor's advice (the soft spoken 'Babumoshai') by candidly mentioning: *"Babumoshai, Zindagi badi honi chaiye lambi nahin…"*

What was the secret of Rajesh Khanna's phenomenal rise as a 'Superstar'?

He had an average look with average features: A flat hairstyle, average height and a broad hip. Yet they say, women prepared to swoon the moment he appeared on screen.

'Andaz', a film starring Shammi Kapoor as the main hero, had Rajesh Khanna in precisely three scenes and one song; not surprising, because his role was billed as a 'Special Appearance'.This was incidentally Shammi Kapoor's last movie as a hero. Again, not surprising because he had started to age, and acquired a lot of fat! It was precisely this one song *'Zindagi Ek Safar hai suhana'* picturised on Rajesh Khanna, which was hummed by people and played repeatedly by All India Radio making this Shammi Kapoor starrer to be identified as a 'Rajesh Khanna film'.

The country had just won a decisive war with her wily neighbour; 90,000 Pakistani soldiers surrendered to the Indian army headed by General Jagjit Singh Arora,which erased 'East Pakistan' to carve out a new nation called Bangladesh. Feel good films was a natural way to rejoice and with seventeen consecutive hits in 1971-72, Rajesh Khanna had become a confluence of the 'Big Three'. Socially relevant issues, soulful lyrics, excellent compositions by stalwarts caressed cinegoers in to a rapturous delight. The films were exciting and entertaining in their content. The success of 'Aradhana' fortunately did not set off a rash of clones to appear. Each of them had unique themes distinct from each other; like taming troublesome In-laws (Haathi Mere Saathi); overcoming a scheming 'Bhabhi' (Do Raaste); saga of Good-Bad in a double role(Sachaa Jhuthaa); spreading a positive attitude when terminally stricken (Anand); reformed alcoholic(Dushmun); evils of Dowry (Doli), the good Samaritan(Amar Prem) and the flow continued unabated.

Even a film like 'Daag' with an ambiguous ending became a hit. Directed by the young turk Yash Chopra, the story was as relevant to the forte of Rajesh Khanna. College mates Sunil (Rajesh) & Sonia (Sharmila Tagore) are in love. Few songs and several scenes later, there is an attempted rape where the hero saves his beloved by killing the assaulter (Prem Chopra). To escape the prospect of being dragged to the gallows, Sunil disappears and resurfaces in a distant hill station with a new name, a new identity and a new look. The benevolence of his new master now compels him in to marrying his daughter Chandni (actress Rakhee). Later, by a strange quirk of fate, his first love appears in the same town and many other twists later the villains are taken care of and his sentence is pardoned. In the end, he is shown living happily ever after, ostensibly, with both the women! While 'Daag' was another feather in

Rajesh Khanna's long list of hits it was also the beginning of Yash Chopra's fondness for societal taboos starting with the unclear message in 'Daag', a decade later 'Silsila' and three decades later a film called 'Lamhe'.

In the choppy waters of Bollywood when other leading men managed to stay afloat, 'Dame Luck' was serenading with Rajesh Khanna. Tickets were being regularly sold in black. Legends abounded and so did gossip. Grapevines emerged to declare that girls 'wedded themselves to his photos'. As fame rose so came wealth; expensive cars, many sycophants, a palatial house overlooking the Arabian Sea in Bombay's Carter Road named as 'Ashirvad' which became a 'must see' spot for locals and tourists. Fame also brought in pride which started clouding his decision making. Parties at 'Ashirvaad' became legendary; a rash of cronies took form who partied till the wee hours. Soon the superstar wrapped himself in a cocoon of hubris.

From the drought affecting the other actors, it appears all the departments of film-making like story, script, music, lyrics seemed to be peaking only in Rajesh Khanna specific films. All the departments, in tandem, were at their creative best only where Rajesh Khanna starred. There is no denying the fact that his charisma and ability aided to their success, yet, it is difficult to imagine 'Aradhana', 'Kati patang', 'Amar Prem', 'Anand', without the music of S.D.Burman and R.D.Burman. Can one watch 'Haathi Mere Saathi' minus the antics of those playful elephants? Slowly and surely arose a necessity to kindle a new fire.

Those sparks were seen in a young man who co-starred in a Rajesh Khanna film called 'Anand'. The man had earlier played the role of a deaf-mute in Sunil Dutt's desert saga 'Reshma Aur Shera' which had flopped badly. But the man was made of steel and refused to let go. He went on to play second fiddle in films like 'Gehri Chaal' which had Jeetendra as the leading man and immediately after played a disgruntled lover in 'Parwana' where he was pitted against the then promising hero called Navin Nischol. He kept his focus intact and very soon landed himself the role of 'Bhaskar Bannerjee', whose grim outlook of the terminally ill 'Anand' is rudely jolted by Anand's personal take and candid confession of how life should really be. Bhaskar Banerjee or "Babu Moshai" also endeared himself to the film's director Hrishikesh Mukherjee who signed him for his next venture 'Namak Haram". The man was Amitabh Bachchan.

In 'Anand', Rajesh Khanna was the 'Titan', so naturally Mukherjee's next 'Namak Haram' was a contest between unequals—A reigning Superstar and an upcoming actor. After its release, equations changed, so did fashions. As 1973 drew to a close, the reign of narrow bottomed pants ended and 'bell bottoms' began. The short hair cut was out and side burns emerged. Very soon, the Rajesh Khanna 'hairstyle' was disappearing; the new hairdo was kept 'over- the- ears'. Rajesh Khanna struggled to maintain this new hairdo while his younger rival had it slick: straight and epic.

'Namak-Haram':

"Yeh dal, chawal key daam badh gaye hain, tumhein kaun bata raha hain?"- Seth Damodar

1973 was a watershed year for that was the time when Rajesh Khanna was on the last leg of his superstardom while Amitabh Bachchan was on the threshold of being crowned as the 'next Prince'. Hrishikesh Mukherjee, the master story teller of middle class icons directed this movie which has the distinction of being their last confrontation. Said to be influenced by the English film 'Beckett'that starred giants Richard Burton and Peter O'Toole, this one was based on a friendship between two unequals: Vicky(Amitabh) and Somu(Rajesh Khanna) that is deep and revered until factors of capitalism and Marxism bring about a state of confrontation in their brotherhood. It was a classic take on the backdrop of socialism when India was unsure about the economic policies she had adopted.

Vicky symbolized the well entrenched scion of a hard hearted capitalist Seth Damodar (Om Shivpuri) supported by the 'licenseraaj' which ensured the safety of his millions through monopolistic rules. Somu played the middle class fellow who was considered loyal, but had to rebel, albeit, in a non-violent way. He was torn between a selfless love for his friend, whose wealth meant nothing to him, and his co-workers whose worrisome poverty and social strife was drawing him closer to them.

Hrishikesh Mukherjee's genius in putting forth a social issue can be seen in several convincing scenes. Aided by Gulzar's dialogues and brilliant music by R.D. Burman the film becomes a landmark mirror of those times..

Rewinding Namak-Haram:

- A furious Vicky narrating his plight to Somu about his tormented pride.

- The proud and haughty Vicky looking down upon the frail frame of Bipin Lal(actor A.K.Hangal) the union leader and asking forgiveness in a hard , venom filled voice. After uttering the *'maafi''* word; without much of a backward glance he swiftly swivels in an about turn to walk away.

- The industrialist father (played brilliantly by Om Shivpuri) advising his son to beg for forgiveness but also "never forget the humiliation in doing so for that will be your strength".

- Vicky livid on seeing his friend beaten up by an angry mob. ("*Ma Ka Doodh'* lines suited Amitabh and not just Dharmendra in those times)

- Somu breaking down the cost of a 'Chivas Regal' peg and equating with the cost of several meals it can buy.

- *Diye jalte hai phool khiltey hain*: Lamps are lighted flowers bloom(Somu & Vicky engrossed in their friendly banter.)

- *Nadiya Se Dariya dariya sey saagar saagar sey gehra jaam*: not a stream nor a river not even the ocean, the deepest point is found in wine. (Somu reading a scribbled note left behind by Alam (actor Raza Murad) a rabid alcoholic who pens down his sorrows when drunk.)

- *Jeene ki arzoo mein marey ja rahey hain log, marne ki arzoo mein peeye jaraha hoon main*: In their desire to live they keep on dying, in my urge to die I go on drinking.(Alam's reply to those who caution him from drinking.)

- *Main Shayar Badhnam*: An epitaph on one of Alam's poems excellently rendered by Kishore Kumar

- *Woh Ek Namak Haram Tha*: Vicky claiming straight faced to the judge the reason for getting his friend killed, emphasizing that his friend was a "traitor".

- Vicky castigating his tearful father that he as his son had to atone for his father's crime; because "i knew your wealth and influence would have freed you. But now you will suffer seeing me in jail just as i do" and goes on to explain the whole essence of his friendship with Somu.

In the economic distress of the 70's, the slogan of *'Garibi Hatao'* by the Congress government failed to find any resonance; when serpentine queues for daily necessities was looked upon as an 'opportunity'and ration card a 'perk' in such times an empty stomach stopped valuing his right to vote.In such a scenario the battle between the protagonists in 'Namak Haram' had to culminate in to a tragic finale. Was he a Traitor or a Martyr?

Rajesh Khanna as 'Somu' in an author backed role did full justice but it was 'Vicky' who stayed back in our minds.

Even though the lanky young man won a Filmfare award for both 'Anand' and 'Namak Haram' stardom was far away.

An earlier release, called 'Parwana', which did not succeed but Amitabh was noticed for his 'cool, calculative, cold blooded master plan'to bump off his beloved's uncle who refuses to agree to his marriage proposal. The film ends with the villain (Amitabh) confessing his crime and committing suicide. People liked him and among them were two evolving writers: Salim Khan & Javed Akhtar.

Phenomenon

'Ek Police Inspector ko maarney ki keemat pacchas hazaar? Bahut Imandaar malum hota hain'!--Sher Khan

Salim Khan and Javed Akhtar, unsung writers of Rajesh Khanna's 'Haathi Mere Saathi', now collaborated on a story which they were confident about. It was based on a real life incident of a police inspector being framed for bribery. Prakash Mehra, a well known director-producer who was fresh from the success of his last film 'Haath Ki Safai, bought it. Prior to this he had made 'Samadhi' which had Dharmendra in a double role and was also a hit.

The script was titled as 'Zanjeer'. Salim and Javed were not only adept screen writers but also keen observers of situations and the socio-politico times.

The country's situation was far from rosy. Dreams and aspirations raised sky high after independence remained largely unfulfilled. The unemployment levels in 1973 were dismal. 'License –Raaj' coupled with a closed door policy kept growth locked and allowed wealth to remain in the pockets of a few. The law was proving to be impotent or too corrupt to deliver justice. Unable to obtain justice generated sympathy from the audience. In such times tales of love had lost credibility keeping them utopian. Wooing a pretty maiden in the foothills of snowy vales was not cool anymore. Need of the hour was some action-not of the fisticuffs kind but of a fighter who could turn all the wrongs on their head. 'Zanjeer' was that spark which set up a wild fire in those verdant vales.

Just as the socio-economic palette of India was changing so was the mind set of the audience. Their image of a hero no longer accommodated the lovelorn pursuits of Rajesh Khanna and his ilk! It will be also worth mentioning that in the cusp of this era two flourishing villains, Vinod Khanna and Shatrughan Sinha, found it relatively easy to make their transition from villain to hero. It was during the same time a struggling actor (Amitabh) who would have fitted well in the boots of a villain was fortunate enough to have found his 'mojo' in such disgruntled time of the 70's. That 'one time villain' of an unknown film called 'Parwana' was pushed by the socio economic times to thunder around and strike lightning through monstrous hits.

The search for an actor to play the role of Inspector 'Vijay' in 'Zanjeer' proved to be long. The script travelled to one from the erstwhile 'Big3: Dev Anand -who felt that a role bereft of songs was not for his asking. From Dev it travelled to Dharmendra who too refused for reasons unknown. As mentioned earlier, Prakash Mehra had earlier directed him in the hit 'Samadhi' where Dharmendra had played a well feted double role: of a good and a reformed bad. Exasperated, Prakash Mehra accepted Salim Javed's recommendation of an actor with "promise" -Amitabh Bachchan; 'Zanjeer' was finally made with him and soon, the genie was now set loose.

After 'Zanjeer', in most of his subsequent projects Amitabh Bachchan became the antithesis of the 'Good' hero. He was everything that went against patent,accepted qualities that were deeply embedded in minds. This 'New Good' never came 1st class 1st in college; most cases he was an illiterate: an 'angootha chhap'.The characters he played were never teetotallers; in fact they polished off bottles with elan!

The troubled economic period and the angst of the common man came to coalesce in Amitabh. The period started from 'Zanjeer' and remained on course till his accident in 1982.

As Vijay Khanna, a police officer wrongly framed by the villain Dharamdas Teja played by Ajit, was nothing new; the newness was in Amitabh's demeanour in acting out the role of no-nonsense 'Vijay' which appeared like he was carrying inside him a lot of venom. Venom- manifested from nightmares left behind by the massacre of his parents, and the unhindered reign of smugglers like DharamDas Teja who stop at nothing; be they mowing down innocent school kids under their fleeing trucks, or framing a police officer because he refuses to toe his line or gunning down reformed henchmen, (example, Vijay's father) lest they start aligning with the law by turning whistle-blowers. Salim -Javed's characterization were all fleshed out distinctively: Vijay Khanna the no-nonsense cop, Jaya Bhaduri as 'Mala' a street-smart girl, Pran as 'Sher Khan' the fiery pathan, Bindu as 'Mona' the moll, Om Prakash as 'D'Silva'the mourning alcoholic who wants vengeance for his sons and Ajit as the cruel 'Seth Dharamdas Teja'.

A Lost Key

'Hamari zindagi agar aapki milkiyat hain, to maut hamari milkiyat hain'--Raj

'Zanjeer' gave way to films which put bollywood entirely in to a new perspective. A new world was taking shape. In the midst of this churning, bobbed a film made by Raj Kapoor. Based on an untouched topic of teenage-romance, he introduced his second son Rishi Kapoor and a new girl opposite him whose name was Dimple Kapadia. The film was 'Bobby'.

In a world set on fire by anger and ruled by storms of fury, Raj Kapoor carved out a path of love where 'Bobby' sashayed away to infinite glory. It did not have killings or vengeance; In its place were barriers of rich-poor divides. It had Pran as the father who turns out a parental villain to oppose his son's love for a girl who is his child-hood'nanny's grand-daughter. Actor Premnath (Raj Kapoor's brother-in-law) played the girl's father: a middle class fisherman who values love and simplicity over wealth and riches. As a film maker, Raj Kapoor was directly on the path blocked by a mountainous rock of violence and revenge. There was no space for him to turn around so he hewed away to carve out a teenage love story that remained believable. After the debacle of 'Mera Naam Joker'it was widely thought that this time he would 'fall in line' and dance to the 'changing tunes' of those times where revenge ruled. The blue eyed man remained true to his inner soul and did what his forte was all about; being naturally inclined towards heroine oriented subjects so what he did was this: He brought alive a teenage love story set between a Hindu boy and a Christian girl under the backdrop of a rich poor divide. There were insinuations, and sniggers that Raj had now reached his nadir. All of them proved to be woefully wrong.The first burst from his cannon was the album rights bought by HMV. Each song was a blistering hit.

- *Mein shayar to nahin* (am not a poet) The young lad, Raj, has just returned home from hostel. At the centre of a grand party hosted by his millionaire father(Pran) where the flirtatious Nima(Aruna Irani) is swaying, he catches a glimpse of a shy rosy-cheeked girl, looking less on confidence, maybe because she has just stepped inside a luxurious mansion for the first time with her granny Mrs Braganza (Durga Khote). That shy girl with rosy cheeks, is Bobby Braganza (Dimple Kapadia). Unable to locate her, he breaks out in to this song about 'equating himself with a poet'.However, when Raj goes over to her house, Bobby is supremely confident and even takes a dig at his chubbiness by calling him "dibba"(square)

  Interestingly, ten years later the same scene is fleetingly felt in Subhash Ghai's 'Karz' when Monty (Rishi) is about to sing and just then his eyes fall on a shy girl (Tina Munim) entering the hall.

- *Hum Tum aur Chaabi kho jaaye* (you me and a lost key). Raj has to make amends with Bobby with whom he has just had a spat. In the lovely valley of Kashmir, the two teens find themselves in a room all alone; with love drizzling their hearts and a setting as seductive as a locked room it was a perfect spot for inserting this song.

- *Na Mangu Sona chandi* (I do not desire gold nor silver) Raju has dropped in at Bobby's place near a wharf, where a quintessential Christian gala celebration is being held; Hosted by her father, the boisterous'Jack Braganza' (Premnath), admired for his energy amd 'joie-de-vivre'. Holding a trumpet in one arm and sipping rum from another, Jack Braganza belts out this song which etches out his principles of life:

"Na Mangu Sona Chandi, Na mangu bangla gaadi, yeh mere kis kaam ki? Deta hain dil dey badley mein dil ke"

(Nor do I aspire for gold nor long for silver, never a mansion nor a motor, I can give my heart and take away yours, for which I crave forever.)

A month later the film released to smash many records. Made within a budget as low as a shoe string, 'Bobby' earned millions for its maker.

Raju (Rishi Kapoor) and Bobby (Dimple Kapadia) are teenage lovers who have been barred by their parents because of their socio-economic divide. But the grittiness of these two sweeps away all opposition to unite in a love story that enthralled the nation. Raj Kapoor's gamble paid off ! Bobby was declared a big winner where both the lead pair grabbed the Filmfare awards in best actor and actress category. In fact that eventful year, 'Bobby's Raju trounced Vijay of 'Zanjeer' and filmdom lit up under two moons, one as different from the other: The vengeful 'Zanjeer' and the love story 'Bobby'. While Rishi Kapoor found a sound foothold due to 'Bobby', its heroine Dimple Kapadia was shockingly whisked away to oblivion by getting married to a much older Rajesh Khanna! Her fans were downcast.

The nation too was passing through a churn. Anarchic factors like shortage of food, a few assassination attempts and an imminent law and order breakdown was being fanned by many political stooges leading to peoples rights and freedom to be throttled. To the shock of all in June, 1975 an order proclaiming emergency was signed by the President of India.

The era of anger and vengeance had risen and land seemed to give way under the Kapoors and the Khannas. The finished products had a gleaming feel over them especially due to the impregnable prowess of Amitabh Bachchan. The media dubbed him as 'The angry young man'. But there was more than just anger in this man. He went on to excel in just about any kind of roles; the botany professor in Chupke Chupke; a criminal on the run (Zameer); Rebel with a cause (Deewar); vengeful son (Trishul); ruthless Don (DON); a lovable 'dada' (AmarAkbarAnthony); unrequited love (Muqaddar Ka Sikandar); country bumpkin (Namak Halaal) and more followed to stamp his authority. The scale reached by him in emoting anger, pain, fury, drunken stupor, comedy, were superb. What started with 'Zanjeer' was soon followed by

'Gulshan Rai produced 'Deewar and immediately after, Ramesh Sippy's Sholay--scripted by the same writers.

The Greatest Story

'The Greatest Story ever Told, the Greatest Star Cast ever Assembled'--Tag line on the posters of 'Sholay'

After their successful 'Andaz' based on an untouched topic of remarriage, this time the 'Sippy' family wanted to create something 'big'. Salim –Javed provided the fodder and wrote a story, that seemed to have been heavily borrowed from the Henry Fonda starrer film: 'Once Upon a Time in The West'. It was 'Sholay'

Two petty thieves, one avenging former cop and one gang of dacoits led by their brutal but efficient leader. It was peppered with measured doses of songs, authentic sets, scenarios and dialogues that entertain and numb you in equal measure. But the sum total of all made the villain walk away to thunderous applause! He was 'Gabbar Singh', played by rookie actor Amjad Khan.

If Gabbar Singh is the writer's muse then 'Thakur Baldev Singh' is their inspiration!! The remaining characters of Jai-Veeru-Radha-Basanti-and the others who even though are a part of the narrative are mere spokes in the wheel for the audience to laugh and take it easy; in the midst of seething tensions such interludes are a necessity.

Jaidev and Veeru (Amitabh Bachchan & Dharmendra) are petty thieves hired as paid mercenaries by master strategist

'Thakur' (Sanjiv Kumar). Their task is to nail the Bandit and bag a sum of 70K (50K is the 'Sarkar's Inaam' and 20K is personal fee from the 'Thakurs *tijori*'). The core narration is the herculean duel of vengeance between the 'Thakur'(victim) and the Bandit Gabbar(perpetrator).

When the rustic 'Veeru' is busy boozing or wooing 'Basanti', the melancholic 'Jaidev' is drowned in thoughts of how to bare his heart to the widowed 'Radha'. In the midst of these swirling emotions master strategist Thakur Baldev Singh is immersed in charting out ways to ambush Gabbar and his gang. For Jai-Veeru, the job taken up is just a means to earn money; for Thakur, it is deeply personal. Towards the end it becomes personal for Veeru too when he loses his friend to a hail of bullets.

Ramgarh and indeed, all the nearby hamlets, are low hanging fruit for this diabolic plunderer whose area of operations is on a land where the long arm of law is invisible even beyond its horizon. For Gabbar, Thakur Baldev Singh is a living example of his gruesome deed. His 'chopping off' act helps him achieve twin tasks: an act of exemplary punishment & unhindered suzerainty.

The fearless cop 'Thakur Baldev Singh' is now reduced to being a walking –talking billboard who reminds all of a terror known as 'Gabbar Singh'. No wonder, childhood fables in Ramgarh are bedecked with ballads of fearsome tales that can scare away a truant child to rush off to the confines of his mother's bosom or otherwise-"*Gabbar Singh Aajaeyga*' (Gabbar will arrive)

This holds well until the day 'Thakur' charts a blueprint for revenge and rise as his nemesis.

Gabbar Singh has no trappings of wealth. While his peers in other films wore leather jackets or fluorescent suits, he wears an old withered garb of some unknown soldier. While they sip Vat-69 and perhaps played out the number on their live-in molls, he chews on cheap tobacco yet, remains sharp as a razor. While they loot millions this man is content in receiving bags of food grains as tribute from the terrified villagers. Indeed the wee bit of vice we see could be the red-carpet rolled out by gun-runners entertaining their 'VIP customer' to a sizzling cabaret by Helen where, one can sense a longing desire in his eyes. Indeed, by modulating his voice and demeanour Amjad Khan conveyed a lot; pointing to the tied up Veeru he reveals his funny side when he taunts Basanti in his lair *"tum dono ka koi taaka bhida hai kya"*? (are you two having a scene?) Or that raucous smirk to the Thakur *"Bahut Jaan hai"* and then a plea, hideously played out chilling the audience-*"Yeh Haath humko dey Thakur"* (give me those arms)

He knows very well that his infinite dominance over Ramgarh is built on the bulwark of fear. This receives a jolt when three of his men ride back like scared prey with their tails between their legs. This is when Gabbar the 'daku' reveals his take in doling out management lessons; in his style. He first explains why their act is a blot on his reputation:

kitney Inaam rakhey hain Sarkar hum par'?. Poore pacchaas Hazaar"

For Gabbar Singh 50,000 bucks is his Equity value and like a bullish trader he desires to hear a higher figure from 'Samba'(actor MacMohan) his right-hand man! A reduction can signal the end of his reign. He also knows his math when the details revealed shows a skewed ratio of 2:3 " *Woh Do They aur Tum Teen*" !

The fearsome three now meek as lambs find their tearful pleas of 'salt & loyalty' (*namak –wafadaari*) being hurled into a game of Russian roulette. To drive home his point he decides to scare the other gang members thru a shock and awe tactic: terming the roulette game as a joke 'played out on himself' he evokes uproarious laughter from his entire gang including the three guilty of fleeing. As their laughter peaks, Gabbar guns down the three point-blank shocking the others in to deathly silence. As a lesson dawns on them, Gabbar softly utters the title of his management manual: " *Jo Dar gaya samjho mar gaya*" (you flee you die)

The next day he launches a raid on Ramgarh where in the midst of a shattered 'holi' celebration; burning tents, upturned carts and terrified villagers, he straddles the village courtyard menacingly to offer his final solution:

"To save you from the wrath of Gabbar only one man can Guarantee-"*Khud Gabbar*" and for this if he demands some food grains it is not a crime. Never again raise your head"-and then proceeds to teach another exemplary lesson: spitting on the ground he hoists his leg on an upturned cart and orders Jai to come and rub his nose on his boots. It is another matter though that Salim -Javed lend a lifeline to Jai in the form of 'gulaal' (coloured powder) blinding Gabbar momentarily.

The legend ends, unconvincingly though, with his lair laid waste by the mercenary duo and the 'Thakur' extracting revenge by crushing his arms; torn away under his nail studded shoes.

Gabbar Singh is now in a jail where his useless arms can no longer help him in a jail-break, Veeru takes Basanti and returns to his town presumably to a life of honesty and wedded bliss. Thakur and his widowed daughter-in-law spend their remaining days in the betterment of Ramgarh.

For us, 'Sholay' and Gabbar Singh continue to enthral!

The film remained unsurpassed for many decades. Almost forty five years have passed but any thing remotely associated, resembling, or even smelling of'Sholay'makes money. From the makers to the stars, the distributors and the writers all made immense money.

From the star cast, barring Amitabh, no one ever could transcend their roles; beginning from Amjad Khan, Dharmendra, Sanjeev Kumar and reaching down to the smallest. Keshto Mukherjee who built his forte in drunken roles is more remembered as the non-boozing barber 'Hariram'.Same is the case with Jagdeep for his role as 'Soorma Bhopali'. Actor Asrani, a talented character actor who has played a repertoire of roles in 350 films as a brother, friend,doctor, villain and even as a hero in one of them, is identified more as the *Angrezo ke zamaane ka jailor"*

'Sholay's success set the flag of Salim-Javed as writers flying high. By inserting audacious messages in film journals they tom-tommed about their invincibility. Their names became the new by-word for success. The super success of 'Deewar' (which preceded 'Sholay' by six months) 'allowed them to dictate terms.

'Deewar' (The Wall) stood for the law-outlaw divide between two brothers. Past circumstances grind their way to create a yawning chasm between them. In the end, the older son Vijay(Amitabh) is shot dead by his sibling Ravi (Shashi Kapoor)

The Characters:

- Nirupa Roy played 'Sumitra Devi': the mother who bears the brunt of suffering from the first reel to the last; from watching her helpless husband disappearing, to being reduced to dwelling in shanties. Years later when she finally senses a hint of happiness on seeing her sons grown up she is yet again devastated to know that the apple of her eye, her favourite 'Vijay', is a criminal.

- Amitabh Bachchan as 'Vijay': the tormented son who is convinced that turning to crime is a logical way to get even with the world. Revenge is wrong, but in this case,'Vijay' was exonerated by the audience.

- Satyen Kappu as their father 'Anand Verma' whose act of disappearing lets loose a barrage of factors which destroys his son.

- Shashi Kapoor as 'Ravi': the younger brother who pays a heavy price for being called honest. To uphold his conscience he has to shoot down his brother.

- Parveen Babi as 'Anita': the resolute and smart girl but with shades of grey. In the world of the 70's Anita smokes, drinks and sins by living in with Vijay. She yet manages to be classified as the film's 'heroine'

- Actor Iftekhar who had by then become the eternal bust of either a detective, police commissioner or an inspector of police was interestingly, cast as the smuggler 'Mulk Raj Dhabar'. It was he who prophesied that the shoe shine boy(Vijay) is a *'lambi Race ka ghoda. Yeh ladka zyada din jootey saaf nahin karega jis din isne speed pakdi yeh sabko peeche chod dega"*. -(-this boy will not end up as a shoe-shine boy forever. He will outrace all.)

- Actor Sudhir in his initial days had acted as one of the martyred soldiers in Chetan Anand's 'Haqueekat'. In 'Deewar' he played the smuggler's sidey where he gained eternal fame as the one who famously flung a coin at the shoe-shine boy only to be met with an unforgettable retort: " *Mein phekey huey paise nahin leta*"(I do not pick money that is thrown at me)

- Neetu Singh as 'Leena' the younger brother's girlfriend who is perhaps the only character in the film who has led a normal life. She is pretty, daughter of a police commissioner has had a proper education and looks forward to wedded bliss with her beloved.

- Actor Madan Puri as the main Villain 'Samant': he is the one who spoils Vijay's triumphant run by killing his girlfriend and pays the price by getting flung off a high rise.

- Actor Yunus Parvez as 'Rahim Chacha': the aged, old hand at the docks where Vijay worked. Rahim cares for Vijay so wants him to remain passive towards all the wrongdoings happening around. He is the one who advises him to keep his porter's badge carefully: the one inscribed with the number '786'

- Actor Kamal Kapoor as the 'Sethji,' who unleashes the threat of blackmail and murder on Vijay's father. The 'sethji' firmly believes that 'spilling blood is more expensive than paying a bribe'.

- Last but not the least, actor A.K.Hangal: as the retired school master whose son Chander is shot and wounded for stealing few loaves of bread. The man is old, retired, frail and can barely feed his family. But his belief that "poverty & hunger should never be an excuse to steal for this can lead to anarchy in society" shakes up the proceedings. This scene changes the course of events which until then was on the side of Vijay. The old man's candid outburst is what gives confidence to Ravi to gather his inner strength and shoot down his delinquent brother.

<u>Scenes:</u>

The clash with sidey gangster Peter's men inside a warehouse where, nursing a 'beedi' between his lips, legs stretched nonchalantly, Vijay challenges Peter's gang of six men to a fight making mincemeat of them singlehandedly.

The grim dialogues with his mother when he exclaims how he was singled out to have a tattoo branded over his arm ("*mera baap chor hai*"-my father is a thief), making it, according to the innocent mind of the wronged child, the single most factor that distinguished him from his righteous brother. When compared with his diligent brother, the child points at the depraving tattoo on his arm and calmly reveals the analogy to his mother: "*Farak toh hai. Sabse bada farak to yeh hai*" (this is that biggest difference)

'Deewar' proved to be a milestone hit but surprisingly Amitabh Bachchan never won any award for it.

The next immortal act was in Prakash Mehra's 'Muqaddar Ka Sikandar':

Prince Of Destiny

'Ek bhai agar doosre bhai ka pet bharta hain to ehsaan nahin karta'
--Sikandar

The invincibility of this writer-duo was reined in by another of Amitabh's hit which was big, if not bigger, than their creations. It was written by character-actor Kadar Khan, who was also a writer, and here was assisted by Vijay Kaul.

Rewinding Sikandar:

An orphan on the verge of starvation receives food from a little girl. But the girl's father ridicules her empathy and soon tosses him out.

Nevertheless, the boy learns life the hard way and soon grows to become the nemesis of smugglers. He is now known as 'Sikandar'-the prosperous and powerful. Indeed, he celebrates his life in style by serenading along the iconic 'Queen's Necklace' of Bombay on a bike, piping aloud philosophically charged couplets:

"Zindagi toh Bewafa hain Ek din thukrayegi, maut mehbooba hain apni saath lekar jayegi".

'Life is treacherous for she will toss us away, death is our beloved and she will take us away!'

Come evenings and he sips his sundowners with buddy Pyarelal (Ram Sethi) at a 'Kotha' brimming with oomph under the shadow of sensuous 'mujras' rendered by the voluptuous 'Zohra Bai' (Rekha) But his life turns messy when the little girl of yore, who is now a fair maiden, loathes him. Sikandar's indebtedness towards the girl had turned reverential and he addresses her as 'Memsaheb' (Rakhee). Her rejection makes him work doubly hard to illuminate the lives of his out-of-work- friend Vishal (Vinod Khanna) and his foster sister Mehroo (Madhu Malini)

Thus rolls out a saga of love, friendship and sacrifice. As claimed by many, this triangle owes its origin to Bimal Roy's 'Devdas'. In creating the character of 'Sikandar' the writers need to be credited (one of them being Kader Khan) for crafting a radical'Devdas'; while Bimal Roy's 'Devdas' embraced alcohol as a balm to soothe his grief, Prakash Mehra's Devdas is anything but that. Sikandar never drank out of sorrow -he drank for the pure joy which he derived, in fact, he polishes off several pegs with elan. When 'Devdas' is drunk he sits as if in a trance under a long spell woven by the chants of Chandramukhi. But the tale of Sikandar is radically different.When Zohra recites her couplet " *Main sunao tumhein baat Ek Raat Ki..*(Let me narrate you the story of one night....")*, Sikandar by then has just downed a 'Quarter'; the one hundred eighty millilitre potion whips up its magic in stirring his poetic streak. Sikandar butts in between to sweep Zohra off her feet with his own take:

"Maseeha tu Mohabbat key maaron Ka hain, ab dava dey humein ya tu dedey zeher, teri mehfil mein yeh dil jaley aaye hain.."

You are a messiah for the ones downed in love; in the pomp of your court we have assembled either give us an antidote or poison.

Pyarelal plays the version of Bimal Roy's version of ChuniBabu, who was the drinking companion of 'Devdas'. In ChuniBabu's company Devdas became suffocatingly melancholic, but over here, the twosome of Sikander & Pyarelal, when punch drunk, weave their own personal domain; a mutual admiration society. The scene where both are drunk and start searching for their house is classic 'Bevdagiri' (a Mumbai slang word for drunken antics).

It is much later, in one scene, where alcohol gets the better of Sikandar and who emerges, is a changed man.

On that fateful day from behind a bar counter, to his utter disbelief, Sikandar watches his love parable torn apart when he sees his 'Memsaheb' cozying up to Vishal on a dance floor (both swaying awkwardly to singer Mahendra Kapoor's *"Pyar Zindagi hain Pyar Bandagi Hain...* (Love is life love is salvation")

At every beat of the drum Sikandar sees red. As they dance away in bliss the sounds become a metaphor for Sikandar's aching heart thudding away. A deafening roar –Sikandar downs a neat peg. The drums keep beating, the pegs keep flowing soon the dancing girls' chants reach a high

"Pyar Sanam pyar Khuda"...the eyes are now a murderous red. He discards his glass grabs the bottle and drinks full throttle.

The drums beat yet again with Vishal clasping Memsaheb lovingly.Then comes the last stanza:

"Dekh Humein Koi jaley, Koi Jaley aur Haath Maley..Aise logon sey kyon darna yahan"(Watch out for the jealous; for he is left behind, why do we fear them ?)

The barb pierces him and he can take it no more; by now the downed 'neats' have taken their toll. His head spins and Sikandar erupts, spits out a barrage of expletives at Vishal and guns him down:*"Zaleel-Kaminey-EhsaanFaramosh"*

Thankfully, his sordid outbursts turn out to be a make-believe nightmare.

Stepping forward from the darkest end of the bar Sikandar now examines reality: the banquet hall with strobe lights is dim; its gigantic candles extinguished, sending off dying wisps of smoke; the buzzing dance floor is now silent and eerie. He can also see tattered bits of his ill-fated love parable struggling to find their place on the velvet carpets. He is calm; venom swallowed back. Deciding to put his broken heart to good use, Sikandar buries his love for 'memsaheb' in his heart, carries the love of Vishal on his shoulders and in the end the corpse of Zohra in his arms. He then begins his 'Harakiric' finale with Dilawar (Amjad Khan).

Vishal & Memsaheb enter matrimonial bliss, while Sikandar perhaps is buried beside 'Zohra's grave, in the same cemetery where the dervish 'fakir' (Kader Khan) lies buried. The same fakir's gospel way back in the beginning of time had given wings to Sikandar's life: *"Sukh to bewafa hai, Dukh ko galey laga,Takdeer tere Kadam choomengi Aur Tu, Mukaddar Ka Badshah Hoga"*

Mukaddar Ka Sikandar was soon followed by another terrific hit called 'Don'. The film was a racy thriller which dazzled us in the many splendoured hues that spelt the city of Bombay; those long car-chases; characters dressed as the quintessential smugglers aided by their crooks and molls, policemen in their distinct blue uniform, local trains darting away and the feverish momentum in its alleys. It was directed by Chandra Barot who ended up as a one-film wonder.

Rewinding 'DON':

"aapka khoon karna chahta hoon ummeed hain aapko koi aitraaz nahin hoga"-Jasjeet (J.J.)

Somewhere in the Western ghats in a glade abounding with fern and wild grass, a crook 'Raj Singh' and his two accomplices masquerading as buyers of gold are mysteriously blasted away. Some shepherds claimed to have seen a tall, sharply dressed man with prominent side-burns, speeding away in an immensely long Toyota saloon. This makes the police uneasy and they soon find their answer at a high chaired meeting by Interpol officer Mallik (Om Shiv Puri) & Deputy Commisioner of Police D'Silva (Iftekhar), where he grimly reveals that Bombay is now the new headquarters of a smuggling syndicate whose operations are controlled by a man known just by a three letter word: DON-no middle name no surname, an alias sounding more like a code!

D'Silva, the police commissioner, immediately gets in to action mode for laying traps and surveillance to nab this elusive man.

Don is an expat living in Bombay; he is wanted in at least eleven countries. Dressed sharply he usually prefers being consigned in his high rise to indulge in slim 555's,expensive whiskeys and fiddle a game of bridge with his lieutenants, notably, Narang (actor Kamal Kapoor who in his last avatar as 'Sethji' had blackmailed the father to sign all papers in 'Deewar), Mac (the Immortal Sambha) and his moll Anita (Arpana Choudhary). With his origins a mystery and having handled operations in eleven countries, his Hindi is coated with a smattering of English; when he shoots down a member planning to rat him out, as the man slides dead Don pours a large drink and to his bewildered men merely whispers *'Cheers gentlemen'*; and another where the slain man's sister Roma(Zeenat Aman) is bashing up one of his baddies; far from getting livid he gently claps in appreciation, likening her feat to a nimble cat: *"Good good, very good! Mujhe junglee billiyan pasand Hain, keep her."* Ever serious and alert, for Don, song and dance is no way to make merry. No wonder, DCP D'Silva's honey trap involving Roma's sister- in- law 'Kamini' (Helen) spectacularly fails. Even though under the garb of blue contacts and a slit gown she swears *"Yeh Mera dil Yaar ka deewana'* desperately writhing her hour glass figure with come-hither looks, yet, elicits no response from the straight-faced pro! As expected, Kamini is dumped dead in some alley.

No wonder 'Don' gloats over his supposed impregnability, to arrogantly proclaim: "*Don Ko Pakadna Mushkil hi nahin Namumkeen Hain'* (Trapping Don is an impossible feat)

One fateful day the cop's surveillance picks up telephonic chatter between Narang and a conduit called 'Tarachand'. Don soon arrives in his Toyota saloon. Emerging unarmed from his car he finds himself staring down a dozen gun barrels. Regaining his composure 'Don' offers to give away his huge suitcase; Staring eyeballs back at D'Silva and his men he audaciously spells out his offer: "*Iss bag mein itney rupaye hain main apni nikal janey ki keemat de sakta hoon!* (this suitcase contains enough money to buy my freedom)

Shocked in to a momentary silence, 'Shut Up' is what 'D'Silva' manages to bark back. 'Don' persists to enact the same deed which he had done some months back at a glade where he hurls the suitcase towards the cops which blasts-off mid-air, giving cover to escape. Pushing hard on the car's pedals 'Don' screeches away. Toppling carts, smashing grills, mounting pavements he races away with D'Silva and his men in hot pursuit. With the city behind them they now race on a highway. Harnessing his past ability in giving the slip in eleven countries, 'Don' maintains a decent head start. Racing towards a level crossing and just when he is need of a few seconds to reach the other side, his luck runs out and the gates slam shut. He is not done yet. Leaping from his immobile car he runs. In his white suit with cops closing in on him- Don begins his final marathon. Soon he sights a train puffing down his path and he knows this is his 'now-or-never' moment. He runs like one possessed. The train is approaching and soon a coach is tantalizingly close. The tired fugitive is almost there, those handrails inches away but like a runner up Olympian he misses. As the train speeds away, the gangster turns and prepares to leap into a foamy river below. Just then a bullet from 'D'Silva's revolver finds a spot on his back. 'Don' leaps but not before giving all a glimpse of his back now bedecked in a deepening crimson.

With darkness soon approaching, D'Silva posts his men and few searchlights on both sides of the bank. Scanning the water and embankments his cops are jubilant. D'Silva starts off to report to HQ. Driving his 'Ambassador' with a smile on his face D'Silva is rightfully at ease. His quarry is either dead or dying,and then, he feels a touch of cold steel on his neck.

To his shock he hears that much hated voice, the same English twang: *"Eazzeeee"*. Even before he can comprehend, a head rises from the back seat; grimy and bruised the white coat now blackened with algae. Those same murderous eyes, threatening, now tortured by the rising pain in his back. D'Silva is now a hostage!

Pointing his pistol at D'Silva's temple, in between gasps of pain he obstinately maintains:*"Don Zakhmi hain to kya phirbhi Don Hain. Chalte raho mujhe is ilaake sey nikalna hain'*. (so what if Don is wounded, Don still remains a Don;keep driving I need to get away)

But it's finito for 'Don'. With the vertebra in his back shattered by the bullet and the lead swiftly eating away his spinal cord, the legendary gangster slides in to rigor mortis, D'Silva can now finally announce that 'Don is Dead'

But he doesn't. He is tight lipped and soon breaks protocol to act out his own secret plan; whose sheer audacity makes him smile. After personally completing the last rites of this gangster, he is soon standing at the doorstep of a 'Chawl' whose tenant is a tall lungi clad 'Gavaiyya' who earns a living by singing paeans on the glory and riddles of 'Bambai Nagariya' and loves to chew on 'paan banaraswala'. This look alike called Vijay is trained to infiltrate the gang and soon he is a perfect fit to impersonate 'Don'. He enters and learns all their big secrets but some times his past of being a 'gavaiyya' pops out in unguarded moments when he mouths, to the sweet surprise of his cronies the following love ballad:

"Hoga tera aashiq zamana auro ka dil hoga tera nishana naaz na kar yun tirey nazar sey aaye humein bhi teer chalana, jo hain shikari unhey khel hum dikhaenge apne hi jaal mein shikaari phas jayenge woh ghadi aayegi aayegi".

The highlight comes when he enthralls all as the 'Item-Man' in the roaringly aggressive *"Arrey Deewano Mujhe pehchano kahan sey aaya mein hoon Kaun"*? dancing along are about seven or eight girls throwing a mighty shout out of *'Don – Don- Don- Don -Don "*. With a posse of crooks and cronies holding a glass or a fag it was a perfect moment to roll out a cabaret; it does, but not in the form of some semi-clad damsel: what we get is Amitabh in a three-piece suit dancing away with amazing gusto! After a great entertaining rigmarole of fights-song-dance-drama it ends.

But what impresses and leaves a larger footprint is that dark persona of 'Don'; dead and buried, in some obscure graveyard in Bombay, a character clearly pencilled on the lines of "The Jackal". For playing the twin roles a Filmfare award was undeniable.

In his next 'Trishul' which brought the makers of 'Deewar' into their second partnership, and as 'Vijay' again, his every plan is laid to upset his 'Illegitimate' father's ventures. He raises seed capital by freeing his father's plot of land from a shark called Madho Singh (Shetty). But before this happens, he has to barge in to his father's chambers and give him some shock and awe tactic by proudly confessing: *"Main paach laakh ka sauda karne aaaya hoon aur mere jeb meing paach phooti kaudi nahin hai"*.(I have come to make a deal worth five lacs and I dont even have five grounded coins). To be one-up on his father the 'Vijay' of Trishul does not resort to joining hands with a smuggler. This was a corporate battle to be fought out in the markets so he converts his father's trusted team-member in to his mole. In both-the element of dishonesty stands out.

In Manmohan Desai's lost-found saga'Amar-Akbar-Anthony' he played one of the three, but ended up towering all. Even though the 'lost-and-found' template was used by many makers, the other template of religion based brotherhood remained Desai's cozy monopoly.

The story goes thus:

Three brothers are lost on the 15th of August. A Hindu cop finds the eldest outside a park, a Muslim tailor picks up the second while the third is found by a priest outside a church. While Amar grows up to be a cop like his foster father, Akbar grows up to be a 'qawaal' singer and the third, becomes the lovable 'dada' Anthony.

Twenty years back, their father Kishanlal (Pran) was working as a driver for Robert "Seth "(Jeevan) a smuggler of gold biscuits whose fleet of fishing boats regularly unload cartels of gold on secluded beaches of Bombay. One day, Kishenlal's master is involved in a hit and run accident. He flees from the scene and coaxes Kishanlal to take the blame on him in return for his family being properly looked after. Upon his release Kishanlal learns that his "seth" has reneged on his promise leaving his family in dire penury. Shocked, he rushes to confront the seth but circumstances prevent him and under tragic conditions later his family is lost and wife struck blind under a falling tree.

The rest is how the separated brothers grow up, keep bumping into each other & their blind mother in various situations. They realize later that they belong to the same 'khoon', re unite to take revenge on the villainous Mr. Robert.

Amar Khanna (Vinod Khanna) is a serious Inspector of police determined to weed out seedy elements from his area, that includes Anthony. He is in love with Laxmi (Shabana Azmi) who he had earlier rescued from a gang of thieves.

Akbar Ilahabadi (Rishi Kapoor) the hyper active 'qawaal' whose one goal in life is to make Salma (Neetu Singh) his begum. He sings 'qawaali' with terrific gusto (the song *parda hai parda* became a trendsetter), makes a mockery of Salma's father opposing his overtures, befriends every body around and shares a mutual admiration society with Anthony "bhai'

Amitabh as 'Anthony Gonsalvez' towers above all. His character is the fall out 'desperado' of those times, who lives like a 'dada', dares anyone out to evict him from his 'basti', brews booze for a living and is willing to atone for it by giving off a part of his earnings to the altar of a church. Rest of his time he would like to woo a pretty Christian girl, Jenny (Parveen Babi) by dressing up like 'Mr. Hyde' at a lavish Easter party, get punch drunk and bashed up in the bargain. Seeing himself bruised all over the next morning, he starts scolding his own reflection in the mirror; 'Anthony Gonzalvez'revealed a comical side of Amitabh Bachchan. His comic timing (as the late Manmohan Desai opined) "was the swinging factor that earned him his Filmfare award".

Cinematically it had many idiosyncrasies and unimaginative moments. Its art direction was shoddy, technically very ordinary, some truly ridiculous scenes. Like the one where the three brothers are donating blood to their blind mother, each unaware of the other's identity, with a sermonizing Mohammad Rafi song playing in the background *"Yeh sach hain koi kahani nahin Khoon Khoon hota hai paani nahin"*; Or the miracle at the Sai Baba temple, where an implausible ray emerges and their blind mother (Nirupa Roy) regains her sight. There is another one where the snarling Robert "Seth" (actor Jeevan) exclaims *"hum soch raha tha whiskey mein taste kyon nahin aaraha hain, hum ice daalna bhool gaya"*, spills a few drops on his shoes and orders the troubled Kishanlal to polish it. In the penultimate sequence the three brothers, though disguised, keep repeatedly singing their names "Amar-Akbar-Anthony" without the villains getting any whiff of their impersonations ! Though comical and absurd in nature the sum total of all was their ability to entertain. It had some vital ingredients like the template of all religions living in harmony which appealed to the masses, unbelievable godly miracles, damsels in distress, the lost-found formula, hit music by the L-P duo and the presence of Amitabh Bachchan in good measure. All these created a tremendous repeat value. The audience deprived of bare essentials came in droves to watch this multi-starred tale of a family fight the ironies of destiny.

However, if there was one rival who excelled in both, comedy and action, he was Dharmendra. In the light as a waffle 'Chupke-Chupke' by Hrishikesh Mukherjee, which was primarily Dharmendra's film, Amitabh played a relatively shorter role; As Professor Sukumar Roy impersonating as Dr Parimal Tripathi it gave us our first peek in to his sense of comic timing and almost immediately after both starred in 'Sholay'the biggest film of their careers. Dharmendra was doubly blessed by acting in one of Bimal Roy's films like 'Bandini'; he also shone bright in Roy's pupil Hrishikesh Mukherjee's works notably 'Satyakam', 'Guddi'and 'Chupke Chupke'. In a strange irony, after snuggling close to us in 'Chupke Chupke' the sweetest family drama of the year, yet, why do they remain in our minds as 'do chor'' is baffling. At the time of their release, in both 'Chupke Chupke' and 'Sholay' Dharmendra was a much bigger star than Amitabh, but somewhere, Dharmendra meandered away; Refusing 'Zanjeer' was a cardinal mistake and the reason attributed to 'Vijay's role being a songless one proves doubtful because the same year he did play the role of 'Shankar', a songless one, ironically in a musical brimming with some of the greatest hits for eternity called 'Yaadon Ki Baraat'.

As the tall man marched ahead in his bell-bottoms trampling all under his long legs, the other side, Rajesh Khanna's career commenced its flight towards descent. As we saw, his flops also coincided with poverty and disillusionment setting in. Economic hiccups triggered changes. Spiraling prices, shortage of essentials, rigged elections, sycophancy in bureaucracy, bribery at every step, in such a dejected mind set of the common man where the adage: "an empty stomach does not care for his right to vote" can well reflect the man's pit of misery which had no bottom. In such an atmosphere of restlessness the romantic hill stations with its gushing water falls turned in to a mirage. A failed monsoon, the wicked step brother, a cunning 'bhabhi' or a crooked 'munshi' become lesser evils. The system of rule had become a larger evil. Ironically, the earlier generation bequeathed a Frankenstein to the next; when a smiling face faded away to bring in brooding eyes and a clenched fist.

In 'Deewar', the reasons for Vijay's detatchment are attributed to his troubled childhood. An innocent Union Leader Anand Verma (actor Satyen kappu) who is Vijay's father committed to the well being of his fellow workers is falsely framed by the wily factory owner (actor Kamal Kapoor) and in the eyes of the workmen he is branded a traitor. Incidentally the factory owner justifies his action to 'Anand Babu; He confesses apologetically by stating *"Main Ek business man hoon, aur mujhe yeh karna accha nahin lagta"* clearly implying that in business spilling blood is more expensive than giving a bribe. To save his wife and two sons from being killed by the 'Sethji's' henchmen, Anand Verma puts his signature on all the papers thrust at him; Soon he is heckled as a traitor in the eyes of his co-workers. The guilt rackles him so much that he abandons his family and sets off alone aimlessly for the next two decades, loitering around incognito leading his life as an uncared destitute; Only to resurface two decades later as a corpse in some train. Fortunately, his soul cajoles his 'karma' to get his pyre lighted by his eldest son, Vijay, where the camera pans on a flaming torch and a depraving tattoo, to send shivers down the audience.

But in 'Sholay' the cause for Jai's quiet demeanour is not explained. While Veeru (Dharmendra) is an extrovert, happy go lucky fellow, Jai is more guarded over what he commits.

The idea of a 'thief' had found a reluctant acceptance in the minds of cinegoers. Lack of employment opportunities and wealth being concentrated in the coffers of few; the role of a thief being played by the new age hero came to roost. So in 'Hera-Pheri' we see the lead pair of Amitabh – Vinod as thieves; In 'Sholay', Jai and Veeru are thieves. The protagonist in 'Mukaddar Ka Sikandar'is a police informer earning hefty commissions from the police by tipping them on the illegal warehouses of smugglers; In 'Amar Akbar Anthony', he brews illegal booze for a living but 'atones for it by keeping twenty percent of his earnings at the altar of a church'; In 'Mr Natwarlal', he dupes other businessman with shady dealings off their money and in Ramesh Behl's 'Kasme Vaade' the character 'Shankar' is a car thief. The new age hero had brought in the concept of 'tit-for-tat' however there was a 'Robinhood' streak lurking inside those so called thieves. All were super hits leading to a new churning. Scripts written from the same mould were finding their way to other peers like Dharmendra, Shatrughan Sinha, Sanjeev Kumar, Jeetendra, Vinod Mehra, Vinod Khanna because this new onslaught by now, had relegated them as second -tier heroes

In an early Era, the hero sighted a rainbow by saying " *Mujhe Naukri mili hain Ma* "(I just got a job Mother), the new mantra now was " *Seth ki tijori mein maal bahut hai*". (There's lot of cash in the locker)

In the seventies Dharmendra too was a right fit where films had action and romance as the two mainstays. With a string of hits in 'Samadhi' (film by Prakash Mehra), 'Jheel Ke Us paar ', and 'Kahani Kismat Ki '(by Arjun Hingorani),and 'Aankhen'(by Ramanand Sagar) a spy action drama he was extremely convincing in action roles and good looking with sufficient brawn too thrown in. Those damsels in distress in such movies were in search of knights, who would hold and protect them. Dharmendra was a knight of the right fit! However, if damsels in distress gravitated towards Dharmendra their knight in shining armour, but men of those times, wronged by a system beyond their control, gravitated towards Salim-Javed's muse.

While Amitabh's films hit bull's eye, Rajesh Khanna's were biting dust. Ajnabee, Roti, Humshakal, Prem Kahani, MahaChor, Bundelbaaz,Aashiq Hoon Baharon ka, Anurodh, Chakravyuh, Mehbooba fell like the proverbial pack of cards. Tickets of Amitabh's films sold in the 'black market' in the *'dus-ka-bees'* category while films of Rajesh Khanna and the others were readily available in 'Current booking'. By the end of 1977, the aura of Rajesh Khanna had completely disappeared. His problem was more telling because Rajesh Khanna never made any attempt in re-inventing himself. However, in the midst of the Bachchan juggernaut he did give few hits like 'Prem Nagar', 'Amar Deep', 'Chhaila Babu','Thodisi Bewafaai', 'Fifty –Fifty', 'Dhanwan'. But they were few, spread over a long period of four years 1977 to 1981. He no longer looked fit and age had begun to show on his face and form. His prancing around with young girls like Poonam Dhillon and Tina Munim looked misplaced.

The success of anger, as a factor, brought in many changes. Herd mentality, coupled with a lack of good stories made producers insist on scripts that had this *'chor-badla'* undercurrent. The alternate heroes signed, were cheaper and were also available to give bulk dates. This started a tidal wave of pedestrian stories with lesser known directors; Where in the name of cashing on a wave gave birth to mindless violence like; vengeance sworn due to a parent's murder, or the rape of a sister, or an oppressive zamindar. The list was long and made people weary. Hundreds of them went down the drain.

Shashi Kapoor and Vinod Khanna did keep themselves busy by having solo hits like 'Chor Machaye Shor' and 'Lahu Ke Do Rang', both heavily based on the lost and found formula. Shatrughan Sinha remained busy from the twin success of 'Kalicharan' his best crime saga and 'Vishwanath where vengeance is unleashed on the villains by a qualified lawyer.

'Kalicharan' and 'Vishwanath', both super hits, brought director Subhash Ghai to the limelight. In later years, he would go on to have a long innings as a successful producer -director. Shatrughan Sinha had just changed tracks from playing the villain into a hero and after a few minor successes it was 'Kalicharan' which spectacularly announced the cross over of a villain scaling up as a hero. Subhash Ghai made his debut as a director with this thrilling tale of a dedicated police official Prabhakar Srivastava(Shatrughan Sinha) who loses his life while trying to expose the true credentials of business tycoon 'Seth Deen Dayal' (actor Ajith). His death is kept under wraps by the police commissioner M.R. Khanna (Premnath) who inserts a look-alike known as 'Kalicharan' and is a criminal on the run whom he trains to masquerade as Prabhakar. Subhash Ghai made a good concoction of drama topped with a double role. Premnath had become set to play stellar roles while Ajith continued the English speaking persona of 'Dharamdas Tejaa' from Prakash Mehra's 'Zanjeer': the same cigar belching honcho who nurses a 'Vat-69' and projects an image of an honest business tycoon. The success of 'Kalicharan' boosted Shatrughna's prospects but could never really make him a serious rival to Amitabh; his way of dialogue delivery bordered more on the theatrical and was amply demonstrated in 'Kalicharan' where the style in delivering his lines flaunted his inherent bombastic approach:*"Aapke haath mein nahin mujhe aapke mooh mein khoon nazar aata hain seth Deendayal "* (a lengthy exchange, its there on 'YouTube')while his 'rival' Amitabh excelled in both, the pompous and the brooding; there was a a line in 'Zanjeer' which had a quiet tone tinged with sufficient venom:

"jab tak baitne ko kaha nahin jaata chup chap khade rahon yeh, police station hain tumhare baap ka ghar nahin."

How to enhance box-office value without having Amitabh Bachchan in their films was the biggest challenge for film makers. How to sustain the interest of the audience bypassing this gigantic factor ? These questions vexed their minds. It was also obvious that only a select few were able to afford Amitabh's price which was rumoured to be seventy lacs plus a territory, avail his dates and so reaped the benefits. Such banners were few and they were Yash Chopra, Prakash Mehra (PMP productions), Manmohan Desai 's MKD films, Rakesh Rumar, Ramesh Behl's 'Rose Movies', Ramesh Sippy's 'Sippy Films'.

The remaining producers had to sell their wares by signing the two-tiered ones to wear the cloak of the 'angry, vengeful man'. But by this they met with little or no success. If the others mouthed dialogues " *Mein tera khoon pee jaoonga*' leading to whistles from the aisles, Amitabh's mere entry on screen with the camera panning his long legs and then on to those side burns led to coin-showers in mofussil towns. To book his film tickets one had to not only be an early bird in queues, but also have the stomach to take in the disappointment when booking windows snapped shut with a 'housefull' board dangling. Those days a joke doing the rounds was "one could get sugar and even kerosene from a government-controlled shop but getting a ticket for an Amitabh starrer always remained a fat chance". No wonder 'India Today' a leading monthly magazine in 1986, had him on its cover under the heading: 'Bachchan-One Man Industry'.

However, actors like Manoj Kumar known as 'Bharat'in all his films beginning from the seventies, did meet success with films like 'Beimaan,''Dus Numbri', and 'Sanyasi'. 'Beimaan' even won him a Filmfare award. Some others which were non-Amitabh hits was Brij's 'Victoria No 203' which had Navin Nischal.

Many producers took in three or even four of the second runged heroes to make a single multistarrer. Those multistarrer had the usual lost-found or, revenge themes. They mainly starred the garrulous Shatrughan Sinha -the frolicsome Shashi Kapoor -knight templar Sunil Dutt -the sombre Sanjeev Kumar -'Herculean' Dharmendra & 'jumping jack' Jeetendra who made teams backed by mid sized producers; one of them being Raj Kumar Kohli. That year Kohli startled all when his multistarrer film 'Nagin', in the midst of Amitabh's 'Adalat' & 'Kabhi Kabhi', turned out to be a big money-spinner.

NAGIN—'revenge of a serpent'.

The serpent in question is a female cobra. In a long primitive past, superstitions on snakes and their activities formed a chunk of folklore which gave rise to many myths : that they 'drink milk', they 'sway to music' played by blowing air through a *'Been'*, that they 'never forget'. Ancient folklore go on to narrate that older species dwelt in deeper jungles where the rarest ones nestle a rock-sized diamond known as *'mani'* perched on their hood. Killing a snake was never considered an act of bravery; in such cases it was claimed it could invite retribution in form of ill-luck. Down south 'Sarpadosha' which means 'ill luck arising from the killing of a serpent', needs to be corrected pronto! Some parables even claim that few of their kinds can take form of any human they fancied. To fortify this theory the starting credits of 'Nagin' reminds you that in the battle between 'Lord Krishna' and the serpent 'Kaliya', after being vanquished, 'Kaliya' appeared in the form of a human to ask for forgiveness from Krishna. Kohli drew up a script based on all these myths, with rewarding results.

Earlier, films based on animal-protagonists did have a successful record, especially where honours were shared with a dog or an elephant. 'Nagin' with its reptile being of prime focus was eerie and a sort of horror-thriller. The 'Adults only' certificate kept away the kids but brought in the elders in droves.

Six friends out on a hunt in a forest watch a pair of serpents canoodling in the form of humans. In an act of foolishness one of the friends shoots down the male. This triggers in to motion an age old parable that the female will hunt them down. She does just that, through well contrived situations, the ' *Icchadhari Nagin*' (Reena Roy) takes '*badla*' by taking forms of the girlfriends of the hunted,(Yogita Bali, Mumtaz, Neelam Mehra and Rekha), and ensnare the men. The screen play was racy and the chase by the 'nagin' and subsequent killings are well enthused with suspense: Who will go next and how-, was the question uppermost in the audiences mind ! The first is seduced by the serpent and is bitten in bed; the second is ensnared in a hotel room to be struck on his head. Shaken by the prophecy turning out to be true the others obtain a holy talisman that can protect them. Not to be deterred the serpent takes up forms of other woman to create blight in the conjugal bliss of the fourth who is forced to part his '*Shivji-waali-taveez*'. The fifth gives it off when his child is held hostage in its black, shiny grip. The sixth, Sunil Dutt, by virtue of his success in killing the hissing cobra survives to be called as the 'hero' of this hunt.

The music by Laxmikant-Pyarelal was okay enough to lighten people's minds while the main theme song "*tere sang pyar mein nahin todna*" is aptly haunting and keeps popping up when ever the serpent is mourning the loss of her mate. With a star cast crowded with mid-sized names like Sunil Dutt, Jeetendra,Feroz Khan, Sanjay Khan, Kabir Bedi, Anil Dhawan, Vinod Mehra, Rekha, Mumtaz, Ranjeet, and Premnath, 'Nagin' grabbed significant market share that year. Kohli again repeated this success with 'Jaani Dushmun': a story of a blood thirsty werewolf on the loose which again,had five leading men; Sunil Dutt, Shatrughan Sinha, Sanjeev Kumar, Jeetendra and Vinod Mehra. Such films led to a rise in value perceived by the masses in cities and towns. Films like 'Nagin' and 'Jaani Dushmun 'were big hits and made a lot of money.

However, Raj Kumar Kohli could not sustain the same formula for long resulting in inane and over the top films like 'Badle Ki Aag' which of course sank instantly even though having had multi heroes Dharmendra, Sunil Dutt, Jeetendra. These were survival tactics to make money. But repeating the same trash only added to the din, making them lose money and further eroding the box office values of these actors. But in this maze actor Feroz Khan won the race with his 'Qurbani'. This slick musical thriller dazzled audience, which was no mean achievement. In the midst of Bachchan's 'Laawaris' and 'Dostana', and Rishi Kapoor's 'Karz', his 'Qurbani' made money on it's own USP's. Even though it was deeply entrenched in stuck formulas of 'friendship –turned-sour- due- to a love triangle', what worked for it was its slick screenplay. Fast paced and riveting it had Amjad Khan for the first time in a positive role of a cop blessed with a 'gift of the gab', Shakti Kapoor as the new villain on the scene who got noticed for turning out to be a 'good looking'villain. With action mostly shot in England, its music honours for the first time were shared by two composers: Kalyanji-Anandji & Biddu; it was Biddu, who composed the hit *'Aap Jaisa koi merei zindagi mein aaye....'*

Though multistarrers was the current norm, DevAnand loathed sharing honours with rivals. So in 'Navketan Films' next project he deviated to chart a new path and decided to instead cast multi villains. Starting from Amjad Khan, Kader Khan, Shakti Kapoor, Ranjeet, Prem Chopra, Gautam Sareen, Narendra Nath to molls like Simple Kapadia and Kalpana Iyer; his attempt in cashing in on the action era resulted in a financial disaster called 'Loot Maar'. The former 'Guide' and the dashing 'Johnny' were now past their sixties. Frailed and shriveled, Dev concealed his frailities by wearing several layered forms of clothing: shirt-jacket-coat-muffler-scarf and tried to blend in the action era in 'Lootmaar' by not only 'riding' a Yamaha bike but even audaciously 'springing' up mid-air to dive under a speeding trailer truck.

The scenario was now swarmed with many such big budgeted disasters. Dharmendra –Zeenat Aman starrer 'Shalimar', filled to its brim with stars from Hollywood like Rex Harrison of 'My Fair Lady' fame, John Saxon from 'Enter The Dragon'fame and actress Sylvia Miles of 'Midnight Cowboy' fame. Produced and directed by an NRI, Krishna Shah, it had great music by R.D.Burman with some of its numbers immortalized for eternity. Shot in some exotic locales and rumored to have cost him four crore rupees the film emptied the coffers of its distributors. Dharmendra as the secret agent 'Kumar'was perfect; with the physical charm of a gladiator, cloaked in a suit, Dharmendra literally redefined the concept of being clean-cut and dapper! Zeenat Aman as 'Sheila', in a well fit business suit complemented him. The film had impressive sets, a star cast studded with the best from both sides, yet it spectacularly failed. In hindsight, the reasons for its dismal performance could have been the huge mismatch between its shrill publicity and the final product. The song *one-two-cha-cha-cha* sung by Usha Uthup had garnered great expectations by music listeners. Images of a large discotheque, gigantic lights hovering over Zeenat Aman stomping away in a slit skirt, was what people imagined but what they actually watched was their favourite chartbuster systematically shredded; instead of Zeenat they watched Aruna Irani doing the 'Chachacha' and the camera boringly sneaking off to pan local trains, handcarts, pedestrians, buses and taxis outside Bombay Central. This listless picturisation, in the very first reel of 'Shalimar', set the tone for its downhill slide. It further strengthened the belief that to make big money, Amitabh Bachchan was a safer bet. In the case of multistarrers it made good business sense to also accommodate the 'Number 1'. This new oracle also helped in furthering the careers of his colleagues in the industry. Shashi Kapoor after solo hits like 'Chor Machaye Shor' and 'Fakira' went on to give about 15 duds. Any other person in his place would have surely disappeared but his timely pairing with Amitabh: starting from the iconic 'Deewaar' to 'Suhaag', 'Do Aur Do Paanch' and 'Namak Halaal'not only helped him remain in public domain but as he himself confessed, "helped me in financing my passion for making my kind of movies under 'Prithvi Films". Rishi Kapoor kind of held his own in hits like 'Hum Kisise Kum Nahin' and Subhash Ghai's 'Karz'. But duds like 'Doosra Aadmi', 'Yeh Vaada Raha' and Nasir Hussain's magnum let-down called 'Zamane Ko Dikhana Hain' threatened to roll him over, if not, for his partnership with Amitabh Bachchan in films like 'Naseeb' and 'Coolie'. Nasir Hussain had kept the fires glowing by making films on his fixed templates of basing love-stories on quaint hilltops; more than the script he loved to focus more on song picturisations.; A hitherto rewarding formula which brought out classics like 'Yaadon Ki Baarat' and 'Hum Kisise Kum Nahin'; this trait proved to be his undoing by manifesting in the form of 'Zamane Ko Dikhana Hain', a mighty flop.

The renouncement by Vinod Khanna owing to 'Sanyas' narrowed the competition. So there was a 'Ram-Balram' directed by Vijay Anand for big budget producers Mushir –

Riaz having Amitabh and Dharmendra. Then came 'Dostana' produced by Yash Johar (father of today's Karan Johar) and directed by Raaj Khosla had Amitabh Bachchan and Shatrughan Sinha, Prakash Mehra's 'Namak Halaal' had Amitabh-Shashi while Manmohan Desai's 'Naseeb' had Amitabh-Shatru-Rishi.

It was now amply clear that for a big budget film to succeed, the star cast had to be led by 'Him'. Many formed partnerships, except the tempestuous Rajesh Khanna.

There was another cluster taking shape. While the A-Listers were trying to scale newer heights, there was a group of smaller heroes who constituted the 'B' category. They were Benjamin Gilani, Vijayendra Ghatge, Mukesh Khanna, Sachin and a young outsider from Calcutta whose name was Gourango Chakraborty.

An Outsider

Gourango Chakraborty strayed in to Bombay to try a shot at stardom. For starters, he did small roles for a living. Having a National Award under his belt and an FTII certificate to boot, producers refused to touch him with a barge pole. He was as they dubbed him: an 'Outsider' in Bombay. But the man's spirit held on. He went through a name change, adopting an alias as unknown as 'Rana Rez', (this name appears when he performed a short dance rendition in a film called 'Mukti). Soon he managed to get a role of the hero's friend in a film called 'Phool Khile Hain Gulshan Gulshan'. This film, produced by a Kapoor and starring a leading Kapoor sank, but that dance item by Rana Rez in 'Mukti' had carved itself in the memory of the audience. 'Rana Rez' later decided to rechristen himself as Mithun Chakraborty. Those days there was an unmet need of a real dancing star. Shammi Kapoor had retired and alongwith with him,dance went on the back burner. While all the so-called dancing stars of those times – mainly Jeetendra and Rishi Kapoor- specialized in moves resembling a PT drill. In fact the 'Om Shanti Om' number from 'Karz' which was a thumping chartbuster in its own right had Rishi Kapoor merely walking around on a gigantic replica of a rotating record while actual dancing moves were left to the chorus girls!

Mithun was just another guy whose sole usp was, as many magazines remarked, 'strange dance movements' which had never been ever attempted by any of the certified 'dancing stars'. However, millions of cinegoers found the same 'strange dance moves', where Mithun jiggled his pelvic- to their liking was instantly lapped up. As he kept on steadying his little boat by bagging insignificant roles in 'Do Anjaane' and 'Amardeep' he finally found some toe-hold by starring as a hero in low-budget smallies such as 'Tarana' from the Rajshri Team, Shakti Samanta's 'Khwab', and 'Mera Rakshak' by the makers of 'Haathi Mere Saathi'. His moment came during 1980-81, when big budget films starring the reigning icons of the Industry, either failed or did less than expected business. Multi Budget films like Bandhan (Rajesh Khanna), Takkar (Jeetendra) Be-Reham (Shatrughan Sinha) 'Burning Train' (Vinod Khanna) and 'Professor Pyarelal (Dharmendra) had been given a big thumbs down at the Box office. A few months later a big-bucks movie called 'Shaan ' made by the creator of 'Sholay', starring the who's-who of the Industry, jolted it by doing less than expected business. A few streets away, in a dilapidated cinema hall, a small budget film called 'Suraksha' was running for several weeks continuously. Made by Ravi Nagaich from the South, he dressed this film up like an incongruous 'James Bond' caper in which Mithun played a spy bearing a code called "G-9". The common people comprising of college students in the morning, and the labour class during the night, welcomed this tall, dark man who displayed new dancing skills by swaying his pelvis and briskly swishing a 'nan-chaku' giving birth to a 'new kind' of action.

Around the same time a film categorized as 'B-grade' called 'Humse Badhkar Kaun' made by producer and director Deepak Bahry was giving decent return on investment (ROI) to it's maker—solely due to the drawing power of this man alone. But admittedly, 'Humse Badhkar Kaun' was a well made film perfectly milking the concept of multistarrers; it had Vijayendra Ghatge, Amjad Khan, Danny Denzongpa and Mithun (as the four lost bros) while the villain's role was played by Ranjeet. In such a daunting situation, came a small time producer called B.Subhash. Perhaps, sensing the lack of a real dancing hero as wished by the masses, he took a calculated risk and dared to make a movie dedicated to this concept. He signed Mithun for a film boldly titled as 'Disco Dancer'. The film went on floors and was soon readied for release.

The outlines was about a boy, famished from poverty who tries to makes ends meet in eking out an existence by singing and dancing under the tutelage of his late father's partner (Rajesh Khanna in a terrific cameo). Circumstances brand his widowed mother a thief –stigmatizing mother-son to be thrown out of the humble slum where they dwell.

They migrate; ostensibly, to neighbouring Goa where the boy grows up honing his innate dancing skill and makes do by performing at weddings or an odd function.

An extremely ordinary story per se but what held the audience of 1982 remarkably captive, was how the young man hits back, by bringing aloft his dancing skills and play out his battles on the dance floor. An ordinary script sewn together with a limited budget, bereft of big stars. But what bound all of them together were six songs, for these captivated the audience.

The first was *"goron-ki-na-kalon-ki*

The young lad prodded by his tutor 'Master Raju' (Rajesh Khanna) dances to the beats skilfully tapping on a bongo, blowing in to a flute and strumming on a guitar. They strut away from the beaches of Bombay to enter in to nearby lanes of the high handed elite, where he incurs the wrath of a 'Sethji' (Om Shivpuri)

The second- a songless foot tapping sequence where the lad is now a young man, starkly alone on an empty road with it's street lights gazing down upon him, smartly trotting away on its median, miming a jig with gestures and movements. Those lights too twinkle away at this incognito dancer whose signature moves bring in a sense of celebration on this solitary path. At its farthest end evaluating him real hard, is his discoverer- Mr David Brown (Om Puri)

Third- *"Ae-Oh-Aah-Zara Mudke.."* this unknown aspirant is now on the cusp of his debut. Dressed in fitting whites, accentuating his well-toned torso-'Jimmy'(Mithun) is ready to grab this moment when, to the shock of all gathered, a stiletto flung by the 'Sethji''s haughty daughter (Kim) lands on the floor. Soon, cries of "Boo'-Sadak Chhap-street singer" rises up from her sycophants and this coterie appear to be well on their way to rattle him away. The organisers are terrified, certain that their new 'pick' would turn out to be their 'Waterloo'. Manager David Brown and his find Jimmy are shaken yet, non-plussed. They know that for them, it's a now or never moment.

The drums roll, beats begin and holding the stilettos in his tight fist-Jimmy fights out another battle; stamping the floor, twirling his heels, he sears that same spot left sordid by those stilettos. The unsure spectators who silently agreed with the shoe-throwing-act by the 'Shrew' are now mesmerized. All signs of tentativeness are swiftly decimated. In a stanza that goes as '*Aisa Mauka Zindagi Mein pehli Baar aaya Hain*'--- wiping his palms casually, as if to shrug off those bits of soil from her stiletto he not only lays the Shrew waste, but makes her coterie blend with his fans; when he bends so do they; when he twirls they jump with joy and when he thrusts his pelvis they shriek in orgasmic delight- A Star is born.

In the fourth- '*Krishna Dharti Pey aaja Tu*', like all villains per se, the 'Sethji' decides to scuttle 'Jimmy's career by laying cohorts on his path. As 'Jimmy' leaves for his first major show they waylay him. What ensues is the usual fistcuffs, flying kicks and finger-snapping antics that stem from the ordinary- after which an almost imminent 'smoke-break' or a loo-break by the audience, is put on hold by the unravelling spectacle of watching an enormously sized 'King's Crown' cut-out across which, lay the longest flute! That legendary Crown topped with a bright peacock plume –with Jimmy symbolically in purple blues pleading 'Lord Krishna' *Chhed dey baansuri geet woh pyaar key* to come, revisit the planet, play his flute and pronounce his sway; dreamy mist swirling around the crown, the flute pointing one end to the sky-Jimmy and the audience became one with the Lord !

In the fifth- it went as *'Say-D-say-I-say-S-say-C-say-O'-DISCO*

This is 'Jimmy's moment of consolidation. Robed in shimmering silver with a matching laurel wreath- Jimmy hurls all his ammo in to the microphone. Strobed lights illuminate his gravity-defying moves where the entire length of his torso rests on his calves drawing out a position of critical impregnability. He reaches out to his audience who have paid to watch him, " *Tumhein maloom jawaani kya hoti hain?*" they reply stupefied " *Nahin maloom*" with Jimmy playing out his signature moves. These were not a creation of any well paid VHX. What was on display was the innate energy that this plucky man brings to chart a continuum of energy.

In the finale, a shattered 'Jimmy' whose soul has been tragically torn apart now sees the guitar as an epitome of evil- gathers his grit to fight back. A face gaunt with grief, he straightens his drooping shoulders to battle out his final woes. Flinging away a 'poncho' draped around his crestfallen shoulders to reveal a sleeveless vest- Jimmi proclaims the shredding of his inner demon. Rippling arms glistening under a thin film of sweat he grabs the guitar like a new found mace. Striking a piercing note on the electric cords, he struts around recollecting his mother's blessings and dares his perpetrators to drown his spirit !

'Yaad-Aa-raha-Hain' indeed, was a battle royale.

'Disco Dancer', made on a shoe-string budget, stitched together by lower-graded actors or out of work ones, pulled along by an ordinary script and led by a struggling 'B-grade' hero- was a perfect recipe for being called as a 'loser in the offing'- but for this man who came in to be shunned as an 'outsider'. With an FTII medal and a National Award under his belt he seamlessly merged in to mainstream cinema.

While makers were either jostling around to sign Amitabh Bachchan or at least partner him with another actor, many were poring over inane scripts twisted and turned to be moulded in old stale formulas of lost-found siblings, or losing money in expensive Hollywood ventures, there was another breed of makers who also remained in their quest for glory. But they were on paths less travelled. They made films on realistic topics with modest budgets. They were oblivious to the embedded tracks of anger and vengeance. Never was there a need for garish sets or snarling villains nor molls or flashy cars. Their films had the fragrance from the wet soil of a village or the dewy sweat glistening on the foreheads of the scores who commute in suburban Bombay. Their heroes wore plain trousers below untucked bush shirts, their leading ladies wore saris with simple hair dos; they worked either as typists or clerks in offices. They earned modest salaries and drew joy in simple pleasures of life. They were films on social issues with performances that stayed with you for a long time.

Prominent among them were Shyam Benegal, Basu Chatterji, Basu Bhattacharya, Sai Paranjpe, Govind Nihalani, Hrishikesh Mukherjee and Gulzar. In the midst of glamour these doyens were making their presence felt in their own quiet ways; Shyam Benegal's 'Ankur', Basu Chatterjee's 'ChitChor','Baton Baton Mein' and Hrishikesh Mukherjee's 'Golmaal' and 'Khubsoorat'. Gulzar was of course a veteran who in his initial days had partnered with Bimal Roy and later Hrishikesh Mukherjee as a lyricist. Even Raj Kapoor and Hrishikesh Mukerjee were different from the current tide. For these legends, making films on social topics gave vent to their creativity. They steadfastly refused to migrate to the more 'saleable' angry phenomenon for the plain fact it was not their forte. One such film was 'Shaukeen' which had an unheard theme.

Rewinding 'Shaukeen':Basu Chatterjee's film had three unlikely heroes, all past their sixties: Ashok Kumar, superstar of 1946 played Chaudhary, A.K.Hangal, the blind muezzin of 'Sholay' and the frail teacher from 'Deewar' played the most stylish role of his career as Indersen and Utpal Dutt, who besides acting in films was a decorated stage actor who conducted Shakespearean plays in impeccable English- played the rustic 'beedi' smoking Jagdish Bhai. The conventional 'hero' played by a young Mithun Chakraborty was relegated to playing second fiddle. A radically thought out humorous film but back then in 1983 was considered to be too bold.

The story was of three elderly men who have fulfilled their familial responsibilities; A voiceover after the credit titles introduces the three: Chaudhary owns a construction business, Indersen who likes to remain stylish in the English way runs a travel agency called "Andersen Travels'(Andersen is actually an English mask of his name Indrasen). "*Accha Khatey hain peetey hain arrey bhai accha kamaatey bhi to hain*" (he eats good, drinks good why not he also earns good) Jagdish Bhai is uneducated *"Matric fail honey key baad unhoney padhaai chhod di"* (after failing his tenth he quit studies)but owns several flats where he gains on rent and also earns interest thru money-lending. Chaudhury's children are married and he lives with his wife, while the other two are widowers. However they still feel 'young' and become restless in the company of young girls or even middle-aged woman. But due to societal frowns they are reluctant to pursue the woman they eye upon; Chaudhary on a young girl who is his neighbor, Indersen on his young buxom secretary and Jagdish on his middle aged widowed tenant. The three, often meet in the evenings for drinks where they discuss their frustrations and inability to give a damn about societal taboos. Jagdish in his kurta-pyjama keeps getting flustered with Indrasen around as he feels he can't match up to his stylish life-style which Indrasen proudly displays by wearing dapper clothes, putting on glares and puffing on a pipe.

Indrasen- *sorry aaney mein der ho gayi*

Jagdish- *zyaada bano mat majnu laila key saath office mein der ho rahi hain laila key saath cinema dekha jaa raha hain"*

Indrasen- *arre bhai Laila nahin Leela. Aur akele nahin bhare cinema-hall mein.*

Jagdish- *toh saala mere saath cinema dekhna aur Leila key saath dekhna ekhi baat hain kya?*

Turning to Chaudhary he asks: *accha woh ladki jo ab aayi thi acchi lagti hain?*

Chaudhury: *sharab peekar jhooth nahin bola jaata, achhi lag ti hain, koi bhi jawan ladki acchi lagti hain*

Jagdish: *accha hum kya sach mooch buddhey ho gaye hain kya ?*

Chaudhury: *kyon tumhein nahin lagta ?*

Jagdish: *pata nahin aisa lagta hain sub kuch khatam nahin hua ab bhi kuch armaan baaki hain*

With their libido on an over-drive Choudhary suggests an idea where the three could go off to some distant place where no one would know them. Under the pretext of 'holidaying' they could then pursue their real motives. To keep their plan hush-hush they even do away with their regular driver and hire a temporary one. This is where Ravi (Mithun) steps in, offering his services as a driver. Ravi is originally from Goa, so when he hears them haggling over which destination should they go to, he shrewdly suggests Goa, since his girlfriend Anita (Rati Agnihotri) lives there. Anita is a crooner at a hotel in Goa and to Ravi's dismay these three men start eyeing Anita. The rest of the film was about the three drawing up meticulous plans to woo Anita and how she and her boyfriend keep parrying their attempts. Of course in the end, the film ends on a happy note with the three realizing the futility of chasing piped dreams. The humour in this film was wrongly deduced as 'vulgarity' by the audience and moreover 'Disco Dancer' had just released so most in the audience were expecting lot of 'dance-situations' making 'Shaukeen' a low gainer.

The period 1975 to 1979 was too fiery. Bachchan's angst vapourized all. Raj Kapoor's 'Satyam Shivan Sundaram' lacked passion and it showed. The story of Rupa(Zeenat Aman) a village belle was meant to be pure and innocent of worldly ways. Standing tall under a waterfall was meant to show her celestially beautiful- titillation was the last thing on Raj's mind. But the unintended came to the fore. The original message of beauty transcending superficial physicalities got buried under Raj's camera trying to focus more on her boobs than her heart.

Hrishikesh Mukherjee tried diluting Bachchan's persona by casting him as a classical, melancholic singer in 'Alaap' which could not survive beyond a few weeks. His 'Jurmana' too met with average success. But a year later, his 'Golmaal', without Bachchan, was a classic hit and a year later came 'Khubsoorat' with the voluptuous Rekha –minus-Bachchan again turning a winner all the way. Hrishikesh Mukherjee hit an unexpected purple patch with the back-to-back success of 'Golmaal' and Khubsoorat'. While actress Rekha bagged her maiden FilmFare award for her role as the bubbly 'Manju', 'Golmaal's' Amol Palekar, a former bank clerk, known more for his off-beat roles, was catapulted as a commercial hero. But Mukherjee's next 'Naram Garam'and an insipid 'Rang Birangi' brought him down.

The Star Sons

In the year 1980, when Amitabh Bachchan had the industry eating out of his hands, straddling India with his monstrous hits, turning ticket counters in to serpentine queues and people from mofussil towns showering coins on the screen when he appeared, a new breed was roosting.

Legendary stars of yore, decided to launch their progeny in to "action 'mode. The pack was led by Sunil Dutt, Raj Kapoor, Shashi Kapoor, Manoj Kumar and Dharmendra. The first dart to be shot out was from the bow of Rajendra Kumar. He launched his son Manoj Tuli, by rechristening him as 'Kumar Gaurav'.

Love Story

Raj Kapoor's 'Bobby' was the last teenage romance made about seven years back, just on the eve of a new era where vengeance was scaling up. In between were films where the average age of the leading stars was touching forty and invisible to naked eyes filmdom's entry barriers to the ousiders were always locked down, by feudatory lords. In such a world bereft of any fresh infusion, 'Love Story' and Kumar Gaurav fulfilled an unmet need.

Ideally as per norm, even after christening, the 'Kumar' should appear as a surname but here Rajendra Kumar perhaps tried to make his son's name appear 'different'; he preceded 'Gaurav' with 'Kumar'. The young man was of average height, slim figured with pink cheeks, rosy lips and dark eyes set above an aquiline nose below a broad forehead crowned with thick curls. In a story whose title was self-explanatory, its main theme was of love between a girl and boy freshly out of their teens. Usual stuff of boy meets girl, sparks fly to kindle true love, and having many moments of humour. The problem soon to loom large, unknown to them, is the sworn enmity of their parents, because of complications from a distant past.

'Love Story'was pretty well made! A rookie director Rahul Rawail (son of producer H.S.Rawail of 'Laila Majnu' fame) soaking the script with his brilliance and written by a bunch of writers who called themselves as 'Mirza Brothers'. Music by R.D.Burman was fresh as those dainties abounding plentifully in Kashmir; *dekho maine dekha hain yeh ek sapna* soared the imagination of the young and built up a veritable nest for Kumar Gaurav; with Amit Kumar (son of Kishore Kumar) rendering his voice for Kumar Gaurav and 'daddy dearest' proving to be a generous producer- Rajendra Kumar was willing to leave no stone unturned to make a perfect debut for his son along with a fresh faced heroine called Vijayeta Pandit (she was the sister of musical composers Jatin-Lalit and actress Sulakshana). He also brought in Amjad Khan to play the role of 'Sher Singh' a bumbling Haryanvi 'thulla'(cop) while

Danny, Vidya Sinha and Rajendra Kumar played the warring parents.

On a same note, Sunil Dutt too had similar aspirations and he launched his son Sanjay Dutt in a film called 'Rocky' directed by himself. It was another matter that the title resembled a Hollywood namesake. 'Rocky' too, had music by the maestro R.D.Burman. This set off a race amongst other senior actors; Dharmendra, Manoj kumar and Raj Kapoor. Though, Raj Kapoor had done the act seven years earlier when he had launched his second son Rishi Kapoor in the very successful 'Bobby', much earlier to that he had introduced his eldest son Randhir Kapoor in RK Films' 'Kal Aaj aur Kal'. However during the beginning of the 80's they all appeared like an unchecked rash. The Industry could never have a bigger example of nepotism than this. In fact the Kapoors never gained in attempting in-bred pairing: father-son-grandson (Kal-Aaj-Kal) uncle-nephew (Heeralal Pannalal, Duniya meri jeb Mein).

Rajendra Kumar's 'Love Story' set the box office ringing. It went on to celebrate silver jubilees across every city. Having descended from the bloodline of rich established stars also ensured that the sons received a befitting debut. Sunil Dutt booked twin theatres 'Ganga' and Jamuna' at Tardeo, Bombay; a grand premiere was held where the entire industry and press was invited. The publicity posters had Sunjay Dutt astride a Yamaha bike with the remaining cast barely visible. But in a couple of weeks it became clear that the audience meted a tepid response to 'Rocky'. Backed by Nalanda films which was Sunil Dutt's own banner 'Rocky' was a big budget extravaganza. It had the producer-director playing the father's role, aided by others like Raakhee, Tina Munim, Shakti Kapoor, Reena Roy and Ranjeet. Music by R.D.Burman was already topping the charts. What it woefully lacked was adequate freshness in its script. It had the age old done and dusted lost and found rigmarole and vengeance as its main theme. Sunjay Dutt's entry scene was copied from Amitabh's 'Mukaddar Ka Sikandar'; when 'Sikandar' zoomed on his bike Amitabh gained glory; when 'Rocky' did the same Sunjay Dut scored a duck! The average success of 'Rocky'and Sunjay Dutt gaining a reputation of a junkie later, did harm his forth coming prospects.

Kumar Gaurav was now the toast of every party and was being signed up all over. Aryan Films, his home banner, launched their next called 'Lovers' opposite Padmini Kolhapure, while Biddu, a music director who gave the sensational *'Aap Jaisa koyi...'* number in Feroz Khan's 'Qurbani' launched his production venture by announcing 'Star'with Gaurav. Tito –Tony whose last hit was 'Mr Natwarlal' with Amitabh Bachchan had just scrapped their recent venture 'Tiger' which was announced with much fanfare by signing him- made way for a romantic film 'Teri Kasam' with Kumar Gaurav. Such was the colossal high reached by 'Love Story' that an Amitabh film was put on the back-burner to accommodate the puny Kumar Gaurav.

Rajendra Kumar became his son's back-end who now advised his son on his film assignments. Producers who made a beeline to sign him up had to first face Rajendra Kumar who had started demanding 40 lacs as his son's fee. When flabbergasted producers told him that Amitabh Bachchan was available for an additional 15 lacs, Rajendra Kumar is said to have retorted " I am giving you something better than him".

In 1969, I was not a witness to the fame of Rajesh Khanna but I did watch the kind of adulation post 'Love Story's release; girls went crazy blushing all over at the mere mention of his name;weekly magazines having Kumar Gaurav's poster were instantly sold out. The next big awaited event was the release of the music cassettes of 'Teri Kasam'. True to expectations R.D.Burman gave excellent compositions. The score was as good as his earlier 'Love Story'. The music became a hit and cassettes and records did brisk business. People, especially the young girls and boys were eagerly awaiting the release of Tito-Tony's 'Teri Kasam'. In an unprecedented mayhem of expectations, the film came and went; so did Kumar Gaurav.

Gaurav's fall was as swift as his rise. While Rajesh Khanna walked a bridge resting on seventeen consecutive hits, three filmfare awards and seven nominations before the down hill, Gaurav was less fortunate. Post 'Love Story' he gave nine releases- all droopy ducts of misery. *Teri kasam, Star, Lovers, All rounder, Hum Hain Lajawab, Ek Se Bhale Do, Romance, Dil Tujhko Dya*. The young man was reasonably good looking, and just a few months back producers and people swore by him, so what went wrong ? The kind of expectations raised by 'Love Story' was not properly sustained by the other directors. In the case of 'Love Story', it had a fresh theme of youngsters running away from home, meeting in distant Kashmir and gradually falling in love. Rather than coming back to the city they build a hut in the mountains and plan to live as a couple.

However, warring parents ensure that their hut is destroyed and they are brought back to the city. This film had those factors which were used in plenty by Nasir Hussain in his hill-top stories and in Raj Kapoor's 'Bobby': where the young lovers elope and perhaps plan to do something similar but the climax is swiftly played to scuttle such a plan; 'Bobby' ends where 'Love-Story' is half-way.

Rahul Rawail the young director of 'Love Story' used the above factors skillfully. Unfortunately, his name got blanked out from the credits because of an unknown rift he had with Rajendra Kumar. While Rahul Rawail worked up the factors to Gaurav's advantage, the same cannot be said of the others like: A.C.Trilokchander (Teri Kasam), Biddu (Star), Ramanand Sagar (Romance) Mohan Kumar (Hum Hain lajawab). They were all relying on Gaurav's laurels from 'Love Story 'to work for them too. But Gaurav was no superstar. His charisma still was at a nascent stage. As a result the young man fell. Four years later, his father did try to resurrect him through his third home production 'Naam' casting Sanjay Dutt as the younger brother 'Vicky' whose character was that of a 'black sheep' of the family. But Salim Khan's script backed 'Vicky's character so much, that it completely overshadowed Gaurav's 'Ravi'.

The damage had been done; the audience started taking a closer look at the second lead-Sanjay Dutt. While Kumar Gaurav was struggling to stem the spate of flops, another star son was launched. Raj Kapoor's third son Rajiv Kapoor was being introduced in 'Eagle Films' new film 'Ek Jaan Hai Hum'.This was loosely based on the english film 'Endless Love ' that had the new sensation, Brooke Shields in it. By the end of its first week of release it was clear that the film was not making an impact. The Mehras of Eagle Films then added a tag line on posters as 'Yahoo days are here again' by comparing Rajiv's resemblance to his uncle 'former rock-star' Shammi Kapoor. Though this film flopped, by the sheer strength of being Raj Kapoor's son, Rajiv Kapoor still had few life jackets at his disposal:

Tito-Tony's 'Aasman', Nasir Hussain's 'Zabardast', and Ravindra Peepat's 'Lava'; each of them drowned. Manoj Kumar's son Kunal too met a similar fate. Prakash Mehra's 'Ghungroo' a film directed by his protégé Ram Sethi (who played Pyarelal in 'Mukaddar ka Sikandar') had Kunal as the young hero which also failed miserably.

Big Small & Lowly

'The Greatest Show on Earth'--tagline on posters of 'Shaan'.

For a brief period, from 1980 to 1983, with focus zooming in on the young brigade, pushed the seniors on their backfoot. Their situation was further exacerbated by the underperformance of many big budget films. Those days the big daddy of multistarrers Ramesh Sippy and the demigods Salim –Javed, came together to recreate the magic of their last cult classic 'Sholay'; the result was 'Shaan', which came nowhere near its predecessor. Taglined as 'The Greatest Show on Earth', costing thrice the cost of 'Sholay' and mounted on a grandeur rarely seen in Bombay, Ramesh Sippy and his father G.P.Sippy spared no expense. The script was loosely based on 'Sholay' but the canvas was changed; From a bandit terrorizing a village, this time it was a 'Dr No- 'Jamesbondesque' kind of gangster striking terror through gadgets. From an unknown village on mountainous boulders forming the backdrop of 'Sholay' the locations this time rolled across through dazzling sets culminating on an island in the Gulf of Scotland. Music by R.D.Burman followed the same path as in 'Sholay': a weird buzzing sound whenever the scene shifts to the villain's lair, a number by Rafi and R.D.Burman which again was on same trajectory as the *'mehbooba-mehbooba'* number and a grand picturisation of the *'Pyar karne waale '*number that had the dazzlingly covetable Parveen Babi leading almost the entire cast on the dance floor. Polydor, a competitor to HMV, sold a lac records even before it's release while its posters with the bald 'Shakaal' (Kulbhushan Kharbanda) in a uniform likened to a 'Nazi SS officer' took curiosity to a steep level. The character of 'Shakaal' was not harped upon, but posters, with his face right above the three leading men, spoke a lot about it. People braced themselves for a 'bigger' force than Gabbar Singh; many magazines even started writing obituaries on Amjad Khan, and soon enough on a wintry day of December, 1980, people thronged theaters to watch it. As the screen came alive with the title track, interesting snippets juxtaposed on the lady clothed in white tights swaying to Usha Uthup's husky voice began to unfold; images of a fiery blast, a screeching car rolling off like a fireball, two shapely girls dancing away under giant strobe lights; a wounded Shatrughan Sinha peering through the cross-hairs of a telescopic gun; Amitabh bashing away at a goon; the bald-pated 'Shakaal' threshing about with his baton, all these images were playing out as a teaser promising the actual unfolding of their 'GreatestShow'. But they were stymied by 'Shakaal's antics: his listless voice,his funny walk and bald pate left them fuming. In the end, when they emerged after watching a line up of stars trying their utmost to entertain, they had only two factors to recall: the slick title song rendered by Usha Uthup, and actor Mazhar Khan as the cripple informant 'Abdul'. The producer, the director, set director, lyricist, music composer, the actors, all gave their best but the characterisation of 'Shakaal', the biggest face on the posters of 'Shaan'sprouted many holes; questions foremost on every one's mind was how could the writers hoist upon us a 'villain' dressed up as a dictator and leading a lifestyle of a maniacal ruler bordering between Idi Amin and a Gadaffi, who should be either planning coups or make menacing moves to blow up the world-be bothered about some 'godowns in Bombay'? Ensconced in a seemingly impregnable island on deep sea, out of reach of any radar, with killer sharks at his disposal and woman-commandos armed with sophisticated weapons on call: why was he bothered about a mere DSP? The lines connecting these dots were staggered and farfetched where the fault lay entirely with the script. After giving masterpieces like 'Sholay', 'Deewar', 'Trishul', 'Don', the resultant arrogance in Salim-Javed's demeanour had dimmed their forte in prying out such irritants. It was therefore no surprise that in its fourth week of release tickets were available on 'current bookings' at Bombay's Minerva Theater; the same theater where 'Sholay' ran non-stop for five years.

On the other hand, Dharmendra, the star who refused 'Shaan' due to billing issues was hit hard by some large-scale flops: 'Professor Pyarelal', 'Ram Balram', 'The Burning Train', 'Krodhi' all suffered the ignominy of doing less than average business. These were films made by reputed directors. The first was Brij whose 'Victoria No 203' was a massive success, who now ventured in to big budget production with 'Professor Pyarelal' starring Dharmendra, Zeenat Aman. Shot mostly in Europe, it failed to impress.

'Ram Balram' was another biggie bringing Amitabh and Dharmendra together after 'Sholay' and directed by Vijay Anand whose track record boasted of names such as 'Teesri

Manzil' 'Johnny Mera Naam' and 'Guide'. Having Rekha with Zeenat Aman, Helen and a host of villains like Ajit, Amjad Khan, Prem Chopra, Sujit Kumar, the film strangely met a luke warm success.

Billed as 'India's First Disaster film' B.R.Chopra's- 'The Burning Train' a massive multistarrer influenced by the English film 'Towering Inferno' met a burning end.

He again suffered a body blow in the form of 'Krodhi' directed by Subhash Ghai. Being a production helmed by one of his family members hurt him doubly hard. In addition stretched time frames, a lack of confidence between the director and the stars made the film suffer.

Amitabh emerged largely unscathed as he had tall hits like 'Mr Natwarlal' and 'Naseeb' vouching for him.

<u>Rewinding 'Naseeb':</u>

"Waqt sey pehle aur Naseeb key baad tere paas agar kuch ho to mujhe dena"-John Jani Janardhan

Co-produced by the industrialists, Hinduja Brothers and Manmohan Desai it was mounted on a lavish scale having all the classic ingredients of the 'lost and found' theme which had become so synonymous with Desai. It was a multistarrer and the core theme had a middle class ring to it. A drunk man unable to pay his hotel bill barters away a five lac lottery for four rupees. On being asked why, he replies *"Saab, apun ka Naseeb phutela hain"* (Sir, my fate is a waste) Four friends, sitting next to his table,agree to this barter- Namdev (Pran) a waiter,

Damodar (Amjad Khan)a photographer, Raghu (Kader Khan) a tongawallah and Jaggi (Jagdish Raj) a band master.

This triggers off events that sweep away the four friends and their families in to a world fractured by greed and deceit,.

The lottery encapsulates the fantasy of the poor. When a poor man with a matching lifestyle is suddenly seen in the trappings of wealth, the reaction from his peers would be some thing like this: *"teri lottery lagi hain kya"*; the nucleus of 'Naseeb' was about this paradox. How a lottery ticket raises hopes of all the four and how it sows greed in two: Damodar & Raghu.

The next morning papers announce their jackpot. While Namdev & Jaggi are jubilant, Raghu & Damu have other plans. They plan to bump them off and after completing the heinous act the usurped share is invested in a Star hotel. On the side lines, Namdev's wives are killed in an earthquake rendering his children effectively homeless and orphaned.

Even though the opening scenes just before the credit titles forebode a sense of misery, it is to Desai's credit that he does not allow the film to meander away as a tear jerker. Unlike Yash Chopra's 'Deewar' which tears you with venom and vengeance, Desai was an antithesis whose protagonists create rainbows by turning their misery on its head; Where his affected protagonists transcend suffering and emerge as happy beings. Desai not only brought this out, again, but also focussed more in rolling out the screenplay on a bigger scale than his latest 'Amar-Akbar-Anthony'. He also retained its core. So even though all the characters are

Hindus, he continues the brother hood act by naming his main protagonist as "John-Jani-Janardhan'. Even though this character is addressed throughout either as "John" or "Jaani"---'Janardhan' is never ever uttered. Similarly, their old neighbour 'Mrs Gomes" (Lalita Pawar) is the quintessential aunty who is largely a throwback from the 1955 'Anari' as Mrs D'Sa and the matron from the 1973 'Anand'. Mrs Gomes and her daughter Julie (Reena Roy) make up Desai's Christian fraternity in 'Naseeb'.

The 2nd generation by now has been reared as per their 'Naseeb' (fate). John the orphan grows up to be a lively waiter who is known for his 'tray-twirling-feats'. He is the 'housekeeping' lifeline of the very hotel set up by his father's killers and also takes pride in affording to educate his younger brother 'Sunny'(Rishi Kapoor) at a convent school in Simla, while Jaggi's daughter is a much sought after singer (Hema Malini as Aasha)

On the other hand, the children of the perpetrators: Damodar (Amjad Khan) and Raghuveer (Kader Khan) are ending up on the wrong sides of life. Raghu's sons-Sunny (Prem Chopra) and Ashok(Shakti Kapoor) have manned out as the proverbial goons. But Vicky (Shatrughan Sinha) who is well on course to attain a fancy degree from London; who begins his day by jogging on a boulevard near the Thames; spends evening at the casino swathed in designer suits- is unexpectedly swept away in unrequited love. A clear case of bad karma affecting the progeny of the perpetrators,

Even though cast as a second lead, Shatrughan Sinha as 'Vicky' spends three-fourth length of his role as an 'alcoholic'. Dejected, he leaves London nursing a broken heart and a swollen liver. While his buddy 'John' (and real-life-arch-rival) is shown twirling trays, wooing a show-gal with his charm and drawing thunderous cries of "jaani-johnny-jaani"from punters betting their stakes on him when he walks in bare armed to fight. Desai further empowers by putting up a long line up of villains, brings in a wee bit of a love triangle, a resultant 'dushmani, some fine dose of sacrifice, a lot of fun filled moments of hindu-muslim-christian bonhomie and of course a long-drawn drunken antic by Amitabh. He then garnishes these with glorious sets, seasons it with local-'bombayiyya' dialogues (by Kader Khan) and signs off with some spectacular thrills. What emerges is an amazing potpourri of bang joining its buck!

In the climactic song-dance routine he relies on his original game-plan of shock & awe. Just as in the second reel he surprised all by bringing in a galaxy of stars like Raj Kapoor, Shammi Kapoor, RajeshKhanna, Randhir Kapoor, Dharmendra, Sharmila Tagore,Waheeda Rehman,Mala Sinha,Simi and many others to light up the antics of the song 'John-Jani-Janardhan', in the last of the twenty reels, during it's climax, the entire star cast of 'Naseeb' –the 1st Gen-the 2nd Gen-and entire villains are assembled in a dazzling revolving restaurant. Under a sizzling chorus number which swears Desai's mission statement- *"Log Tamasha dekhenge -taali baja key jayenge"* he puts forth his multistarrers to gate-crash into the final party of the offenders dressed in colourful 'mufti:

Amitabh as a 'Matador'- Shatrughan Sinha as a 'gypsy'- Rishi Kapoor as a 'Chaplinesque' clone-Hema Malini as a Spanish 'flamenco'--Reena Roy as a 'harem girl' and Kim as the lady from 'Pygmalion'. On carpeted floors, with villains nursing wine & scotch, they all sing, sway and swing and then erupt to fight. The battle royal in medieval style begins; Spears are flung, battle axes hurled, swords are swung. The perpetrators finally meet their fate, everything sorted out and the victors team up in the end to own up their star hotel. They even gift a lifelong membership to that 'bevda' who had bartered his lottery in the beginning of time.

Indeed, 'Naseeb' made enough bucks to be called the biggest that year and it was not written by Salim-Javed.

Manoj Kumar's 'Kranti', a film that was based on events presumed to have occurred on the sidelines of the mutiny of 1857. Though it did not delve in to the events of 1857, instead, Manoj made a kind of hotch potch from various factors. Even though he had a successful legacy of making films that had patriotism portrayed from the heart as in his earlier films like 'Purab Aur Paschim', 'Upkar'and the unforgettable classic 'Shaheed'. Even his 'Roti-Kapda-Aur Makaan' was a seemingly realistic mirror of those times. He usually had a character actor playing a prominent stellar in all his films: What Pran was to 'Upkar', Madan Puri to 'Shaheed', on similar lines Premnath played an important one in 'Roti-Kapda-Makaan' where as a sanguine Sikh, he slays the three men responsible for bringing misery on a young woman; those three symbolized the three pillars for middle-class-indians: a landlord, a tailor and a grain merchant. The pitiable rape scene is shot in a granary where under a heap of 'atta'(wheat-flour) the dastardly deed is committed.

But in 'Kranti' he went overboard, junked off patriotic pretensions and became more of jingoistic. Quite telling in the proceedings was a ship that resembled a 'Roman galley-ship' from the Hollywood film 'Ben-Hur'. The ship is owned by the 'Angrez' and the 'Krantikaris' made up of 'beta Bharat'(Manoj), 'bhai Karim Khan' (Shatrughan Sinha) rowing away in its underhold are being whipped by Madan Puri dressed as a jailor but behaving like a 'roman centurion'. On the deck above, heavy rains are lashing where Meenakshi (Hema Malini) is tied and being forced to sing a song for the lustful eyes of the perennial 'angrez'of the hindi film industry (actor Tom Alter). For a lady who never went beyond showing a dainty ankle she was made to writhe and crawl under heavy rains in a 'choli'. As the song is played out, the ship gets hijacked by an arm-less soldier of the 'krantikaris'. However, there were certain scenes which did lighten our minds like the one where 'Sanga' (Dilip Kumar) gets in to a friendly jig with a little English girl !

Kranti's biggest USP was bringing Dilip Kumar finally out of his seemingly permanent retirement drawing him in to a great second innings. Perhaps the most surprising fact about 'Kranti' was about its writers- incongruously written by Salim -Javed!

The next was 'Karz made by Subhash Ghai. After the debacle of 'Krodhi' this some how salvaged his reputation. 'Karz' was based on the subject of reincarnation. The last films made

on this theme successfully were Bimal Roy's 'Madhumati' which had won accolades for the director and 'Neelkamal' which had Raj Kumar and Waheeda Rehman. A topic largely untouched 'Karz' was partially based on an English film 'Reincarnation of Peter Proud'. Casting Rishi Kapoor as Monty, a rising Rock star who is actually the reincarnated scion of a tea estate tycoon aroused sufficent interest from cinegoers. Simi Garewal played the role of 'Kamini' the cunning gold digger who drives a jeep repeatedly over her husband Ravi (Raj Kiran) to usurp his vast property. Prem Nath as 'Sir Juda', her handler who is dumb so communicates with his lieutenants in a weird kind of 'morse code': where he keeps tapping those thick rings abounding his fingers on his whiskey glass; In fact this stunted Premnath's role in the film leaving him nothing much to do. Laxmikant Pyarelal's music, both soulful and thumping, really brought in people; the number *'Om Shanti Om'* imaginatively picturised on a stage with a gigantic gramophone record revolving with Rishi Kapoor jiggling away on it and that hypnotic signature tune on the guitar which triggered images from Monty's past and lastly the climactic dance-ballet *'Ek Haseena thi ek deewana tha* whose seven minute choreography brilliantly showcases the short life of Ravi and reveals the true face of Kamini.
(so what if it appears inspired from a similar one played out in the Dilip Kumar starrer- 'Dastaan'.)

'Karz' was appreciated, but with Feroz Khan's 'Qurbani' breathing down its neck, money wise made less than expectations.

The industry could yet draw relief from the still tall charisma of Amitabh Bachchan. 'Kaala Patthar' based on the coal-mine tragedy at Chasnala and 'Dostana' based on a friendship saga, did good business but they were not super hits like say, 'Mr Natwarlal' and Prakash Mehra's 'Laawaris'. The fluctuating performance of the two releases slightly dented his armour. This became more pronounced by the split of the immensely successful duo: Salim -Javed.

Towards the close of 1981, the topic of taboo topics again clouded the mind of Yash Chopra. A theme on forbidden love seems to have been a topic dear to his heart. This had manifested in the 1974 'Daag' which fortunately was a hit. It again manifested itself in 1977 through his protégé Ramesh Talwar's 'Doosara Aadmi' which was not a success. This time Yash Chopra took it under his mantle and made a product that was his wont: large and lavish. It is not clear how could a topic based on extra marital relations impress Yash Chopra. Even though he never admitted it was clear he wrongly believed that by casting a 'real life triangle' he could be on the cusp of a new age: an ensemble cast of Jaya-Amitabh – Rekha, good music by new pair called Shiv-Hari,Sanjeev Kumar in a mature role of the 'silent husband' and beautiful, virgin locales of Amsterdam. He also asked Javed Akhtar to write the lyrics. Amitabh even danced and lent his voice to the evergreen 'Holi' song *Rang barse bheegi chunariya"*, Rekha looked bewitching as the coquettish third angle but all these well thought out factors failed to scorch the screen resulting in Yash Chopra and Amitabh's fruitful association to end with this debacle. With 'Silsila' putting sudden brakes on the magical persona of Amitabh Bachchan, the industry was now bereft of new ideas.

Soon, a flash of light rose up from South India.

K.Balachander, a respected director of Tamil cinema decided to remake his telegu film 'Maro Charitra' in to Hindi by casting the same hero who was exceedingly talented and was much feted by the name of Kamalhaasan, in the lead. The result was 'Ek Duje Ke Liye'. The film released without much of fan fare and hardly any publicity,yet serenaded in to instant acclaim.

'Ek Duje ke Liye' had an unconventional story of love between a young Tamilian boy and a Punjabi girl which tragically ends due to various machinations piled upon them by their parents. Kamalhaasan, already a veteran of more than 75 films, in Tamil, Telegu and Malayalam cinema was a master in essaying emotional roles. As 'Vasu' the Tamilian neighbour in 'Ek Duje Ke liye', he was merely re-essaying the role he played in the original'Maro Charitra'. Interestingly, the Hindi audience reacted the same way as the southerners and Laxmikant-Pyarelal's music also gave it an added fillip. The film was a grand success and the lead pair of Kamal Haasan and Rati Agnihotri found an instant home in Bollywood.

Kamalhasan made all the right moves. He could act well and was a trained dancer. With the failure of Kumar Gaurav's 'Teri Kasam' and Amitabh's 'Silsila' it seemed he could go for the kill. It did appear possible, with prestigious projects in his bag like Barkha Roy's 'Sanam Teri Kasam' Balu Mahendra's 'Sadma' and 'Zara Si Zindagi'by K.Balachander.

'Sanam Teri Kasam' in hindi parlance had all the makings of a great entertainer; it had music by R.D.Burman, several dance sequences, lost-and-found son, shot mostly in Simla and decent direction by veteran Narinder Bedi, but it turned out to be a fifty-fifty success. One theory could be his typical Dravidian looks appearing incongruous in those disco sequences. He also sounded off track when Kishore Kumar lent his voice. It was a tactical error committed by the makers of 'Sanam Teri Kasam'; post 'Ek Duje Ke Liye'they should have stuck to S.P.Balasubramaniam as his voice suited him better. As for his dancing skills the one that he performed and drew in gasps of appreciation in 'Ek Duje Ke Liye' were the bike-riding feats that he played out in *'Hum Bane tum baney'* the second one was the strenuous 'bharat natyam' which he performs in front of Sandhya(Madhavi) when he gives vent to his frustrations. But his moves in 'Sanam Teri Kasam' which bordered purely on the emerging disco style made no impact. Moreover, the producer made another error by inserting her boyfriend, a small time actor called Mahesh Anand, who swayed under dark silhouettes to the credit title music, made Kamal's moves appear ordinary. Anyways, the audience those days had reserved their appreciations in that category for rising star Mithun Chakraborty. Lastly, two of his films 'Sadma' and 'Zara Si Zindagi' were too much of the depressing kind. The two appeared to have been made with the single objective of making the audience weep; which they had already done in the last scene of 'Ek Duje Ke Liye'!

In his short career in Bombay he did act in several A-listed films and even one with Amitabh in S.Ramanathan's

'Geraftaar' which was a success. In the end Kamalhaasan remained in memory as a talented actor who won the FilmFare award for 'Sagar' and exited by taking in Sarika, a failed heroine turned starlet, as his girlfriend to Madras. Kamlhasan continued making waves in Tamil cinema but there were no more offers from Bombay.

For now, there were no more launches and very soon, Mushir and Riaz, the deep pocketed producers of Bollywood who were famously known to have produced big budget films like, Bairaag,(a flop starring Dilip Kumar) Mehbooba (a flop starring Rajesh Khanna) and Rajput(a huge multistarrer that netted average collections) this time, collaborated with Ramesh Sippy to produce a film based on a script written by Salim -Javed (before their split). It was named 'Shakti' and the main roles of father and son were to be played by Dilip Kumar and Amitabh Bachchan. A casting coup indeed! The film's focus was on an ambivalent father, doting mother but a rebel son. Dilip Kumar was on a high, a year ago he was appreciated in his come back film 'Kranti'. There always existed a school of thought whose takes clashed whenever there arose an immensely debated question: how far did Dilip Kumar influence Amitabh ? In that context this casting was certainly a coup. If 'Deewar' had a blend of both 'Mother India' and 'Ganga –Jamuna', then 'Shakti' had lots of 'Deewar' in it.

See the similarities:

1. Ganga Jamuna: younger brother guns down older brother because of Law and Outlaw divide.

2. Mother India: Mother guns down her dearest son because of his unacceptable way in extracting revenge from the 'baniya' by abducting his daughter.

3. Shakti: A decorated police officer reluctantly shoots down his son who is a criminal on the run.

'Shakti' was lauded for Dilip Kumar's stirring performance as the father who is just not able to know the reason behind his son's alienation from him. The agony is festered due to the son stubbornly refusing to bare his mind. The Vijay in 'Shakti' seemed to be a continuation of the Vijay from Deewar: the ghost of Anand Verma his father in 'Deewar' who out of shame had abandoned his family, was brought back by the writers in a different form in to 'Shakti'as Deputy Comissioner of Police Ashwini Kumar. He is fiercely protective about his family but one day, his little child who is kidnapped to extract a quid-pro-quo deal, overhears his father daring the kidnappers on phone *"Maar dalo mere bête ko, Haan Haan maar dalo, jo karna hain karo magar mein Yashwant ko nahin chodoonga"*. (Kill my son, go ahead and kill him do what you want but I will not release Yashwant.)

These words remain embedded in his mind just as a depraving tattoo was carved out on his arm in 'Deewar'. Like the tattoo, this telephonic conversation rose up to stand in the form of a permanent 'deewar' between father and son. The character of

Sheetal (Raakhee Gulzar) as his mother has shades of Sumitra Devi (Nirupa Roy) from' Deewar'. Similar to Sumitra who is torn between the love for both her sons, is Sheetal who is her husband's pillar of strength but falls miserable and sick out of grief when her rebellious son walks out of home. While the 'Vijay' in 'Deewar' or 'Zanjeer' never burst out in to a song, the 'Vijay' in 'Shakti' is a 'less tormented soul'so a duet with his girl friend Roma (Smita Patil) is perhaps plausible. Smita Patil as Roma has shades of Anita (Parveen Babi) from 'Deewar'. But she is not a rebel or a street walker like Anita. Roma is an independent, working girl and unlike Anita she does not indulge in vices like smoking or drinking and yet, does not mind inviting Vijay to move in to her apartment as a live-in companion. In 'Zanjeer', Mala (Jaya Bhaduri) moves in to live-in with Vijay due to problems from Teja's goons (ostensibly the physical element is left untouched)

In 'Ganga Jamuna' the older brother Ganga stood tall and not Jamuna the cop who gunned him down. In 'Mother India' she was Radha (Nargis) and not her son Birju(Sunil Dutt) whom she gunned down. In 'Deewaar' it was the rebel Vijay not his younger bro Ravi, but in 'Shakti' Dilip Kumar (as DCP Ashwini Kumar) the father, stole the show; the soul of Anand Verma could now rest in peace! 'Shakti' won an award for Dilip Kumar in the 'Best Actor' category further cementing his second innings in Bollywood. However, collections wise, 'Shakti' never rose to the levels of the other iconic hits of Amitabh Bachchan. For Ramesh Sippy it was another futile search for transcending 'Sholay'.

Before people could delve deeper in examining the balance-of-power left after 'Shakti', Amitabh cascaded again to erupt in 'Namak Halal'. Produced and directed by Prakash Mehra, who had just licked off the wounds left behind by his recent experiment of casting Shatrughan Sinha in the forgettable 'Jwalamukhi'. Since the time he made 'Zanjeer' Amitabh Bachchan had become a permanent fixture in his films and post 'Zanjeer' every single film of his, except 'Jwalamukhi',was a money spinner;   the naughty 'Hera Pheri', the exciting'Mukaddar Ka Sikandar' which was one of the pillars that harnessed Bachchan's charisma and his latest one called 'Lawaris'.

'Namak Halaal' vindicated Amitabh's charisma by casting a magical cloak over the audience, who were enthralled watching a rather ordinary film. It turned a super hit only because every frame is ruled by a character called 'Arjun Singh'; a simple waiter at a hotel by profession but extremely principled in character. He has structured his life on three simple lessons imparted to him by his 'Daddu (grand –pop Om Prakash)

Sheher mein aane sey pehle mare daddu ne teen baatein sikhayin:
Anyaay ke samney kabhi Sar nahin jhukana
Parayi Aurat parayi daulat pey nazar nahin rakhna
Jiska namak khaon uski Namak Halaali karna

"Before leaving my village Grandpa taught me to follow three principles: never bow down to injustice, never covet others' wealth or wives, and be loyal to your employer."

'Namak-Halal' as was the norm those days, was a multistarrer. It had Shashi Kapoor as the 'malik' whose loyal servant is Arjun (Amitabh), while Smita Patil and Parveen Babi played the female leads and Ranjeet the villain. But the entire narration is mainly played out between Arjun Singh and his 'Daddu' Dashrath Singh (played by Om Prakash).

The film was a One-man show. Its biggest USP was Amitabh and to an extent Bappi Lahiri's music. Every frame where Arjun Singh appears is worth a repeat. Remove him and the film is rigor-mortis. Shot entirely in studio indoors, no special effects, no great dialogues, just simple lines which linger on even after the film.

Scenes worth their 'salt':

- Arjun Singh agreeing with his 'Daddu's take on the growing pangs of youth:

  "mujhe bhi masti aawey, tarang uthey, aur seeney mein armaan jaagey"

  (I too get tickled by my blooming youth, those ripples of desires and soul seeking pleasures)

- Arjun Singh in search for a job reaches his pal Bhairon's house who is known in his village as a 'big shot' for having crafted a successful living in the 'Shaher'(city) as a photographer (actor Ram Sethi). But there he watches his friend getting hilariously walloped by many, which ultimately reveals 'Bhairon's true status in the city.

- Arjun Singh dressed up as a true son of the soil in elite 'Haryanvi' style, complete in a sherwani and 'pugree' enters a 'Five star' hotel. Staring wonder struck at all the glitter around and without mincing words he talks about it aloud ' *Bhai bahut badiya bhai bahut badiya*', much to his friends dismay. Even though he feels himself to be in an uncomfortable zone he just cannot afford to ignore his friend's advice that if he sings then the job is his.Faced with a daunting prospect of making an impression on his prospective employer he breaks out in to a classic country number blended with disco beats: the chart buster '*Pag Ghungroo Bandh Meera nachi*' a lengthy number that speaks vociferously about hard work, honesty, loyalty and love. What starts off as a small 'gharana' styled stanza ' *Buzoorgo nein farmaya ke apne pairon pey khadey hokar dikhlao*", changes gears and goes on to thump around with the next stanza "*Paanisa Mapaani re re re re ga re ga*" when he acts out his shoe-losing episode to the dancing girls who are falling all over his country charm; the next stanza he casts direct aspersions on the Manager (Ranjeet) his future boss by exclaiming "*aapka to lagta hai bus yahi sapna ram ram japna paraya maal apna*", in the last "*Mausam-e-ishk mein machley huey armaan hain hum, dil ye kehta hain aap apni hain paraayi nahin*", he bares his heart out to a beautiful woman (Smita Patil) whom he has just glimpsed.

- Poonam (Smita Patil) who heads the 'Housekeeping' department trains Arjun in answering a guest's query.

But the guest of Room number 666 (actor Dev kumar) makes a pass at her in his presence by trying to gift her a Nose-ring to which, Arjun gives him a piece of his whirring mind: *"Aur jo thaari behen nahin hovey to ma to hovegi usko Pehna dena, Samajh gaye Mr Teen Chakkey !"* (If you do not have a sister you should be having a mother; give it to her she will remember you until death and beyond; understood Mr 666)

- The song *'Aaj Rapat Jaaye'* we watch, first time, the transformation of actress Smita Patil. Clad in a low waist saree and drenched to the skin, turned her 'arty' image on its head.

- To test his grandson's character after migrating to the city, 'daddu' discards his dhoti kurta dons a suit, puts on a hat and arrives as an NRI with an alias of 'San Francisco Contino Decosta Rodriequez'. The interludes are extremely hilarious.

- Arjun Singh with a knife in hand and the villain(Satyen Kappoo) tied up under his chair, warns 'Zalim Singh'(Ranjeet) " *ab aap hamare Raja babu key hathkadiyan khol dijiye varna hum aapke daddy ka bahut kuch khol dalenge*- The knife is pointing at 'Daddy's crotch !

- The number*'Raat Baaki Baat baaki'* is the eternal conspiratorial song; with assassins lurking in the shadows, foreheads turning sweaty, eyes unusually darting about; just like the eternal cabarets of yore that takes you to a point where the script swerves to leave behind a twist.

As the makers and distributors of 'Namak Halaal' poured out the bubbly, a south Indian producer duo, Satyanarayana & Suryanarayana, signed S.Ramanathan to direct a hindi version of an early Kannada hit called 'Shanker Guru' in which an actor called Raj Kumar an icon of the Kannada film industry, had played a triple role. They signed Amitabh to essay the same triple role. The film was named 'Mahaan' which means 'Great' but the product was far from it.

'Mahaan' went overboard in milking the persona of Amitabh but it failed to impress people who found three Amitabhs too many to digest ! Not that he was bad. As a good actor he gave his best to a story where he played a father to two sons. His wife and his two sons have been separated due to circumstances created by the villain (Amjad khan). One grows up to be a cop Shanker (Amitabh) who has a stern expression through out. As Shanker, the script tries to offer the audience a run down Amitabh of the 'Zanjeer' era. The second son whose name is 'Guru'plays a 'nautankiwala' (a dramatist) where again the script puts forth Amitabh's comic timing as a highlight. While the father (Amitabh again) plays 'Amit' a lawyer whose make-up is on the lines of an earlier hit called 'Adalat'-same grey wig, beard and dark glasses mounted on a serious expression. To tackle three Amitabhs spread over two generations the script demanded multi villains so 'Mahaan' had Amjad Khan, Kader Khan, Sujit Kumar, Shakti Kapoor and the perennial side-kick, MacMohan.

'Mahaan' met with a thumbs down by the critics but being a big budget multistarrer would have by the strength of its initial weeks would have broken even and made some overflows. It did not burn holes in the pockets of the distributors but yes, it was not a money spinner like 'Namak Halaal'.

As the year 1982 traversed we saw the star sons brigade had mostly failed. Kumar Gaurav, the much touted Star met a tepid response to his second release 'Teri Kasam'. Script writers Salim-Javed suddenly decided to split citing 'creative differences' and big stars failed to produce a hit.

But on 27th July, 1982 Bollywood got hit where it hurt most. Their biggest star since a decade was injured on the sets of Manmohan Desai's 'Coolie' rendering him out of action and bringing him to the brink of death. Clouding all under a pall of gloom, the accident put Bollywood and the nation on tenterhooks. He was confined inside a hospital room and later at home for months. The people of India, literally, stopped going to theatres and instead rushed to temples to pray for his recovery.

Big budget projects with crores riding on him came to a halt. But there were many filmmakers who fortunately for them were not in the line of fire; one of them being Subhash Ghai. He was hired to direct a multistarrer named as 'Vidhata' produced by Gulshan Rai (producer of 'Johnny Mera Naam', 'Deewar' and 'Trishul') starring Dilip Kumar-Sanjeev Kumar-Shammi Kapoor-Sanjay Dutt- Padmini Kolhapure. 'Vidhaata' was about a middle class man 'Shamsher Singh' seeking vengeance for the brutal killing of his son and daughter in law. The killer is Jageera (Amrish Puri) a poacher and smuggler who has spread his network in the jungle to steal ivory and among his many victims, is an honest cop (Suresh Oberoi) who is Shamsher's son. This sets Shamsher in to conflict with God-('Vidhaata'), making him swear that he is now an aetheist and shall hence forth be the master of his own destiny. He comes in touch with a man from the underworld known as Sir John Mizia (Dr Sriram Lagoo) and after his death inherits the mantle of becoming the boss of his powerful crime syndicate called the 'Mizia'(similar sounding to'mafia'). With his leadership skills Shamsher becomes the supremo of 'Mizia' and entrusts the care of his grandson to Abu Baba (Sanjeev Kumar) who is a widower and an epitome of honesty, sincerity and loyalty. The grandson grows up as Kunal (Sunjay Dutt) who dotes on Abu Baba. But the risk of running a 'mafia' gang manifests itself in the form of Abu Baba getting killed and the grandson blaming his grandfather for it. The film had the best of old legends in Dilip Kumar,Shammi Kapoor and Sanjeev Kumar. To draw out their best each one of them had long drawn out scenes which was a treat for viewers; like the one where as locomotive drivers, Shammi Kapoor and Dilip Kumar, sifting through coal sing aloud their personal takes on 'taqdeer'(destiny) and 'tadbeer(plan); there was another one in a face-off encounter which had Dilip Kumar and Sanjeev meet eyeball-to-eyeball. But it was Sanjay Dutt who just could not stand up to them and his labored efforts showed him in bad light.

The film was a success but it was said that Subhash Ghai had a tough time handling Sunjay Dutt who had become a hapless victim of drug abuse. The experience shook Ghai to such an extent that he swore to never again work with him. For his own production titled 'Hero'where he had originally thought of casting Sunjay Dutt, his search began all over again for a man who could fit the bill. Sunjay Dutt with the help of his father, the benevolent Sunil Dutt, went off to the Americas to get cured in a Rehabilitation Center. For his new project Subhash Ghai now decided to hurry his search for new discoveries.

Few months earlier, an old struggler, Mithun Chakraborty had his first certified solo hit in B.Subhash's 'Disco Dancer'. His stock by now had grown and was regularly being signed up by big producers from Bombay and the South. Navketan Films, the banner owned by Dev Anand, that prided itself in making films on socio topics, launched a film called 'Swami Dada'. The subject delved upon was whether to tackle the issue of evil through godliness or violence. As was his wont, Dev Anand cast himself as both- the 'Swami' and the 'Dada'. While Mithun Chakraborty played a parallel hero it also had Shakti Kapoor as the villain and a lanky man called Jackie Shroff as his crony. Son of a Gujarati father and a Turkish mother, Shroff earlier dabbled in modeling where he was the face of 'Charminar 'cigarettes and 'Savage' shaving blades. During one such shoot an acquaintaince advised him to go give an audition for Subash Ghai's 'Hero'. As they say, Lady Luck comes knocking unexpectedly. He had recently shot for a tiny role in Dev Anand's film so nursing no expectations, Jackie auditioned for the role and was shocked to learn that from the scores that day who had come to try their luck, he turned out to be the chosen one indeed; the 'Hero' of Subhash Ghai. His selection became the talk of the nation and Subhash Ghai announced it in style ! A fortnightly film based bulletin called 'Screen'which was an Indian Express publication, brought out a four page pull-out edition where the back of a lanky man, with a gun-belt wrapped around his waist, wearing jack-boots was stamped under dark bold caps as: 'Hero'. A week later, 'Screen' front-faced the young turk as Subhash Ghai's 'Hero'. With Meenakshi Sheshadri as his heroine Ghai positioned Jackie as- 'my answer to the star sons'. Jackie did not let his mentor down; 'Hero' was made, released and became a hit celebrating a golden jubilee catapulting Jackie Shroff straight in to the league of A-listers making Subhash Ghai and his banner Mukta Arts a force to reckon with. The music also was a stupendous sell out. Thank God for small mercies even though Bappi Lahiri was ruling the roost Subhash Ghai stuck on to his regular composers Laxmikant and Pyarelal; songs like *'nindiya sey jaagi bahar'* spoke aloud about the beautiful greens gently awakening from a nightful of sweet slumber; the next was the fast-paced *'Ding Dong baby Singa song'* where bike borne 'Jaikishan' and his gang of lovable goons who have happily hoodwinked Radha (meenakshi) zooming down forests of Himachal with Subhash Ghai throwing in a fleeting appearance a la 'Alfred Hitchcock style'; another was the qawaali strain of *"Pyar karne waley kabhi dartey nahin'* where both declare love 'cheek by jowl'in Mughal-e-Azam style and yes, that lilting tune played on the flute by the gun toting 'Jaikishan' alias 'Jaggu Dada'. The songs alongwith his protégé Jackie Shroff climbed the popularity charts while Meenakshi Sheshadri got a rebirth, after her debacle debut in 'Painter Babu' which was made by Manoj Kumar to introduce his brother Rajeev Goswami.

The 'King of Kings'was still out of action. With the traditional producers going in to creative bankruptcy, Bombay was a sitting duck. On such an unsure note we saw 1982 coming to an end with dejected producers waking up to competition engulfing them from the South.

Raiders From The South

Amitabh's accident had sent shock waves of concerns not only throughout bollywood but across the entire spectrum of the masses. The accident was regularly mentioned over media and discussed in every home. Treatment was done in the best hospitals under the watchful eyes of famed doctors. Tense weeks later Amitabh was declared out of danger. The nation in unison heaved a sigh of relief but it did put their icon out of active service for some time. Shortage of essentials remained a daily occurrence and people were resigned to their fate. As a nation it was not going anywhere. Those were the golden years of 'babudom' and red tape. Single window clearance was beyond the realms of anybody's imagination and against such backdrop of a tattered socio-economic scenario, bollywood too had lost its imaginative skill. Insipid fare in the name of entertainment was being doled out. From the churning out of regular trash a few would succeed which again spawned numerous 'me-too'.

This was the period when a new invasion occurred. It's epicenter originated from distant studios in Madras. The style was 'Madrasi' where most of them were remakes and their preferred 'totem' was Jeetendra. To digress, Jeetendra had already bettered on his links with south Indian stalwarts. He had since more than a decade been working with producers from the south and in fact, the first film that made him a

'Star' (and immortalized those white shoes)-was the 1967 film 'Farz'. Made by a Madras team and shot entirely in Madras, 'Farz' was a 'desi Bond' kind of caper made by Ravi Kant Nagaich who specialized only in such type of templates to work upon: 'Agent 116 (also known as Gopi) works as a secret agent for a secret service arm of the government of India. On a template borrowed from 'James Bond', the director makes 'Agent Gopi(Jeetendra) gallivant in snowy landscapes, canoodling with various girls-just before he gets a "call from Headquarters'; 'Farz' proved to be a cheap copy of a Bond film, but- well injected with localized styles of the prevailing times; a boyishly handsome secret-service agent, a pretty beloved (actress Babita), car chases (of the 'Impala' kind), the villain's lair fitted with fluorescent gadgets, excellent music by Laxmikant-Pyarelal- all added up to put forth a successful product making it the first true-blue box office hit for Jeetendra. His dancing skills or rather, an ability to roll up a jig, helped him carve out a niche for himself. The success of 'Farz' in turn, made him a favourite with South Indian producers who found in him a safe bet. His south assignments heavily outnumbered the ones from Bombay so naturally Jeetendra's association with directors like Dasari Narayan Rao and T.Rama Rao kept growing. He even turned producer by launching his own banner 'Balaji Pictures' where he formed a veritable mutual admiration society with them. His production forays too were directed by South Indian directors. No wonder inspite of having lesser assignments in Bombay, his schedules were jam packed. In one of his interviews to a leading magazine he claimed to be "living off a suitcase most of the time because I usually had one leg perched in Bombay while the other stood in Madras". Every film of the early 80's that starred Jeetendra had the stamp of either 'made in Madras' or 'made in Hyderabad' – 'Jyoti Bane Jwala' a saga of vengeance, 'Judaai' –marital troubles spawning two generations,'Maang Bharo Sajana'—a triangle, 'Pyasa Sawan'-marital neglect, 'Prem Tapasya'-terminal disease, all made good money.

Their production values, especially sets, styled same way as in their originals: palatial houses where each floor is decked up with carpets, dining tables as broad as the Marina beach on which stood gigantic bouquets of flowers and lamps that could light up an entire locality. Outdoor sets were erected in villages on the banks of the rivers Tungabhadra or the Cauvery, dreamy song sequences shot on the sands of Kovalam Beach and fight scenes emphatically based on the 'dhishum-bhishum' kind which had bald, obese shaped stuntmen from Kodambakkam, a suburb in Madras. Many years ago two stalwarts did try their hand but without much of luck; Gemini Ganesan in 1957 in 'Miss Mary' and 'Devta', and one of their top stars Sivaji Ganesan who could claim equality with Dilip Kumar also forayed in to Hindi movies but failed to make an indelible stamp in Bombay. Kamalhaasan did erupt through 'Ek Duje Ke Liye' in 1981 but as explained earlier, he could not sustain further.

When the going was good, there was one film that made him digress from the south. A film called 'Deedar-E-Yaar'. Casting Rekha, Rishi Kapoor, Tina Munim and himself, he chose H.S.Rawail to direct this Muslim social. Rawail had exquisite Muslim socials in his resume like 'Mere Mehboob' with Rajendra Kumar and 'Laila-Majnu' with Rishi Kapoor. Its screenplay and story was by Rawail's son Rahul, who had turned famous after 'Love Story'. But this several-crored film made mincemeat of him leaving Jeetendra into a financial doldrum. In Jeetendra's own words in an interview he claimed to "have lost two crores so I had to activate Operation "khadda-bharo"; if true, then this would have been equal to about sixty five percent budget of 'Sholay' and fifty percent of 'Shalimar'. Left in a precarious state Jeetendra hoped for a miracle.

The lazy squall of his films from the south soon took the form of a hurricane when in March 1983, a film called 'Himmatwala' released. Starring Jeetendra, Kader Khan, Amjad Khan, Shakti Kapoor, Waheeda Rehman, Asrani, and Swaroop Sampat, it launched a leading actress from Madras named Sridevi as its heroine. This film belonged to the 'Padmalaya' banner owned by Krishna, a veteran actor and producer of Telegu films. The film dumped all the prevailing socio-eco times which had become so symbolic of the failures and successes of Bombay releases.

The film in brief:

- Ravi(Jeetendra) an engineer returning back to his village, alights from a second class coach wearing a designer jacket, matching trouser, expensive shoes and carrying a branded suitcase. He walks to his village and discovers that his mother and sister are living inside a tiny thatched hut working as domestic helps for a living !

- The village is ruled by a tyrant (Amjad Khan) whose name sounds like a hindi-parsi combo-'Sher Singh Bandookwaley'. His daughter Rekha's(Sridevi) friends are of the 'ghagra-choli-lehnga' kinds but she struts around in black leather trousers and jacket.

- Sher Singh protects his tyranny by quelling all sorts of protest or disobedience in a rather chilling way: he ties them up and leaves them at an unmanned railway crossing with speeding trains doing the rest.

- Sher Singh's manager is 'Munimji' Narayandas (Kader Khan) a shrewd buffoon. By being obsequious to his master he extracts toll in the form of his dim-witted arrogance with people at large.

- Ravi has been sent to his village by the government for constructing a dam, which will drown more than half of Sher Singh's fields.

- To scuttle Ravi's plans they capitalize on his sister's love for Shakti(Shakti Kapoor) who is 'munimji's son. Getting them married they arm twist Ravi by torturing her.

- Ravi and Rekha gang up to teach them a lesson where Rekha pretends she is pregnant, making her aghast father beg for forgiveness.

'Himmatwala' was basically a comedy stitched together by extremely hilarious situations, pithy dialogues, garishly colorful songs and innovatively choreographed dance sequences: one of them had Sridevi dressed up as some celestial nymph with Jeetendra in matching whites and a thousand copper pots laid in the midst of giant silvery cutouts, at some secluded sand-bed off the Marina beach. Wriggling away to Bappi Lahiri's *"Naino Mein sapna sapnon mein sajhna, sajhna pey dil aa gaya"* those thousand pots jangled to ring in the most profitable innings of Jeetendra; why they made him wear a wig beats me !

Dipped in tomfoolery, almost every character outdid the other in clowning around. The lyrics were inane and the dialogues silly, yet, the audience loved them all:

"Taki o taki o taki taki taki re jab sey tu aankhon mein jhaaki:

This song translates as "from the moment you peered in to my eyes" (however the word' Taki" defies any translation !)

"Chadha na mein ghodi par, baati naa mithai, phir bhi khaney lagi tu kyo khattai ?" I never mounted a horse nor given away sweets; yet you keep gorging away on salty treats!' (this alludes to imminent pregnancy)

The dialogues by Kader Khan had a proper noun inserted in some form or the other:

- *"sarkar is gaav ke sar hain to mein us sar ka seeng hoon. Jo meri baat nahin manta mein usey seeng markey 'Singapore' bana doonga"*

- *Agar tumney baat nahin maani to tumhari naukri 'Godavari' ho jayegi.'*

- *Zara bhi gadbad ki to mein tumhara 'Nanga Parbat' bana doonga'*

- *Malik aapko 'Uttar Pradesh' ki kasam"*

- *Tumhein Patna sey uthakar, Madras mei girakar Dilli pahuchadoonga "*

As the audience gaped in amazement at the comical atrocities unspooling, 'Himmatwala' went on to be the biggest hit of 1983. In Bombay alone it celebrated silver jubilee runs at two theaters: Central and Hindmata located in its busiest localities. A record that remains unbroken.

In hindsight 'Himmatwala' actually rode on four pillars; the introduction of Sridevi, music of Bappi Lahiri, Indeevar's lyrics, Kader Khan's dialogues and the way he enacted the character of 'Munim Narayandas'. In order to put across the effect of his inane dialogues Kader Khan masked his voice; As 'Munim Narayandas' he cleverly joined those dialogues with artful tomfoolery by modulating his voice.

After 'Himmatwala', Sridevi became the next hot sensation while Jeetendra got the miracle he wanted. But the biggest change unseen to the others was the transformation of veteran dialogue writer Kader Khan. Much before the invasion from the South, Kader Khan was already around as a talented and eminent dialogue writer. Films like 'Mukaddar ka Sikandar', 'Roti', 'Amar Akbar Anthony', 'Laawaris' 'Coolie','Naseeb' were testimonials of his skill. He wrote all kinds: philosophical, realism and even the comical. He had the ability to write dialogues for both: the high heeled or an underdog. To quote film critic Shoma Chatterjee: "Hindi films have the unique quality of different characters speaking different varieties of Hindi according to their social status".

Tereko (to you), dikhtaich(visible),kayko (why),kat le (buzz off),mamu (Cop),lafda (fight),chikna (fair),sutta (cigarette),vatle (go away), bindass (carefree) chal phoot (get lost),

Readers can recall many such words which have evolved down the years as 'bombay slang'.If the credit in creating the template of the 'angry young man' is given to Salim-Javed, the same should be shared with Kader Khan, who lent soul through dialogues written for many of his films

In the iconic 'Mukaddar Ka Sikandar, his dialogues dramatically spelt the conflict between destiny and practicality in vivid forms:

"sukkh to bewafaa hain aur dukh apna hain. Dukh to apna saathi hain. Isliye Sukh ko thokar maar aur Dukh ko galey laga. Takdeer tere kadmo mein hogi aur tu Mukaddar ka baadshah keh layega'

"zinda hai woh log joh jo maut se takrate hain..murdon se bhattar hain jo maut se ghabratey hain".

Those funny ones in 'Amar Akbar Anthony: *Aisa toh aadmi life mein do time bhagta hain. Olympic ka race ho ya police ka case ho"*

And now, a decade or so later, the lure of the green had altered the ink in his pen. He climbed down several rungs to write dialogues that bordered more on the comical:

- *Ek toh waise teri shakal kharab hai, upar se royega aur manhoos lagega'*

- *Beimani ke school mein Shaitan mujkse tuition leta hain '!*

- *Tum jis school mein beimaani sikha hain mein waha ka principal hoon*

- *Mujhe khud is baat ka shaq hain yeh mera beta nahin hain; ya hospital mein bacchey badal gaye they ya phir mein isska baap nahin hoon!*

Kader Khan was not only a prolific writer but also an excellent actor. Filmdom is dotted with his characterisations and in playing strong stellar roles, he was perhaps, second only to Pran. While Bombay recognized him as a poignant writer-actor, films from the South,turned the poignancy on its head,sadly turning him in to a perennial 'jester'.

'Himmatwala's huge successs sent Bombay film banners in to a tizzy. Bellwether banners like 'Yash Raj Pictures', 'Mukta Arts'and 'Sippy Films' were pushed in to a corner.

'Padmalaya Films'which had the goddess Padmalaya as its emblem was not exactly a new comer to Bombay. It had a couple of years earlier made 'Takkar' and 'Meri Awaz Suno' with Jeetendra. Both were average performers and for strange reason back then 'Meri Awaz Suno' was on the brink of being banned, supposedly, for content pertaining to politicians which was found objectionable by the censor boards. The film managed to get an 'A' certificate and made good money riding on this curiosity factor. But with 'Himmatwala' people all over the country sat back to enjoy their new-found comedy pair of Kader Khan-Shakti Kapoor; their dialogues, their antics and the Jeetu-Sridevi dances garnished with Bappi lahiri's music, those wares were lapped up in glee. Such a joyous moment was last seen during the peak of Rajesh Khann's stardom and the Bachchan onslaught.

There was a movie every fortnight from their stable. 'Padmalayas' followed it up with their next called as 'Mawaali' which also brought the people in droves. After two months of a house full release distributors released posters of 'Mawaali' with the tag line of 'Craze of the Nation' ! It was again that same team of 'Himatwala' with the addition of Jaya Prada and deletion of Amjad Khan. From the success of 'Mawaali' it was clear that 'Himmatwala' was no fluke. People had got tired of the continuous spectacle of 'lost-found' sagas and the fights against a system which now found acceptance, as a bitter truth. They were now in the mood for something new which could give them colours and reason to laugh and put up their feet- however absurd it might seem. Slapstick was welcome. 'Himmatwala' and its many cousins was just what the people imagined; The ability to make them laugh and guffaw from comedy that was 'ear catching' and romance that was naughty - not Classic. Here, the romantic angle had the hero subdue the heroine by his 'masculine charm'; where the heroine was again placed as a 'badly brought up girl' to be taught a lesson by the sermonizing hero.

In continuation of this trend in 1983, 'Laksmi Productions' introduced Rajnikanth, who was the biggest star of Madras. Today he is known as 'Thalaivva' the 'Super Lord 'of this universe who can right every wrong. Back in those days in Madras he had scaled the rungs to be known as 'Superstar Rajni'. Ironically, most of his hits were remakes of the ones that had made Amitabh a Star; like 'Thee' (Deewar), 'Billa' (Don),'Shanker-Salim-Simon' (AAA) where he 'added value' with his cigarette flipping antics.

'Andha Kanoon' the film that introduced him had cleverly roped in Amitabh Bachchan in a 'special appearance'. This could be seen as a well thought out factor to insure the film from unforeseen failure. Indeed it proved to be so: the 'special appearance' became a stellar role and at the time of its release became the highlight of 'Andhaa Kanoon'. The film was a hit and launched Rajnikanth as a known face in Hindi but the film is remembered more for the forest officer 'Jaan Nissar'(Amitabh) who has his own legible take on the Law of the land. But these were fleeting mentions.

An industry which churned out approximately 350 to 400 films every year the share from the south was a mere 10%. The modus operandi used to be few known banners of the south signing a known established name in Bombay, usually for projects which were remakes of hits in their lands. But the 1983 hit of 'Himmatwala' saw south indian banners hanging around for a longer time—1983-1984-1985-86; it was the proverbial 'gold rush' with several banners from the south coming in to spread their wings. Jeetendra no longer remaining their exclusive totem; the others like Rajesh Khanna, Shatrughan Sinha, Dharmendra, Mithun Chakraborty, Amitabh Bachchan and even Dilip Kumar were ensnared in their net. Soon started a long chain-link: Shatru-Jeetendra combine in 'Qaidi' (whose story was of a prisoner on the run, borrowed heavily from 'First Blood'- of the Rambo series) Rajesh-Jeetendra in D.Rama Naidu's 'Maqsad', Amitabh in T.Rama Rao's 'Inquilaab', Jeetendra-Dilip Kumar-in 'Dharam Adhikari' and many more that defy memory.

However dismissive we may be about the quality of their content, it was a widely accepted fact that the south brigade had many other factors working to their advantage. They were more disciplined when compared to their Bollywood counterparts; a clear time frame for their project; a turn around time of five to six months, a bound screenplay, pre arranged locales and a team of actors and actresses who were usually consistent. With Sridevi and Jaya Prada becoming mandatory, stories abounded about their rivalries; each turning oneup on the other. The success of this new juggernaut riding on films like 'Himmatwala', 'Mawaali', 'Justice Choudhury', 'Farz Aur Kanoon', 'Jaani Dost' and several more had reduced these two extremely talented actresses to mere song and dance routines. Besides hiring these ladies as heroines, these film makers also started inserting sizzling cabarets by girls having weird screen names like 'Silk Smitha' 'Disco Shanti', 'Nylex Nalini'. Considering the fact that the Internet had not been invented and television prime time being occupied only by Doordarshan, the same became reasons for repeat audiences. Of the two, Sridevi was notches higher than her rival Jaya Prada. The baby-faced look of Sridevi looked suitable for enacting any role that required a young girl breaking in to silly (thigh -tapping) songs. That way, she did have an edge, and scored over Jaya Prada's perfectly chiseled features, making renowned director Satyajit Ray to one day declare Jaya Prada as "the most beautiful face of India'.

Sridevi continued to climb higher. 'Himmatwala' had made a permanent place in the minds of viewers. But with continuous hits she became bigger by the day and so obviously increased her fees. This put off some production houses, especially the 'Padmalayas'. To arrest their over dependence on her, 'Padmalaya' films on the advise of Jeetendra decided to introduce another girl from the crowded South -Radha, in their next flick "Kamyaab". Giant posters of 'Kaamyab' introduced her saying "this is not Sridevi this is, Radha." But it failed to shift the audience away from Sridevi. 'Kaamyab' predictably flopped.

During 1983 the medium of viewing films was either through theaters or television. Lazy Sundays were ruled by India's only television channel 'Doordarshan' beaming old films. Theaters continued to be of the appalling kind. Be they in mofussil towns, suburbs or even a metro where walls with peeling paints, torn seats infested with bugs and rats scurrying around in stinking urinals was the norm! In such bleak conditions appeared the VCR or the video cassette recorder. Just as television was the purview of the few during the seventies, so was the VCR in the eighties. This small humble box did throw out piracy laws to the wind and set up a spurt of 'mom and pop theaters'. Upper middle class households put up black boards on their doorstep where messages written in chalk announced the screening of the next Jeetu-Sridevi flick. At the price of an 'Upper-stall' ticket which was inclusive of a cup of tea served by the household, not only one could get to watch a latest film a week before its release but also escape the hassle of queuing up to buy it in 'black'. Coincidentally that time'Justice Chaudhry', a big Jeetendra –Sridevi starrer was being readied for release. Distributors woke up on a Saturday morning, to find their Friday collections dismal.

The trail led to pirated video cassettes already in the market since a week ago. By these mushrooming 'video parlours' the curiosity value of films was being killed so the first two weeks collections which is a make-or-break factor, especially for a big-budget film, suffered staggering losses. Even Hollywood was not spared; 'Octopussy' the latest James Bond flick was also circulating all over.

Naysayers predicted that an industry already reeling from a success rate of barely 20%, video parlours would quicken its demise. However, the indomitable spirit of the industry proved them wrong !

Towards the end of 1983, the much-awaited 'Coolie' released. Even though the blurry prints of its pirated video cassettes had already made its rounds, people still thronged theatres to watch their coolie who was now 'immortal' for he had just defied death. Those pictures of him lying in hospital faded away when people clapped watching their 'Coolie' walk like a knight cloaked in red, pacing long strides on a train's roof top, nonchalantly puffing on a 'beedi'and petting a falcon perched on his shoulder. For the audience it was a Friday to rejoice for their icon had returned in a Manmohan Desai film; with four hits in a year notched up on his holster: 'Parvarish', 'Chacha Bhatija','' Dharam –Veer and 'Amar-Akbar-Anthony' the 'Man' had a terrific record. A year earlier he had directed and produced the lavish 'Naseeb'. In the black and white era Desai also earned the distinction of directing the Kapoors: Raj Kapoor in 'Chhalia' and Shammi Kapoor in 'Bluffmaster'.

Desai and Amitabh Bachchan tossed away the 'VCR' threat and 'Coolie' had a stupendous opening. (I had watched both- the blurry print at a 'mom and pop video parlour' and also the first show at a theatre). Bachchan playing a 'coolie' changed equations making the coolie no longer a mere 'porter' but a supreme underdog; therefore to oppose this 'Coolie' with a larger-than-life image, Desai had to draw in a string of villains: Kader Khan, Goga Kapoor, Om Shivpuri, Suresh Oberoi and not to forget the man who punched him in this film: Puneet Issar. It also had the Marathi stalwart Nilu Phule in a stellar. The near fatal accident on the sets quadrupled the film's curiosity and repeat value. If ever there was a film that could generate a publicity blitz on it's own then it had to be 'Coolie'. Inspite of the huge clouds of doubt kicked up by the advent of the VCR, 'Coolie' strode like a colossus. Shattering records and reviving the black marketeers.

In March 1984, a film called 'Akalmand' starring Jeetendra – Sridevi-Kader Khan-Shakti Kapoor which was an umpteenth one in the long chain of South films, flopped badly. This effectively brought an end to the rollicking run this team had been enjoying. Thankfully, the 'VCR' was not singled out as the reason. It was the obvious 'Law of Diminishing Returns' catching up with all; Jeetendra, Kader Khan, Shakti Kapoor and all those film makers out to make fast mega-bucks. But the only one who emerged unscathed was Sridevi. As the proverbial queen bee by the sheer weight of her charisma and hard work she was in a higher orbit. Jeetendra's best phase effectively came to an end. He would go on to star in few more movies opposite other entrants from the South like

Bhanumathi, which would help him to hang around for few more years before fading away to rise again in the distant future as a content producer for television. 'Padmalaya Films' time too was up and their persistence never paid off. Their last project called 'Simhasan', a film based on a story made up of fabled kingdoms and palace politics mightily failed.

In the world of villainy where kingpins comprised of either dacoits, capricious money lenders or suave gold smugglers, there now emerged a new breed –one of corrupt politicians.

After coaxing dacoits to surrender under Vinobha Bhave's amnesty scheme, or by enacting the dreaded MISA to rein in smugglers, the entire mantle for 'conning' now fell on the politicians. The entire machinery of politicians and the police was turning in to a nexus of creating ill gotten wealth. Keeping this unholy alliance in mind, Lakshmi productions' made 'Inquilab' with Amitabh-Sridevi-Kader Khan-Shakti Kapoor-Utpal Dutt.

On the other end, Rajesh Khanna, the perennial hopeful in making 'comebacks' was further buoyed by the unexpected success of his two recent releases which was 'Souten', a love triangle with Tina Munim and Padmini Kolhapure directed by Sawan Kumar Tak,who had a successful reputation of having carved out a small niche of his own by making woman oriented themes. The title is actually the scourge of all married woman, the word 'Souten' is not only the second name for a mistress but also a stigma on the lawfully wedded wife that she, inspite of being a legal wife, has been a misfit in her husband's conjugal bliss.

Sawan Kumar the maker shot 'Souten' in the lovely locales of Mauritius where pristine beaches and blue waters dotted with luxurious yachts gave it an unlikely 'unique-selling-point; foreign locations always added that additional oomph to the narratives. It partially also showcased the labour class migrating from India to Mauritius to find employment just as generations before them had migrated to the West Indies. 'Souten' begins with a young man, Shyam (Rajesh Khanna) having big dreams but without the backup of any inheritance. He is in love with an heiress (Tina Munim) of a large company. They soon get married but later, after the honeymoon period, the young man's scrupulous principles prevent him to accept any rich goodies from his in-laws. With sheer hard work and a visionary mind he soon sets up his own business. Very soon financial trouble comes, in the form of unexpected storms that sink his merchant ships. Financial losses notwhithstanding, 'Shyam' also has to thwart the designs of his in-laws (Prem Chopra and Shashikala) and also undergo the test of fidelity because he had during his good times financially helped one of his employees (Dr. Sreeram Lagoo) and his daughter Radha (Padmini Kolhapure). He also has to bear the loss of his unborn child due to the careless ways of his wife.

Speaking of actor Prem Chopra, the man was good looking: tall, fair with those rosy Punjabi looks, high cheekbones, a silky mop of hair and Elvis-styled sideburns. Starting off as one of the martyrs in Manoj Kumar's ' Shaheed', his career unfortunately did not hit the high notes of a hero. To stay relevant he turned to 'villainy'. His good looks scored over what Ranjeet lacked, but where booze,women and salacious remarks ruled,Ranjeet was a compulsory choice. After playing a range of villains like the two-timing lover of Asha Parekh in 'Kati Patang', raping Sadhana in 'Aap aye Bahar Ayee' Amitabh's dubious friend in 'Gehri Chaal', the wayward son in 'Purab aur Paschim', the one-eyed sumuggler called 'Paapi Singh' in 'Kaala Sona' strangely, the man is mostly remembered for a single line from 'Bobby' '-*prem naam hain mera-Prem Chopra*'. This led to other directors put in a dedicated one-liner for him. So in 'Kranti' as the evil brother-in-law of the king he mouths: '*Shambhoo ka dimmag do dhari talwar hain* and in 'Souten' he rattles out: *Main woh bala hoon jo patthar ko sheeshey sey todta hoon*"

With hit songs and decent performances 'Souten' was a hit and immediately after, the Mohan Kumar banner released 'Avtaar' which had Rajesh Khanna in a path breaking role. The main core was about a father's revenge on his opportunistic sons. Rajesh Khanna played 'Ram Avtar' who owns a garage. His wife (Shabana Azmi) whom he had married by eloping since his rich In-laws did not approve their daughter marrying a 'lowly garage owner'. He has two sons, played by Gulshan Grover and Shashi Puri. But the sons prompted by their greedy wives swindle their own father of his property. Rest is all about how the old 'Avataar' works hard, becomes rich and beats his unscrupulous sons at their own game.This struck a chord and the film was rightfully declared a hit. But the pompousness of Rajesh Khanna made him shout from the rooftops that ' I have arrived'! He was now approached by another set of producers to be signed for a film called "Aaj ka MLA'. Since the success of 'Avtaar' had kind of given a second lease to the fading, ageing, ex-superstar he insisted in inserting the word 'Avtaar'. So the film got renamed as 'Aaj ka MLA- Ram Avtaar'. The media insisted and believed that the first to release would be the winner. 'Inquilab' and 'Aaj ka MLA' raced away each trying to outsmart the other in getting released first. What we expected was a nail biting finish but instead, an anti-climax occurred with both of them falling off the cliff !.

Speaking of sons, Dharmendra was scouting for a script to launch his son Sunny Deol. Javed Akhtar wrote a script, titled it as 'Betaab' and sold it to Dharmendra. The script was liked and he signed Rahul Rawail, the actual director of 'Love Story'. He wanted a new girl opposite his son and signed Amrita Singh,(an only child of Delhi socialite Ruksana Sultana). 'Betaab' was a super hit and Sunny Deol was launched successfully. His shy looks coupled with a brawny physique set him apart from the other star sons. Betaab's super success made veteran journalist Devyani Chaubal to give him the sobriquet of 'Dharamputra' Sunny Deol.

In times,where Amitabh ruled as that towering character battling out for the underdogs-as a dock worker, as a 'coolie ' or even as a taxi driver, Jeetendra was busy fighting crooked 'munshis' and struggling to solve love triangles. When Shatrughan Sinha and Dharmendra battled smugglers and Star sons fought warring parents- the nation was facing a new kind of threat. It was terrorism and separatism.

When The Cat Was Away...

The 'Khalistan' movement had started taking a deadly form. The state of Punjab had become a hot bed of strife and discord which threatened to boil over. This happened sooner than thought of and by June 1983 this resulted in a warlike situation coded as 'Operation Bluestar'. Never before since Independence had the Indian army been asked to resort to warfare, inside Indian soil, against its own citizens! It was a difficult decision but the surgery had to be done; the army stormed the Golden Temple and flushed out the terrorists.

Four months later the Prime Minister Mrs Indira Gandhi was assassinated. Immediately after, her only living son Rajiv Gandhi elevated by a gigantic wave of sympathy, took over as the Prime Minister and insisted that his childhood friend Amitabh Bachchan assist him. Promptly calling a press conference the mighty 'Crusader on-screen' decided to renounce films and venture in to the real world where he perhaps, hoped to begin life as a real-life crusader. He was given a ticket in distant Uttar Pradesh where he stood against H.N.Bahuguna- a proven heavyweight. Amitabh defied all pollsters and won the elections with a huge margin bringing him in to his new studios---the Parliament House in Delhi. However, it was hard to believe of a filmworld without its tallest force.

During the void created by his renouncing films, there were a few being readied in the interim, for release. The first was Prakash Mehra's 'Sharabi'. As expected it was a big hit to again vindicate Amitabh Bachchan's grip as a mass entertainer.

"Aaj untna hain maikhane mein jitna chod diya kartey they paimane mein" — Vicky Kapoor

Alcohol, considered as vice all along, was turned on its head by the character Vicky Kapoor (Amitabh). He is most of the time 'high' and his debilitating love for alcohol is traced to a troubled childhood: millionaire widower's (Pran) business tours gets hampered by his crying, mother less child. To quieten the bawling baby, a few sips of brandy had done its trick and as time passes the bawling baby grows up into a 6' 2" handsome Vicky, who now considers this potent liquid as a part of his daily diet. Only son of a wealthy father, Vicky passes his days in the company of wine, poetry and Munshiji, who has been his care taker since childhood (Om Prakash). Apparently, the father does not mind his son's daily tipples but he is certainly concerned for his son's lack of business acumen. Much to his chagrin, Vicky Kapoor keeps giving off his father's money to the needy. The father loses no opportunity to put him on the backfoot by reminding him thru cracky one-liners, like *"Khali Botlon ki bhi keemat hoti hain'* and very soon the friction between father and son is not due to his fondness for alcohol or his charity; It rises because of his love for the beautiful Meena (Jaya Prada) who is not only a poor girl but makes her living by singing and dancing at stage shows. The father charades his son's love for Meena by equating the sum total value of his "expensive carpets, priceless chandeliers, exquisite furniture and opulence" to zero value of Meena the dancer! In bombastic 'Mughal-e-Azam 'style Vicky Kapoor the scion rebels. With his beloved 'munshiji' in tow he leaves his father's mansion. How events culminate outside and how they in turn help his love triumph over his father is what the film is about. Amitabh's drunken antics in other films were well known; as Sikandar in 'MukaddarKaSikandar' where he and his drinking buddy in moments of drunken tomfoolery start 'searching for their house'; that classic 'bevdagiri' as Anthony from 'AmarAkbarAnthony' where he is giving a 'dressing down' to his own reflection in second –person style. But 'Sharabi' was a different ball-game. He is not that quintessential 'bevda'. Even though 'high' in every frame, alcohol does not get the better of him. As was the case in that one scene in 'Mukaddar Ka Skandar'; unlike Sikandar, Vicky Kapoor when high is in control of himself, his speech and his thoughts. 'Sharabi' rose to be another example of a one-man show riding to box-office glory.

In Laxmi productions 'Aakhree Raasta' a remake of a Kamalhasan film which was made originally in Tamil, made money again in it's hindi remake. Unlike 'Mahaan' this had an unusual theme. Usually, the son exacted vengeance for the wrongs done on parents, brother, sisters; In 'Aakhri Raasta' where Amitabh enacted roles of both father and son, interestingly, it is the father who wreaks vengeance on the perpetrators who had tormented him in his youth. The son (young Amitabh) who is a cop, seems to be just filling in for the lighter moments of song dance and some fights. The focus is clearly on the father; old but not withered; grieving but not broken. The transformation of the loyal simpleton David (Amitabh Senior) in to a man, who is now on a hunt for the depraving three: the rapist Minister played by Sadashiv Amrapurkar, the heinous Doctor played by Bharat Kapoor and the corrupt DIG Police-Dalip Tahil. Just out of prison after having spent two decades for a crime he never committed, he is now meticulously working out a plan to kill them and that plan is what kept audience on their toes. What was the plan by David and how he eliminates each one without leaving any clue for the cops is what the gist of the film was about. In fact, 'Lakshmi Productions' had already played out Rajnikanth in a similar facet in their earlier 'Andha Kanoon'. While Sridevi merely lent glamour and oomph to her insignificant role, it was Jaya Prada who stole the show. However in the case of Sridevi there certainly was a case of 'conflicting interests' because actress Rekha (all along considered to be the real-life-heart-throb of Amitabh) dubbed all the dialogues for Sridevi. A rare brainwave from the makers!

The next release was Manmohan Desai's 'Mard'

"Sirf Patiyala kyon hum to saara Hindustan lenge"-Mard

With a leading magazine 'India Today crowning Amitabh Bachchan with the title of 'One-Man-Industry' Manmohan Desai's 'Mard' was like the hindi medium equivalent of a 'super-hero'. The story was based on a princely state being usurped by the British. The members of the 'Indian National Congress' seemed to have not appeared on the scene even though armoured tanks and planes are shown in ample measure! Few years earlier, Manoj Kumar's 'Kranti' and its events did convey a half baked sense of a supposedly Pre-1857 times; in contrast- 'Mard' was confusing and, terrible. If Amitabh had great script writers and directors to hoist him on to success then the opposite was also true.

Film makers like Desai who post 'Coolie' had exhausted their creative juices to a trickle put Amitabh to greater risk by making him star in hackneyed films like 'Mard'. This 'Mard' like his predecessor in 'Coolie', takes on the bad guys by playing the role of an underdog, this time as a 'tongawallah' who takes on the might of the 'Angrez'. For authenticity you even have one of the 'angrez' called as 'Curzon Saheb' (played by the light-eyed Kamal Kapoor) and to strike a sort of balance there is a sympathetic English woman known as 'Lady Helena' (played by Mithun Chakraborty's ex-wife Helena Luke). Taking a leaf off from Lee Falk's 'Phantom' comic strips, Desai even planted a dog and a horse as the 'Mard's companions. The ridicule of this 'mard' continues; he is forced to face the whiplash of an Indian princess. He in turn as a 'Macho' Mard abducts her, whips her in return and then rolls her down over salt pans. She in turn gets turned on by his 'machismo' to croon in a song that went *"will you marry me"*?

The audacity does not end, in fact, as more reels of film unspool, the proceedings become tortuous. The british masters are shown as allies of an oppressive king who clones slaves by extracting blood from his subjects!. Such a laughable depiction of the English rulers would make even Warren Hastings roll over in his grave.

People did express their bitterness at being let down by the Desai-Bachchan team by not giving it the response that Desai expected. Another reason for 'Mard's average performance perhaps was that Desai's forte lay in injecting the 'Bombaiyya' way of life in his films: 'Parvarish, Amar Akbar Anthony, 'Naseeb' were pointed examples. If these films were crowning glories that defined Manmohan Desai's glory then 'Mard 'was a pathetic obituary.

Manmohan Desai, the man whose films formed pillars to Bachchan's bulwark, rued the lack of good scriptwriters and also mulled handing over his 'MKD' banner to his son Ketan Desai.

After the premature renouncement by Vinod Khanna in 1979 followed by the abdication by Amitabh Bachchan in 1984, the throne of Bollywood lay vacant. Vinod Khanna, one of the busiest stars of those times earning good money cited his inclination towards sprritual fulfilment. A life of hubris perhaps did take a toll on him. Donning orange robes and opting to live life as a 'yogi' under Swami Rajneesh (more well known as Osho),Vinod Khanna deserted his country, his family and career. Nothwithstanding their absence the place was crowded with many contenders. But the highs scaled by the Big3 during the 50's, the superstardom of Rajesh Khanna in the 70's and the One-Man-Industry title earned by Amitabh, was a near impossible task for these contenders to reach. Shatrughan Sinha, Dharmendra, Jeetendra, Rishi Kapoor,Rajesh Khanna and Mithun Chakravorty. The sizzling energy from 'Disco Dancer' had spread fast. Post 'Disco Dancer', Mithun had started giving regular hits: 'Swarg Se

Sundar' (family discord), 'Ghulami' (desert-saga), 'Pyar Jhukta Nahin' (marital discord), 'Ashanti (multistarrer), 'Muddat' (thriller), 'Dilwala' (thriller) were a few from the many that hit bull's eye. But former A-Listers were now being relegated to stellar roles in the 'Senior Category'. Any fresh attempt made by them as a solo hero met with disaster. Dharmendra met some leeway through two of his hit's; 'Naukar Biwi Ka' by 'nagin' maker Raaj Kohli and 'Hukumat' made by Anil Sharma.

With contenders now turning seniors there was enough room for new entrants. The Modelling world threw up a few like Deepak Parashar, Anand Balraj, Dalip Tahil. Deepak Parashar, a tall lanky fellow had become the face of 'Digjam' suitings while Dalip Tahil with his bushy hairstyle was well known for the 'Modella' ads. Another aspirant doing the rounds from his theater days was Raj Babbar. He was introduced by B.R.Chopra in his film 'Insaaf Ka Tarazu'. Depicting the aftermath of a closeted subject like rape 'Insaf Ka Tarazu' was a well made remake of an English film 'Lipstick'. Raj Babbar played the fiend 'Ramesh' who rapes woman as a matter of lifestyle. As an actor he was effective and in fact welcomed as a dedicated one. He also had the rare distinction of having signed thirty two projects even before the release of his debut film! Nevertheless, Raj Babbar was not the flame that could set film lore alight. Nothing worked for him.Not even the strategy by mid-sized producers to pair him with Deepak Parasher. Films like 'Aap To Aise Na They' and 'Armaan' starring these two that rode on the disco-chugging *Rambha Ho-Sambha-ho* proved to be failures. Except for B.R.Chopra's

'Nikaah' which was a Muslim social based on 'triple-talaaq'. A new actress from Pakistan called Salma Agha was introduced as the main protagonist in 'Nikaah' who faces the onslaught of 'triple-talaaq' for no fault of hers. Raj Babbar and Deepak Parashar, chief protégés of B.R.Chopra, greatly benefitted from its success.

Two decades ago Muslim socials was the forte of only H.S.Rawail (Rahul Rawail's father). As a producer and director he had earned his stripes by making 'Mere Mehboob' with 'jubilee star' Rajendra Kumar and the extremely beautiful, Sadhana. The film was all about falling in love but besides this prime casting of top stars, the joy derived was about love and stolen glances from, the veiled custom of the muslims: the 'Naqab'. The setting of the film opens up in a college, presumably managed, by a Muslim social organization where everybody: the principal, the teachers, staff and students, all are Muslims. The film celebrates that strata of society where Muslims shine under a beacon of culture which we all know as 'Tehzeeb'. Rajendra Kumar and Sadhana as 'Anwar' and 'Husna',the students in love with each other, made the viewers fall in love with them. Their love blossoms when both collide outside the library and as he helps her in picking up her scattered sheets of papers, he gets allured by her dainty fingers clasping them. Since she is wearing a 'Naqab'(veil) he is not able to see her face and those fingers are his only clue. This incident is tenderly narrated in its title song penned by Shaqueel Badayuni and its lilting music by Naushad made 'Mere Mehboob' an extremely endearing film for all across. Since then, Muslim socials had its own nascent audience.

After H.S.Rawail it was B.R.Chopra who also brought his forte to Muslim socials. After the successful 'Nikaah', B.R.Chopra brought out another muslim-social film called 'Tawaif' casting Rishi Kapoor and Rati Agnihotri and like 'Nikaah' this too was based in a world where all characters are Muslims. 'Tawaif' was another muslim social which unlike 'Nikaah, that was based on the elite, 'Tawaif' based on the middle class Muslims was simple yet very interesting. It narrated the story of Sultana (Rati Agnihotri) a nautch girl falling in love with Dawood (Rishi Kapoor) a jolly fellow who ekes out his living working as a clerk at a small publishing house owned by Sulaiman (Deepak Parashar). He also finds himself falling in love with Kaynaat (Poonam Dhillon) who is an aspiring author. The film soon becomes a triangle of sorts with the nautch girl walking in to his life and sweeping him off his feet.

Of the star sons, all barring one or two, had vanished. While Sunny Deol followed up his 'Betaab' success with 'Arjun', Sunjay Dutt after a successful treatment for drugs at a Rehab centre in America was lucky to see his 'comeback ' film, the little known 'Jaan Ki Baaazi,' opposite the beautiful Anuradha Patel, get appreciated. Immediately after this he got a new lease from the Mahesh Bhatt directed 'Naam'.

While 'Arjun' was written by Javed Akhtar, 'Naaam' was scripted by his former partner- now- rival, Salim Khan. The irony of 'Naam' lay in being an Aryan Films venture. It was made to help revive their scion Kumar Gaurav's career. 'Naam' was a brilliant success and helped prove the rise of director Mahesh Bhatt. After the path breaking 'Arth' and the commercially successful 'Lahu Ke Do Rang' Mahesh Bhatt proved he was no flash-in-the-pan. But Naam 'failed' in what it was meant to achieve. Instead of Gaurav, Sanjay Dutt came to the fore, as Vicky, an unemployed youth from Bombay who gets sucked in the murky world of drug dealers. Three years back, as Kunal in Subhash Ghai's 'Vidhaata' he drew sniggers from the audience; three years later at the same theatre now screening Mahesh Bhatt's 'Naam' they saw a new Sunjay Dutt; the visible disinterest in those hollow eyes of Kunal was gone, what they saw was a toned down face with eyes mirroring the fire in his belly. The audience believed in Vicky's struggles and the pain he felt for his family; when he coughed out blood as the hunted Vicky those people had tears rolling down their eyes. Salim Khan's 'Vicky' failed to bag any award but he gave a reincarnation to Sunjay Dutt.

Jackie Shroff who gate crashed in to the big league as 'Hero, sustained his glory with 'Teri Meherbaniyaan'. It was made by K.C.Bokadia who had earlier made 'Pyar Jhukta Nahin' which had consolidated Mithun Chakraborty's position in the industry. There was another new entrant who also belonged to the star son category. But his father was no star, but a little known film producer whose name was Surinder Kapoor. His banner was known as 'Narasimha 'films. This producer's son, whose name was Anil, entered the industry through smaller films like 'Rachana'; opposite an actress called Bina(actor Pradeep Kumar's daughter), and a hardly-known film called 'Kahan se Guzar Gaya' made by M.S.Sathyu. Later came his first major role; albeit a small one in Ramesh Sippy's 'Shakti' where he appeared on screen briefly as Amitabh's grown up son.

Those days Surinder Kapoor, perhaps, to give his son a better footing, produced a small budget film called 'Wo Saat Din'. He hired the services of Bapu, a veteran director, from the South. This medium budget film was liked and helped Anil in gaining a foothold. Anil Kapoor's dedication is what held him in good stead. His commitment and diligence made him stand apart.It would also not be out of place to mention, in the crowded world of clean shaven heroes, Anil Kapoor (and Jackie) stood out with their 'chevron ' styled mustache.

Anil Kapoor was also making his presence felt through socially moving films like 'Saaheb'. Remake of a Bengali hit of the same name which had starred Tapos Pal, a top star in Calcutta. Tapos Pal had earlier tried entering the Hindi film domain through 'Rajshri Productions' 'Abodh' where his leading lady was a young Maharashtrian girl whose name was Madhuri Dixit. 'Abodh' flopped, dashing Tapas' hopes. Madhuri Dixit continued her efforts in securing herself by signing her next with Rajshri Productions called 'Swati'. But 'Swati' had Meenakshi Sheshadri in the title role while Madhuri Dixit played her younger sister.

After 'Saaheb' came a string of mild hits or average successes as said in film distributors' parlance. They were 'Chameli Ki Shaadi' with Amrita Singh, 'Mashaal' written by Javed Akhtar and sharing equal space with Dilip Kumar, 'Andar-Bahar' with Jackie Shroff, Subhash Ghai's 'Karma', Rajeev Rai's 'Yudh'; then the biggest, 'Mr India'. With Sridevi now being declared as the No 1 heroine in Bollywood she decided to shift to Bombay permanently and sign on scripts which had her as the 'prima donna diva' resulting in the prestigious 'Mr India'.

From the Big 3, Dev Anand failed to propel his 'National Party' which was a ragtag vehicle to launch film stars; old and young in to the world of politics. His political foray failed and so did his films: 'Swami Dada', 'Hum Naujawan' and 'Anand aur Anand' unfailingly failed!

Dilip Kumar as seen, was raking in acclaim in his second innings having just won a Filmfare award for 'Shakti'. Raj Kapoor gave us a memorable film in 1985 in 'Ram Teri Ganga Maili. It also introduced a young starlet called Yasmin Khan. Keeping in line with his banner, he rechristened this girl as 'Mandakini' to become the latest 'R.K.girl', the last being Dimple Kapadia in 'Bobby'. As was back then in 1974 and so it was a decade later, Raj Kapoor remaned true to his forte; keeping his fondness for woman oriented themes intact.

"Zinda insaanon sey dar lagta hain baba,murdon sey kya dar"-
Ganga

The gist of Raj Kapoor's 'Ram Teri Ganga Maili' was a tale whose backdrop is based on the river Ganga, as she traverses from the Himalayas towards the sea. As the mighty river flows on caressing all with her abundance she gathers pollutants caused by man's reckless living. The girl 'Ganga', is a metaphor for the river 'Ganga'. Just like the river, she descends from the mountains in search for the father of her child and how she faces lecherous men in the guise of samaritans. The film was not only a big hit of 1985 but also gave a lifeline to Raj Kapoor's second son Rajiv Kapoor, even though, his disappearance later was preordained. Yasmin Khan, now known as 'Mandakini' for good, went on to emerge as one of the top five heroines, until she was seduced one day by the allure of an Underworld don.

Master of Romance, Yash Chopra, was going through a rough patch. His dream 'Silsila' was history. The media rubbed it in by calling it as "Silly-Sila". After this large scale disappointment coupled with more disappointing films made by his protégé Ramesh Talwar, he and his banner of 'Yash Raj films' were left out in the cold. 'Baseraa 'starring Shashi Kapoor, Rekha and Raakhee failed. So did 'Sawaal' made with Shashi Kapoor and Sanjeev Kumar. While 'Baseraa' could get a benefit of doubt about it's quality, 'Sawaal' -a mish mash of Deewaar and Trishul was a real bad one. For Yash Chopra the writing on the wall was clear- he had to get hold of a good script. It arrived soon in the form of Javed Akhtar's 'Mashaal'; Very soon he got to assembling a cast made up of Dilip Kumar, Rati Agnihotri, Waheeda Rehman, Amrish Puri and Anil Kapoor. 'Mashaal' did have the ripple like effect of the erstwhile duo's (Yash-Amitabh) earlier hits; the clash between good and bad, where both protagonists have their own justification. Mentoring transforms the bad in to a Good. But extraneous circumstances later make the good mentor go against the law. Dilip Kumar played the upright journalist 'Vinod Kumar' whose pen spouts venom against a smuggler S.K.Vardhan (Amrish Puri). Waheeda Rehman and Rati Agnihotri provided the romantic interests. But, it was Anil Kapoor as 'Raja' the vagabond 'tapori' who stole the show. Slim physiqued, tall, lush hair, dark stubble, and puffing on beedis did to an extent - capture the demeanour of 'Vijay' from the epic 'Deewaar'.

Raja from 'Mashaal' was the new age 'tapori' of the 80's. While Vijay of 'Deewar' had a wounded psyche hounding him every where, Raja was a normal product of Bombay's slums where hundreds like him reside. Raja also believes in giving back in the same coin to bullies who torment people from the lower strata. That is where the similarity with Vijay begins, and ends. Raja was not having any element of vengeance inside him; for him being poor and earning a living as a cinema ticket black-marketeer is a way of life; narrating about his father's untimely death, *'Baap mera local train sey gir gaya'*, is not a reason to be felt oppressed but is matter of fact; thousands commute daily, by dangling themselves perilously from speeding local trains.

Though Anil Kapoor won his maiden Filmfare award for this,'Mashaal' was not exactly a hit making Yash Chopra's wait to extend further. He decided to make a love story where warring parents and illegitimate offsprings could tug at heartstrings. He cast Sunil Dutt and Rekha as the older generation lovers and introduced Farha Khan and Rohan Kapoor (singer Mahendra Kapoor's son) as GenNext. Produced and directed by himself, 'Faasle' proved to be bad, if not, the worst of his flops. The ordeal was tortuous for a man whose three decades career was studded with milestones like 'Dhool Ka Phool', 'Waqt', 'Daag', 'Deewaar', 'Trishul', 'Kabhie Kabhie'.

After being noticed in 'Mashaal', Anil Kapoor was now able to come across as a good actor even though he was not yet a 'star'; like Jackie Shroff. However, both became a bankable team for multistarrers. One such was called 'Andar-Baahar' directed by Raj Sippy who had gained notoriety from copying English films. He began with 'Inkaar' a successful one based on Akiro Kurusawa's 'High and Low'; then came 'Satte Pe Satta' copied from 'Seven Brides for Seven Brothers' starring Howard Keel and Jane Powell. He now wanted to make a hindi version of the Eddie Murphy-Nick Nolte starrer '48 Hours' by casting Anil Kapoor in the role of Reggie and Jackie Shroff in the role of the cop, Jack Cates. For novelty's sake, for the heroine's role,he brought in Moonmoon Sen from Calcutta; daughter of the beautiful Suchitra Sen, an extremely talented actress in Bengali Cinema, who had starred as 'Paro'in Bimal Roy's 'Devdas'. But the daughter in her hindi debut titillated in a bikini that left little to the imagination! 'Andar-Bahar' met with reasonable success and Anil-Jackie became a much sought after pair. After the earlier star pairs of Dharam –Amitabh, Amitabh-Shashi, Sanjeev Kumar-Shatrughan Sinha, Rajesh Khanna-Jeetendra, Amitabh-Rishi Kapoor, on those lines these two, became a hit 'jodi'.

In the same year, Ramesh Sippy the maker of India's biggest action hit, now planned to bring alive a forgotten pair.

Bobby Returns

"Mere Naukar mera Namak khaatey hain"-Madam Kamladevi.

Typical of the Sippy's, their 'big bang' projects buzzed from the day of their 'muhurat' till the day of its release. Based on a script by Javed Akhtar, Ramesh Sippy signed up Rishi Kapoor and Dimple Kapadia. This was indeed a casting coup. Even though not towering like his 'Shakti' which bagged giants Amitabh Bachchan and Dilip Kumar, this was certainly controversial. A decade ago when Raj Kapoor roared back thru 'Bobby', the young lead pair had nestled in some romance till it got nipped in the bud. Rishi Kapoor moved on while 'Bobby' remained Dimple's only film.Twelve years later when 'Saagar' released, those who had watched this pair debut, were now in the age-group of fifties and their kids back then, would at the time of 'Saagar's release, be in their twenties. At the age of eighteen or something she had won a Filmfare award in the best actress category and after that her dream marriage with then superstar Rajesh Khanna, had waded into rocky terrain. But after twelve years and two kids later, Dimple still looked stunning; the puppy-fat in 'Bobby' was long shed. 'Saagar' was made to reveal the siren concealed within and was also made to unlock the brand equity lying dormant since 'Bobby'.

'Saagar' (The Ocean) was a love story set as a triangle. The third angle was played by actor Kamalhasan whose memory had more or less dimmed from the minds of the Hindi belt. 'Saagar's' basic theme was rich boy-poor girl-and equally poor, silent suitor. Like all of Ramesh Sippy's films 'Saagar' too, was lavishly mounted. Justifying the banner's value it was released befittingly and Dimple Kapadia was given a warm welcome. Production values were excellent; on the banks of a riveting blue sea rested a quaint village made up of hard working fishermen. The entire set was well conceptualized by art director Bijon Das Gupta.

The fishermen earn a living by selling their catch to a haughty 'Madam's' fishing company (played exceedingly well by Madhur Jaffrey). The hardnosed 'madam' is being influenced by her step-nephew –cum-CEO (Shafi Inamdar) in taking over the entire coastline by launching motorized trawlers which can quadruple the company's revenues. Unknown to them, her grandson Ravi (Rishi Kapoor) is wooing a young girl from the same fishermen community. The girl Mona (Dimple) is the only child of a tavern owner (Saeed Jaffrey). Breath taking photography and Rahul Dev Burman's intoxicating music completed Ramesh Sippy's ouvre of romance.

Scenes exemplifying the Ocean:

- The opening scene where credits flash and R.D.Burman's orchestra comes alive. The camera lovingly pans the sunrise, slowly turning around to kiss the vast sands and gently moving ahead to meet the pier at the far end of the beach. All the while with

R.D.Burman's two versions of background music playing, where each: a fusion of symphonic melody and the other a soulful medley of whistles which later personifies the two forms of love coursing through it; the love between Mona & Ravi in tandem with the quiet ripples of the ocean and the other tune narrating unrequited love, emulating the easy going and hassle free 'Raja' (Kamalhaasan)

- Ravi walking down the beach and in a beautiful cove discovers the lady emerging from the sea a' la mermaid' style.

- Raja witnessing his own heartbreak when he watches Mona and Ravi in each other's arms. Shocked out of his senses he turns around and bolts away like a maniac only to collide against a rock and land face down. The next scene shows twilight descending on the waters and on one of those rocks; the heartbroken Raja is drowning himself in alcohol.

'Saagar' had uncanny similarities with 'Bobby'. The boy Raj was from a rich family so was Ravi; 'Bobby' lived in a village full of fishermen so does Mona; it was a hindu-christian love story, ditto in 'Saagar'; during its climax, the son in 'Bobby' gives a tacit threat to his father of taking his life, so does Ravi to his granny. And, thats not all-'Saagar'also had a scene, similar to the split-second towel drop moment in 'Bobby'. Sippy bewildered all by inserting a shocking blink -and -you -miss topless moment by Dimple. As brief as a nanosecond , it was mysteriously deleted after week one of its release.

But, 'Saagar failed to neither reignite the magic of 'Bobby' nor set a benchmark. Shafi Inamdar's villainy did not strike terror nor were the romantic interludes between the two young lovers, as heartfelt as should have been. As a result, the crackling intensity of 'Bobby' was absent. That left only Kamalhaasan, who as 'Raja', the unrequited lover, stood out with a performance rendered from his heart. He won a Filmfare award in the Best Actor category while Dimple Kapadia won her second Filmfare award in her second film. To sum up, 'Saagar' though appreciated, never became the landmark film as it was expected to be. 'Saagar's' average performance made Ramesh Sippy take a break from the big screen which he had ironically immortalized in 70mm. He now found refuge in a 21 inched television set, then known as an'idiot box'. He made 'Buniyaad' an epic serial for television based on post partitioned India. Back then, like the Chopras and the Sagars, Ramesh Sippy proved to be one of those few who had the far sightedness those days in perceiving the power of television

On the side lines of the launching and mentoring of sons and wives, producer Gulshan Rai, who bank-rolled mega-buck hits like 'Johnny Mera Naam' 'Deewar', 'Trishul', 'Vidhaata', broke waves to give his son Rajiv Rai a break as a director. Daddy dearest spared no expense and the glitter was seen it its casting; the product was 'Yudh' starring the bankable new 'jodi' of Anil-Jackie, heroines Tina Munim and Hema Malini with Shatrughan Sinha, Danny Denzongpa, Pran, Madan Puri and others. Though 'Yudh' was an average success, as usual, Anil Kapoor stood out. In one of the double roles that he played his dialogues were preceded by a word that had no meaning nor placed in any dictionary: the word was '*Jhakkaas!*' This exclamation of a 'feel-good factor' soon became a by-word in daily conversations that referred to anything extraordinary!

Around the same time, far away, in the United States of America, 'Osho' Rajneesh was handcuffed by the American police and deported back to India. The dream of a 'free society' floated by him came crashing down. Like a stock market whose value comes down to penury, Rajneesh came back to the land of his birth and no one was the wiser.So did hundreds of his followers, Vinod Khanna being one of them; with all his money depleted in futile spiritual pursuits he could sought out only one possible option: He discarded his orange robes, his beard, his grey hair and rushed to Bombay. For the producers, hungry always for a controversial topic, Vinod Khanna the 'retired sanyasi', found many takers. His first film after his return was 'Insaaf' directed by an upcoming talented director Mukul Anand. Also starring Dimple Kapadia, Suresh Oberoi,Dalip Tahil,Shakti Kapoor, and Kritika Desai 'Insaaf' a well made film became a hit at the box office. Vinod's performance in the film never showed him out of sync nor belied his long absence. As the credit titles proclaimed "re-introducing Vinod Khanna' - it proved rightly to be so. With 'Insaaf' being declared a hit Vinod Khanna would have then perhaps realized the futility of frittering away his golden time in the pursuit of spiritual fulfillment. While Vinod Khanna was finding fulfilment in his comeback, his colleague Dharmendra, too was basking in his extended innings primarily due to the success of 'Hukumat' made by Anil Sharma whose claim to fame was a socio drama 'Shradhanjali' made a few years back. Dharmendra played a cop out to tackle a 'desh drohi' called 'Deen Bandhu Deena Nath' short -formed to DBDN, and played by Sadashiv Amrapurkar. It was an utterly forgettable film with loud theatrics and inane dialogues stretched beyond imagination. But the film was lapped up with ease in the entire Hindi belts, making it a big hit of 1985. His son 'Dharamputra' Sunny Deol was standing tall with the success of his debut 'Betaab' and the next 'Arjun'. For Dharmendra the spectre of 'Zanjeer', a big opportunity frittered away was too painful a memory. He decided to bring about a synergy by casting both of them in a big film. He consulted producer Arjun Hingorani, who was also his mentor and discoverer and both of them partnered to rope in Mukul Anand to direct this lavish spectacle called 'Sultanat'. The film was technically polished, extravagantly mounted and bedecked with a plethora of stars starting from Dharmendra, his son Sunny, Sridevi, Shashi Kapoor's model son Karan Kapoor, latest Miss India Juhi Chawla and Amrish Puri. Where he perhaps erred,big time, was basing this desert fantasy tale in a fabled region which appeared to be the middle east and all the characters, from the lead to the sides, bearing names such as Shah, Khaleed, Yasmeen, Al Jabbar, Zarina etc fleshed out from a distant caliphate. The film was rejected outright.

Mithun Chakraborty, well ensconced as a busy Star was now stepping higher with B.Subhash's next big film 'Kasam Paida Karney waley Ki'. The trumpets playing in the title song 'O *bereham tune kiye kya kya zulm kya situm'* was a befitting bugle to salute the arrival of the'Disco Dancer'. However, the film had music and dance sequences directly lifted from Michael Jackson's 'Thriller'. The masses being totally unexposed to those hit chartbusters saw B.Subhash's 'Kasam Paida Karne wale Ki' and Bhappi Lahiri's music as a laudable 'proof' of talent. Mithun Chakraborty and Salma Agha serenading alongside a cemetery was a direct lift from its video. Bappi Lahiri's penchant for pinching, helped in the effortless success of 'Kasam Paida karne Wale Ki' adding to Mithun's growing clout in the industry.

In the interim period before 'Dance-Dance', B.Subhash came out with a 'quickie'; in bollywood jargon a 'quickie' means a project made with new actors, completed within a short time frame and out of a modest budget. After plagiarizing the 'moonlighting' walk from Jackson's 'Thriller' he now set his eyes on an English film: 'The Ape Man' –a Bo Derek and Richard Harris starrer. His quickie called as 'Tarzan' brought in Hemant Birje as the beefy jungle boy and 'Thums Up'model Kimi Katkar in his version of 'Jane'. With Bappi Da's music rattling up the 'Wambasi' drum beats feel from tales of the 'Phantom' there was another one that went as *'Do-Re-Me-Fa-So-La-Te-Do'* which was clearly pinched from the English film 'Sound of Music'. Coupled with the stark sex appeal of the gorgeous Kimi Katkar, this quickie-more of-copy minted a lot of money.

The success of 'Tarzan' placed Kimi Katkar on Filmfare's cover, blew off Hemant Birje and added to Subhash's desire in coming out with a 'magnum opus'. He signed Mithun again for his next, an ambitious one called'Dance Dance'. The announcement was published thru 'Screen' under the heading 'a dance spectacle never seen before'. The female lead was the sought after heroine Mandakini, and Smita Patil an acclaimed actress, whose demise later unwantingly added to the film's prerelease publicity. 'Dance Dance' made good on it's costs but was nowhere near the earlier cult hit, 'Disco Dancer'.

As the average response to 'Dance Dance' had sunk in what turned out to be the first major puncture in Mithun's career was Mukul Anand's 'Main Balwan'. Soon enough a large oracle written in caps appeared above: that the dance floor was again in need of fresh blood.

The road for a take over was clear, and it happened soon. Towards the end of 1986 a young boy called Govinda Ahuja set the dance floor on fire in Pahlaj Nihalani's 'Ilzaam'. His dance act in the song *Street Dancer* pushed away Mithun's pelvic moves made famous six years back in 'Suraksha', reaching critical mass in 'Disco Dancer'. The trend of signing each and any script that came their way was an indication of 'quality be damned'. Stars of the 80's signed films mindlessly. Such breed never really cared for quality nor did they ever perceive that poor quality actually eroded their value. Most of them cited "insecurity" as the chief factor. Perhaps, the fear of a Friday afternoon carrying a noose, just a week away hung above them like the proverbial 'Damocles' sword. Mithun Chakraborty's fading away into oblivion was precisely due to this. From 1988 till 1989 he gave an unprecedented thirty six failures in a row!

After the success of 'Ilzaam' Govinda now became the new poster boy in tinsel world. He harvested his usp of being a good dancer to the hilt. In his debut year he had about sixteen releases -like 'Tan Badan'-'Pyaar Karke Dekho'-'Love 86'-'Duty'-'Ghar Mein Ram Bagal Mein Shyam'.Each of these had the "govinda dance' as it's pivot. As an actor he was average so unlike Mithun, he could never foster a cult following

The New Showmen

"Oopar wala kya mangey ga humse koi jawab.Hisaab aur jawab hum mangenge".---The unemployed protaganists in 'Ankush'.

After the profound success of 'Hero', Subhash Ghai began to love the epithet of 'Showman', an appellation reserved until then for Raj Kapoor. Stalwarts like Yash Chopra, B.R.Chopra, Manmohan Desai had their chips down. With the inundation of the South brigade breaching moribund, the coast was clear for Subhash Ghai to fill the vaccum. After the success of 'Vidhata' he furthered his association with Dilip Kumar. For his new project he signed him, Anil Kapoor, Sridevi, Anupam Kher, Shakti Kapoor, Naseeruddin Shah,Dara Singh and of course, Jackie Shroff. This was called 'Karma' and was based on the new villainy that found greater power and wealth from terrorism. The basic story line also had a bit of 'Sholay' as its undercurrent. Mid- way, while shooting was in progress, he also inserted full page ads in 'Screen,' a fortnightly film magazine, promoting newbie Madhuri Dixit as a 'Complete actress' who incidentally had also been signed for 'Karma 'to make a special appearance. The lady from flops 'Abodh' and 'Swati', certainly did not take those as a verdict on her and continued her auditions to will support from Subhash Ghai. We shall come back to that later.

Rana Vishwapratap (Dilip Kumar) is a benevolent jailor. He believes in treating prisoners with love so that post completion of their sentence they may turn over a new leaf. All reverently address him as 'Dada Thakur'. But his run in with a terrorist proves costly, as a result of which he loses his entire family to an act of revenge. By flipping certain main characters the maker offers old wine in a new bottle. The dacoit from Sholay (Amjad Khan as Gabbar Singh) is now a terrorist (Anupam Kher as Dr Dang). From the old, infirm, bespectacled B.V.Pradhan in 'Saaransh', Anupam Kher made an effortless crossover as 'Dr Michael Dang'.The two thieves (Amitabh-Dharmendra as Jai & Veeru) are now reformed criminals (Anil-Jackie) who are hired to form his mercenary team. Old faithful Ramlal (Satyen Kappu) in Sholay, is replaced by Dara Singh. While criminal unrest during the time of the Sippy's was from the pistols of smugglers or from the gun barrels reared in ravines. India during the eighties, was deeply embroiled in warding off terrorist activites from internal unrest like the 'Khalistan' movements aided by unnamed "foreign-support". The name 'Dr Dang', sounding Hispanic or Chinese actually never aided in the guessing game. 'Dr Dang' wears a suit and peers through spectacles with a hexagon frame like what 'Emile Locque' wore in the James Bond film 'For Your Eyes Only'. The prefix of a 'Dr' is not clear in what context it is mentioned, perhaps to make him come across as 'truly global' well-read man who claims that "his father was hanged after independence"; alluding that his father was a traitor and so explains the reason behind his 'hatred for Hindustan'. The jail is nestled somewhere in the Himalayan foot hills. However, one day the jailor loses his temper with fickle tantrums and unreasonable demands made by the newly lodged high profile terrorist leader, who insists that his cell be repainted and fitted with the latest amenities. To end his rabble rousing which reaches a shrill pitch, the Jailor silences him with a stinging slap.

Rattled by the slap, Dang swears vengeance: *"Rana VishwaPratap Singh iss thappad ki goonj ki goonj sunaai di ? Dr Dang declares war"* This showdown between the jailor and the terrorist leader is a harbinger of the mayhem rained down upon the jail by his terrorist organization called BSO (Black Star Organization) who also massacre his family. The Jailor swears vengeance and takes help from three convicts; Jackie, Anil and Naseeruddin Shah.

'Karma' though a big success was qualitatively a slip shod film. It lacked the finesse of Subash Ghai's earlier hits; the musical 'Karz' nor the racy 'Kalicharan'. The writers of 'Don' seemed to have taken in a whiff of 'Kalicharan'; In 'Don' a gangster is killed in an encounter who is replaced by his look -alike simpleton and then trained by the DSP to impersonate as the gangster. Similarly in 'Kalicharan', an honest police officer is killed and in his place a convict on the run was trained to masquerade as the police officer. Influences apart, for Subhash Ghai and the lead players in 'Karma', it's success was an occasion to cheer. However, the much-touted appearance of Madhuri Dixit was struck off on the editing table.

Anil Kapoor, followed it up with his next success'Mohabbat' opposite the 'Love Story' girl Vijayeta Pandit. Directed by the well know south director, Bapu, the film was based on a love story set in a village with Amrish Puri playing the role of a conservative village headman who frowns on his daughter meeting Anil because their betrothal was nixed after the groom's mother insisted on a fat dowry. Its success yet again proved that remakes were a safe bet. Since remakes brought an entire project in ready-made form, such projects were usually safe as a business proposition but never created a brand nor a new genre.

Yesteryear star Feroz Khan, had created his own separate niche in film making skills. Though he made few films, his record was unblemished- 1972 'Apradh', 1977 'Dharmatma', 1980 'Qurbani', 1986 'Janbaaz'. His films made under his banner 'F.K. International' held their own against the onslaught of reigning superstars Rajesh Khanna -when 'Apradh' released and Amitabh Bachchan -when 'Dharmatma' and 'Qurbani' released. His films generally basked on western influence where he cleverly used them in course of their narration; in their pulsating music, stylish sets and dazzling thrills. Feroz personally, had a penchant for trappings that bespoke of things from 'Yankeeland'. Speaking with a twang, liberally interspersing his dialogues with English buzzwords and never missing an opportunity to wear a cowboy hat or lighting a cigarette James Dean style! The eldest of four brothers, Sanjay, Sameer & Akbar, it was Feroz who was the most successful. Debuting in 1959, he went on to take part in stellar acts and even win a Filmfare award for his negative role in B.R.Chopra's 'Aadmi aur Insaan'. He later consolidated his career by standing out in supporting roles in hit fims like 'Arzoo' with Rajendra Kumar and with Rajesh Khanna in 'Safar'. He later graduated to main leading roles and one of them was the 1973 film 'Khote Sikkey'. It was a curry western whose story line was similar to 'Sholay'where villagers hire five men to protect them from a gang of dacoits. It preceded 'Sholay' by two years but was soon forgotten. But Feroz had his heart set out for making his own films and he did just that. His directorial debut 'Apradh' a crime thriller shot on foreign locations, turned a hit. Three years later, his 'Dharmatma', borrowed heavily from the English film 'Godfather' became a bigger one.

'Dharmatma', was in a way a big budget film considering the line up of stars: Hema Malini, Rekha, Premnath, Ranjeet, Sudhir, Imtiaz Khan, Jeevan, Dara Singh, Farida Jalal, Danny Denzongpa and himself. Shot mostly in virgin areas of Afghanistan, satisfied not only his native instinct but was also best adapted for Coppola's 'land of afar'; the Mediterrenean island of Sicily. In the context of films being made with crime and punishment as the backdrop, 'Dharmatma'was indeed a well made copy. The masses lapped up this story of a young man, son of a larger than life father who has turned into a messiah for the poor, yet, who dispenses justice based on the premise of 'tooth for a tooth and eye for an eye'. The son Rajesh (Feroz) abhors his father's ways and decides to live separately on his own terms. He goes off to Kabul where his father's old benefactor lives and there he falls in love with Reshma (Hema Malini) a gypsy girl. This was very similar to the phase in 'Godfather' where Michael Corleone leaves America and goes off to Sicily where he falls in love with an Italian girl, Apollonia. In the original, the murderous link from America sets out to assassinate Michael but instead end up killing the innocent Apollonia. Similarly in 'Dharmatma', the notorious duo (Ranjeet & Sudhir) sent to Kabul to assassinate Rajesh, but end up killing his beloved Reshma. Heart broken, he returns back to India where he is caught in the midst of gangwars that leaves his father dead. The reluctant son, much like Michael Corleone, is drawn into the murky affairs. In order to protect his mother and sister he has to take defensive measures and search for his father and Reshma's killers.

'Dharmatma' was a hit and he again came back four years later in his biggest hit, 'Qurbani'. This slick musical thriller dazzled the audience, which was no mean achievement. In the midst of Bachchan's 'Laawaris', 'Dostana', and Rishi Kapoor's 'Karz', 'Qurbani' made money on it's own USP's. Swiftly paced it had new touches apart from well orchestrated action sequences; the music honours were shared by two composers: Kalyanji-Anandji & Biddu. Especially Biddu because he composed the hit *'Aap Jaisa koi merei zindagi mein aaye"* sung by his discovery-the very young and pretty Nazia Hassan.

In 1986, with his pal Vinod Khanna far away in the garb of a 'sanyasi', he made 'Jaanbaz' with Anil Kapoor and himself. While 'Qurbani' had gold smugglers as its villains,'Jaanbaaz' had narcotic growers as its evil syndicate. Technically brilliant 'Jaanbaaz' was a step ahead of 'Qurbani' but to the dismay of the censor board, there were scenes inserted as metaphors that gave an insight of the 'highs' and a sense of 'ecstacy' gained by inhaling 'smack'. If you watch the film and recall certain scenes you just might agree; chicken eggs rolling and suddenly bursting from an inner energy, a poisonous tarantula spider crawling dangerously close to the swaying limbs of a dancer, oblivious to approaching death. Soon in the next scene one watches the sea rising, tall as a tidal wave to the beats of loud psychedelic music, then swirling to roll over with a gigantic splash alluding to a feel of triumph; all of these appeared to convey the ecstatic feeling after inhaling drugs. With a top cast led by himself, Dimple Kapadia, Anil Kapoor, Amrish Puri, and with Sridevi in a special appearance 'JaanBaaz' seemed to be the logical continuation of 'Qurbani'. As was his style, he looked to English films for borrowing some adrenalin. Fight scenes from 'Sudden Impact' and 'Mad Max' dominated the action while the story was loosely based on the Gregory Peck starrer 'Duel In The Sun'.

But, 'Jaanbaaz' was a mixed success and did not surpass the impact left by 'Qurbani'.

In the same year, small budget films with unheard actors and unknown directors were releasing quietly. One of them, which hit the high scale came from the interior suburbs of Bombay. N.Chandra, a film editor of films like 'Mohabbat' and 'Woh7 Din' brought out all his savings to make his labour of love called 'Ankush' (the fire). The film was helmed by unknown theatre artists: Nana Patekar, Madan Jain and Arjun Chakraborty as the protagonists Ravi-Shashi-Arjun: these symbolized the new youth of India who were stuck in an abyss of corruption and deprivation.

N.Chandra recreated the angst left unfinished after 'Deewar' by conceiving different situations; workers' rights trampled under paid goons, colleges run by bigots, examinations that turn into a farce due to mass copying, but chiefly, the issue of unemployment.'Ankush' laid bare raw human emotions. Painful truths were shown in a frightfully naked form. Street fights that resemble riots where fused bulbs, tubelights and bricks are used to inflict maximum damage. The young men led by Ravi(Nana Patekar) are the face of Bombay's suburbs on whom the axe of injustice has fallen, ripping apart their psyche and compelling them to lose their belief in the law. When their patience runs thin they tear away not by mouthing long dialogues but by hitting anything that they can lay their hands on; an empty bottle, a cycle chain, hockey stick or just their fist.

'Ankush' surprised every one by its stupendous success. Earning revenues that grossed twelve time its price per territory, easily lifted N.Chandra into the big league.

Subhash Ghai continued his good run by being signed for an outside production which was produced by N.N. Sippy and based on Javed Akhtar's fourth script, called 'Meri Jung'. The hero and the villain, both, are criminal lawyers, both successful in their profession. Amrish Puri as 'Judge G.D.Thukral, advocates violence; not by plunging daggers into bowels but in doling out death sentences. He also euologises the practice of capital punishment, citing *pachattar misaley* (75 examples). However, they have an old case which makes them grind an axe. It was a case executed two decades back where judge G.D.Thukral (Amrish Puri) had sentenced Arun's innocent father to death. He further exacerbates his action by attempting to molest the man's wife. Exuding confidence a 'la Bachchan', Anil Kapoor played lawyer Arun Kumar, while Amrish Puri played the role of the crafty 'G.D.Thukral'. 'Meri Jung' also introduced Javed Jaffrey (comedian Jagdeep's son) in a land mark song and dance sequence *"Bol Baby bol rock and roll'* rendered by the maverick Kishore Kumar. Javed Jaffrey showed promising shades of turning out as our very own Fred Astaire but the world of hindi films walks on an unusual path; a villain can become a 'hero' but a dancing villain could have no slot.

Miss India

'Aap yeh nahin dikhayi denewale profession mein kab se hain?"
-Seema

Even though Salim Khan and Javed Akhtar were no longer a team, they were busy in their independent assignments. Soon enough a belated 'blast from their past' soon hit filmdom. An unsold script originally written keeping Amitabh Bachchan in their mind was now bought by Boney Kapoor and called 'Mr India'. It was the last script from the pen and ink pot of Salim-Javed.

A sci-fi film, it broke away from the stereotypes of the 'Madras formula'which had Bollywood in it's grip for three years. It was produced by Surinder Kapoor and directed by a new whiz kid called Shekar Kapur. He was an aspiring actor who perhaps entered the industry by virtue of being Dev Anand's nephew. Being a qualified Chartered accountant he was bitten by the desire to act. He did get acting offers (the utterly forgettable 'Toote Khilone) but none made him what he wanted to. Unknowingly, he gravitated towards direction. In this medium he found his true love and a film called 'Masoom' was born.

Mr India had the "real Hero' in an invisible form while the visible 'hero' was shown as a timid character who gets beaten up by goons and finds it hard to arrange two square meals for the orphans under his care. As a result, for all good reason the role of the heroine had to be stronger.

Arun (Anil Kapoor) is a poor music teacher. Inspite of his ordinary means of income he also shoulders the responsibility of taking care of a dozen orphans. Arun is docile and would never hurt a fly. But the moment he wears a magic belt on his wrist he turns invisible, his voice is resonant and baritone, indicating a powerful genie in motion. The moment he removes the belt he is back as the visible Arun— the cowed down, 'aam aadmi'.

With this 'hero' in 'aam-aadmi' mode most of the time, we therefore have 'Seema' (Sridevi) who treats the audience to an excellent fare of singing, dancing and fighting. The other stellar in this science fiction fairy tale was 'Mogambo'. The film tells us in the beginning that a *baahar ki taaqat* (external power) was behind all the blasts occurring in the country. 'Mogambo' is supposedly that *baahar ki taakat* played with consummate relish by Amrish Puri. Shown as some sinister leader of 'dictatorial' origins whose sartorial look seemed to have floated down from far away times. A pictorial comic strip came colourfully alive; where he wears a uniform resembling French emperor Napoleon Bonaparte's and a hair style neatly flattened with curls that brings alive some 'Lord', from the 'British East India Company'; precious gems sized as little boulders set in rings, adorn his thick fingers; sitting languidly on a throne whose armrests have lighted models of the globe on which this wannabe conqueror keeps tapping those fingers in thoughtful felicity. With boots gleaming like a pair owned by the Egyptian Pharoahs, and his followers paying obeisance thru a 'nazi salute'it was Shekhar Kapur's directorial brilliance which made 'Mogambo' comically fierce and not blood-curdling. Amrish Puri as 'Mogambo' gained immortality through his lines *'Mogambo Khush Hua'*. Few years later the character spurred small time filmmaker Anil Sharma, to borrow the 'Mogambo' character and turn it topsy turvy in his film 'Tehelka'; The character concocted was called 'Dong,' a slit-eyed Chinese looking despot played by Amrish Puri who bosses around yammering *"Dong Kabhi wrong nahin hota"*.

'Mr India'went on to be come a big hit further cementing Anil Kapoor's stock and vindicating Sridevi's hold on the number one position. The breezy narration peppered with the chirpiness of a supremely confident Sridevi as a journalist, got her an immortal place in movie lore. Those moony eyes conveyed 'heaven on earth'. Her various acts; as the giggly 'Miss Hawa Hawaii' out to smell out the smuggler's hideout; as the impersonating Charlie Chaplin at the illegal gambling den; as the hapless tenant who has to cope with a dozen orphans staying in the same house and, as the lady in love with her invisible admirer, Sridevi was awesome. Her seductive dance in a rain drenched blue georgette to the lilting *'Kaatey nahin kat tey…'* held people spellbound. We wondered whether we were watching 'Mr India' or-a Miss India?

Post 'Mr India' the equations in bollywood were now redrawn: Anil Kapoor and Jackie Shroff were the two top stars in Bombay while Sunny Deol, Govinda and Sunjay Dutt appeared in the second rung. Mithun Chakraborty, whose torment had stretched beyond thirty six consecutive losers, was staring down an abyss of uncertain Friday's.

In the midst of this redrawing of lines, far away in Sweden, a radio station revealed a nexus between the masters in Delhi and 'AG Bofors', a Swedish company that had recently won a contract for supplying mortar guns to the Indian Army. This delicate matter became a cause of friction that singed Amitabh Bachchan's ties with the Gandhi family. Unable and unwilling to face this taunt, Bachchan resigned as an MP. After a hiatus of four years, this unsavoury incident perhaps proved to be a blessing in disguise- the actor returned. The immediate fallout was Tinnu Anand's 'Shahenshah', the next big release the nation was looking forward to.

His return seemed incidentally timed to herald the release of this film. Though signed after his recovery from that fateful accident on the sets of 'Coolie', unknown to his fans, another debilitating and unheard disease called 'Myasthenia gravis' had sent his shooting schedules into disarray which had further delayed the under production 'Shahenshah'.

Just like the tale of 'the prodigal son', Amitabh Bachchan's return rekindled people's curiosity and imagination.

The man who ruled and gave a lot to the masses in the form of unbridled entertainment had suddenly walked far away to leave a void. Those were the dark years when the common man felt stifled in his cries. For five bucks he derived immense joy watching this man single handedly pummeling the injustice around to grab his rights. It was as if 'he' had won while the saviour which he sought by casting his piece of paper in a ballot box was alas, lost in a labyrinth of a dark bottomless pit. The law had appointed leaders in the form of ministers to draft rules and Union Leaders who promised relief in the next election cycle. That would be a wait for months or even years. After turning into a political 'avatar', people had reluctantly reconciled to this fact that their tallest entertainer had succumbed to calls from a greener pasture. It is not that filmmaking shut due to his absence or theaters closed down; As they say' life goes on', so did film making. When the Big3 of the 50's decided to call it a day, as 'matinee idols'they had reached well past their prime. It was not the same in the case of this star turned politician. At the time of his renouncement he was just 42 years old. This gave ample opportunity for his peers to make hay. Sadly, no one had it in him to dethrone this man.

'Shahenshah' had been pre-booked by distributors for all territories at the time of its announcement. The posters of 'Shahenshah' –giant cutouts ouside theatres all over, where the man is shown having a salt-pepper beard, wearing an armour made of chain-link, tossed over a leather jacket matched below with long boots- all added up to the mystique of this mysterious protagonist named 'Shahenshah'. Dotted below those gigantic posters and cutouts were pint-sized pictures of Meenakshi, Amrish Puri, Pran and Prem Chopra. Theatres braced themselves for an all-time rush. Screens were suddenly in short supply. The curiosity factor had ballooned due to his hiatus; People were willing to pause their daily chores to watch him (as I did that day); Not just watch but expect an adrenalin rush in their lives.

Back then, the recipe to harvest the magic of a heightened curiosity factor at the Box office, lay in grabbing the first two weeks. That was the pre-internet age where 'fastest-fingers-first ' never existed so reviews hinged on word-of-mouth. According to distributors and producers of those days, for a big –budget film a period of two weeks could make even a bad film to break even, provided the curiosity factor was sky-high. To ensure this, distributors in mofussil towns would allot one single print to feed two or even three theaters by slightly altering the show timings: a 'three-to-six show' would actually turn out to be a 'three thirty-to-six-thirty' slot.

Analyzing his earlier hits, we agree that he was a master in both: anger and comedy.

'Shahenshah' set in motion both these traits. One was as Vijay Srivastava- a paan chewing bumbling police official and the other was the stern, unknown vigilante known as 'Shahenshah'. 'Vijay Shrivastav', seemingly, lives on the bribes doled out by crooks and criminals. But there is also a vengeful story in place where long time ago, Vijay's father (Kader Khan) was framed in a case to be falsely implicated as corrupt. Unable to live with the taint of disrepute the father hanged himself casting an indelible scar on his little son's mind. The boy is then brought up by his close friend and colleague, inspector Aslam (Pran). Young Vijay grows up under the tutelage of his uncle but the stigma his father had to bear is alive in his heart. Just like his late father and uncle, he grows up to be a police officer. But unknown to them, he also dons another lifestyle. In the guise of a tough, bearded crusader he stalks the streets at night to rid the city of rowdy sheeters. Calling himself as 'Shahenshah' his exploits starts disturbing the easy life of goons and criminals like J.K.(Amrish Puri). As 'Vijay Srivastava' he regaled in 'Arjun Singh' style of humour from 'Namak Halaal' and soon comes his run in with a milkman-turned gambler Mukhtar Singh (played by Praveen kumar who had gained fame playing the role of 'Bheema' in the serial 'Mahabharata').

As the reels unspool, displaying the laughing antics of 'Vijay Srivastav' the next one shifts to the introduction of this man as a 'vigilante': It is close to mid night, the streets are deserted and as bit of fog swirls around, the man emerges whose unmistakable face partially hidden under a long salt-pepper lock of hair, cloaked in leather jacket, a steely chain armour dangling from his shoulder and tall boots accentuating those unmistakably long legs. A coil of rope is looped around his shoulder which perhaps is a tool for dispensing justice. As the title song rendered by Kishore Kumar rolls on, this vigilante, the audience feels, has been emphatically introduced.

The next scene is in villain J.K's lair, where a lavish party is being held. Gang members wearing suits, holding glasses, wait for their boss, who emerges from the swimming pool (Amrish Puri with a near perfect torso). As they discuss the threat of this mysterious 'Shahenshah', the vigilante strikes again, somewhere. The audience craved for more.

However, after the first two interludes, this 'vigilante' started stressing the nerves of the audience; The problems of diminishing returns also arose after the interesting interludes between Srivastava, Shalu(Meenakshi) and Tarachand Badlani

(Jagdeep) come to an end. 'Shahenshah's perpetual frown and the repetitive guffaws of Srivasatava further stalled its rise.

They say 'absence makes the heart grow fonder', but 'Shahenshah' proved the opposite to be true. It celebrated a silver jubilee- a muted one, but could not recapture the magic of his superstardom days.

Soon after the average response to 'Shahenshah', came two blockbusters from two of the biggest bankrollers of 'The One Man Industry' syndrome-Prakash Mehra's 'Jaadugar' and Manmohan Desai's 'Toofan'. Both annihilated the charisma of Amitabh Bachchan.

The demi god who galloped unhindered for more than a decade, soon waded into muddy waters. The fault did not lie in the actor but more in the inadequacies of script writers and directors. Prakash Mehra had reached a corner where creative excellence had disappeared but in the case of Manmohan Desai, handing over the reins to his son Ketan Desai certainly was a case of wilful nepotism. 'Toofan' directed by his son was utter crap!

The dock worker, construction magnate, an underworld Don, a 'catholic dada', an introvert mercenary, a police Inspector with pentup emotions searing him from within, a framed murderer, a loyal servant, the lovable alcoholic, a hard-hitting porter--all amalgamating to mould out as the greatest entertainer.

With this giant lying still, felled by bodyblows in the form of 'Toofan ' and 'Jadugar', with Yash Chopra too waiting on the side lines, it was Anil Kapoor who kept the cash registers ringing: propelled by the superhit status of 'Karma', 'Mr India', 'Meri Jung' and the musical thriller 'JanBaaz'.

Sunny Deol after giving a super hit in 'Arjun' hit a roadblock, yet again, when two prestigious films: 'Dacait' and 'Samundar' (both by Rahul Rawail) failed. Anil Kapoor's modestly budgeted 'Saaheb' did more business than 'Samundar' produced by deep pocket producers Mushir and Riaz with most of it shot in the exotic island of Mauritius

Govinda, by now, had well entrenched himself as a 'dancing' star. He became known for epitomizing the formulaic films where songs-dance played a large role in drawing audience. Though he continued connecting with the youth, he kept walking the same path where his predecessor had erred- of spraying the youth with mindless inane stories. However there were a few exceptions like Rakesh Roshan's 'Khudgarz' and his home production called 'Hatya'.

Rakesh Roshan, son of music director Roshan, composer of many timeless songs, was an average known actor from the late 70's and early 80's. Under his banner 'Film Kraft' he had produced films like 'KaamChor' (meant to re-establish himself as an actor), and 'Bhagwan Dada' which had himself, Sridevi, Rajnikanth and, his teenage son Hrithik. One fine day he decided to reinvent himself. He turned a director with 'Khudgarz' which became a surprise hit, more so because the public and his peers, alike, never expected a low runged actor like Rakesh Roshan to give such a huge success and that too as a director-producer. Besides being a hit, it also threw up

Shatrughan Sinha, after a long time, to be remembered in a pivotal role. As the 'bihari-babu' he was indeed the soul of 'Khudgarz' and this rightfully was something for him to harp upon.

During the spring of 1987, Govinda's biggest USP was his ability in making the youth sway to his moves. This USP would make him survive for long until the day when Roshan's son would replace him as the next dancing sensation.

Yash Raj Films was also in dire need for some reinventing.

Post 'Faasley' his reputation as a film maker had taken a dip. This frustration made him clutch at straws; He was now convinced that an all-out big budget film, on the lines of 'Waqt' with a story bearing a whiff of 'Trishul', might just rescue him. Firm in his resolve, the next task was to find a partner who could finance this mountainous budget. His efforts sought out a partner from the South; rich money bags Mr Subbirami Reddy from Hyderabad who had his fingers in practically every pie: construction, hotels, theaters and, politics.

Ironically he titled this film 'Vijay'; a name that had become Yash Chopra's passport to success. By abdicating away from 'Vijay' he had careened away into a dark abyss. Bringing a casting coup in a fare called 'Silsila' he got egg on his face. He then cast his dice on a young romance (which was certainly his forte)but 'Faasle' singed his reputation. The one who had given Bombay and the entire country, classics like Waqt, Ittefaq, Daag, Deewar, Trishul, Kabhie Kabhie, had also seen success in the modest 'Noorie' and swelled in the pride of watching his discovery Poonam Dhillon bloom. He also mentored protégés like Ramesh Talwar to espouse his off track scripts as in 'Doosara Aadmi'. For 'Vijay he whipped up a veritable army. He cast robust stars like Anil Kapoor, Rishi Kapoor, Meenakshi, and a new girl called Sonam; seniors like Rajesh Khanna, Anupam Kher, Hema Malini, Saeed Jaffrey and also fringe stars like Raj Babbar and Moushumi Chatterjee. 'Vijay' had every thing, except his midas touch, and on the anointed day in 1989, this magnum opus called 'Vijay' came crashing down.

The First Khan

'Kya ishq ney samjha hain, kya husn ney jaana hain, hum khaak nashinon ki thokar mein zamana hain'-Nasir Hussain Films

As Yash Chopra cringed, dismayed over losing his mastery in crafting love and drama, there was another dream merchant of his times, the ebullient Nasir Hussain who specialised in 'sing along musicals' shot in hill stations. He was now readying for the second phase of his life. Famed for making all time entertainers like the colossals 'Teesri Manzil', 'Yaadon Ki Baraat, 'Dil Deke Dekho' Nasir Hussain, now old, introduced his son Mansoor Hussain Khan as a film director. This love story, written by Mansoor himself was titled 'Qayamat Se Qayamat Tak' had everything going against it: a rookie director, the heroine Juhi Chawla who was a spillover from her debut film-cum-flop 'Sultanat' and the hero Aamir Khan -a thin, wiry looking boy who appeared slightly famished. The film's tag line appearing on 'Screen', a popular fortnightly from the Express group, proclaimed it under broad caps: "Love- Crime of the Century". Nonetheless it went on to become a baffling hit. The reasons were many which can be chiefly brought down to basics like: having a fresh story, zero audience expectations, soulful songs by music-duo Anand-Milind, heart warming performances by the protagonists, and above all, Mansoor Khan's clever handling of the script.

The story resonated with the youth, where, eloping and setting up a house away in the mountains was a cherished fantasy. Nine years ago 'Bunty' and 'Pinky' from Rahul Rawail's 'Love Story' had done the same; setting up house in the mountains; elements of parental animosity against the other and there the similarity ends. The bitter animosity between parents in 'QSQT' was less about ego and more on the lines of deep rooted hate that led on towards a horrific finale. Mansoor Khan set this 'Rome Juliet' tribute, amongst warring Rajput families. The story sketch was as follows: A man whose sister is pregnant guns down her reneging lover and is sent to jail for a decade. Years later his son Raj (Aamir) falls in love with a girl who is a niece of the slain man. Mansoor re -cast Juhi Chawla as 'Rashmi', a shy Rajput girl which was dramatically opposite her newly-baggged cosmopolitan 'Miss India ' status and his cousin Aamir Khan as the young 21 year old boy strumming on a guitar about his *Papa's advice......"*, both becoming instant hits. They fall in love and decide to elope as they know that to keep their love alive they need to move out of the orbit of hate. The love of Raj and Rashmi had the blessings of the audience but the script, had other plans. They spend their days living frugally where they sing about their being alone in this world " *Akeley hain to kya gam hain"*inside their little abode in a far off rocky cave which is soon invaded by assassins hired by the girl's parents. As the bullet riddled Rashmi tumbles down the rocky boulders, the tearful Raj decides to follow her.

When Raaj & Rashmi breathed their last, there was a long pause in the audience. Usually, the audience starts walking towards the exit when the unspooling reels reach their last tether. The magnitude of the tragedy unfolding kept them rooted. As the tragic strains of *'Papa kehtey they bada naam karega'* waned away followed by the curtain slowly falling over the screen, they continued to remain seated. They were unable to take into the fact that two and a half hours of fondness for Rashmi & Raaj, would end in such a monumental sorrow.

The parents in 'Love Story'with a city bred wealthy air, their animosity- at the most, made us frown.The parents in 'Ek Duje Ke liye' indicated the presence of divisive fissures, which still runs across the country. The warring families of 'QSQT' had a more conservative backdrop of elite Rajput parents where 'diktat' is given precedence over wishes, where unsheathing a sword is the most accepted norm to protect 'khandaan ki izzat'; where 'honour-killing' is still a reality.

Jut when every one lay under the boughs of their thoughts, stupefied by the tragic finale in QSQT, their reverie was jostled by another gate crasher: a short, silver haired man called N.Chandra who had earlier grabbed eyeballs in 'Ankush'. He had now put his second step towards climbing the Big League as an A-Listed maker. His new film 'Tezaab', meaning 'acid,' was literally an acid test for rising star Anil Kapoor who had anchored his career through 'Karma' but, had shared honours with Jackie Shroff. After the success of 'Mr India' he had faced bouquets with 'Miss India' written on them. Even 'Meri Jung 'which had celebrated a jubilee run at many centres was ridiculed as 'Meri Junk'. Finally it was the 1989 film 'Tezaab' that separated Anil Kapoor from the boys and propelled him several notches higher than his colleague Jackie Shroff.

This was his first big film as a solo hero, rightfully a fly or fall moment for him. It also had Madhuri Dixit a lissome beauty who had earlier failed to shine in her debut film 'Abodh' and 'Swati', both from the house of the Barjatya family's 'Rajshri Productions'. The supporting cast also had Chunkey Pandey as Munna's friend 'Babban' (he narrowly missed the filmfare trophy in the 'supporting category' for this). Here let me digress. Two years back, Chunky Pandey was launched in a big way by Pahlaj Nihalani, owner of 'Vishaldeep International' in the film 'Aag Hi Aag'. He was touted as the 'next big thing'who could supposedly dazzle Bollywood. Nihalani earlier, had been credited with the successful launch of dancing sensation Govinda and had started taking his 'prince-maker' status quite seriously. He announced Chunky Pandey as his 'hero' for 'Aag hi Aag'which had Dharmendra and Shatrughan Sinha playing the main lead roles. While Dharmendra played a dacoit with a heart of gold, reminiscent of his halcyon days from 'Samadhi', Shatrughan Sinha played a cop who looked the same, acted the same as in any of his earlier films. Chunky and Neelam played the younger generation.

Chunky Pandey, though not a star son, has glamorous doctor parents whose long list of clientele also included a few A-Listers. His father Dr Sharad Pandey was a cardiologist and his mother Dr Snehlata Pandey a gynaecologist who had celebrity clients like Rekha as one of her patients. Perhaps, this background gave the young Chunky to be within reach of the tinsel world. Old legends reveal that Chunky bumped into Nihalani inside a loo of Hotel Searock at Bandra when he was asked to give an audition. 'Aag hi Aag' came and went but Chunky Pandey did not set the Box office on fire. It was followed by few more like 'Paap Ki Duniya' but he continued to remain on a plateau.

The tag line of 'Tezaab' read as 'A violent love story'; It lived up to it. The disappearance of Amitabh Bachchan did not mean that emotions of anger and revenge had walked away with him. They remained, steadfastly waiting to be wrapped around a new icon. In 'Deewar' where 'Vijay' ended his saga by being shot dead by 'Ravi Verma', metamorphically, Mahesh Deshmukh alias 'Munna' was his new avatar. Like the other Vijay in 'Kaala Patthar' as the humiliated captain of a ship who lay battered under a heap of insults, withdrew to become an incognito coal-miner. On same lines, Mahesh Deshmukh was a decorated naval cadet looking forward to a promising career but is instead reduced to becoming a dreaded 'Tadipaar Tapori' who lives off 'haftas'.One of his many dialogues *"Teri zindagi aur maut ka faasla Munna ki chaaku ke dhaar sey zyada nahin, time khoti mat kar police station mein haazri dene jana hain""* harked back to that era.

Just as 'Deewar' was about injustice and vengeance, 'Tezaab' recreated the same commotions but in line with the prevailing times of the late 80's: Joblessness worsened by rising corruption. It was backed by a strong team: director N.Chandra, fresh from the spectacular success of 'Ankush', Anil Kapoor, who had earlier showcased his 'anger' in 'Mashall ' very convincingly, Anupam Kher and Madhuri

Dixit. After playing the maniacal 'Dr Dang', he played the much believable role of a man in love with easy money and free booze. As Shyamlal in 'Tezaab', he makes it believable by perfectly enacting that rare fiend, who does not mind trading his wife or his young daughter for expensive booze and a free hand at playing the dice.

The actress from two failed films of Rajshri Productions Madhuri Dixit, this time as 'Mohini', sent the audience into a tizzy. Men, after a long time went into 'lust' mode. The dance number 'Ek-do-teen' written by Javed Akhtar not only became a top number but also made the men of India love and lust for her in equal measure.

Thus came to an end the year 1988. With the triumph of a debutant director, the introduction of a wiry actor called Aamir Khan, actor Anil Kapoor catapulting to the big league through 'Tezaab' and yet another failed attempt by Yash Chopra. As these films played on screens across the country no body paid much glance at an advertisement being shown during the intervals; it was an ad for 'Lakhani Hawai chappal' where a slim young man was shown pedaling away on a cycle. The young model's name was Salman Khan.

The Second Khan

"Ek ladka aur ladki kabhi dost nahin hote"---Jeewan.

Three decades ago, the young boy's father Salim Khan had harboured desires of becoming a hero. But fate found him space as a legendary script writer. He had left his home town of Indore to step into the tinsel world of Bombay. He did play small roles but the big break never came. Destiny had other plans. She made him partner with another writer whose name was Javed Akhtar, and write scripts that altered the course of bollywood. Now-Salim Khan's son Salman was ordained to fulfil his father's unrealized dreams.

Film banner 'Rajshri Productions' had grown as a banner synonymous with films that could be "watched by an entire family". Bereft of heavy dosed fights, villains, garish sets or shiny cabarets they became known for making wholesome 'family entertainers' which thrived in tier-2 towns and mofussil areas. Their key drivers for content were family spawned socially reflective films espousing friendship (Dosti), Revenge (Jeevan Mrityu) and several romantic ones with rural backdrops like '(Geet Gaata Chal) love story, class-barrier(Sawan Ko Aane do), Joint families and their rigors (Piya Ka Ghar), tragic (Ankhiyon Ke Jharokon Se), family bonding (Nadiya Ke Paar), atonement (Shikshaa), sacrifice

(Tapasya), a rare spy flick (Agent Vinod) and an off beat but mercurial (Saaransh).

Their modus operandi was formulated on few simple basics; a social story, affordable actors, music which endeared but composed by affordable musicians. But in 1989, the scion of the Barjatyas, grandson of their patriarch Tarachand Barjatya, decided to keep aside his family's rule of hiring outside directors. He voiced his desire of directing one, all by himself. His name was Sooraj Barjatya. In his hand he had a detailed script written by himself that had a plain no-frills title: 'Maine Pyar Kiya'.

The hunt for the lead role of 'Prem' was long. Sooraj wanted an untouched freshness loaded with charismatic abilities. After several auditions conducted with many models and aspirers, Sooraj signed one of them: the slim, slightly beefy Salman Khan to play the role of the persistent lover-'Prem'. The other side he cast Bhagyashree, an actress fresh from doing few television serials, as 'Suman'. Bhagyashree was as fresh as the morning dew while Salman Khan brought in a terrific innocence mingled with charm and brawn. Besides being a love story'Maine Pyar Kiya' was also a tale of friendship between their fathers. It had the time tested story of the rich-poor divide but interspersed with ample content of familial ties. Prem and Suman as the young lovers who have barely understood their moments of love, are rudely set apart by warring fathers. Unlike Raj and Rashmi, the lovers from QSQT--Suman and Prem could never dream of eloping. To unite, they prefer to fulfil the conditions put forth by Suman's father . 'Maine Pyar kiya' went on to become that year's and for the Barjatya's, their biggest success since its inception in 1947.

The tag line *'dosti ki hai nibhani to padegi"* sanctified love and tossed away those blurs which accused the youth of "mixing friendship with love"; in fact friendships that blossom in to love is the greatest blessing. Its tag line became a much loved line for young India. It also catapulted Rajshri productions to the same level as any big Banners of those times.

After the successful launch of Salman Khan, the 'first Khan', Aamir, dented his star power status in B.Subhash's 'Love Love Love'. Post QSQT, it was a clear case by this producer of moving in early to encash its euphoria. By signing both Aamir and Juhi Chawla the move was brilliant and the producer's math was perfect. But he failed in putting up a decent story. The film deserved to bomb. 'Love Love Love' did dampen the box office, but it soon sizzled with Subhash Ghai's 'Ram Lakhan'. The 'showman' stamped a bigger footprint with this blockbuster. After the emphatic 'Tezaab' this was Anil Kapoor's consecutive release. 'Ram-Lakhan', besides being a success also brought in many inclusive growths for its team members; it enhanced the durability of Anil-Madhuri as a hit pair; Dimple Kapadia-Jackie Shroff received invaluable relief after their super flop 'Allah Rakha' which was made by Manmohan Desai's son Ketan Desai. Gulshan Grover, an hitherto ordinary villain who made a living by being either the bad son, bad brother, meek son-in-law or a small- time goon, suddenly gained cult status by mouthing his "bad man' dialogues. The music by Laxmikant –Pyarelal was another big time factor: *'Ek*

Do Teen from 'Tezaab' soared the charts, Ram Lakhan's *'One-Two-ka-Four-four-two ka one"* matched it !

Another reason for 'Lakhan' to shine away was he plays a cop who is in direct contrast with 'Ram' who is, an honest cop. 'Ram' is straight as a ramrod while 'Lakhan'is two-faced; this distinct characterisation helped Anil Kapoor to 'monkey' around: he wears his police cap in a tilted way; swings his police baton and dances away to his winking one-liner " *My Name is Lakhan*'to an audience too happy in giving him a long ovation.

Moonlight

"Mera naam Chandni Mathur hain. B.A.paas hoon, shorthand typing jaanti hoon. Uske baad zindagi jaisi ruk si gayi hain"-
Chandni

Yash Chopra, badly bruised from a string of unloved films was almost felled by the colossal failure of his latest release'Vijay'. He had poured in everything to carve out 'Vijay' as a big entertainer. He had implanted a canvas as vast as 'Trishul'; for each of the characters he had cast big names, hoping, to recreate an aura of a long time ago. Its failure perhaps proved to be a moment of epiphany for the greying legend. He hurled the old spectre of Vijay and his angst away, lay quiet for some time and started working on a new script. He cast his heroine as the 'hero' and gave her the name he seemed to be besotted with: Chandni.

Subburami Reddy his new partner(a deep –pockets businessman from Hyderabad) suggested that rather than introducing a new girl he proposed to place it on a large canvas. Casting a balance and following his partner's advice, he cast numero uno Sridevi as 'Chandni' opposite established actors Rishi Kapoor and Vinod Khanna. Sridevi and Rishi Kapoor had already given a super hit in 'Nagina' three years back where she played an "Icchadaari nagin'where the film catered to age old superstitions.

In 'Silsila', the man wallowed in a love that he wants to retain through adulterous means; he therefore cries out a Javed Akhtar prose that spells out his dilemma in continuing their hush-hush liaison:

"Deewar jo hum dono mein hain aaj gira dein, kyun dil mein sulagte logon ko bataa dein haan humko mohabbat hain,mohabbat hain".

Having turned over a new leaf, Yash Chopra commissioned his writer either Sagar Sarhadi or Anand Bakshi, Iam not sure, to write pure unadulterated love notes for his new 'Chandni'; no hush-hush liaison.

> *"Sham ka dhalta suraj tumhein champai rang ke phool pehna raha hain, aur tumhare khushboo sey mera badan mehak raha hain, Jab raat apna aanchal failati hain to tumhari kasam tum bahut yaad aati ho.Poonam ka chand apni gardish bhool kar tumhara roop dekh raha hain; mein aankhen band kar leta hoon aur Chandni mere dil mein utar aati hain."*

'When the setting sun is adorning you with reddened jasmines the sweet fragrance emanates from my being;when the dark night spreads its cloak I pine for you. When the full moon pauses to gaze at you, I close my eyes and feel your radiance in my heart'.

The charming, vivacious Chandni is thrust on a cross road when the love of her life is crippled in an unfortunate accident. The film show cased the enormous talent of

Sridevi and resurrected the reputation of Yash Chopra. The middle class Delhi girl (the city of Delhi incidentally was Yash Chopra's favourite) is wooed by rich boy Rohit Gupta (Rishi Kapoor). They meet at the wedding of a common friend where Cupid strikes the two. After revelling in days soaked in courtship, a tragic accident renders Rohit a cripple which in turn instigates guilt feelings that prompt him to create unsavoury conditions, that compel Chandni to walk out of their relationship. Distraught, she leaves her parents, her friends and her city of Delhi to start life anew in distant Bombay. There, she meets Lalit (Vinod Khanna) a suave business tycoon who, like her, is nursing a broken heart. He is drawn to her aloofness but Chandni, is unsure. Back in Delhi, goaded by his brother in law (Anupam Kher) Rohit goes off to Switzerland to enroll in a physical rehabilitation centre and gets cured. He immediately rushes to Bombay in search of Chandni where even Lalit is waiting to confess his love for her. This puts her again, at a crossroad.

Yash Chopra packed his film with middle class values and lifestyles of the rich. He also added an exclusive exuberance by clothing Sridevi in soothing white salwar-kameez with 'leheriya dupatta' which is visible in that phase of her relationship when she is with 'Rohit'; and vibrantly coloured chiffon sarees, making her daintily sway beside gushing brooks and streams on the green meadows of Switzerland making her look desirable as never before; significantly overshadowing the near immortal wet look from 'Mr India'. It was also a kind of double role; As Rohit's beloved, the sprightly fun loving girl who does not mince words, her confidence sky-high; then comes her opposite as Lalit's Chandni -where the whites are discarded, she is aloof, withdrawn and has lost her ability to laugh and these stark opposites is beautifully spelt out in the song *"Tu mujhe suna main tujhe sunaoo apni prem kahani"*. Indeed, the film's climax kept one on tenterhooks.The screen play and direction was perhaps the biggest tribute to womanhood; where the customary 'heroes' (the males) were relegated to the sidelines. The 'villains' were the mother –in-law (Sushma Seth) assisted by her daughter (actress Bina); During her stay in Bombay and her trepidation in responding to Lalit's feelings she finds a steady hand from Lalit's mother (Waheeda Rehman). In fact, even the physiotherapist at the Switzerand commune who treats Rohit, is a woman.

'Chandni' became a big success and brought Yash Chopra back from the wild. Incidentally Yash Raj Films hit a purple patch after 'Chandni' and this long-found success, would continue till the Millenium and beyond. His bad phase finally came to an end.

But it was Sridevi who was now shining beneath a new halo. Immediately after as the success of 'Chandni' gushed all over, Sridevi grew taller with her double roles in her next called 'Chalbaaz'. Made by Lakshmi Productions, a production house which a decade back launched Rajnikant in to hindi through 'Andha Kanoon'. In a double role, as a timid and a vixen performed by a talented actress like Sridevi 'Chaalbaz' was preordained to be a hit. Historically, most of the double roled films had given producers good returns. Another reason for Chalbaaz 's success was it's director Pankuj Parasher. He had earlier made 'Jalwa' which came to be called as 'art actor' Naseeruddin Shah's first serious attempt to hoist himself as a 'Hero'.

It was a pleasant surprise to watch Naseer, the God of art films, casting away his plain bush-shirts and getting in to a pair of blue denims, knee length boots with 'Ray-Ban' glares and leaping mid-air with a pistol juttin out of his holster fighting drug peddlers. Set in the backdrop of Goa's virgin beaches (back then it was a Union Territory where a plate of 'fishcurry-rice' came for a mere five bucks). 'Jalwa' brought Goa in to mainstream Bollywood, a good two decades before 'Dil Chahta Hain'. The seven minute title song by Remo Fernandes playing in the background with newbie ArchanaPuran Singh cascading down the edge of what appears like the periphery of either Aguada Fort or was it Chapora ? It starred a clutch of actors from the theater and television circuit like Rohini Hattangady, Akash Khurana, Pankaj Kapur,Satish Kaushik and a new comedian Johnny Lever, whose forte lay in mimickry. They were all led by Pankaj Parashar who had just gained fame from a well made television serial called 'Karamchand'. Jalwa was slickly made, technically polished for those times whose slickness was carried forward to 'Chalbaaz'. It was a decent success and well appreciated, period. It was unable to create a 'hero' out of Naseeruddin Shah.

As Yash Chopra's urn of romance 'Chandni' soothed people, film maker Vidhu Vinod Chopra, who had bared his lateral talent in a thriller called 'Khamosh'came out with a crime saga called 'Parinda'.

It starred the reigning pair of Anil Kapoor –Madhuri Dixit, with Jackie Shroff completing the trio. Similar to the angst shown by director N.Chandra's 1985'Ankush', the story of 'Parinda' dealt with crime syndicates run by gangsters within Bombay. Boldly tag lined as the 'Most Powerful film ever made', indeed, the script derived power from these three:

The subdued cries of Karan (Anil Kapoor) the muted angst of Kishan (Jackie Shroff) and Nana Patekar as the ghastly 'Anna Seth'. 'Parinda' was a dark story where innocent souls in love are marooned in a world monitored by hate and revenge. Like a seasoned craftsman Vidhu Vinod brought in various metaphors to depict uncertainty; flock of pigeons swirling away aimlessly, boats bobbing away in still waters, quiet glow of an incense stick turning in to flames enveloping a screaming figure and a ghostly lilt streaming from a flute that frighteningly veils the muted screams of a killing.

Anil Kapoor played 'Karan' the lead protagonist with Jackie playing 'Kishen',his older brother. Bred in the slums of Bombay circumstances throw Kishen in to a vortex of crime pushing him to align with 'Anna', the kingpin. As he grows into manhood 'Kishan' earns ill gotten wealth that feeds him a life of plenty and helps send off his brother Karan to America for higher studies. Since Kishan is now a trusted partner of Anna, he has turned a blind eye to Anna's nefarious deeds and sadistic methods of elimination; be they traitors or opponents. Such as: personally sawing off an informant's leg under a wheel-turner or even burning his own wife to death ! Karan returns from America and is excited about his future. He is absolutely unaware of his brother's dark life. As events unfold Karan loses his childhood friend Prakash (Anupam Kher terribly wasted in an insignificant role) to a hail of bullets whose smoky trail leads to Anna.

The memories of Nana Patekar's earlier 'Ankush', where he mirrored the country's youth cheated out by politicos and the system, was still fresh in our minds. So was his role from the Marathi film 'Maficha Shakshidaar', where he reprised real-life serial killer Rajendra Jakkal who had struck terror in Pune during the eighties with his cold-blooded killings. As heinous as can be, people were impressed by this character of the cold blooded 'Rajendra Jakkal' from 'Maficha Shakshidaar' seamlessly flowing in to 'Parinda' as 'Anna',who has a business-like approach in eliminating his opponents. As 'Anna' he brought in a new act of villainy where candid observations and brutal killings was chillingly played out under a psychotic smile or a maniacal laughter. The unconventional looks of Nana: those dark eyes appearing lifeless, a conical head that bespeaks a kind of full-grown 'Down Syndrome'Nana's antics actually matched his looks. Surprisingly, in this maniacal world where Karan was the hunter, it was Jackie Shroff who held the film as the subservient Kishen. In face of all odds and misfortunes he is patient but when he erupts- the film ends!

With 'Tezaab ' having just catapulted Anil-Madhuri in to the big league, those fans were perhaps disappointed. As 'Mohini', the young lady had just sashayed in to the hearts of the males through the sizzling 'Ek-Do-Teen' number. She carved out yet another milestone over here as the warm and caring 'Paro'. But their disappointment rose manifold when they were not taken in by Anil Kapoor's 'Karan'. Caught between Nana's 'Anna' & Jackie's 'Kishen' they found Anil's 'Karan'too labored.

No wonder, Jackie Shroff, hitherto known as a 'wooden actor' won his first Filmfare Award as the 'Best Actor'; that picture of Jackie receiving the trophy with his infant son Tiger Shroff in his embrace remains frozen for posterity. Indeed, if 'Tezaab' belonged to Munna & Mohini, and to an extent 'Shyamlal (Anupam Kher), 'Parinda' belonged to Jackie Shroff and to Nana Patekar who redefined heinousness as a new form of villainy. Because the film was dark there was no scope for inserting songs. But Vinod and RD Burman found opportune moments to fit in a few everlasting ones like *'Tume se milke aisa laga tumse milke'* sung by the off-beat Suresh Wadkar and Asha Bhonsale. This song perfectly conjured images of huge lotuses blooming in a heap of swamp.

Rewinding 'Parinda':

- A black Fiat with tinted glasses arrives near a slum. A lanky Kishan(Jackie) steps out, taking off his shirt,dark glares and expensive watch. Wearing a vest tucked in to jeans and the camera focusing on his sinewy arms helped us relish a vintage Jackie from 'Hero. Parrying sword wielding goons and slashing their guts out, he strides up a water-tank to meet Moosa (Tom Alter).

- Anna (Nana) murmuring on his phone, presumably with a local politician where in between guffaws he is heard brokering a quid-pro-quo deal: " *Aaap hamara khayal rakho hum aapka, chotasa kaam hain..kardo*"

- An oil producing factory hums up with unusual activity in order to remove traces of a murder. As the wail of sirens die away, Inspector Prakash (Anupam Kher) in full tow with his cops comes charging inside; *"Kahan hain woh"*? *"Woh Gaya Worli ka gutter mein."* Holding Abdul (Suresh Oberoi) by his neck *"saaley tu bhi jayega Worli key gutter mein"* Abdul erupts *"Abdul ko haath lagata hain"*! When he is just about to pounce, Anna intervenes and in a rare sermonizing manner restrains Abdul *"Chod Abdul, Kahin to Hindustan Zinda hain uski izzat karna seekh;"* his words mirrored those unalloyed cops who are above bribes. The strong baritone of Suresh Oberoi momentarily dims the persona of 'Anna'. Unfortunately, the character of 'Abdul' remained stunted.

- In the last scene, long after the din of the massacre has died away, Anna believes that Kishan still owes allegiance. He hugs him close to his heart and tells him to " *Bhool jaa, chal beedi jalaa"*. Kishan, now alone with Anna, finally erupts and with a mere flicker of his lighter sends his master to bathe in fiery flames.

As the year came to a close, Amitabh Bachchan was now well past middle age. The call for a smooth changeover from a full blown hero –to some one more in sync with his age became the need of the hour. One day those lines joined a dot in director Mukul Anand, whose scarred reputation post 'Sultanat' had been rejuvenated by the success of 'Insaaf', now decided to recast and revive Amitabh's wounded image in a flick inspired by the Al Pacino starrer 'Scarface'. The project was 'Agneepath' and the mantle of being its producer was picked up by Yash Johar's 'Dharma Productions' the 'big daddy' of big-budget films who had earlier produced big names like 'Dostana' and 'Duniya'. 'Agneepath' had a serious subject of a wronged teacher whose family has to face rough shod. Amitabh Bachchan played 'Vijay Chauhan' (or Scarface), Mithun Chakraborty is 'Krishnan Iyer Yem Yey" (or 'Alejandro Sosa'), Neelam Kothari as Vijay's younger sister reprised 'Gina Montana' and Rohini Hattangady was 'Mama Montana'; the mother who despises her criminal son. In a way for Rohini it was an extension of playing her 'Kasturba' look from the film 'Gandhi'. Cleverly interspersed with poems by Harvanshrai Bachchan based on verses from the 'Gita' added a spiritual halo around it and with a fair amount of publicity and curiosity value 'Agneepath' was released.

But the viewers stopped, shocked in their tracks; according to them, Amitabh Bachchan as 'Vijay Dinanath Chauhan' was suffering from a loss of baritone. That rich voice of his seemed to be afflicted by a terrible 'sore throat'. The 'sore-throat' factor was nothing but a new facet added to Amitabh's role where he dubbed modulating in husky overtones; a la Don Corleone from the film 'Godfather'. Mukul Anand had overseen the fact that, Marlon Brando and 'DonVito' may have been iconic in America but in India, bulk of the population had never heard of this film called 'The Godfather'. This 'sore-throat' thing did not go down well so bad publicity by word of-mouth spread and 'Agneepath' was in grave danger of facing sudden death !

Pushed back to the drawing board the entire team advised the reluctant director to recall Amitabh and re-dub the dialogues in his normal voice so as to stave off depleting ticket sales! Sore-throat or not, the film was well made though. An exodus of unemployment and strife in Cuba as in the original 'Scarface', is replaced by Mandwa, a little island supposedly near Bombay where a righteous teacher loses his honour and life. As typical in scripts so wont of anything transcendental, the little boy 'Vijay Chauhan' struggles doing odd jobs but never forgets the torment thrust upon his parents by 'Kaancha Cheena', a reigning don played by Danny Denzongpa.

The villainy of 'Kaancha Cheena' was a great departure from the stereo- typed urban villains; like Tejaa (Ajit), Dr Dang(Anupam Kher) and . Robert Seth (Jeevan) who symbolized urban, English speaking villains in loud suits and dialogues interspersed with fancy English. In 'Agneepath' 'Kaancha' was the new suave. He lived a king-sized life, displayed six packs, gelled his hair, wore expensive suits and possessed a toned body made solely for thongs. His lifestyle was probably sketched from the template of an unknown 'banana republic' leader sans a military uniform; no wonder, 'Vijay Chouhan', with appreciation glistening from his 'kohled' eyes, praises his enemy's sartorial sense by whispering softly: *'Appun ko tumhara kapda pehnney ka style bahut accha laga"* (I am impressed by your style of dressing). Unfortunately the character of 'Kancha Cheena' is invisible in the 'Great Rogues Gallery of Bollywood' which lies adorned with the names of Gabbar Singh, Mogambo and Dr Dang. 'Agneepath' won Amitabh a National award and Mithun Chakraborty a Filmfare trophy.

The year 1990 saw efforts of just-born-stars consolidate their status by sweeping the box office. The first was Aamir Khan-Madhuri starrer 'Dil' directed by rookie Indra Kumar. It was about a middle class boy in love with a girl from an affluent family. It was not the usual love story because the script, had an amusing angle which belonged to 'Hazariprasad' (Anupam Kher) the boy's father who is a merchant trading in old newspapers, rejected goods ('kabadiwala)' and a miser, but dreams that providence one day will shower him with goodies. He looks upon his son 'Raja' (Aamir) as a means to become a rich man by trading him off in exchange for a plum dowry. His plans fail to attract 'potential' families until one day he meets Mr Mehra an Industrialist.(Saeed Jaffrey). Mehra's lifestyle is the one of envy for Hazariprasad and whet his greed when he learns that the millionaire Mehra is the father of an only daughter.

Anupam Kher as Hazari Prasad, was a huge deviation from his last role as ShyamLal in 'Tezaab'. In 'Dil' he had the same diabolic attitude but in a style hugely comical. Madhuri Dixit proved her self yet again. Besides carrying dollops of the oomph factor she proved that she was first- an actress of substance whose oomph was a peripheral.

Music by Anand-Milind was another driving factor where one of them *'Khambe jaisi khadi hai'* sounded like an Elvis Presley composition, became a chart buster. 'Dil' became a major hit, erased the bad memories of 'Love Love Love' for Aamir Khan, won Madhuri Dixit a Filmfare award and made Indra Kumar an 'A' lister. The success of 'Dil' brought in to focus the magic which this new pair could re-create. There were talks of big banners planning to cast them together.

Dil's success gave an impetus to Bollywood to project the 'new hot pair' of Aamir-Madhuri. After 'Tezaab' 'Ram Lakhan' and 'Parinda' there was a growing impression that she paired well only with Anil Kapoor. But 'Dil' put this thought on hold. The boyish looking Aamir did prove to be her Prince Charming and people braced themselves for their second release called ' Dewana Mujhsa Nahin'. Unfortunately, 'Deewana Mujh Sa Nahin' made by an obscure banner sank, putting paid to the aspirations of those wanting to encash on this pair.

The various processes of film making were known and each maker were well adept, but none knew about any process that could lead them to a perfect formula. Audiences were willing to lap up any film provided it appealed to them. The term of 'a one-man –industry' had turned archaic and had surely ended. After the success of 'Dil'a love story, what next followed was an action film: Dharmendra's action oriented 'Ghayal' starring his son Sunny Deol. It had revenge as its main motif.

After a tepid response to his last starrer 'Ram Avtaar' which had Anil Kapoor-Sridevi, and 'Nigahen' that was basically a sequel to the earlier 'Nagina', Sunny Deol roared mightily with 'Ghayal' which was a bigger hit than 'Dil'. It stupefied not only the audience but even its makers - who won landmark awards for posterity and also made their bankers. Dharmendra won a National award as the producer of 'Ghayal' in the 'Most Entertaining Category; while his son won both- Filmfare and a National award. It also shot in to limelight Raj Kumar Santoshi, the brains behind 'Ghayal'. While Rajkumar Santoshi was hailed as an emerging one, another great from a distant past-Dev Anand, tried again to raise his famished 'Navketan' banner by now signing up Aamir Khan for 'Awwal Number',a film based on cricket. But it turned out to be one of those slip-shod matches which save blushes by getting washed away under untimely rains! After the disappointing'Deewana Mujh Sa Nahin'', this was another body blow for Aamir Khan. To save him from drowning, an unexpected lifeline appeared in the form of 'Tum Mere Ho'. This was made by his father Tahir Hussain (producer of the 70's 'Caravan' and 'Yaadon Ki Baraat') this small time success staved off Aamir's fears of getting washed out.

There occured another ripple. A regional hit film was hoisted over hindi speaking regions by dubbing Hindi over the original Tamil. Kamal Haasan had practically completed all his assignments in hindi and had decided to focus completely on his home ground. This was not difficult, rather a cake walk for him. As far as the Tamil film industry and the Tamil masses were concerned their 'Kamal' had merely gone off to 'play' in the hindi heartland. For them he had definitely proved himself through films like 'Ek Duje Ke Liye' and crowning his sojourn by bagging the Filmfare trophy for 'Saagar'. He was welcomed back to Madras enthusiastically where his films made money. One such new hit was 'Apoorva Saghodarargal'. An obscure distributor from Bombay bought out the dubbing rights of this Tamil hit and released it as 'Appu Raja'. People liked and marveled at Kamal's twin roles: of a normal man and the other as a midget. Through 'Appu Raja', Kamalhaasan revisited Bollywood but it was not a comeback film that could bring him back to Bombay. He remained where he was good at- entertaining Madras and winning Awards!

The Pirate

" Hello, hi chodiye Jai Mata Di boliye"--a popular bhajan.

Since the time silent movies gave way to sound, the art and the joy of movie making was complete. Sound throbbed life in recreation and art opened the way for music to emerge as a natural accompaniment; music brought in songs and paved way for dance. Songs became an integral part of every film: today one cannot imagine films to be bereft of songs. Along with film makers, music composers and singers too played an important role in a film's success; many a times bad films turned to be unforgettable because of its excellent music.

As the decade commenced away - in between the blow hot blow cold successes and the uncertainty over Bachchan's future, appeared a maverick called Gulshan Kumar. Before the onset of the nineties he had flooded the market with his T-series brand of cassettes jolting the market monopolized until then by the highly feted 'HMV'. After the exit of its lone rival 'Polydor', 'His Master's Voice' (better known as 'HMV) had been enjoying unrivalled monopoly. Cassettes and records of HMVwere priced beyond affordability which deprived the teeming millions from enjoying their choice of music at their leisure. Gulshan Kumar an ardent devotee of the famed goddess of Jammu 'Ma Vaishno Devi', those days was managing his family's sugarcane juice shop in Daryaganj which is a suburb in Delhi-a place well known for its book shops scattered inside its narrow alleys. One fine day when his customers were sipping their sweet juice and being caressed by Lata Mangeshkar's fine melodies playing in the shop, the innate businessman in him realized that HMV had created an unmet need. To capitalize on this he set up a cassette manufacturing factory in Noida, near Delhi. Peering through a loophole in the Music Act of India, which he soon exploited to the hilt by cleverly recording all the classic hindi songs originally sung by Lata Mangeshkar, Asha Bhosle, Kishore Kumar, Mohmd Rafi, Mukesh, through their sound-alikes like: Sonu Nigam, Kumar Sanu and Anuradha Paudwal. These, like many others, were those struggling singers waiting in the wings for an opportunity. Many made a living singing in orchestra troupes or small time 'bhajan' singers; 'bhajans' formed a big part of his pie. The people did not mind a Sonu Nigam singing Rafi's *'Meri Dosti Mera Pyar'* or a Sanu Bhattacharya trying effortlessly in recreating Kishore's *'Yeh Sham mastani'*. Even Hemanth Kumar and Mukesh were not left unturned.

On a cassette manufactured in his factory, songs recorded by these ghosts at his recording studio in Noida, Gulshan Kumar sold these cassettes at one-tenth the price of HMV.

As he went smiling all the way to the bank, the money earned helped him in bagging music rights of films for his 'Super Cassettes/T-Series banner. The first big film he bagged was Mansoor Khan's 'Qayamat se Qayamat Tak'. Though he had some sense of music as to what kind could enthrall people, he never had any artful inklings of what good films should be about. Gulshan Kumar was not a follower of arts nor did he have any vision for making films. But he was an ambitious man and keeping in line with his desire for making a lot of money, he kept pursuing his efforts in mining the industry. After revolutionizing the music industry the 'Mogul' - as the 'pirate' was now called, set his sights in making films. He created a 'bank' of songs sung by the same ones who were hand picked by him. He hired lyricists to write songs that would cater to all sorts of emotions: Love, heartbreak, break-up, patch-up, weddings, distress you name it ! These 'ready- to- use songs' could be inserted in films depending on situational requirement. Ready with these, he now produced a small budget film called 'Lal Dupatta Malmal ka' (A scarf of silk) and joined them together by casting small time actors. It had eleven songs, all taken from this 'Bank'. The film was never released in theaters but was available in video cassettes (manufactured by his company of course) where people could buy and watch in the comfort of their homes. This unusually marketed film did give good returns to Gulshan Kumar and well appreciated (only for its music) in mofussil towns all over North India. 'Lal Dupatta Malmal Ka' indeed, made Gulshan Kumar's 'T-Series' brand a house hold name. His entry in to Bollywood-first, as a cassette maker and then a producer, was watched keenly by the Satraps with most of them dismissing him. But that did not deter, for he now stood on the cusp of a curve which would make him stride like a colossus. He not only revolutionized the music industry but also turned an entrepreneur by churning T-Series into a brand spawning varied goods like cookers and televisions. He also brought out 'MayaPuri' a film based weekly in Hindi. From a lowly 'pirate' he was now a Mogul ! Thereon, T-Series & Super Cassettes Industries chugged on to hold suzerainty over the Hindi film industry. His next big step was to have alliance with directors who needed deep pocket producers like him. Very soon, Vishesh Films (Mahesh Bhatt) and Super Cassettes came out with 'Aashiqui', which was actually an off shoot after sourcing 12 songs from his bank. A love story was scripted on which the songs from his bank were embellished. The film basked under Gulshan Kumar and Mahesh Bhatt's well thought out marketing strategy of having new actors. Bhatt screen tested many aspirants and the chosen ones were models Rahul Roy, a well known model who shared his face for 'The Wearhouse', a Bangalore based apparel group and Anu Aggarwal who modeled for 'Marvel', a deodorant soap from the house of Godrej. Its release spurred by the success of its songs, set the din.

The eighteen rupees worth cassette of 'Aashiqui' played at every nook of the country; from cassette players of the 'rickshawalah', to the humble radios of the teeming millions and inside the walkmans of the well-heeled:

> *Nazar ke saamne jigar key paar;Bus ek sanam chahiye;Mera dil tere liye;Tu meri zindagi hai;Ab tere bin jee lenge hum;Dil Ka Aalam;Jaan e jigar jaaneman;Mein duniya bhula doonga;Dheere dheere sey*

Among the many firsts, 'Aashiqui' also introduced an unknown pair of musicians: Nadeem Saifee and Shravan Rathod who very soon came to be known as 'Nadeem-Shravan'.

A nation that had once upon a time grooved to 'disco' was now getting weary of 'shrieks' being churned out in the name of 'disco'. The plagiarized list of Bappi Lahiri had failed to grow further. Musicians Anand-Milind, who had gained acclaim by fashioning their offerings influenced to a great extent by R.D.Burman, were also facing dearth of ideas. In such mediocre times, Nadeem & Shravan turned this on its head when they based their music on the template of the 'olden times'.The drums and guitar were pushed in to the foreground while the 'tabla', 'dhol' and the flute ruled the forefront. The scientific reason behind this success was not the radio, but proliferation of affordable music cassettes. As far as we were concerned, the film ran, but lacked the Mahesh Bhatt signature. The film suffered, from Mahesh Bhat's lack of creative overdrive. For a better part of the nineteen-nineties Super Cassettes and the ace musicians Nadeem-Shravan would bring the country under their musical sway. This music duo would now dictate terms with producers and turn this industry a veritable playground for the underworld to roost. Very soon the rise of Nadeem-Shravan led to a slide in content. Song sequences was taking precedence and projects were being woven around songs. The upstarts soon started tom-tomming their sway by inserting pompous insertions self praising their successes.

As the first year of the nineteen-nineties appeared, it was clearly exit time for seniors like Jeetendra, Shatrughan Sinha, Dharmendra, Vinod Khanna and Mithun Charaborty. In Mithun's case a serpentine list of flops had started preceding his name. His fans disappeared and so did his kind of hairstyle; sans-sidelocks. Guys like Chunky Pandey who were launched with much fanfare had no takers because their films with inane plots had laughable titles like ' Aag Ka Gola', 'Aaj ke Shahenshah', 'Doodh Ka Karz' 'Maati Maangey Khoon'. Stale subjects, uninspiring direction, headache inducing music had turned theaters chillingly empty. The ones that could bring in money were few. There was another small niche, that was churning out horror films and infested with plenty of cheap titillation catering to smaller towns and the interiors.

Sunny Deol and Sanjay Dutt inspite of their pedigrees were not able to follow up on their hits. 'Ghayal' did give a formidable impetus to Sunny but Sunjay Dutt was some how trying to stay afloat so wereAnil Kapoor, Jackie Shroff. Salman Khan was the only one standing steady with 'Baaghi' and 'Patthar Ke Phool'.

Rakesh Roshan kept behind the tepid response to his 'Kaala Bazaar' and resumed with a new 'K' factor called 'Kishan Kanhaiya'. The film proved a smasher with Anil Kapoor who, for the second time, played double roles. The success of 'Kishen Kanhaiya' bolstered the star status of Anil Kapoor. A rewarding effort by director-producer Rakesh Roshan whose directorial debut 'Khudgarz' had changed his fortunes and he was now much sought after. However he preferred making films under his own banner. He was now commanding the same leverage like a Chopra or a Ghai !

'Kishen Kanhaiya' got a boost for two reasons: a double role which historically has proved to be a winning formula and second being Rakesh Roshan himself. He had, as proved by his successes, become a master inserter of entertainment. To tie down monotony he had an intriguing knack of turning them around to make it exceptional and absorbing. In the business of film making Rakesh Roshan had his ears to the ground. The concept of a double role in itself can present a bagful of entertainment and has been attempted quite many times. Such stories were usually coupled with a lost-found theme which was prolific during the 70's. In the lead theme of double roles there had been notable successes like 'Ram aur Shyam', 'Seeta aur Geeta', 'Don', 'Kasme Vaade', 'Chalbaaz', 'Bol Radha Bol' and now 'Kishen Kanhaiya'.

Conversely many failed, like 'Dastan' which had Dilip Kumar in a double role. The reason could be because one was a young character with grey shades while the other an older middle-aged character with a poorly written characterization. There was 'Humshakal' which had Rajesh Khanna yet was a flop; both the look alikes in 'Humshakal' were not two extremes but a reflection of the same personality. Unlike 'Saccha Jhutha' which had Rajesh Khanna where the two characters had their zones clearly marked:one was a simpleton the other was bad.

The mention of 'Kishan-Kanhaiya'also reminds me of the time when 'mogul' Gulshan Kumar furthered his 'vision' by hoisting his younger brother, Kishan Kumar, as a hero. In the lookwise department he was as dull looking as a dishwasher. The star son's of the 80's, contrastingly,at least had a fair degree of pedigree that naturally carried an element of curiosity. The 'mogul' was obviously aware that his brother was zilch, yet lay his bets on him. The next best thing for him to do was create a blitzkrieg for his brother. So he got about in the act by plastering his face in all the inner jacket of his T-series cassettes: bhajan, ghazal, films, all had Kishan Kumar's face peeping out alongwith a mention of his debut film'Aaja Meri Jaan'.

Needless to say it toppled and fell flat, but what needs to be mentioned is the persisting 'Big bro' announced a new 'lemon' starring Kishan Kumar every month!

While the young ones were steadying themselves, old veteran Amitabh Bachchan sadly slipped due to a strange film called 'Ajooba'. Produced and directed by Shashi Kapoor, his screen brother during his heydays. 'Ajooba' was generously backed under the Indo-Soviet production which was a loose confederation of the Russian government and some Russian film producers. Under their scheme shooting at locales in Russia proved cheaper than in any other part of the world. This story was about a mother's love for her orphaned son. The problem was the 'mother' is a dolphin and the son is Amitabh. This 'Arabian Nights' fantasy style film starring Amitabh-Rishi Kapoor-Dimple Kapadia –Sonal was a flop whose reverberance was felt throughout Asia. This was Shashi Kapoor's second dud as a producer after the 1984 'Utsav'.

While an old giant was stumbling away, the much touted Rahul Roy of 'Aashiqui'was being tom-tommed as 'the next Big thing'.

Producers were falling over each other to sign him up. Naturally, Rahul Roy did not disappoint and grabbed all with both hands. The nation too, especially teenage girls eager to applaud, were awaiting his next release. The film was 'Pyar ka Saaya', it was a remake of the 1989 hollywood hit 'Ghost'. So we had Rahul Roy as Patrick Swazye, an unknown actress Sheeba as Demi Moore and Amrita Singh as Whoopi Goldberg. Made by none other than 'scavenging' filmmaker B.Subhash, who post-Aashiqui, was the first one to board the bus of Rahul Roy. With music by Nadeem-Shravan it proved to be a disaster on the very first day of its release. The verdict was out: "Rahul Roy could not act to save his life". One had to admit that Mahesh Bhatt had certainly erred in trying to mould out an actor from the dead pan expressions of this ex-model. His expressions could put a piece of wood to shame. It is a sheer mystery why Mahesh Bhat persisted in casting him in each of his film. The flop of 'Pyar Ka Saya' certainly brought a 'ghostly' end to his career.

While all were examining the imminent fall of Rahul Roy, another young pair was being readied by Subhash Ghai: a young plain looking boy called Vivek Mushran who Subhash Ghai claimed was ' as pure as plain water', but it was Manisha Koirala, a young aspirant belonging to the ruling political family of Nepal, who was noticed for her pretty looks.

Subhash Ghai by now, had become unstoppable. His every action was a humdinger. Be it the casting, the music, their publicity or his premieres. Black marketeers looked forward to his releases. His films ensured them 100% return on their investements. This time his casting was on an overkill mode he brought by bringing in Dilip Kumar and Raj Kumar together. Even though he had carefully nurtured his reclusiveness, Raj Kumar over the years had built a loyal fan base who lapped up his loud and theatrical style of delivering dialogues. Lower down the pecking order he stuffed in several characters and signed a long string of performers: Mukesh Khanna, Dipti Naval, Anupam Kher, Amrish Puri, Archana Puransingh, and new finds Manisha Koirala & Vivek Mushran who were the fulcrum. For all stakeholders-the audience, the black marketeers, and those Raj Kumar fans -'Saudagar' was much looked forward to. The story was familiar; love blossoming between two love birds from warring families; each faction headed separately by Dilip and Raj; both were bosom pals long ago untill villains sowed seeds of misunderstanding fomenting into a hatred for each other.

'Saudagar' was another plume in 'showman' Ghai's fast filling cap!

But his discovery Vivek Mushran, failed to take this success forward and got buried under several failures like 'Satwan Aasman', 'Love Letter', 'Prem Deewane'.

While Dilip Kumar was in the thick of his second innings, his late friend and colleague Raj Kapoor's film 'Henna' was lying unfinished at R.K.Studios. The exemplar showman's death had put his last film 'Henna' lying in limbo. It was more than three fourth incomplete. Zeba Bakhtiyar a girl from Pakistan who bagged its title role was chosen after auditioning a bevy of beauties (which included Dimple Kapadia). His forte in introducing new girls to play compeling characters was legendary. In continuation of more than a dozen classics, 'Henna' was another heroine oriented story from Raj Kapoor, which was no surprise. Owing to his death, his oldest son,

Randhir Kapoor stepped in to finish it. 'Henna' saw the light of day in its release and was appreciated. The effort of its stand-in director was also appreciated. Ironically none from his lineage could carry forward the torch of his glorious legacy. After a few failed films and a failed marriage the Last Lady from R.K Films, Zeba Bakhtiyar, too faded away in to oblivion.

The same time a young man called Rajiv Hari Om Bhatia was given a screen name of 'Akshay Kumar'. A hard working lad who tried his hands at bartending, cooking and martial arts instructor, got himself a break from old-style director -producer Pramod Chakravarthy for 'Deedar'. However, lack of cash delayed 'Deedar's release making another film 'Saugandh' his first. Both proved to be flops but Akshay's acrobatic skills got him noticed with other makers helping him to hang out tenaciously.

Former 'angry young man' was now nearing his twilight. Film makers were still bent upon harnessing his charisma. There were twin reasons; first was the man's glorious past and second, a belief that there was still some fire within.

Mukul Anand's 'Agneepath' produced by 'Dharma Productions' was the first step in harnessing it. 'Vijay Dinanath Chauhan', that fiery gangster, reveals rather candidly to the top cop that his age is: "*Chhatees saal nau mahiney*". This brimming confidence assuaged the audience with a flourish that 'Vijay' of the 26 something could still battle at 36 plus! On similar belief, Mukul Anand brought out his next called 'Hum'. With Rajnikanth, Govinda, Danny, Kimi Katkar and

Anupam Kher as the film's ensemble cast and a budget as striking as its name -Mukul Anand promised a dazzling product: Big names befitting a Bachchan multistarrer, giant billboards showing a clenched fist and a number that went *'Jooma Chumma dey dey'* zooming up the charts. All of these ensured a stupendous opening.

Amitabh played 'Tiger' who works at the docks and stays with his step mother and two step-brothers. With penury and exploitation being faced constantly from the gangster 'Bhaktavar' (Danny) the workers face no respite and have to pay 'hafta' (a euphemism for protection money). Tiger is in love with his friend's sister Jhumma (Kimi Katkar). The area also falls under the jurisdiction of local cop Giridhar (Anupam Kher) who is corrupt and always in search for an opportunity to make fast bucks. That moment comes, when Bhaktawar stabs Jhumma's brother to death as he has been fomenting trouble to raise unrest against his sway. The crooked cop Girdhar creates a situation where he burns down Bhaktawar's mansion alongwith his family and orchestrates the entire drama in such a way that Tiger gets framed for it. Having no other option Tiger flees the place taking away his kid brothers to start life anew. Years pass. Tiger is now greying but his mission in bringing up his orphaned brothers turns out fulfilling. One grows up to be a Cop (Rajnikanth) while the youngest (Govinda) is in his final year of college. The three brothers live in a large farmhouse where Tiger tills their land and is living happily with his brothers, sister in law and a little niece. The brothers are totally unaware of his violent past but very soon circumstances bring up obstacles on their path in the form of his nemesis Bhaktawar returning back. The rest was about Bhaktawar wanting to hunt him down and Girdhar doing all he can to keep buried his old secret. Besides an interesting narrative what kept the audience rooted was its style, the outdoor filming in the enchanting locales of Mauritius, Govinda's dances, Rajnikanth's cigarette stunts, the insertion of Kader Khan in a double role: as the stern army general and his double, a bumbling small-time stage actor and its song picturisations. The 'piece-de-resistance' was the picturisation of the song 'Jhumma Chumma dedey' in a hall the size of a mini stadium which had a hundred dancers in blue overalls, thumping beer mugs, spilling it's froth on stony floors swinging away to unhindered glory, with Kimi Katkar in a Spanish styled flamenco and Amitabh in his 'Deewar' styled knotted shirt matching them with gusto, turning this 'Hum' in to a huge humdinger !

It was also distinguished for some more facts; It was the last one to bring together the two superstars of Hindi and Tamil cinema; It also earned Amitabh his 5th Filmfare award; the music by Laxmikant-Pyarelal was thumping and fast- which was a departure from the Nadeem-Shravan styles prevailing those days. To me, the picturisation of 'Jumma-Chumma', seemed a large scale glamourized version of the number 'Ek Do Teen aaja mausam hai rangeen' from the 1951 'Awara'(available on YouTube). The dark side of 'Hum' was the music-duo Laxmikant –Pyarelal directly pinching the 'Jumma' song from African singer Mory Kante's album. They had also used a portion of its music in the earlier 'Agneepath'.

Reminiscing on music, though Mahesh Bhatt's 'Aashiqui' was heralded all over, it was a widely known fact that the film's music cassettes were selling more than its tickets. Mahesh Bhatt therefore had a point to make which he made- in September 1991.

That point came as a joint venture with T-Series called 'Dil Hai ke Manta Nahin'. In 'Lehren', a video magazine, Mahesh Bhatt candidly confessed that he was 'guilty' of copying an old English film -'It Happened One Night'. However, Mahesh Bhatt was not the first. Thirty six years ago, a Raj Kapoor-Nargis starrer 'Chori-Chori' was based on exactly the same story and was a hit. Mahesh Bhatt's remake was also a hit making big bucks for him, and the former 'pirate'.

The roles reprised by Aamir Khan and Anupam Kher are worth watching even today. Nadeem-Shravan's reign continued with the hit music of this film. 'Dil Hai Ke Manta Nahin' proved to be a god-sent for Aamir Khan that kept intact his image of a lover boy.

To repeat, DHKMN was the story of a rich heiress. To avoid an arranged marriage she leaps from the steamer of her tycoon father and swims over to the shores. Dodging lookouts placed by her father she inadvertently is 'rescued' by a reporter Raghu Jaitley (Aamir khan) who actually is in search for a juicy scoop to boost his dull stint as a reporter. Gradually, the two fall in love and the reporter after knowing the real reason behind fleeing her tycoon father, now wants to put things in their right perspective.

Aamir Khan and Pooja Bhatt rekindled a love story with their true feelings. This is exactly what 'Aashiqui' lacked. The love in DHKMN delighted the audience and gave a firm footing to all involved. The former juice seller, and the lucky mascots all went laughing to the bank.The icing on the cake of DHKMN's success had just been savoured when two more thunderous hits appeared:

Lawrence D'souza directed 'Saajan' and Mahesh Bhatt's hattrick –'Sadak'. Both had music by Nadeem-Shravan.

Both were different from each other. The only common factors were Sunjay Dutt and Nadem-Shravan. 'Saajan' was a sensitive love story, where a fan falls in love with a poet, whom she admires for his soul stirring couplets.The poet is actually a handicapped man who writes his poems under a pseudonym named 'Saagar'. But Saagar is not only a handicap he was an orphan adopted by a benevolent couple who took him in as 'Aman' bringing him up as their own son, alongside their real son who grows up as Akash (Salman Khan.) The real son gets smitten by the same girl and with his foster brother's permission wants to masquerade as the poet 'Saagar' so as to make the fan gravitate towards him.This naturally, leads to heartbreak on all sides putting Saagar the poet on the cross road of a dilemma.While Salman Khan played his then, usual self role of a lover boy gallivanting with girls, it was the unusual casting of a tough looking Sunjay Dutt as the limping poet, who stems his grief by penning poems and this is what touched the audience. This was a great makeover for the actor who until then mainly specialized as an action hero.

The second biggest factor was the music by Nadeem-Shravan. Each number was enthralling, vindicating the duo's prowess over their medium. The locales of Ooty added to the film's beauty while T-Series the music banner scaled newer heights. Sanjay Dutt not only overshadowed Salman Khan, he also displaced his peers. Before they could even contemplate their next course of action they were again jolted by 'Sadak', the Dutt's next hit. Produced by Mahesh Bhatt's home production called as 'Vishesh Films' which literally means 'Special Films' this again was a love story garnished with palpable violence which heightened its thrill quotient. Mahesh Bhatt was a shrewd maker. His 'Arth' if at all autobiographical, did express extremely violent mental battles between the characters. The duels between Pooja (Shabana Azmi) and Inder (Kulbhushan Kharbanda) because of the other woman Kavita (Smita patil) were all equally devastating, if not more, than the blood and gory tactics of 'Maharani,' the villain in 'Sadak' (actor Sadashiv Amrapurkar)

"Maharani' a eunuch, runs a whore house in suburban Bombay. A young girl (Pooja Bhatt) on the run is ensnared in a dragnet run by 'Maharani'. A chance meeting between a cab driver and the helpless girl gets transformed in to imminent love. This sets in motion a plan to permanently rescue her from this illicit business. The movie was a big hit and all credit definitely goes to Mahesh Bhatt. But his recurring successes raised muted whispers of English films being remade and dipped in the 'Bhatt emotion': The Frank Capra directed 'It Happened One Night' for DHKMN and now, Robert De Niro's 'Taxi driver' for 'Sadak'.

As Gulshan Kumar was opening up his kitty to make more films, and Mahesh Bhatt had cast off the tag of art films, few of the Big Guns were readying for a title clash;

Yash Chopra's Anil Kapoor-Sridevi starrer 'Lamhe, Ramesh Sippy-Mushir Riaz's 'Akayla' starring Amitabh Bachchan, and a Salman Khan starrer titled 'Love'.

Dwarfed in the midst of these biggies was a film called 'Phool Aur Kante' where a new lad called Ajay Devgan, son of veteran fight director Veeru Devgun was being introduced. The outcome was as follows:

Ramesh Sippy directed 'Akayla' was produced by deep pocket producer team of Mushir-Riaz who had bankrolled several lavishly mounted names in their resume. 'Akayla' was one of them. Written by Salim Khan and starring Amitabh, Meenakshi, Amrita Singh, Shashi Kapoor this film could have been anything but a hit. Being several years in the cans was its terrible undoing. The characters felt stale. Names like 'Vijay Verma' had stopped impressing the audience. Time gaps created continuity issues to further damage its screenplay.

The second to flop was 'Love'. Just fresh from the recent success of 'Saajan', it was perched on Salman's shoulder. However, people found this 'love' laughably ridiculous.

The third was Yash Chopra's 'Lamhe'. Cities were plastered with publicity posters. With pictures of a slightly greying Anil Kapoor locked in a tight embrace with a very bubbly looking Sridevi, baffled people. Incidentally Anil Kapoor's last couple of releases had fared below-average. In 'Benaam

Badshah' he was cast as a reformed criminal who rapes the heroine, met with a big frown from the audience. The next to fail was 'Jeevan Ek Sunghursh' which had Madhuri and Raakhee. Produced by D.Rama Naidu, a movie mogul from Hyderabad, directed by Rahul Rawail and script by Javed Akhtar made this project indicate a bejeweled back-end. But it failed.

With 'Lamhe' on the eve of its release, Anil Kapoor hoped to recover lost ground. For Sridevi too 'Lamhe' was an important film. After the twin successes of 'Chandni' and 'Chaalbaz', she had to face the brunt of 'Heer-Ranjha's failure. This made Sridevi extremely cautious, giving room for Madhuri Dixit to quickly scale up the ladder. 'Lamhe' opened to fantastic reviews and a very good initial response in Tier-A cities. Its treatment in all departments; direction, camera, locations, costumes, music had been finessed with extreme elan. Rajasthan- the backdrop of this film, was captured beautifully; especially those eternal sand dunes near Jaisalmer. Visually it was a labour of love by Yash Chopra. Nevertheless, the story of Thakur Viren Singh (Anil) in love with Pooja (Sridevi) daughter of Pallavi (Sridevi) for whom Viren secretly nursed a deep crush, made the Indian masses attach the tag of 'incest' to it. Even though the character 'Pallavi' had no inkling that 'Viren' was besotted with her, Yash Chopra's script mightily failed. By putting across a weak view point, people felt that the much older 'Viren' had no business falling in love with the daughter of a woman whom he once had loved secretly. Unwittingly for Yash Chopra, 'Lamhe' came across as 'Lolita'!

As one tabloid put it 'the failure of Lamhe was one of those bizarre moments in hindi cinema that cannot be explained'. The debate rages on.

The one to succeed was indeed a dark horse called 'Phool aur Kante' which successfully launched the son of veteran fight director Veeru Devgun. His introduction scene of standing astride a pair of bikes remains rooted in posterity. However, the bigger star in this was the music duo Nadeem-Shravan. Their juggernaut rolling ahead, the duo boasted about "refusing films with folded hands".

The successful induction of Ajay Devgan coincided with a big breakthrough being orchestrated by the P.V.Narasimha Rao government. On the advice of his finance minister Manmohan Singh, India decided to open up her economy and invite foreign investment to create jobs.

While in the industry too few milestones were being passed big names had soon started fading away. Or being offered worthless stellar roles. Dharmendra had as many as six releases; snarling the same kind of dialogues in his same old style; tight jaw-below-flaring nostrils. Shashi Kapoor after the debacle of his directorial dream 'Ajooba' with drew completely. He started nurturing 'Prithvi Theatre'. His children; Kunal Kapoor from 'Ahista Ahista', 'Vijeyta'; Karan Kapoor the brand ambassador of 'Vivaldi' shirts of the textile company 'Bombay Dyeing'and who had debuted with Juhi Chawla in Dharmendra's 'Sultanat'; Sanjana Kapoor who had played a princess in her father's 'Utsav' (where Shekhar Suman had debuted,) all of them could never really make a mark. Rishi Kapoor was still afloat since his 'Henna' was an above average success.

The indomitable Dev Anand was still plouging away aimlessly. The doyen of 'Navketan' was tirelessly making films. None of them touched our hearts while his discoveries remained incognito.

In the meanwhile Rajesh Khanna was now stationed in Delhi as an elected Member of Parliament. Manoj Kumar, who as 'Bharat' wore patriotism on his sleeve for which he drew praise from late Prime Minister Shastri and the man responsible for turning around actor Pran and launching Dilip Kumar's second innings, seemed to have lost himself in utter mediocrity; his brother failed courtesy 'Painter Babu'; his son failed courtesy 'Do Gulab','Kalakaar', 'Ghungroo'and he failed courtesy his own-'Clerk'.

1991 brought down curtains on some old legends but also gave many things to cheer about. It was the successes of films like 'Hum', 'Saajan','Dil Hai Ke Manta Nahin',the continuing juggeraut of the duo Nadeem and Shravan. It also answered some pertinent issues on Amitabh Bachchan.

The titan of two decades was now well beyond middle age. He was few months short of celebrating his fiftieth. Inspite of it his box-office appeal could not be ignored. Turning a blind eye to his ability to draw in the masses would be an incalculable loss. Even though it would not be prudent to cast him as sole lead, but the very name of the man appearing in a project translating in to big money, could never be tossed out. Long before 'Hum' the old and the young persona was played to great success. Examples being Feroz Nadiadwala's 'Adalat', the 1982 'Mahan' the 1985 'Aakhree Rasta' and now ' Hum'.

The success of 'Hum' emboldened Mukul Anand to rope in partners and plan a film bigger than 'Hum'; That big project bore the name of 'Khuda Gawah' on a landscape wide enough to fit in big names like Bachchan, Sridevi, Sunjay Dutt, Danny Denzongpa, Shilpa,Kiran Kumar and a line up of several more names reaching all the way up the 'Hindu Kush mountains....

On an other side there was Raj Kumar Santoshi who had created 'Ghayal' the fighter and warded off obsolescence for the Deol family. This time he wanted to create another crusader but, in a feminine form; a woman who refuses to toe the line of the males in a family where she is supposed to remain a 'pati-vrata' wife; a meek 'bahu'. Thus came in a film called 'Damini', where he cast Meenakshi Sheshadri. The script was interesting and so was its music and dialogues. Even though Sunny Deol is shown as an alcoholic lawyer, cleverly interspersed dialogues, like the cocky *"dhaai kilo ka haath"*, ensured the spectre of his tough guy image to loom large in the film.

Whispers suggested that Santoshi was so smitten by Meenakshi that he wanted to not only make her his wife but also get her a National award. On the contrary, the National award and the Filmfare trophy went to his friend-later-foe Sunny Deol while Meenakshi did not bag a single one. 'Damini' went on to celebrate good success and as Santoshi held the Filmfare award for the Best director, in private, he was left nursing a bruised heart. Shrugging off his besottment, his next focus was in creating a comedy classic. He got hold of a script where two youngsters run away from their homes to ensnare a rich heiress. For this he managed a casting coup by signing on Salman Khan and Aamir khan. Then suddenly every thing went in to a cold freeze leading to budgetary deficits, freezing the entire project in to a long time warp.

After 'Damini', woman power soon got its biggest booster dose. 'Maruti International' the makers of 'Dil' added another hit called 'Beta'to their kitty. The high point of 'Beta' was Madhuri Dixit all the way. Woman -power grappling with blind societal rules thrust by male chauvinism. Saraswati (Madhuri) is an astute woman. As a lover she is skilled in the art of seducing her husband and as a wife she is ever alert to protect the same innocent -to a fault - husband from the scheming ways of his supposedly 'close-knit' family. The songs too were chart busters. *Dhak Dhak karne laga'* was a popular number which also got brickbats from critics who likened Madhuri's rhythmic thrusts to a sense of 'vulgarity'. In a realm dominated totally by the hegemony of music directors Nadeem-Shravan, few players like Anand –Milind the composers for 'Beta' were able to hold out on their own.

Madhuri Dixit as 'Saraswati' actually behaves like the goddess 'Durga'. Refusing to take in the injustice heaped in the name of 'duty'her grittiness is of the same kind like the girl Geeta from the film 'Seeta-Aur-Geeta'. She gives back in equal measure to her crafty mother in law (Aruna Irani) who is also excellent in her role winning this veteran a rare Filmfare award in the 'Best Supporting actress" category.

The sartorial tastes of hindi film heroes was also put to good test here where Anil Kapoor wore a dhoti through out. He looked elegant and breathed life in the role of an illiterate yet well-off farmer who considers his step-mother the epitome of motherhood. Not able to see through the machinations of his crafty step mother he is almost killed when, putting aside his wife's timely advice he goes ahead and drinks medicine laced with poison. That becomes the turning point of this tale.

The success of 'Beta' won both Anil & Madhuri filmfare awards and cemented Madhuri Dixit's rise as the Queen Bee of Bombay.

As Anil Kapoor raced ahead, young lad Aamir Khan was distraught. What with Santoshi's' Andaz Apna Apna' lying indefinitely in the cans and the recent debacle of 'Daulat Ki Jung' and 'Afsana Pyar Ka'. Two big flops preceding his name, Aamir Khan was rightfully a worried man. In a career of 4 years since the iconic success of QSQT it was only 'Dil' and 'Dil Hai Ke Manta Nahin'which had suceeded. His debut director Mansoor Khan, for reasons unknown had gone in to hibernation for a few years. He soon returned with 'Jo Jeeta Wahi Sikander'giving hope to Aamir.

'Jo Jeeta Wahi Sikandar' was perhaps the first known attempt in making a film based on adolescence; the joys of desire and the pain of heartbreaks in a backdrop of senior schools where the protagonists are studying. Where adolescence is just being breached and seeking their first stepping stone in to adulthood. JJWS was a story where this emotion is the tipping point; where villainy blooms when rival boys covet the same girl; the dicey task of dealing with over bearing parents; where being cool is sharing a few puffs from a single fag by three friends. A phase always tricky at that age when barriers of parental dominance still beats down upon them and where the concept of hard work is yet to take root in these minds. JJWS tried to focus on that thin strand of life between the last days of adolesence and the budding beginnings of youth.

Territories with economical barriers are clearly demarcated: On one side is an elite school called 'Rajput' where children of affluent parents study and on the opposing side is 'Model School' where middle class children envy the opposite end. Aamir Khan, Ayesha Julka, Mamik Singh, Aditya Lakhia, Deven Bhojani formed the group from 'Model'. While Depak Tijory, Sooraj, Deb Mukherjee formed the team from 'Rajput'and Pooja Bedi played the role of one of the much chased girls from 'Queens college'. Jatin-Lalit's music sang the pangs and unsurety of the late teens; '*Chhaey tum kuch na kahon maine sun liya*', still has an inherent magic to coax your heart to beat a bit faster; whether you are young or old doesn't matter, it can still send you flying in to a rapturous mood. It was a gigantic love-note that shows up when you face those blues while baring your heart to your girl (or guy); no grades no class yet you find meaning in the clouds and '*zameen*'. When the boys sneak away from their morning assembly lines and share a fag amongst themselves by justifying " *jo sab karte hain yaaron woh kyon hum tum karein yunhi kasrat kartey kartey kaheko hum marein, gharwalon sey teacher sey bhala hum kyon darey,Yahan key hum Sikandar*" felt like a snippet from our teenage days.

The response to the film was good-from critics and Tier-A cities helping it win a Filmfare award in the 'Best Film category' but smaller towns gave it a thumb down making Aamir's wait a little longer. Its average success money wise, forced Aamir Khan to rethink his strategy of keeping more films in his bag.

While Aamir Khan the actor who catered mainly to young girls in the audience was trying to find a proper anchor to his career, old lover boy Rishi Kapoor, was in the midst of extending it through an editor-turned-director called David Dhawan who was holding up a script titled 'Bol Radha Bol'. David Dhawan had in his resume notched up names of average and below average films as a director. The first was 'Taaqatwar' which had Sunjay Dutt and Govinda and produced by actress Anita Raj's family. It was an average 'chalta hai' kind of film. However, his second film,'Aandhiyaan' proved to be the flop debut for Bengal star Prasenjit and old actress Mumtaz's failed comeback. David Dhawan also tried hands in directing a terrible film titled 'Gola Barood' which in critical parlance had actually 'crossed its expiry date'.

Rich producer Nitin Manmohan (old time villain Manmohan's son) who back in 1984 had launched Vinod Khanna's second innings found his favourite director Mukul Anand, unduly busy. Nitin found David Dhawan as an ideal replacement and he agreed to make him the captain of 'Bol Radha Bol'. As they say, this film succeeded in announcing David's entry with a loud bang.

Set in the vales of Ooty and foothills of Himachal, the film smelt of a Nasir Hussain thriller. Rishi Kapoor as a rich, 'young man' coming across a village belle 'Radha' (Juhi Chawla) carousing in his inimitable style with his 'dafli' on Hussain's template of the sixties was filled to its brim with songs, dance and comedy. The advantage of being Rishi Kapoor was that besides having a 'lover-boy's image he was also a music composer's delight; he not only emoted well but also put in a little twist and a few twirls. The story meets an exciting bend when the villain crops up in the form of his look-alike.

The biggest benefit from 'Bol Radha Bol' was derived by Rishi Kapoor. It was a massive lifeline for his career. 'Henna' was a prestigious film but not exactly a super hit; 'Bol Radha Bol' was just what the doctor ordered. In a double role to boot Rishi Kapoor vindicated that his 'lover boy' image still had some embers glowing. To further boost his career and prove that 'Bol Radha Bol' was no flash in the pan there followed another important release for Rishi Kapoor. Directed by rookie director Raj Kanwar and cast opposite a young actress called Divya Bharati, who was nearly half his age, that film was 'Deewana'.

The Third Khan

"Aisa Kya karoon tumhein yakeen aajaye ? Jaan dedoon ?---Raja

'Deewana' was a love triangle where the third angle was played by a new actor called Shah Rukh Khan. As was the trend, music by Nadeem-Shravan played a major factor in sustaining the success of most films. With 'Deewana' they were in their successive hat trick of pulling out unbelievably massive hits. It starred Rishi Kapoor as 'Ravi' and, it was to his credit that even after the 1980 'Karz', more than a decade later he was still able to pull off roles of a 'stage-singer'. In almost every film of his Rishi Kapoor had the ability to climb up a stage where a song could be inserted; *'Sochenge tumhein pyar karein key nahin'* in 'Deewana' was the last in his long list of films where he appeared on 'stage' in silvery whites and a colourful jacket. But the most subdued was the debut of Shah Rukh Khan as 'Raja'who appears only after the interval. The interested audience leaned forward to watch this new boy with brown skin, head covered with a thick mop of hair that almost kissed his eyelashes, and a pair of eyes whose hypnotic stare could enthrall a goddess. His introductory scene, in a jeans and white round neck tee, shows him biking around in Bombay mouthing *'Koi Na Koi Chahiye pyar karne wala'* sung by Vinod Rathod to become the first song of his career. Next was another melodious song *'Aisi Deewangee dekhi kahin nahin'* (Vinod Rathod again since Kumar Sanu was allotted to Rishi

Kapoor) where in a turquoise blue shirt, matching trousers and a deep dimple adorning his cheek serenaded with Divya Bharati firmly clasped around his waist, leaving a mark on the audience. Being a young man of twenty six or so he did come across as a logical suitor for the young, issueless widow. Even though post interval, her deceased husband Ravi reappears, the director makes him a martyr so that the young widow can find wedded bliss with Raja. The return of the middle aged Ravi did not draw sympathy and was rightfully bumped off in the climax. The ending where she goes off with the 'third angle' found acceptance with the audience. Analytically, this love triangle, pitted against an older star, may have actually helped Shah Rukh Khan to cement his debut. One film analyst while critically dissecting 'Deewana' observed that 'the most difficult part for a woman is sleeping with the first man and then falling in love with the second' therefore the death of Ravi gave an easy way out to the widow. 'Deewana' was a hit and Shah Rukh Khan, a complete outsider with no links with the industry had arrived.

As a logical step forward in furthering his career in the Mecca of hindi films Shah Rukh Khan, a theater actor from Delhi had migrated to Bombay with his young hindu wife Gauri. Even though 'Deewana' was his debut film but in the world of acting he was no rookie. He began with television serials starting with 'Circus' and later 'Fauji' under the tutelage of Aziz Mirza. The appreciation received after 'Deewana' made him sought after. The early birds were producer Hema Malini's directorial debut 'Dil Aashna Hain', Aziz Mirza's 'Kabhi Haan Kabhi Naa', Eagle Films Rajiv Mehra's

'Chamatkar', producer Shabnam Kapoor's ' English Babu Desi Mem', and Venus Records 'Baazigar'. But 'English Babu Desi Mem ' and 'Hema Malini's directorial debut did less than average business, where the only saving grace was ShahRukh's presence.

A similarly rooted man, Akshay Kumar, saw to his delight his film 'Khiladi' with rookie director duo Abbas-Mustan being well appreciated. It finally established Akshay Kumar as a 'lambi khiladi ' (long distance player) and the industry took notice of this director –duo who were always cloaked in scrubbed whites.

The music world was being knocked around under the baton of the musical duo Nadeem-Shravan. Old veterans like Laxmi-Pyare, Kalyanji-Anandji were into forced retirement, R.D.Burman had passed away and Bappi Lahiri had been sent packing. Among singers, Kishore Kumar had passed away while Asha and Lata Mangeshkar were never in the preferred list of singers for Nadeem- Shravan.The industry indeed was eating humble pie.

Early 1992, Mukul Anand's 'Khuda Gawah' had progressed to wards the finishing line.Enroute Sunjay Dutt had walked out citing 'personal differences' and was replaced by Nagarjuna, a popular actor from Telegu cinema.

Amitabh played 'Badshah Khan', a fiery Pathan from Kabul who is the chosen leader of his tribe. Truth and bravery are his hallmarks. The sport of hunting, known as 'Bazkhashi' in 'pashtun' is his passion. He is also in love with an equally fiery woman, 'Benazir' (Sridevi). After a great deal of bravado and chivalrous wooing, 'Badshah Khan' succeeds in sweeping 'Benazir' off her feet and the two get married.

The song *'Tu mujhe kubool mein tujhe kubool'* heralding their 'Nikaah' is a dazzling spectacle befitting a Pathan leader; resplendent with golden awnings, dancing girls, booming guns.

Post marriage some circumstances arise which compels 'Baadshah Khan' to leave for India. The scene where he is standing at the threshold of the Khyber -Pass is the stuff that creates legends:" *Sar- Zameen –e-Hindustan. As-Salaam-ale-kum Mera Naam Badshah Khan hain'*, raising his rifle and offering salutations in his heavy baritone voice, made us brace for more:

This is where the saga erupts and starts going deeper and deeper in to tragic overtones. The excitement wanes when the larger than life 'Baadshah Khan' who is supposedly an invincible warrior, is now reduced in to a grieving convict by the script. The film was mounted on a gigantic scale because of which 'Khuda Gawah' might have been termed as a hit. However, a larger loss in value could have been prevented if the director had pulled reins on a script that was tethering, between pride and a serious case of self-pity.

On this side of the 'Hindu Kush', the Yash Chopra directed 'Parampara' released. One of those rare films which he directed for an outside production. Produced by Firoz Nadiadwala of 'Paravarish' fame this one too, had an A-List casting.

Vinod Khanna, Sunil Dutt, Aamir Khan, Raveena Tandon,Ramya and a new star son-Saif Ali Khan, the son of Sharmila Tagore and former cricket captain Mansoor Pataudi.

The film became a victim of the proverbial 'All the king's men and the entire Kings' horses". It crashed like no one expected.

Even though it had a screen play by his son Aditya Chopra and direction by Yash Chopra the film proved to be a disaster.

Mahesh Bhatt by now had been totally commercialized. What mattered to him was the box office. After emptying the resonating heartbeats from his chest in the form of 'Arth', 'Naam' and 'Saaransh' the much in demand Bhatt started rehashing English hits; 'Sadak'from 'Taxi Driver' was a super hit. This emboldened him to plagiarize more. The Nastassia Kinski starrer 'Cat people' was made as 'Junoon' with Rahul Roy. But this terrible concoction could not be saved even by Nadeem-Shravan's music.

Just as Salim-Javed as story writers hogged the maximum limelight by the sheer presence of their names ensured an early booking by distributors, similar way Nadeem-Shravan and Gulshan Kumar were ruling the roost in 1992. Just then a small spark from the south lit up the vast Bollywood sky.

The film was 'Roja' by Mani Rathnam. It starred a Tamil hero Arvind Swamy and actress 'Madhoo, who had just peeped in to the world of hindi films vide the Ajay Devgan vehicle:'Phool aur Kaante'. The music was rendered by an unknown music director called A.R.Rahman. 'Roja' was termed as a film which churned the Tamil industry.It's maker Mani Rathnam had earlier stamped his mark through a very hard hitting 'Nayakan'; a biopic based on a Bombay gangster Vardharaj Mudaliar. Kamalhaasan played the title role and ' Nayakan' had become a cult film; It even went on to be India's entry to the Oscars. 'Roja' was technically and thematically very slick. The pangs of a young wife whose husband is kidnapped by Kashmiri militants resonated with the audience. Even the role of their leader (played by Pankaj Kapur) exudes fierceness laced with flashes of being benign..

In the past there were films made where terrorism was a factor. But 'Roja' perhaps was the first that focused on militancy arising from the Kashmir Valley. Even though 'Roja' was never shot in Kashmir, Mani Rathnam skillfully, under clouds of fog, converted Ooty in to a much believable 'Kashmir'.

Mani Rathnam's song picturisations brought in pure poetry to life. While one song *Dil Hai Chhota sa* encapsulated the essence of nature's bounty and the heart's desire to fly high, Mani let the camera potray the images playing in his mind: caressing gushing streams; the terrain glistening after being kissed by rains; a little girl playfully leaping around with the flame of a lamp glowing incandescently. The song *'Rukmini… Rukmini…'*.played out on their nuptial night is perhaps the only song danced with gusto by a group of septuagenarians!

The songs of 'Roja' melodious to their core had a great deal of differentiation from the ubiquitous fare being dished out by the gang led by T-Series.

Aamir Khan's next was called 'Daulat ki Jung' which was a sort of treasure hunt that did not find its' pot of gold'; The box office discarded this 'treaure hunt'. Shah Rukh Khan's 'Chamatkar' made by Eagle Films' top honcho Umesh Mehra (Jaal, Ashanti) had Urmila Matondkar opposite him. She had earlier been launched in N.Chandra's Sunny Deol starrer 'Narasimha'. Now she was opposite Shah Rukh Khan in 'Chamatkar'. For Urmila there were no dearth of 'breaks'; what she now badly needed was a Hit. 'Chamatkar' had melodious numbers by Annu Malik like the deeply romantic *"Yeh hai Pyar Pyar, yeh hai pyar pyar'*. It also had Naseeruddin Shah in a stellar role. But 'Chamatkar' (which translates as brilliance) could not weave it's 'brilliance' on the audience.

Having established themselves much earlier, the two senior Khans were in search for sustaining their Star status, while Shah Ruk Khan the 'Junior', had to toil more. While the two were cautious, the 'junior' didn't care much about 'sustainment'. He had been noticed in the TV serials 'Fauji' and 'Circus', so films was a logical path, and he had got on to it. He was content that his break was a hit. But lest he became a fading memory he too yearned for a 'biggie hit'.

On the sidelines, the 'Twins' who clothed themselves only in white and who gave Akshay Kumar his first hit in 'Khiladi' were now closeted in a meeting with the producer brothers of 'Khiladi',who also owned the Venus Records Company. They had a script in their hand whose title was 'Baazigar'.

Coincidentally, around the same time, Yash Chopra was toying with an idea of making a film that would be based on a triangular love story, but, the third angle would be 'Villainous' and this factor would be based on 'obsessive love'. Since Sridevi had scaled up big time she was interested only on projects focusing on her (by now she had begun to age and been gently nudged out by a youthful Madhuri Dixit was another matter) so Yash signed Juhi Chawla (who had earlier done a special appearance in his 'Chandni') with Sunny Deol and named it 'Darr'.

For the third angle-the obsessively inclined with maniacal undertones, he went for a lateral casting. He wanted to cast a conventional actor so offered it to Aamir Khan. The first Khan agreed and signed on the dotted line. Shooting commenced but after a few schedules he shocked Yash Chopra in adopting a complete retreat by returning the signing amount. He explained to a distraught Yash Chopra that his role was having undertones of a 'villain' and how it was 'risky' and would go against his image. He hurriedly left, leaving 'Darr' in the lurch. Shah Rukh Khan who had no qualms in doing any role grabbed it. In fact he considered himself lucky to be taken in a Yash Chopra film!

Six months later, during the festival of Diwali 1993, Abbas-Mustan's 'Baazigar' released. This film transformed the television actor in to a full-blooded film Star and the man entered the realm of Solo Hero films. Ironically though 'Baazigar' had him as a hero, his actions were more or less villainous. Five months after 'Baazigar', Yash Chopra's 'Darr' released to bumper biz. It was Sunny Deol's big hit after a prolonged gap. 'Darr' steadied Yash Raj films after the debacle of 'Lamhe'. But 'Darr' in its entirety belonged to this new blue eyed boy called Shah Rukh Khan. His stammering signature made him a craze, *"ka-ka-kiran"* entered in to the 'Hall of Famed' dialogues. Whenever the film entered in to the mandatory song and mushy romances, the stammering whisper *"ka-ka-kiran"* chilled the audience.

'Darr' was preceded by 'Baazigar',whose script was radically different from the usual vengeful sagas.

The story had a boy growing up with violent memories of his parents being duped by their business partner. The boy grows up swearing revenge and enters the treacherous man's life by befriending one of his two daughters (Shilpa Shetty); drawing her in to a one-sided love. Ensuring that he has her firmly in his entrapment, he orchestrates her cold blooded murder by cleverly disguising it as a 'suicide'. But in this dangerous game of entrapment he actually falls in love with her younger sister (Kajol Mukherje). As 'Ajay' and his alias 'Vicky Malhotra', Shah Ruk Khan was a hero whose brazen acts of villainy intersperses the film. His act of ruthlessly pushing off Anjali (Shilpa Shetty) from the ledge of a hi-rise, turned out to be a radical moment for the audience, when, a hero and a villain appeared conjoined; the line between good and bad appeared blurred and the outcome anarchic . But as the film progressed, their shocked numbness transformed into an astonishing excitement. The end of 'Ajay', who is torn between his oath of vengeance and his love for the daughter of his foe, was foregone. In mortal pain during its climax, Ajay (alias 'Vicky') mourns aloud the untimely demise of his love. But his victory is well surmised in those lines uttered much earlier in the film

Teen Sey Chhey

"haar ke jeetne waley ko Baazigar kehtey hain"

Shah Ruk Khan's unabashed performance as the remorseless killer, Kajol's acting filled with substance and Shilpa Shetty's fresh debut with Annu Malik finally blooming to infuse better-than-the –rest music serenaded 'Baazigar's success.

These two successes, in one swift stroke, pushed away long time contestants Sunny Deol, Jackie Shroff and Anil Kapoor. It also jolted the other two Khans.

Shah Ruk Khan further proved his prowess over his craft in his next release which was, conventionally, low budgeted when compared to his latest two: 'Baazigar'and 'Darr'. This one was made by theatre specialist Kundan Shah and named 'Kabhi Haan Kabhi Naa'. The story was about a boy called 'Sunil' (Shah Ruk) who is the proverbial underdog. He hates his studies; at best is average at worst he fails; hides his marks card; silently adores his neighbour's daughter Anna (Suchitra Krishnamurty) and resorts to lying when faced with competition from a smarter, dapper and much in demand rival-friend whose name is 'Chris' (Dipak Tijori).

'Sunil' is rightfully apprehensive because 'Chris' is the only son of rich parents, good in his studies and may also gain a good job. As the underdog 'Sunil', Shah Ruk Khan excelled in a role that reminded you of a besotted bunny.

The three laterally different roles: of the cold blooded 'Vicky', the demented 'Rahul' and the charming 'Sunil' turned the concept of heroes having 'Images'on its head. That year, history was created on the Filmfare awards podium when this Khan bagged two filmfare awards for both the characters: 'Vicky' the 'heroic villain' and 'Sunil' the underdog.

The rise of Shahruk Khan threw up a new era. Destiny, for a long time would fan the winds of good fortune to blow his way.

Yash Chopra's next production was a part of his extended projects where his protégé would hold his baton. Decades back Ramesh Talwar was his favoured protégé. But this time it was more business like where the Yash Chopra banner would bankroll the talents of known, talented hands and back them in their endeavours. His one time assistant Naresh Sharma brought out 'Yeh Dillagi'. This one had two unlikely heroes; Akshay Kumar, a tenacious man after 'Khiladi'and Saif Ali Khan who had a baggage of flop films. 'Yeh Dillagi' infused life in Saif. The young lad was better known for his flop debut and his untimely marriage to an ungainly woman years older to him. In the proverbial jungle, the pedigreed Saif Ali Khan was a little boy lost. Yash Chopra's 'Yeh Dillagi' was the oasis that gave him the recognition he deserved. Playing the role of a charming playboy, which came naturally, Saif impressed: the song *"jab bhi koi ladki dekhe..mera dil deewana boley Oley oley.."* heightening the effect.

Post 'Khuda Gawah', Amitabh Bachchan's charisma began to peer in to a giant window of wane. Going through a great deal of introspection and prodded by family and close friends he ventured as an entrepreneur. The thought formed in to a company based on his own name 'ABCL' (Amitabh Bachchan Corporation Limited). It was a business house headed by professional managers where they would dabble in the world of entertainment through many verticals: Films, Music and Events. With his name now lionized as 'BIGB', pumping his own money and borrowing huge loans from banks, the former 'Monarch of Bollywood' looked to even greater glory in his new innings under a corporate name

Underbelly

'Mujhe Duniya ka Sabse Bura Aadmi banna Hain'-- Ballu Balram

Films were earlier financed by businessmen and other deep pocketed sources who had a finger in every pie. In the seventies, the lure of glamour, glitz caught the fancy of smugglers like Haji Mastan. Corporates too funded films: there was one far back in 1960 when construction firm, Shapoorji Pallonjee's big bucks, bankrolled K.Asif's 'Mughal-e –Azam'. Down the decades many evolved, like Kishore Biyani-founder of 'Big Bazaar'; Bharat Shah a diamond trader.

It was more pronounced during the nineties when it was observed that the underworld was finding ways to penetrate the film world. They were present very strongly in real estate and match-fixing-betting. Shadow boxing was evident in the whispers concerning many films where the trail led to Dubai. After the flight of Don Dawood Ibrahim to Dubai, many actors, directors, actresses, starlets, producers hobnobbed at lavish parties thrown open by him. Chartered flights used to be arranged where entire plane loads from the fraternity flew across to entertain him and his ilk. It was a quid pro quo. For this adulation, the fugitive'Don', it appears, laundered money and bankrolled several film productions. An actress whom he coveted (Mandakini of 'Ram Teri Ganga Maili) even became his concubine. Bombay wined, dined, and danced with him.

Thankfully, the established and known film makers avoided him like the plague. But many did succumb to his overtures which led to an unwanted rash of cacophonic movies. In their bid to outdo the other only led to all tripping over each other leading to a long list of instantaneous failures. Unheard 'exponents 'of films sprouted, who apparently, were frontmen of the tainted.

A huge bubble took shape in the form of multi releases every Friday. Films like 'Dil Ka Kya Kasoor' starring Prithvi & Divya Bharti, 'Jaan Tere Naam' starring Ronit Roy and Farheen, and 'Milan' starring Jackie Shroff & Manisha Koirala,failed to be a success. If at all, they earned wee bit of money and presence, it was solely on tainted finance from unknown sources and pure music by Nadeem-Shravan.

The rot soon surfaced when Hanif Kadawala and Samir Hingora, two ambitious partner brothers who were rumoured to be frontmen, opened a video film house called 'Magnum Video'.This company was in the lucrative business of buying the video rights of films and reproducing them through video cassettes that could be legally bought and watched in the comfort of homes. The concept was excellent and in line with the times. Every middle class household had a VCR and multichannels on TV was still at a nascent stage. (those days only Zee and DD produced content). Their next foray was film production which was a logical step. They launched a project called 'Sahibaan'. It had a star cast of Sunjay Dutt and Manisha Koirala. Sunjay Dutt fresh from the super success of 'Saajan' and Manisha Koirala just blooming after the release of 'Saudagar' were prized assets.Distributors were willing to lap up this project at any price. The brothers were now on a huge high.

But soon after, a terrifying incident happened that rocked not only Bombay but the entire country. Unfortunately, the bedrock was Bollywood.

On Friday 12th March, 1993, a day usually slotted for filmi duels, instead, a dastardly event occurred. The capital of Hindi film industry, Bombay, was quaked by twelve consecutive bombings that went off in the span of an hour. Two hundred fifty seven were killed and thousands maimed. The trails led to several clues and one of them reached the producer duo of Hanif-Samir. An intensive interrogation with them further led the cops to a shocking find: actor Sunjay Dutt.

Subhash Ghai, the man who launched many faces, was now well known as 'The Showman'. A decade ago, after directing 'Vidhata' for Gulshan Rai's Trimurti Films', he had sworn to keep away from Sunjay Dutt. He had been so harangued by Sunjay Dutt's drug induced behaviour, that the ordeal prodded him to cast an 'outsider' in his 1984 hit "Hero'. After several successes down the years he made 'Hero' which lacked star power, yet with it's inherent strengths of sincere performances and stupendous music stretched way across a superlative 'Silver Jubilee'run. Then came 'Karma'where the film- making-entrepreneur brought up a multi star cast. The patrioitism laced 'Karma' paved the way for'Ram Lakhan'which was a conflict of brotherhoods having their own take on tackling oppression and inequalities. The next resounding success was 'Saudagar', where the casting overshadowed its script. Going forward with his profitable alliance with Dilip Kumar he managed a coup by getting the reclusive and eternally temperamental Raj Kumar to act alongside him. His next one, again, focused on ensnaring another casting coup and the catch this time was Amitabh Bachchan, to star in a supposedly ambitious film titled 'Devaa'. After a few shoots, the 'Bofors' scandal erupted to engulf the country and this according to Ghai, seemed to 'singe' Amitabh's reputation. Subhash Ghai, immediately cited 'creative differences' and to the disappointment of the entire country, shelved this mighty project.

Few years later Subhash Ghai, decided to eat humble pie, and as a fair-weather maker ignored his earlier vow. He did the unthinkable - he went ahead and signed Sunjay Dutt for the role of 'Ballu' in his magnum- 'Khalnaayak'. But then on hindsight, since he wanted to make a big film with a top A-Listed cast, Sunjay Dutt indeed was an obvious choice. Not only was he a big star, he had also got rid of his junkie demons.

However, by washing his hands off by shelving 'Devaa', in this case, Subhash Ghai could not abort a fully developed baby on verge of delivery. On the eve of 'Khalnayak's release his leading man was facing pointed fingers where his patriotism was being questioned. Posters of the film were being garlanded by strings of footwear making distributors brace for 'sudden death'. But that fear soon took the form of a double edged sword: one side was a catastrophe owing to this huge trust deficit, the other side it ballooned in to a huge curiosity factor. In the end even though Sanjay Dutt was incarcerated in to spending his time in a notorious cell in side Bombay's Arthur Road jail, 'Khalnayak's march towards prosperity went unhindered !

The public enjoyed 'Khalnayak' but remained puzzled and started debating over Sanjay Dutt's actual role, if any, innocent or framed, in the conspiracy to blow up the city. As they questioned their own sensibilities, Nana Patekar the crusader from 'Ankush' and the fiend of 'Parinda' galloped in as a 'hero'in 'Krantiveer'.

Its maker Mehul Kumar was an average filmmaker. After being known as maker of several Gujrathi films, he later crossed over to Hindi and earned recognition through his hit 'Marte Dum Tak' starring Raj Kumar-Govinda-Farha. In the case of Nana Patekar, as 'Annaseth', the 1989 'Parinda' had bracketed him, rather firmly, as a villain. But the memories of 'Ankush were not yet distant from public memory and the versatility within him refused to remain strait-jacketed. 'Krantiveer' strengthened the possibility of Nana Patekar standing tall as a main hero. The film belonged to him and so was its success. No surprises that it bagged him a FilmFare award in the Best Actor category that year.

On the other side the '2nd Khan' of the new age (Salman Khan) had a terrible release called 'Chandramukhi'. A story, whose 'idea' is credited to Salman Khan, seemingly appeared to be a period film. The budget appeared big since it had Sridevi as the heroine and various special effects. But like his similarly delayed film 'Andaz Apna Apna, 'Chandramukhi' too had dragged towards indefinite deadlines making the period film look jaded, tired and stoned. 'Chandramukhi' released and immediately burnt its distributors to cinder. The brand equity of Salman Khan which was few notches upgraded by the unexpected success of the average-budgeted 'Sanam Bewafa' was lost. As in the famed game of 'Snakes & Ladders' Salman Khan badly needed a rung to hold onto.

Mahesh Bhatt, nothwithstanding the failure of 'Satwaan Aasman', this time came around with a kind of a rescue act which was reminiscent of him a decade back when he made 'Naam'. This time he did it for himself and the '1st Khan' – Aamir, who was stuck in a quick sand of failures. Seven years back Bhatt had whipped up his magic to rescue Sunjay, the "Deadly Dutt" (this nickname was earned after he got a new hair-style, gained star status and conjoined with several link-ups). This time he rescued Aamir in the actor's home production: 'Hum Hain Rahi Pyar Ke'. Produced by Aamir's father Tahir Hussain who had given lifeline hits earlier to Jeetendra, in the gypsy tale 'Caravan' and to Rekha in a well made thriller called'Locket'. Two years back Aamir's uncle's 'JoJeetaWahiSikandar" directed by his first cousin, Mansoor Khan, had actually failed the acid test of all film makers: in leaping across the hurdle called 'box-office'.

'Hum Hain Raahi Pyar Key' had a story as pure as a rippling stream. A young man Rahul(Aamir) is coming to terms with the loss of his older brother and 'bhabhi' in an accident where by default the responsibility of their children comes to him. To add to his woes he has to fast track a shipment of many thousand garments to clear a debt, or, as per terms, consent to get married to the lender's (Dalip Tahil) only daughter whom he loathes (actress Navneet Nishan).

In walks a runaway girl 'Vyjayanthi' (Juhi Chawla) who sneaks in his house helped by the three orphans. What then follows is an uproariously funny series of anecdotes that tickles the audience repeatedly. But the film has its moments of seriousness where 'Vyjayanthi' actually falls in love with Ravi (Aamir).

Prior to 'Hum Hain Raahi Pyar Key,' both, Aamir & Mahesh Bhatt were weighed down by flops. Bhatt's 'Satwaan Aasman', and the big budget 'Gumraah' with Sunjay Dutt and Sridevi were unsuccessful. His much touted but less feted telefilm, 'Phir Teri Kahani Yaad Aayi' was boringly damp.'Hum Hain Raahi Pyar Ke' was mostly, a 'shining knight' for him as much it was for the 1st Khan.

In the middle of this fourth year of the nineties, the first Khan heaved a sigh of relief after the much needed success in 'Hum Hain Raahi Pyar Ke'.

The second Khan,Salman, had thundered in with the refreshingly large 'Hum Aapke Hain Koun', the third, Shah Ruk,was rejoicing in the reality of having gained a robust foothold in Bombay.

Madhuri Dixit too reached the pinnacle of her stardom. After the chart-buster 'Saajan', 'Hum Aapke Hain Kaun' was the second big hit from this pair. It redefined collections in every city, town and village where all erupted to *Didi Tera Devar Deewana*'. For the Barjatyas it was a vindication that their son's 'Maine Pyar Kiya' was no fluke. So confident were they of this success that they had pre-booked the leading twin theatres in Bombay: Liberty & Liberty Deluxe. Every household endeared. The critics assailed it with their sarcastic jibes of being 'the longest ad for a toothpaste'.Whatever little negativity floated in the forms of such silly barbs was lost in the deafening din of success.

The Elders: Dharmendra, Jeetendra, Shatrughan Sinha were still 'kicking' around. They, or rather, certain breed of filmmakers refused to give them a farewell; result being a huge tranche of headache inducing films like 'Aazmaish, Janam Kundli, Paapi Devatha, Policewala Goonda, list is long. Ditto for Mithun Chakraborty, Jackie Shroff, Sunny Deol, Anil Kapoor. Even so for new stars like Sunil Shetty and Akshay Kumar. Anil Kapoor's prospects got badly hit due to colossal flops like 'Roop Ki Rani Choron Ka Raja' and the unexpected dismal show by Rakesh Roshan's 'Khel'.

"Ek-do-teen-char... Anil no longer superstar"; this was the refrain that summed up Anil's low point. The path of stardom for Anil Kapoor had suddenly zigzagged in to desolateness. Few years back he was close to be crowned the Numero Uno. But big flops by invincible film makers ruined his chances; Rakesh Roshan's 'Khel', D.Rama Naidu's 'Jamai Raja', Yash Chopra's 'Lamhe' and Prakash Mehra's 'Zindagi Ek Jua'. Yes, in between there was 'Beta', a grand success that earned a lot of money for its makers and even won a Filmfare award for Anil. But this solitary success was swamped under the weight of the Satish Kaushik directed 'Roop Ki Rani Choron Ka Raja' (trumpeted as an Indian version of a successful English film called'The Duchess & the Dirtwater Fox).

But in the early spring of 1994 came Vidhu Vinod Chopra's '1942 a Love Story'. Four years ago his 'Parinda' with a tag line of ' The most powerful film ever made' had a terrific opening. But in the ensuing four years Anil Kapoor's value had thinned. This new release called '1942- A Love Story' promised to make a correction.

The film used the 'Quit India' movement of 1942 as its backdrop. It delved in to the love story between the daughter of a freedom fighter and a young man, who have remained largely untouched by the freedom struggle engulfing the quaint hilly town of Kasauni in the foothills of the Himalayas. Anupam Kher played the freedom fighter who is known as a' teacher' to the outside world. He comes to Kasauni alongwith his pretty daughter Rajjo (Manisha Koirala) ostensibly to nurse an ailment. But the real plan, known only to a select few, is to assassinate a British general, who is due to arrive at Kasauni in a few weeks. With Rajjo unaware of these plans, she is instead swept away by the charm of the picturesque Kasauni and falls in love with Naren (Anil Kapoor)

With story credited partially to Sanjay Leela Bhansali, the first half is like being caressed by the gentle gaze of a poet. Terraced hill ridges, colourful glades, misty mornings, throbbing rivers and foamy waterfalls come alive under a blue sky, resonating with the infectious laughter of 'Rajjo'. Javed Akhtar's lyrics and late R.D.Burman's compositions picturised on 'Naren' equating his love to "the eternity in the fragrance of sandal, the piety of conch blowing in a temple,like the exotic blooming of a rose, like a deer in search of an elusive fragrance, like a poet's dream' and many such exquisite metaphors set in motion the giant wheels of audience expectations..

Unfortunately, after the interval the focus moves away from 'Rajjo' and 'Naren' and shifts to 'Shubhankar'(Jackie Shroff) the revolutionary who has come to assist his master (Anupam Kher). Suddenly, events become dangerously volatile. This pushes away their love to the back-burner. The second half which focused more on the conspiratorial events lacked the creativity of the first-half, turning this promising outing in to an average performer.

The decay of high expectations had also started roosting inside theatres. Seats chewed away by rats with their inner fillings made of coconut coir hanging loose, dirty urinals whose stink wafted in to 'Rear Stalls' to rise up to the 'Balcony'. Lesser revenues from flop shows were keeping the proprietors of such theatres tight fisted. They were resigned to their fate who believed that this slide would remain forever. But unknown to them an edifice in the form of India's first mall was being drawn out near Bombay's sea-front that would soon revolutionize the experience of watching movies.

Govinda continued his insignificant run through loud films, like 'Rock Dancer' (produced by the cacophonic Bappi Lahiri) This one had an item number performed by the busty Samantha Fox where Govinda danced to laughably ridiculous lyrics: "*You are my chicken fry you are my fish fry, kabhi Na kehna*

Kudiye bye-Bye' ! Another in the same league was 'Gambler' where he jostled to unimaginative moves to a rap-style song:

'Madhuri Dixit mili Rastey mein khaaye chaney hum sastey mein "

But very soon David Dhawan, who had earlier brought back Rishi Kapoor from the brink of extinction with 'Bol Radha Bol', life jacketed Govinda in 'Coolie No 1' With this Govinda discovered a new talent; flair for comedy. David Dhawan continued his rosy streak with Govinda and both successfully rolled out films with the suffix: "No 1"

Epoch Moment

'23 years of Raj & Simran'--poster put up at 'Maratha Mandir' theater, Mumbai.

As the year was turning out to be a dampener, all eyes were now on Yash Chopra. The occasion was a soon to be an epoch moment for him and his banner - his son Aditya was being launched as a director in their new offering titled 'Dilwale Dulhaniya Lejayenge'. It was not only a huge important test for Aditya but also for Shahruk Khan. His recent releases like 'Guddu', and 'Ram Jaane' released a few weeks back were torn apart by the public. Fortunately for him, this came at the right moment proving to be a serendipitous success and joy for its maker and performers. Its title was similar to a song from the 1974 Shashi Kapoor starrer 'Chor Machaye Shor'. Switzerland, which until then, was revealed by Yash Chopra in bits and parts, was captured full blast by his son : Eurail travels, car sojourns, zipping along the Alps, picture perfect station-side curio-shops, jingling cow-bells, and a chilly 'rum-soaked' night inside a swiss barn.

Trailing his beloved, all the way from one end of the world to 'mustard-flowered' fields of Punjab, the young 'dilwale'-the NRI Raj, who infiltrates to scuttle the impending wedding celebrations masquerading as an 'investor', who also keeps parrying inquisitive queries soon realizes that his task of whisking away his 'dulhaniya' is stuck deeper underground because of a naughty prank he had played on the girl's father.

In the end, his persistence pays off.

It rose to be the biggest success from Yash Raj banner and Aditya Chopra's advent brimmed with promise for the future. For trivia, it had a very young Karan Johar probably in his early twenties, playing Raj's friend who keeps getting rapped on his head. In a long innings, destined for the 3rd Khan in enthralling movie buffs- 'Dilwale Dulhaniya Le Jayenge' or its short-formed 'DDLJ',proved to be the spearhead. It's success at that time was so prevailing that it brushed aside Shah Ruk's dismal flops which happened a few weeks earlier in the form of Prem Lalwani's'Guddu', Eagle Films' 'Ram Jaane', Ketan Mehta's 'Oh Darling Yeh hain India' and Ramesh Sippy's 'Zamana Deewana'. In fact, the failure of 'Zamana Deewana' effectively scotched any further attempts by makers of the iconic 'Sholay', in nursing any more comebacks.

On the sidelines, Rajkumar Santoshi's ambitious 'Andaz Apna Apna' finally broke through its womb and released. The phenomenon of films getting warped up indefinitely were many; There was Shekhar Kapur's ambitious 'Joshilay' and an old Salim-Javed leftover called 'Zamana' but with four years being in limbo 'Andaz Apna Apna' lagged the longest. Continuity in the film was affected and it showed; Adjacent theatres showing 'Hum Aapke Hain Kaun' had Prem (Salman Khan) in a crew cut while 'Andaz Apna Apna' had him (also as Prem) with lustruously long hair in some scenes and crew cuts in others.

At the time of its release it was panned by critics and given a cold shoulder by the audience; For good reasons they perhaps found its humour loud and bordering too much on slapstick. A delay of four years had also harmed its continuity and curiosity factor.

'Amar' (Aamir Khan) and 'Prem' (Salman Khan) are two young boys who come from lower-middle class families. They are the epitome of good-for-nothings living off their father's frugal earnings. They also dream of becoming millionaires and gain a rich lifestyle through a 'quick-fix way'.

'Amar' is the son of Murli, a barber (Deven Varma) and 'Prem' the son of a tailor Bankelal Bhopali (Jagdeep). Amar keeps pinching money from his father's cash-counter to keep pace with fashion trends such as getting an expensive 'french-styled 'haircut at a suburban 5-star hotel. Prem an aspiring actor conducts a photo shoot for himself by hiring photographer 'Johnny' (Mehmood) at his studio called 'Wah –Wah-Productions':The name 'Wah-Wah Productions' is a throwback from one of Mehmood's earlier belly-aching laugh riot called 'Pyar Kiye Jaa' where Mehmood had teamed up with actor-singer Kishore Kumar. Through the photo-shoot Johnny has promised Prem to get him a 'launch' in films provided he can arrange some hard cash. To ensnare Prem, Johnny makes his assistant call him on his phone from an adjacent public booth and pretends that it is a call from film maker Subhash Ghai. The gullible Prem is sold on this idea and surreptiously sells his father's house (who is out on a 'tirath yatra') and gives the cash to Johnny. Incidentally at the same time, newspapers announce the arrival of a rich heiress

Raveena(Raveena Tandon) from England accompanied by her assistant Karishma(Karishma Kapoor), yes, their real names was also their screen names, who on the instructions of her millionaire father Mr Bajaj (Paresh Rawal) is on a visit to India presumably in search of a groom. The news is read by both – Amar & Prem and both set out to win her hand, as gold diggers.

The rest is about the two boys who use their silver tongue to get out of rough patches, impress the heiress and try to win her hand with their bumbling yarns. The tickle felt by the audience was not about those yarns but the terrific confidence the duo displayed in uttering them.

Amar the bully gets the better of Prem and in this race to gain the hand of the heiress Amar appears to be the hare but in the end it is Prem who, to Amar's shock, wins the right girl making Amar realize rather late that he had been cosying up to the wrong one.

Even though, it had old, worn out comedians like Mehmood and Jagdeep, their cult value was still intact. Mehmood during his heydays used to end up overshadowing the leading men of his times, while Jagdeep was publicly crowned by Mehmood as his successor. The others too contributed in no less measures; Paresh Rawal in a double role as the millionare Ram Bajaj who makes his aspersions on the boys clear when he says " *tumhare naam Amar aur Prem kisi ghatiya film ka naam lagta hain*" and his notorious twin brother Shyam Bajaj alias 'Tejaa' who wants to hoodwink him of his diamonds and use it as capital to open a 'one-stop' shop of poultry and bakery products under the following tagline : *"Bread ka Raaja aur Omlette ka baadshah: Bajaj-hamaaaraa bajaj"*; his henchmen Bhalla (old actor Ajith's son) who is perenially devising a goofy plan to impress his master and, eyeing them all from the sidelines is 'Crime Master GoGo' (Shakti Kapoor) who claims to belong to a lineage of erstwhile thieves that traces its bloodline to Mogambo (the Despot of 'Mr India').

The film was an average performer in 1994. Strangely, two and a half decades later it has seen several re- runs and emerged as a cult film. One of the reasons could be that in today's times when the two have gained an armour of impregnability around them, the joy of watching the two partnering in laughably silly antics, and people realizing that an 'Andaz Apna Apna' can never occur again, has created a repeat audience in today's generation.

The next year also saw some star sons and some Hollywood influences. The Deol family's second scion Bobby Deol's launch vehicle 'Barsaat' was being chiseled by their blue eyed boy Raj Kumar Santoshi and the girl opposite Bobby was Twinkle Khanna, daughter of ' ex –superstar' Rajesh Khanna and former 'mermaid' Dimple Kapadia. The second was Boney Kapoor, shadow king maker of the successful Anil Kapoor, who chalked out a similar start for his youngest brother Sanjay Kapoor; The film was 'Prem' introducing him and Tabu, (actress farha's younger sister introduced earlier as an adolescent by Dev Anand in 'Hum Naujawan').'Prem' was originally visualized as a big budget, blue blooded release with Shekhar Kapur as its director, Javed Akhtar as its writer and deep pockets producer Boney as its maker.

But then, as was his wont, Shekhar Kapur started distancing himself, letting this film like the promising 'Joshilay' earlier to drift away in to a dark valley. To salvage the project in came Boney's trusted man, director Satish Kaushik. He was a conscientious employee and gathered all his creativity to do a good job for his master. But this untimely resuscitation failed to revive 'Prem'. Sanjay Kapoor never really recovered after this.

'Barsaat' had all the potential to be a big hit but turned out to be an average runner. This was a major setback for Santoshi whose recent 'Andaz Apna Apna' also had failed. Rumours of Santoshi feeling suffocated in the company of the Deol clan was also swirling around which perhaps curbed his creative juices to flow in to 'Barsaat'. Even though an average performer, its lead players Bobby Deol & Twinkle Khanna, having the advantage of blue blooded surnames did manage to shrug off the luke warm response to their debut film. Bobby got an extended headstart by signing up big ticket deals like Venus Productions' 'Soldier' while some thronged at Twinkle to sign her up for their future projects opposite the 'Three Khans' and Akshay 'Khiladi' Kumar.

On the other hand, Sanjay Kapoor who was staring down helplessness post 'Prem' got some sweet moments of sunshine when he bagged Ashok Thakeria-Indra Kumar (makers of Dil, Beta, Kasam) new project called 'Raja'. Backed by two big factors of success in those days, Nadeem-Shravan, (they lifted an evergreen tune for this from the Rock Hudson-Gina Lollobrigida starrer 'Come September') and Madhuri Dixit,

Sanjay Kapoor could not have asked for more. 'Raja' was a hit but Lady Luck had favoured 'Raja' and not Sanjay.

In the midst of all came few remakes based on English hits. The first was 'Kramer Vs Kramer' remade as 'Akele Hum Akeley Tum' by Mansoor Khan and had Aamir Khan & Manisha Koirala. The second was Robert Redford-Demi Moore starrer 'Indecent Proposal' made in to a college romance called 'Sauda'. The third were a rash of films based on the Julia Roberts starrer 'Sleeping with the Enemy': The first in the list of plagiarized versions was 'Yaarana' which had Rishi Kapoor-Madhuri Dixit-Raj Babbar who played the three protagonists as shown in 'Sleeping with the Enemy'. The second was the Abbas-Mustan directed flick which again had Rishi Kapoor and Juhi Chawla as the abused wife where Salman Khan's younger brother Arbaaz Khan played her villainous husband. The third, was a production made by the famed Thackeray clan of Bombay (Bal Thackeray's son produced it) starring Jackie Shroff and Manisha Koirala as the married couple in bliss and Nana Patekar as the husband from her past.

Box office verdicts for 'Yaarana' was dismal, 'Daraar' average while 'Agnisakshi' a hit.

'Yaarana' tried to do too many things; It tried to flog Rishi Kapoor's just ressurected second innings post 'Deewana'; recreate the *Ek Do teen* magic from 'Tezaab' by installing *Mera Piya Ghar aaya O Ramjee* where Madhuri Dixit twists and twirls upon a thronging audience while Raj Babbar, as the oppressive husband, was ineffective in striking terror. In

'Darrar', the young debutant Arbaz Khan played the haughty husband suffering from 'ocd' who stole the show from the ageing Rishi Kapoor. In 'Agnisakshi', Nana Patekar whose forte lay in enacting roles filled with fear and dread, instilled terror in 'Madhu'his wife which aroused sufficient interest in the audience, turning this one a hit.

But the chief patron that year was certainly the success of the 'Double- Khan' starrer: Salman Khan and Shah Rukh Khan in Rakesh Roshan's 'Karan Arjun' It was the first project which brought both together. Rakesh Roshan had this uncanny knack of looking in to the crystal ball. This time he brought out a screen play based on the reincarnation theme, then weaving a revenge story around it in which two brothers (Karan & Arjun) are killed and are reborn to return and avenge their deaths. Metaphorically the names sounded an unlikely union between two brothers; the names are actually sworn foes from the epic 'Mahabaharata'. The story had Rakesh Roshan's slick treatment jack-booting its way to commercial glory. The Shah Ruk- Kajol pair brilliantly replaced the 'Jodi' of Anil-Madhuri. Mamta Kulkarni, a perpetual starlet and heroine in waiting finally gained stardom by being Salman's girl in this one. While Salman Khan, who was overshadowed by Madhuri Dixit's impishness in 'HumAapkeHainKaun' and darkened by the lack lustre performance of ''AndazApnaApna' finally found true solace here. He also managed what was thought unassailable; as Karan,in the epic 'Mahabharata', he overshadowed the mortal Arjun (Shah Ruk Khan).

After the flop of Aamir Khan's take on 'Kramer-vs-Kramer' in the badly made 'Akele Hum Akele Tum',these two Khans gave a lot to cheer.

Exactly a year back, the second Khan had inked his prowess in the big success called 'Hum Aapke Hain Kaun'. The third had lighted up the skyline with 'Dil Wale Dulhaniya Le Jayenge'.

It was now high time for the first to let out his cry of triumph. Which he did through the colourful 'Rangeela'.

Ram Gopal Verma, the diminutive guy from the south had carved out a niche for himself through a film called 'Shiva'. It had violence as its content in the backdrop of college campuses and their control by local politicians. 'Shiva' had given a more telling and graphic version of the youth being used by politicians, than the 1986 hit 'Arjun' which had Sunny Deol. He later made 'Raat' based on the horror genre, which was thankfully, not the kind developed by the Ramsay brothers. In fact 'Raat' was rightfully expressed by writer Avijit Ghosh as ' a smartly crafted supernatural'. His next was ' Rangeela', a love story with comic and dramatic moments intwerwoven through out.

If 'Prem (Salman Khan) was the goodie goodie 'devar-beta-bhai'living in a 'bhartiya' joint family then Shah Ruk Khan's 'Raj' brought in the pangs of growing up as a motherless child of an NRI millionaire. As Munna in 'Rangeela' Aamir Khan eptomized the ubiquitous 'Bumbai ka Tapori' who has grown up as an orphan and takes life one day at a time. 'Rangeela' was important for all concerned. This was Verma's first attempt in making a film in the comedy genre. It was also

A.R.Rahman's debut in to hindi film dom. Urmila Matondkar who had literally been shown the door due to her two releases 'Narsimha' and 'Chamatkar', this was a do or die window for her to bag a hit.

'Munna' (Aamir Khan) is a local 'tapori'. 'Tapori' in Bombay lingo means an uneducated kind of harmless ruffian who does odd jobs for a living. 'Mili' (Urmila Matondkar) is an aspiring actress who lives in the same locality. She works as an 'extra' in film shoots and dreams of making it big in the Industry. 'Kamal' (Jackie Shroff) is a big film star who tragically is a loner because he had lost his beloved in an accident. Munna loves Mili but always fails to enlighten her about this fact.

One day, the shoot of 'Kamal's' film comes to a halt because the leading lady has eloped with her driver. Coincidentally, 'Kamal' happens to watch 'Mili's' early morning workout regime on the beach. Impressed by her looks, and rhythmic agility he recommends her to his producer (Avtar Gill). Mili gets the role and transforms in to a rising star. 'Munna' is happy for her success but is now hesitant to clearly express his feelings for her as he feels, in the current scenario, 'Kamal' should be her rightfull suitor. After some minor heart-aches, tears songs, Munna and Mili are united.

'Rangeela' was a thorough treat. The screenplay, dialogues, music, made it feel less of comedy and more of a happy film. Manish Malhotra's costumes accentuated her flawless figure while the camera caressed Urmila's elfin charm to almost redefining the way heroines should be. The music by A.R.Rahman made people wake up to a world beyond

Nadeem and Shravan. After a long time, Asha Bhosle crooned her best: the zestful *"Rangeelaa reyyyy"* took us back to her *'Dum Maro Dum'* era. Dialogues hammered to perfection by Aamir in matching situations drew laughter from the aisles endearing 'Munna' & 'Mili' to the audience.

The film also mirrored the disorderly ways of working schedules in film studios.

'Colourful Scenes':

- The producer(Avtar Gill) sermonizing his director Steven Kapur(Gulshan Grover) that an 'Item' number is a necessary ingredient for the success of any film; he cites 'Tezaab' and 'Khalnayak' to back his argument.

- The producer thinks it is necessary to bend over backwards to amuse the mother of his heroine, which actually alluded to age old gossip of film lore, when heroines were managed and chaperoned by their mothers (film magazines were agog those days about the heroine-mother chaperoning like Neetu-Mrs Singh, Hema-Mrs Chakravorty, Sridevi-Mrs Rajeshwari, Zeenat Aman-Mrs Heinz))

- Munna selling tickets in black outside a suburban theater. When the customer insists his preference for "two corner tickets', he retorts: "sure, one from one corner the other from the other corner ".

- Munna resting his legs on an aisle seat. When the man objects Munna rebukes " *tu pair dekne aaya hai ya picture* ? (you are watching the film or my feet?)

The film bagged Fimfare awards for Jackie Shroff and A.R Rahman but the best actor category was awarded to the character of 'Raj' (ShahRukKhan in DDLJ) leading to a self imposed ban by Aamir Khan on himself, from attending any award functions.

Dark Queen

*"Haan Mein Phoolan hoon behen#$%!*d"*-Phoolan Devi

As the people were savouring the mischievous dialogues of 'Rangeela' they were jolted by a Shekhar Kapur directed film which was based on the pathetic life of Phoolan Devi. The film was 'Bandit Queen' and the result: a highly toxic content spewed in the name of entertainment, by a seemingly delighted film maker, who had impressed us with 'Masoom' and 'Mr India'.

The story of 'Bandit Queen' was based on the life of Phoolan Devi, who had gained notoriety during the eighties when she and her gang, lined up twenty four men against a wall and gunned them down in a village called Behmai in Uttar Pradesh.

Shekhar Kapur's direction laid bare the reality of the caste system in Uttar Pradesh; India's largest state. The happenings make a mockery of the Indian Constitution and its principles. Murders, coercions and rapes flourish under deep rooted caste barriers. 'Bandit Queen' was a stark and dark visitation by a film maker in giving us the other side of the Chambal Valley. It depicted the inhumanity meted out to low caste people where a gun is the only refuge for survival. The painful journey of Phoolan (Seema Biswas) from the tender age of ten to middle age is full of torment: rape being the prime factor. She is married off at pre-pubescent girlhood to be raped by a husband double her age and discarded, then lusted by the 'high-caste' neighbor hood boys and beaten black and blue by them for trying to ward off their advances. She is later abducted by a dacoit and raped and then again-gang raped by a group of 'thakurs' of Behmai, turning the shaky, timid Phoolan into a foul-mouthed dacoit, tingling for revenge,leading to the vengeful massacre towards the end.

So, what troubled us? Those endless cuss-words that made us miserable, profane barbs from the 'thakurs' to Phoolan; the marriage of a ten year old Phoolan and its immediate consummation. Then came the scene where dacoit 'Babu Gujjar (Aniruddh Agarwal) repeatedly penetrates Phoolan in full view of his gang in an unpalatable rape scene--making us wonder which period in India was the worst? Pre or post-independence?

What relieved us? It was the brilliant cinematography by veteran Ashok Mehta which made us forget the violence by framing many magical moments; those long boats ferrying people across sand banks on shallow sides of the Chambal; the pathos of those who aspire for a square meal and a roof, those long walks by Phoolan along rail-tracks with her uncle chatting away; the pealing laughter of little Phoolan and her friends playfully splashing in the Chambal waters and, the soulful music by Nusrat Fateh that caressed all of Ashok's work.

To give the devil his due, Shekhar did infuse the film with fine creative strokes of his genius. For argument's sake, as Shekhar justified in an interview, remarked "remove the rape scenes and you lose the fury of Phoolan". But for a viewer, a certain threshold exists between artistry and gros. For the viewers, it was akin to conducting a medical surgery without administering anesthesia.Nonetheless 'Bandit Queen' bagged several awards. It got Shekhar Kapur two FilmFare awards but this proved to be his last stint in India. With a new wife in tow, he migrated to England to fufil his cherished dream of entering Hollywood. While one left for greener pastures, his friend Anil Kapoor still loitered around to regain his stardom through two under productions. The first was a south production 'Mr Bechara' where Anil Kapoor aped the styles of Raj Kapoor and the emotive style was borrowed from Kamalhaasan's 1982 film 'Sadma'. The second was a medieval styled 'prince-princess' fantasy film called 'Raj Kumar'

'Mr Bechara' looked good on paper. It had Sridevi as his heroine, and a large element of 'amnesia'. Even though the film was well made with Anil Kapoor adopting the Raj Kapoor style amalgamating with his 'Mr India' fervor, it failed to match agreement with his audience resulting in 'Mr Bechara' disappearing from theaters in it's second week.' Magazines topped their reviews as 'Bechara Anil'!

Anil's other release 'Rajkumar' was ambitious and promising. It had a perfect casting and had almost everything going for it: Madhuri Dixit as the princess, Naseeruddin Shah as the rogue king and Danny as the loyal chieftain. Helmed by rich producer Pradeep Sharma and Pankaj Parasher as its director to whom, many producers were willing to raise a toast owing to the huge success of 'Chalbaaz' which had Sridevi. Set in an imaginary period of the 'fairy-taled' and 'fantasy kind' filled with period styled drama, costumes, music and action in place. The song picturisations were innovative, especially the one where Madhuri dances in an 'afro-styled' makeup with her hair curly and skin ebony. However 'Rajkumar' failed and the worst to be hit, again, was Anil Kapoor. Though he wore the badge of being successful, yes- but he was now no longer in the race. He was now a survivor and no longer a contender.

Producer –Director David Dhawan's self-discovery of his penchant for comedy found a perfect muse with Govinda in 'Coolie No 1' (the first in the No1 series) and their second success in 'Sajan Chale Sasural' cemented their teaming.

The flavour of comedy did not dim the power of action. Buoyed by the success of his latest'Mohra', Akshay was now a confirmed A-lister. It was also a shot in the arm for its maker Rajiv Rai who had met a bloody face in his last 'Vishwatma'. 'Mohra'doled out large sized benefits to many in its embrace: maker Rajiv Rai, heroes Akshay Kumar and Sunil Shetty; heroine Raveena Tandon and villain Naseeruddin Shah. Akshay Kumar cavorting with Raveena in the *mast mast* number made her perennially known by it.

'Mohra' had the stamp of belonging to the banner of 'Trimurti Films' which had given iconic films that remain embedded in the minds of cinegoers: 'Deewar', 'Trishul', 'Johnny Mera naam', 'Vidhaata'. Sunil Shetty, the beefy hulk from the 1992 hit 'Balwaan' too prospered from the success of 'Mohra'. After Dara Singh from the fifties, Sunil Shetty was perhaps the only actor of early nineties with muscles that stretched his shirt-sleeves to tearing point; in fact his muscles did appear to overwhelm the "dhaai kilo" claimants. Another distinct possibility that had emerged was the disinterest of the 'Khans' to collaborate as successful pairs. In that context 'Mohra'achieved, what Sajid Nadiadwala's 'Yeh Waqt Hamara Hai' could not: With the Anil Kapoor –Jackie Shroff pair reaching the end of their brilliance, a replacement in their form came up. But the career paths of both skewed in different orbits and only one could reach his zenith.

Even before the magic of 'Mohra 'could wane, Akshay Kumar blitzed several notches ahead with another film, which unwantingly adopted the 'Khiladi' tag:

The film was 'Khiladiyon Ka Khiladi' which was made by an unlikely team of old time producers Mehras who owned the 'Eagle Films' banner and the Ramsays who were known as the 'horror specialists'. Directed by Umesh Mehra and produced by Kiran Ramsay, the film was an out and out action thriller. Having those 'WWF' wrestlers featuring 'The Undertaker' in its proceedings added a realistic element making Akshay's skill in martial arts engaging. In a lateral change, actress Rekha, for the first time, played a negative role as the boss of the baddies, which she did convincingly, winning her awards and accolades. 'Khiladiyon Ka Khiladi' was that big light which dispelled darkness from the career of Akshay Kumar. It was an effective vehicle which showcased his prime skill: martial arts. As in the past, when it came to powerful roles, Rekha remained the preferred choice. A decade ago she had impressed as 'Jyoti' the timid wife- turned- vixen, in Rakesh Roshan's revenge saga called 'Khoon Bhari Maang'. A decade later even though she was well past middle age, her dialogue delivery and her persona lent that chutzpah to the role of 'Maya'. By turning the spotlight on her she made the heroine a mere wall flower. The word 'Khiladi' though not needed in the context of this film, found final immortality as a tag line for all Akshay Kumar films. That word, even two decades later, finds resonance in the stardom of this waiter-model-karate exponent.

The year 1996 witnessed some star sons to be launched, some extensions, failed Fridays and few big successes.

N. Chandra, the feisty film maker, who had given a head start to big actorsNana Patekar and Anil Kapoor dipped further away in to oblivion after making 'Beqabu'. This film ostensibly meant to be a relaunch vehicle for the flopped and the damned Sanjay Kapoor, in hindsight, seemed a byproduct of nepotism. Its posters had a huge image of a neighing horse on its poster, which figuratively galloped away to being consigned to the ultimate graveyard of flops. It had Mamta Kulkarni as the leading lady and Mohan Kapoor as the villain. Mohan Kapoor those days had gained eminence as a star anchor in a series called 'Saap Seedi' a game show on Zee TV.A man whose forte lay in extracting heightened performaces from theatre artistes, seemed weird that he cast a Television anchor, that too, as the main villain in 'Beqabu'. The dizzy heights reached by the success of 'Tezaab' perhaps proved too much to be digested by N.Chandra. 'Beqabu' was his second big budget flop after the much touted 'Narsimha'.

Another son hoisted upon us that year was a young man called 'Puru Rajkumar', son of the eccentric actor 'Jaani'

Raj Kumar. The actor who three decades ago impressed with his performances in films like 'Waqt' and 'Pakeezah' later, perhaps due to the Bachchan onslaught and to remain relevant, styled his persona through loud dialogue delivery in an exaggerated and pompous way. Nevertheless, this appealed to a niche audience. Also, his notorious takes on his colleagues coupled with a weird sartorial sense kept him famous. Puru Rajkumar found a sturdy director in Prakash Mehra. After all, Prakash Mehra had given an equally sturdy vehicle for the Big Super star Amitabh Bachchan. He was also the man behind the biggest hits of Amitabh, Vinod Khanna and Dharmendra. This film was called 'Bal Brahmachari' where Puru Rajkumar potrayed all the virtues of Lord Rama's faithful savant known to mortals as 'Hanuman'. But this was not a Salim-Javed script, not did it star Amitabh and Prakash Mehra had not bettered on his track record of introducing successful debutants. In Bollywood nepotism never works, it can just give some blue-blooded offspring a headstart; nothing less nothing more. 'Bal Brahmachari' disappeared faster than the batting of an eyelid. Puru Rajkumar branched off to do villainous roles and mighty maker Prakash Mehra, maker of big blockbusters like *Rampur Ka Lakshman, Haath Ki Safai, Zanjeer, Mukaddar ka Sikandar, Laawaris, Namak halal, Sharaabi* got swept off under the age old adage: "Old generals do not die they just fade away".

After this failed son's entry, there was another 'star pair' waiting to be launched. Producer Salim released 'Raja Ki Aayegi Baraat' which had Amjad Khan's son Shadaab Khan alongside the grand daughter of the Mukherjee clan (and,

Kajol's cousin) Rani Mukherjee. The film flopped. While Shadaab went off in search of other pastures the young Rani dug her heels and waited.

Her wait was further lengthened due to the decadence of writers leading to virtual absence of interesting scripts the hindi film industry found itself to be staring at an empty bowl of scanty morsels. In such a scenario fly-by-night-operating filmmakers out to make a fast buck took to an easy way out by lifting ideas from American films. So out came 'The Hard Way' a Michael J.Fox starrer in the form of Akshay Kumar-Saif Ali Khan starrer 'Main Khiladi Tu Anari'. As is the wont in Hindi filmdom, a hit film with two heroes is immediately taken up for harvesting by others to encash on its success. This one too was meant to encash on the pair's latest hit "Yeh Dillagi' made by Yash Chopra's banner which again was a copy of an old American one called 'Sabrina'. The film was produced by the Jain Brothers who had produced the first 'Khiladi' which had given Akshay Kumar a strong lifeline for survival. This one came to threaten to undo the good done. Now both, Saif Ali Khan and Akshay Kumar were being relegated to 'a heap of kabada raddis' (wasteful newspapers). The other half of Akshay---actor Sunil Shetty, who also happened to be an entrepreneur having interests in boutiques-distribution-acting, was also wallowing in shallow waters. "Krishna' a big budget film having Karishma Kapoor as the heroine and most importantly for Sunil, was a solo hero film, failed to make a mark.

Karishma, the petite and pretty grand daughter of Showman Raj Kapoor, had well entrenched herself through 'Prem

Qaidi'. Though a confirmed hit it was an unlikely debut for a pedigreed debutant. Reason being, she was originally slated to debut as Bobby Deol's heroine in 'Barsaat' but that did not materialize beyond speculation. She had to instead debut in a D.Rama Naidu film (a movie mogul in telegu cinema) opposite a little known guy called Harish (whose earlier brush with hindi films was as a child star playing the boy Rajnikanth in 'Andha Kanoon'). Even though she gave a mixture of flops and hits, she was shipwrecked by two: 'Sapney Saajan Key' and 'Paapi Gudiya' made by Lawrence D'souza who had been heralded after the block buster 'Saajan'. Rescue came her way in the form of Sunil Darshan's 'Raja Hindustani'.

Sunil Darshan had earlier directed Sunny Deol –Juhi Chawla in the decently successful 'Lootere'. In 'Raja Hindustani', he adapted the 60's hit of Shashi Kapoor starrer 'Jab Jab Phool Khile'. 'Raja Hindustani' was successful to be termed a hit, but it did not make a 'raja' out of Aamir Khan but rewarded a Filmfare trophy to Karishma Kapoor and gave her reason enough to be a 'rani'.

The same year, the man who reveled in being called mad, evil, maverick and 'bastard' Mahesh Bhatt by now, had also smoked out his autobiographical sagas; last being his 'Janam' extrapolated as 'Zakhm' the one that had Nagarjun, Pooja Bhatt & Ajay Devgan. Even though Ajay won a National award the film did not rise to leave a mark. The molten glow of the lava inside him which had stupefied people a decade back had now lost its fiery charm. They were dull repetitions. His banner 'Vishesh Films' and 'Bhatt Productions'with brother Mukesh and himself as custodian, are venerated brands.

It was churning out films supposedly, on taut, sensational themes. But the end products failed to repeat his signature successes; a love story called'Papa Kehte Hain' which had Jugal Hansaraj the kid from 'Masoom'as the puppy faced hero and lastly 'Chahat' starring the en -route-to-numero-uno Shah Rukh and his daughter Pooja. With his nephew Vikram, they also rehashed many English films. But he was also a shrewd spotter of opportunities. This time he zoomed in on the 'Miss Universe' pageant which had just given India's very first 'Miss Universe' in Sushmita Sen. He promptly signed her for his new project 'Dastak'. A film based on 'obsessive love' where the main protagonist goes to maximum extremes to gain the affections of a beauty queen whom he stalks. This was in the same genre as Yash Chopra's 'Darr'.

Comparatively 'Dastak 'appeared juvenile. The failure of 'Dastak' left the Mahesh Bhatt discoveries; Beauty Queen Sushmita Sen, model turned aspiring actors Rahul Dev and Sharad Kapoor fending for themselves in the choppy waters of stardom.

On the other side former 'Movie Monarch' Amitabh Bachchan –aspiring to be its 'Mogul' was literally sinking.

Amitabh Bachchan's 'ABCL' was literally swamped in the colour Red. His films not only failed, his ambitious foray in hosting the 'Miss World Pageant' in Bangalore left his business bleeding profusely landing him under a colossal debt. He now did the unthinkable: ABCL decided to re-introduce Amitabh Bachchan in his own production.

So the 'BiG B' who had supposedly 'retired' for the second time was again coming back to perceived glory, blazing guns all the way ? The following happened:

'Mrityudaata', starring Amitabh with Dimple Kapadia and Nana Patekar, produced by ABCL and directed by Mehul Kumar who was poised to become a 'something big' cult director after the deafening success of 'Krantiveer', met a shameful fate. After Manmohan Desai's 'Toofan' and Prakash Mehra's 'Jaadugar', ABCL and Mehul Kumar completed the ignominy of orchestrating the complete fall of Amitabh Bachchan.

The year 1997 was largely dominated by many such ambitious films which unfortunately flopped. The year also saw the release of highly touted films like 'Ghulam-E-Mustafa' that ended whatever 'hero-like' aspirations was raised by Nana Patekar after the twin hits of 'Agnisakshi ' and 'Krantiveer'. The latter had touched raw nerves by dwelling on jingoism to rant aloud it's lessons on anti-corruption, nationalism and communalism. That scene from 'Krantiveer' where Nana stamps a rough stone on his muslim neighbour's fingers and himself ranting away to *"yeh hindoo ka khoon yeh mussalman ka khoon '* was recited dramatically in his trademark yelling style. It not only became a money spewing project but also gave this character actor-turned villain-turned leading man the ultimate honour, of bagging the FilmFare award in the 'best-actor-category!

The next was Rahul Rawail's 'Aur Pyar Ho Gaya. The usp here was Aishwarya Rai, a former model and the just-crowned

'Miss World' at a prestigious and resplendent event held in South Africa. However, the film written by Honey Irani (Javed Akhtar's wife) failed to remind us of Rahul Rawails past laurels of a not very distant past. The failure of 'Aur Pyar Ho gaya ' was a blow to Bobby's career but the young man could stomach it, thankfully, due to the success of Rajiv Rai's 'Gupt' which was a 'who-dun-it thriller' having Kajol and Manisha Koirala.

The quick rise of Nana Patekar was quickly decelerated by two swift flops: Mehul Kumar directed 'Ghulam-E-Mustafa' and Anil Mattoo's 'Yeshwant' which had a featherbrained tag line' *Ek Macchar saala aadmi ko hijra bana detu hain'* ("a mosquito can turn a man in to an eunuch").

While Nana Patekar was walking back to the pavilion, reconciling to the fact that he would never be a 'hero', actor turned politician Sunil Dutt was struggling to get a bail for his prodigal son Sunjay. He left no stone unturned to get him freed. From propitiating the God of the famous 'Siddhivinayak' temple, to lobbying hard with powerful colleagues in Delhi, of which he was an eminent member, to also appealing the charismatic and tempestuous leader of Mumbai: Bal Thackeray. Efforts paid off and the courts offered him succour in the form of a bail. Promptly father-son set off for 'Matoshri' the residence of Bal Thackeray to pay obeisance to the uncrowned king.

Balasaheb Thackeray was a man who had his ears to the ground. Through feedback from his cadres and his own deep rooted network he was convinced that Sanjay was no terrorist nor was he a wilful pawn but had unknowingly got himself entangled in this horrid mess. Though he could walk free from jail, this did not exonerate him completely. The 'Damocles' sword was still dangling above as the final verdict by the TADA court was not pronounced yet. Rather than brood in this interim period Sunjay Dutt decided to bury himself neck deep in work. He also decided to marry his long time girl friend Rhea Pillai, who, for months used to stand outside Arthur Road jail to catch a glimpse of her beloved.

After Varma's super hit 'Rangeela' there were whispers of his unspoken spat with Aamir Khan. Shrugging off he moved ahead and launched 'Daud. The film had the 'newly released' Sanjay Dutt basking in his new hairstyle and Urmila Matondkar in an 'Ursula Andress makeover'. Barring these two, 'Daud' was an ill conceived film, badly made and bereft of anything praiseworthy. Unlike 'Rangeela' which connected with the audience, 'Daud' disappointed them.

Rakesh Roshan's 'Koyla' too met an uphill terrain. It had Shah Rukh and Madhuri with Amrish Puri. It was about feudal exploitation and avarice. Shah Rukh played a mute, bonded slave under the shackles of the zamindar (Amrish Puri).

Even though 'Koyla ' was not that big a success as all anticipated, Shah Rukh pulled himself up with Subhash Ghai's 'Pardes'. Ghai brought in a new girl called Mahima Chaudhury whose claim to fame earlier were her 'Pepsi' ads with Aamir Khan.

The theme of this film was based on the subject of an arranged match between an NRI and an indian girl. The girl rejects the

NRI's downgrading attitude towards Indian thoughts and beliefs as "old" and instead gets attracted to his friend who seems to be sharing her beliefs. In his trademark style of big scale mounting and a larger emphasis on its music coupled with Shah Ruk Khan's success of being a serious contender, made 'Pardes' a hit. It also brought back Subhash Ghai as a film maker.

Shah Rukh hit bull's eye again with Yash Chopra's musical 'Dil To Pagal Hain '. It had Madhuri Dixit (after the negative pairing with him in the repulsive 'Anjaam') and Karishma Kapoor. The film was colourful in its central theme of handling love and its many hurdles. These two back to back successes helped Shah Rukh gain more head start over the other Khans.

But the biggest one who stood out that year was film maker J.P.Dutta, who came all guns blazing in 'Border':

On 2nd February 1991, the world woke up to news of fierce ground battles being fought on the deserts of Kuwait, codenamed 'Operation Desert Storm', between the armies of a belligerent Iraq and a Coalition army led by America. Two decades prior to 1991, on the Thar Desert of Rajasthan, India had fought out her own 'Desert Storm'. Just as CNN beamed the battles live for the world to watch, J.P.Dutta made us relive India's triumphant victory through 'Border'.

"Chidiya naal main baaj ladava taan Gobind Singh naam dharava"
-Subedar Rattan Singh

'Border' was based on the events leading to the night of 4th December of 1971, when West Pakistan launched an attack on the BSF post of Longowal, near Jaisalmer. Crossing in to India with a fleet of Patton tanks (gifted by their cold war ally) these were given a befitting reply. The thrill of watching Pakistani battle tanks under the cover of a moonless night audaciously crossing over the Indian borders, with an Indian platoon trailing them for an opportune moment to ambush, made us sit back and rediscover the valour and legacy of our brave soldiers.

The last film based on war as a dominant theme was the 1972 hit 'Upkaar' made by Manoj Kumar. Prior to that was Chetan Anand's 'Hakeeqat' based on the Indo-China border row. In 1976 came 'Hindustan Ki Kasam' which was again made by Chetan Anand but failed to leave any mark. To J.P.Dutta's credit 'Border' was a well researched project with a taut script. Soulful lyrics by Javed Akhtar helped by Anu Malik's rare, creative upsurge brought to life the spirit of patriotism pained by the pangs of separation. Javed Akhtar won a FilmFare trophy and the film earned a well deserved National Award.

J.P Dutta always reveled in basing his stories on Rajasthan's Thar Desert as a backdrop. This stood out right from his 1985 'Ghulami'. Slightly glorifying the night attack of 4th December, it poignantly brought to the forefront a soldier's moment of glory which can come unannounced to his doorstep. How each of the characters use this event to stand tall and pause their familial ties, is what the script narrates. The film had a fighting fit ensemble cast of Sunny Deol, Jackie Shroff, Sunil Shetty, Akshaye Khanna, Puneet Issar, Sudesh Berry and many more representing the fighting Indian soldiers. However, no known face represented the Pakistanis.

The Millenium was fast approaching. The nation that year, would be celebrating 53 years of freedom from British dominance.

The Millenium

"Computer ji, option C ko lock kiya jaaey"--Kaun Banega Crorepati

The economic turmoil of the seventies spreading right across to the eighties was on course in becoming a distant memory. This was largely helped by the demolition of the 'License Raj' in early 1991. Lifestyle brands representing international food-chains and many more had now become well entrenched in a country, whose economic rise was being carefully examined by major brands ruling various sectors world wide. Indian companies spread their wings by turning exporters. A wholly owned Indian company called 'Infosys' was one of the earliest to lead the country's growth; largely helped by the rise of the internet where people were soon creating their own email addresses and, the swarming of cell phones, leading to tremendous efficiency and more jobs for the evolving youth.

Television had gained prominence and its reach would now breach critical mass.

'Star Television' entered in to a JointVenture with 'SKY' to sell Direct To Home Telecast, for which they were awaiting clearance from the government.

The city of Bombay known for being the 'Mecca' of Hindi films was being rechristened: In line with fulfilling this long cherished desire of the Marathi polity, Bombay or, 'Bambai'- was now named 'Mumbai. An old song " *Yeh Bambai shaher haadson ka sheher'* had very enthusiastically eulogized the energetic 'Bambai'. Even though 'Bombay' changed to 'Mumbai' –'Bambai' continued to linger. The crown of Mumbai, "former angry man" Amitabh Bachchan, had described the paradoxes of this city in the song ' *Eee hain bambai nagariya'* –'This is the city of 'Bambai'and, after influencing an entire generation, was now being looked down upon as a failed businessman. To stake claim over his throne several knights had fought long drawn battles. The first were his contemporarians: the ever modest but hugely talented Dharmendra, the ever pompous Shatrughan Sinha, and eternal rival Rajesh Khanna followed by Jeetendra. Each displayed his own expertise but could not scale up. Early eighties saw the focus deflected by the brisk birth of many star sons; Few succeeded, most of them thrashed and trashed. Soon followed the serious contenders:

Anil Kapoor with his four Hits; 'Mr India', 'Eeshwar', 'Ram Lakhan' and 'Tezaab' and there was Jackie Shroff with 'Hero','Teri Meharbaniyan' and 'Tridev'. The king makers: Yash Chopra the master maker and his peers: Subhash Ghai and N.Chandra. But the ever continuation of formulaic films forced them to either reinvent or face the perils of obliteration. The appearance of young Turks with spearhead alliances chased the wind out of their sails: Shah Rukh –Aditya Chopra; Salman-Sooraj Barjatya; Govinda –David Dhawan. Age old formulas bowed out. Titans were reaching the end of their tether; the low point was Amitabh Bachchan playing second fiddle to a Govinda in David Dhawan's 'Bade Miyan Chote Miyan' where even the title song granted one-upmanship to Govinda in its amply clear lyrics: *"Bade Miya to Bade Miyan -Chhote Miyan Subhanallah'!*

Anil Kapoor, the promising knight from the late eighties, made a minor comeback vide Priyadarshan's 'Virasat'. This film maker called Priyadarshan per se was not a Hindi film maker. He was a known film maker down south who picked up on hits and remade them in Hindi. 'Virasat' was the remake of a Tamil hit called 'Thevar Magan'which starred two of the biggest icons of Tamil cinema: thespian Sivaji Ganesan and Kamalhaasan. Priyadarshan sensed a winner, bought the rights and decided to remake this cult classic in to Hindi.

Anil shone in this film where the original role in Tamil was played by Kamal Haasan and Sivaji's roled was reprised by Amrish Puri. PriyaDarshan brought in Mushir-Riaz as producers and they made hay by merely xeroxing it. Anil Kapoor and Amrish Puri towered on screen, as well as the two titans of the South, and rightfully so, the success too was met in tandem.

However, the mood in the industry soon numbed. The whispers during the nineties that tainted money was being ploughed in to certain projects with dubious producers, brimmed over when the 'Mogul'Gulshan Kumar was brutally shot dead in broad daylight outside a temple in Mumbai. To the shock of all, the police pointed their finger towards music director Nadeem Saifi. This terrible turn of events halted the suzerainty of the 'T-Series' banner for a long time. The murder of Gulshan Kumar literally put a lid on the further aspirations of T-Series. He was the company's main honcho. Since its inception, it was his brains steering the company through the nitty gritties of film making, music planning, sourcing. The short, diminutive man was well on course to make his company the bellwether of Bollywood. He succeeded to a certain extent until being felled, unbelievably, to the bullets of a hired assassin. Incidentally, music director Nadeem fled to England which further added fuel to the rumour that there was certainly more to what one would believe. The question every one was asking was, why did Nadeem flee? Was he involved? If not then certainly he could stick around to prove his innocence. Parallels could be drawn between Nadeem and Sunjay Dutt: one fled while the other remained rooted to prove his innocence.

As the big heroes were exploring all stops to keep oblivion away, there was one die hard guy who squeezed maximum mileage by keeping aloft his old template. Three decades ago, Mithun Chakraborty was branded by the media as a "poor man's Bachchan' but he shrugged off those barbs to become a star in his own right; There came a time when he shared equal space with the phenomenon. The aftermath of a long felt insecurity and his old incubating days, fraught with poverty and homelessness, lured him to guillotine his hard earned star status through inane films. Third rate producers and out of job directors exploited the rustic appeal of this son of the soil leading to thirty-six consecutive flops. This blanked out his appeal but his innate nose for survival worked out an immensely profitable formula.

So, after the demise of the 'Mithun' brand, Gorango Chakraborty retired to the verdant hills of Ooty where he started his own 'parallel' bollywood. In his mind he had a workable business plan that smelt of good return on investments: scripts based on old templates of vendetta were dug out and recast; where 'Prabhuji' (Mithun's new moniker) played the honest man or a good cop; villain would be a corrupt politician or a corrupt cop; in between there would be a wronged mother, some B-lister as a heroine, few moments of slapstick comedy, some crass song picturisations with hot-pants wearing buxom belles sweating out with Mithun either on the dance floor or on meadows of the Ooty hills to hurriedly composed music, and voila: a film was ready for release; the only condition being entire shooting had to be done in the hills, nooks and cranny of Ooty. This arrangement worked out well for two years. While he also managed his huge hotel business more than fifty of his films were rolled out and none of them lost money. These found an eager audience in B -towns where they were screened in old, dilapidated, single -screen ramshackles.

While Mithun and Jackie Shroff were in search for survival, the rest were doing no better.

Salman Khan gave an average with Twinkle Khanna called 'Jab Pyar Kisise Hota Hai'. Anil Kapoor tried to do a different act in 'Jhooth Bole Kauva Kaate' made by old legend Hrishikesh Mukherjee. Anil's next 'Kabhi Na Kabhi' made by Priyadarshan of 'Virasat' fame failed to reignite the Anil-Jackie pair. Further, the old pair well past their forties wooing a Pooja Bhatt who was half their age, did not arouse interest. Dilip Kumar of the original Big-3, was handed a final salute by the resounding flop of 'Qila'. It not only nudged the thespian to enjoy full and final retirement but also brought finito to all concerned.

Dev Anand, the other surviving link from the 'Big-3' was still wriggling his dice. This time he made a film as ridiculous as its title: 'Main Solah Baras Ki'. Nothing much was heard of the film nor the actress whom he introduced.

Ageing monarch Amitabh tried to prop himself up with the last of his ABCL production: 'Major Saab'. As the grim faced army captain, this film was way off the mark. All that it could achieve was to add a deeper tone to the red shade enveloping the balance sheet of 'ABCL'.

Feroz Khan, the Pathan with a yankee accent, was preparing to launch his son. Feroz still had recall value in the minds of people and now that he was introducing his son Fardeen, which kind of aroused more curiosity. People thronged the first day shows of 'Prem Aggan' (Fiery Love). The result was anything but fiery. 'Prem Aggan' was not only a bad film it had nothing 'Feroz Khan' about it; The father had unwittingly finished his son's career even before it could take off!

N.Chandra's seriously ambitious film 'Wajood' with Nana Patekar and Madhuri Dixit was where he seemed to be making amends over his past.'Wajood' failed. Subhash Ghai tried dipping in to the cauldron of his past hits and pulled out 'Ram Lakhan' to be remade as 'Sham-Ghanshyam' with Arbaz Khan and Chandrachur Singh. For the first time, a film made under the much feted 'Ghai' brand failed to sell tickets.

Aamir Khan too faced rigor mortis with the flop 'Earth' made by off beat maker Deepa Mehta. Only Govinda managed to whip out a hit with the laugh riot 'Dulhe Raja' made by Harmesh Malhotra. 'Dulhe Raja' aided by the comic timing and funny dialogues between Kader Khan & Johnny Lever increased the laugh quotient to make the audience happy and contented.

Next came Raj Kumar Santoshi. Tired of his shackles with the Deol family he desperately wanted to break out. He chose a script which was lateral for those times. It was partially based on Akiro Kurosawa's 'Seven Samurai' but with a twist. Santoshi's 'Seven Samurai' were men past their sixties, entrusted with the task of protecting an obscure village from the menace of a dacoit. He brought in a new actor, Manish Tiwari to play the dacoit. The film was 'China Gate' and Santoshi put all efforts in projecting Tiwari as a terror reminiscent to old legend 'Gabbar Singh' (he even gave him the garb of a dirty uniform resembling a CRPF soldier). He tried instilling fear by making him mouth dialogues like *"mere man ko bhaaya mein kutta kaat khaya"*. He did try to bring the thunder of Classic westerns by making scores of horses kick up a furious cloud of dust in an unknown gorge. He also tried to receate the boisterous beat of *'mehbooba* from 'Sholay' where he made Urmila Matondkar sway to *'Chamma Chamma'*. To sum it up he thought about everything except for anything original. When creativity hinges on plagiarism such an endeavor is bound to fail. At the end of the day comparisons with 'Sholay' was obvious.

Mahesh Bhatt also tried to be different. He shrugged off his autobiographical nuances and decided to accept Dharma Productions' offer called as 'Duplicate' having Shah Ruk Khan in a double role with Juhi Chawla and Sonali Bendre who still had her equity intact from the A.R.Rahman number ' Humma Humma'.

Overall 'Duplicate' was an average hit. It fortified the rise of Shah Ruk Khan and made Mahesh Bhatt whistle a sigh of relief.There was another reason for Mahesh to smile. His nephew Vikram Bhatt had just given a big hit called 'Ghulam' which in turn made Aamir Khan let out a sigh of relief!

'Ghulam' in itself was an impressive film. Like his uncle Mahesh Bhatt, Vikram too had a penchant for either lifting or remaking English hits without acknowledging or crediting the originals. There were scenes in 'Ghulam' which were clear lifts from the Marlon Brando classic 'Waterfront'. His first, a sexo-thriller called 'Fareb' was based on an English film called 'Unlawful Entry'. 'Fareb' had Aizaz and Suman Rangnathan with Milind Gunaji as the cop who covets the attractive wife of the doctor.

The success of 'Ghulam' also gave succour to a girl called Rani Mukherjee whose pedigree descended from the blue blood of the 'Filmalaya' founders. Her debut 'Raja Ki Aayegi Baraat ' opposite Amjad Khan's son, Shadaab, had just flopped.

'Ghulam' by Vikram Bhatt, was about two brothers. One is an accountant who works for a local goon and the younger brother, is a jobless guy but also follows an interest in boxing. He does not mind doing some odd jobs for the goon who also nurtures an interest in boxing. One of the highlight was a song rendered by Aamir Khan, or rather silly banter that went as "*Aati Kya Khandala*', but for Aamir Khan the success of 'Ghulam', shored him up to enter seamlessly in to the millennium.

As the clock ticked, the dawn of the new millennium was just a year away.

Indeed, times had changed; The heroes, their perspectives and the way the people led their lives. The villains and their origins had also changed The aspiring emotions of the new born nation had given rise to the 'Big 3' and in them Dilip Kumar epitomized emotions, tragedies and patriotism. Dev Anand embodied the middle class youth who set afire dainty hearts with a blink and a mere nod of his head.Raj Kapoor gave the underdogs from all walks of life, a feel that they were the wheels which gave motion to the world around.

In their quest for the common goal of establishing the triumph of truth, they also had to embattle negative forces in many forms like: the evils of caste system, oppressive land owners, the vagaries of the weather, villains within families, pitfalls of love and above all, poverty.

Many times they also set aside morbid topics to indulge in swash buckling tales of prince and kingdoms.

Shammi Kapoor had symbolized that new Indian who defined chilling out. Emerging from a night club, wearing a tuxedo and strumming a guitar gave an insight of those high points in society where poverty was being stamped out.

Rajesh Khanna's films engulfed the youth in a single focus one stride style in which the world was dipped in the ink of romance. But the era of the seventies with it's tidal wave of unemployment and gloomy tidings shattered that ink pot !

Thus began the Bachchan onslaught where Bollywood witnessed a dramatic U-Turn. Love was saved for the end. The rest would be spent in destroying inequalities, injustice and poverty so that in the end, love remained inclusive.

The ageing Amitabh gave leeway to many 'me-toos'. But the scale reached by him was difficult to breach. A 'Munna' from Tezaab could never deskill 'Vijay Verma' of 'Deewar' and a 'Ghayal' was no match for a 'Sikandar. Soon enough with advancing age and descending stars, the Superstardom of Amitabh Bachchan, now neared its tether.

Every Friday meant a duel between contestants. Giving one hit brought one closer to the throne. It was bad business sense for two big films to clash on a common Friday. The Deol brothers, Akshay Kumar, the three Khans, to an extent Ajay Devgun and Govinda were the prominent A-listers. Govinda like his predecessor Mithun was soon on the path of his predecessor where a string of flops, the poor faring of the "Number 1" suffix and the call of politics derailed his chances and instead turned this contestant in to a 'Member of Parliament'.

The nineties had a strong stamp and feel of movie mogul Gulshan Kumar and his satraps. T-Series towered over the others, helped also largely by the unwavering success of music directors Nadeem Saifi & Shravan Rathod. The tide soon turned: one was killed while the other turned a fugitive.

Indeed, the tone for the approaching millennium was set by two film makers.

The first was Ram Gopal Verma and the other was a newbie. He was the son of Yash Johar who owned Dharma Productions and his name: Karan Johar.

Ram Gopal Verma who five years back gave Aamir Khan a big hit in 'Rangeela' had won awards and hearts. A year later he butchered his reputation by a thud called 'Daud' where he had taken Sunjay Dutt. In his own words he had candidly confessed, "I almost screwed up Sanjay Dutt's career". Now, a year later, he came with one of the most authentic film ever on the 'growing' Mumbai underworld. Made on a modest budget with relatively unknown actors like Manoj Bajpai, Saurabh Shukla, Shefali Chhaya (presently Shefali Shah), Makrand Deshpande, Govind Namdev and Chakravorty (who appeared in Verma's 1991 hit 'Shiva'as Nagarjuna's friend),and of course, Verma's muse- Urmila Matondkar.

The film was 'Satya', based on a story –screenplay jointly written by Saurabh Shukla and Anurag Kashyap. Chakravorty played the title role while Manoj Bajpai played the unforgettable 'Bhiku Mhatre'. His earlier known outings before this were in a tiny role in Mahesh Bhatt's 'Dastak' and Shekhar Kapur's 'Bandit Queen'.

Just as 'Rangeela' dwelt on the humorous side of a harmless Mumbai' 'tapori', his 'Satya' revealed the dark other side of the same coin. 'Satya' showed diligently, how goons operate within territorial rights by dissecting the city through blood and mayhem and how the nexus between politicians and criminals is well-oiled. Varma locked down the narrative in suburbs like Pydonhie, Byculla and those large tracts of slums in Dharavi which helped him in revealing the grossness in Mumbai's dark underbelly. The anger of the seventies was more on the side of righting a wrong, but 'Satya', showed an entire society riddled with violence. The migrants of the seventies who came to Bombay immediately faced the prospect of encountering suitcase lifters, pickpockets and stark realities of sleeping on crowded pavements,'Satya' brought out crimes embedded in various forms all over; from politician who wears white and hobnobs with criminals, right down to your unknown neighbour who might just turn out to be a member of the underworld. One of those most chilling scenes was the killing of the character 'Bhiku Mhatre': with no struggle, no duel, no pain-induced monologue---just one bullet inserted point-blank into his head! The film took everyone by storm and was a success all over. One of its biggest gainers was actor Manoj Bajpayi. From that blink and miss scene in the 1996 'Dastak', he became a star overnight. 'Satya' perhaps was the first film which had a host of stage actors who collectively spun a super hit. For Ram Gopal Verma the mishap of 'Daud' had just turned an aberration. The old sin was purified with one huge splash called 'Satya' turning his fledgling RGV productions in to a truly big banner.

The success in narrating just one chapter from the Mumbai underworld opened up a new vista for Verma. For the next decade or even more he would be milking it perennially.

Just as Varma revealed the violent underbelly of Mumbai, another young man, from the same city, put his heart and soul in to a love story. The film was 'Kuch Kuch Hota Hai' and the man was Karan Johar. The film had the endearing pair of DDLJ: Shah Ruk Khan and Kajol Mukherjee with the newly emerging hottie, Rani Mukherjee. Where love stories were either 'love at first sight' or "fight at first sight' blossoming eventually in to love- this one had a departure in the form of 'friends falling in love'; with the other friend thrown in to create a triangle.

The first half of 'KuchKuchHotaHai' brought to life the 'Riverdale college campus' from the Archie comic strips: those expensive sporty bicycles, those roller-coasters, those fluorescent tees, matching head- bands, a college canteen that reminds of 'Pops Tate' and a principal-teacher duo who have shades of 'Prof Weatherbee' and 'Ms Grundy' !

Rahul (Shah Rukh) Anjali (Kajol) and Tina (Rani Mukherjee), were Karan Johar's beaten down indianized versions of 'Archie-Betty-and Veronica Lodge'.

Karan Johar then turned this sweeter than sugar film in to a pool of copius tears by removing one friend, due to complications arising out of labour pain and bringing back his other friend- 'Anjali' who is already bethrothed to 'Duh! Big Moose' like character, Salman Khan. Covering unexplored foreign locales the way Yash Chopra excelled in, Karan broke tradition by skipping Chopra's favourite Switzerland in favour of other regions like Austria and far off castles in Scotland. Nevertheless, he won big time; earning laurels, awards and cash. It swept the Filmfare awards and without doubt carved Shah Ruk Khan's number one status, in stone. It also established 'Dharma Productions' to tower above the existing ones. 'Dharma Productions' now had it's scion as its director just as the Barjatyas of 'Rajshri Productions' had their very own in Sooraj Barjatya.

Shah Ruk Khan further consolidated his throne with Mani Rathnam's 'Dil Se' where a pretty girl called Preity Zinta, fresh from winning the 'Miss India' title, debuted.

After the superb success of 'Roja' in its dubbed Hindi version, it was obvious that Mani Ratnam would make a bilingual. By dubbing in Hindi the film ensured top-up revenue. This practice was earlier followed by many Hindi film makers prominent among them were Shakti Samanta: he dubbed his Hindi hits 'Aradhana', 'Amanush' and 'Barsaat Ki Raat' in to Bengali. On similar lines came Kamal Haasan's 'Appu Raja' followed by Mani Rathnam's 'Roja', then came his 'Bombay' which was also a bilingual. In his next 'Dil Se' the same two-pronged strategy was applied: having Shah Ruk Khan & Manisha Koirala in the leading roles, it was mainly meant for the heavily numbered Hindi audience so dubbing it in Tamil stemmed any loss of revenues down south. But 'Dil Se' never helped Mani reignite the embers left behind by 'Roja'. The pathos of 'Roja' the wife, crying away at every pillar to help save her husband never transferred on to the angst of the pretty lady turned human-bomb in 'Dil Se'. The film piggy backed on the bulwark of hindi filmdom's newest superstar and partly, on an innovatively picturised item song *'Chal Chhaiyya Chaiyyan* 'on the roof of a slow moving train on a narrow gauge line between Mettupalyam and Coonoor near

Ooty. Malaika Arora, who sizzled on this train, became the hot new 'Item girl'.

Before the curtains could be brought down on the 90's, some more meteoric incidents occurred. Few shone bright while the rest burnt out like shooting stars. The first, was the impending release of 'Hum Saath Saath Hain' from Rajshri productions.

Sooraj Barjatya, post 'Hum Aapke Hain Kaun' was a man to watch out for. The film having turned into a much discussed topic at dining tables in homes all over had made barriers disappear; by giving them a subject to communicate this film broke down all walls. The old with the young trooped in with their grand children in to theatres to revel in this grand entertainer. He had almost become a symbol of familial necessity. The matinees, the noon shows, screening 'HumAapkeHainKaun'in theatres all over, had become the favoured ground for such an audience. Since then, this segment, which constituted bulk of the nation's population waited, anticipating an encore. But 'Hum Saath Saath Hain' highly awaited as a connecting dot to complete his hat-trick, jolted all to enter in to that 'Hall of Wane' where promising lights turn fleetingly bright and then turn out to be quiet wisps of smoke.

The next was 'Dharamputra' Sunny Deol. The brawny hero, introvert other wise, decided to launch himself as a director in 'Yeh Dillagi'. He perhaps fancied himself as a better visionary than his 'employee' Raj Kumar Santoshi who had directed 'Ghayal' and friend Gurinder Chaddha, an NRI filmaker, who had gained international acclaim through her last release 'Bend it like Beckham'.

Soon came Rishi Kapoor, deciding to wear the hallowed robes of his Iconic director father and confident that he could prove to be a chip off the old block. The title 'Aa Ab Laut Chalein' was reminiscent of an old song from his father's iconic film 'Jis Desh mein Ganga Behti hain'.

The next big thing was Indra Kumar and Aamir Khan teaming up for making 'Mann', a pale remake of the fifties hollywood classic 'An Affair to Remember'.

Then there was Ram Gopal Varma, again, flying high after the great success of 'Satya' who tried to carve out another radical. He made a film called 'Mast', which was self confessedly based on his adolescent fascination for an A-Listed heroine.

Casting his muse- Urmila Matondkar played that character of an actress who fascinates a young boy.(played by Aftab shivdasani, a former child star in Sridevi's 'Chalbaaz')

But the Report card from the Box office showed all the above projects epmhatically as 'Failed'.

The Sunny Deol directed 'Dillagi' starring himself alongwith brother Bobby Deol had actually been rough shod due to many last minute changes; The original heroine Karishma Kapoor had to walk out; The original director 'Gurinder Chaddha who had gained worldwide acclaim with 'Bend it like Beckham' also had to walk out. Reasons not known. In came Sunny Deol wearing the Captain's cap that brought in Urmila Matondkar. But 'Dillagi' lived up to its name: as a box office 'joke'.

The other newbie director Rishi Kapoor's, 'Aa Ab Laut Chalen' generated well deserved curiosity. He was the son of Raj Kapoor and by the virtue of his pedigree made him 'entitled' to lay his claim. 'Aa Ab Laut Chalein', like Sunny Deol's 'Dillagi, never allowed money to come between it's conception; a big star cast in the form of Akshaye Khanna and Aishwarya Rai; shot in locales almost entirely in America; big and expensive character actors like Moushumi, Alok Nath and big stars like Rajesh Khanna with Kader Khan. The only thing that rose as a mountainous deficit was the lack of creative abilities from its maker. 'Aa Ab laut Chalein' was probably destined to be the last film from the R.K banner. Rishi Kapoor never again dared to wield the director's baton again. He now focused in enjoying his retirement.

The other side, his erstwhile colleague, Amitabh Bachchan, was now neck deep in debt. That year 'ABCL' filed for bankruptcy. Lenders brought the invincible 'Sikandar' to the brink by sending him a notice which spelt out their plan to auction his palatial house 'Pratiksha'which was, and luckily still is, his official residence. But the financial world of bankers and lenders never factored in his uncanny ability in extricating himself out of every bottleneck; being destiny's favourite child had its advantages. In the corridors of power and unknown to his troubled mind, there were crucial things happening.

By dislodging the fragile BJP government a cartel of many big and small regional parties had joined in an unholy matrimony called as the 'Third Front'. But in thirteen odd months, the BJP jostled up the required numbers and conquered Delhi.

One of the firsts that they sanctioned was to open up DTH. This led to an explosion of the Television industry which was, hitherto, held sway only by Zee.

Saif Ali, an underdog Khan, popped up and sunk again with Mahesh Bhatt's 'Yeh hai Mumbai Meri Jaan '. Akshay kumar lost yet again with 'International Khiladi 'and 'Jaanwar' made by his one time mentor Pramod Charavarthy. But the 'Three Khans', each gave a hit which strengthened their lairs. Aamir Khan tossed away the failure of 'Mann' by giving the hit 'Sarfarosh'. Shah Ruk Khan stamped another hit called 'Baadshah' made by his lucky macots Abbas-Mustan while Salman topped with 'Hum Dil Chuke Sanam'. The last year of the nineties belonged to two young makers: Sanjay Leela Bhansali for 'Hum Dil De Chuke Sanam' and Mahesh Manjrekar (a veteran film maker from the Marathi film industry) for 'Vaastav'.

Sanjay Bhansali, a gifted screen writer who worked as an assistant to Vidhu Vinod Chopra in his 'Parinda' and '1942-A Love Story' launched himself as an independent director with 'Khamoshi'. The film was co-produced by Sony Pictures and had Salman Khan and Manisha Koirala alongwith Nana Patekar & Seema Biswas. It was a moving story of a young girl struggling to cope with the plight of her deaf and mute parents. Even though it moved people to tears -it failed to win their hearts. Three years later he came back with 'Hum Dil De Chuke Sanam'. He gathered all that he had and gave it his best shot. Fresh music by Ismail Durbar, lavish sets, picturesque locales and above all, a tale of love and sacrifice spoken from the heart, won Bhansali a clutch of awards.

He also revealed his penchant for turning film making in to poetry. By making not only the actors to emote his line of thinking but also using other elements like- sets and costumes which not only gave a visual treat, they also personified his content. 'Hum Dil De Chuke Sanam' is also said to be the beginning of a tumultuous romance between its two stars that climaxed in to despair.

The second wonder was a film called 'Vaastav' (Reality). The incarceration of Sunjay Dutt in the '93 Mumbai Blasts case had put up a gigantic question mark over his future. Ten years before that,after he had just debuted, when he had checked in to a rehabilitation centre in America, the same question was put forth. Spending five months at the Rehab he swung back, fit as a fiddle, with a never expected hit called 'Jaan ki Baazi'.

Now, with a bigger catastrophe hovering over him, he swung back with 'Vaastav'.

To digress, during the seventies, the social diaspora of Bombay had been jolted by a crippling strike which shut down almost all the textiles mills. The culprit was a doctor-turned –union leader called Datta Samant who like his ilk, never really knew the dark side of shutting down businesses. Collateral, in the form of lives of thousands was cruelly upturned which led to an increase in crime. The effect engulfed the next decade and the story of 'Vaastav' is set in that scenario. Raghu (Sunjay Dutt) is one of those many young men, a by-product from the morass of poverty that arose by the closure of those mills. Living in a chawl where people crave for food clothing and shelter, Raghu borrows a small sum of finance from his father to fund his dreams of subsistence and worthiness by putting up a 'paav-bhaaji' stall. Alongwith his friend and companion nicknamed as 'Ded Futiya' (actor Sanjay Narvekar) and buoyed by the brisk business of his 'Paav-bhaaji' stall, Raghu is well on course in achieving his objective of contributing to the household income. Then one day, disaster strikes in the form of an unnecessary spat with drunken goons who eat and refuse to pay. An argument spirals in to a brawl that ends up as a brutal murder. Soon, 'Raghu' and 'Ded Futiya' are forced to be on the run. In dire need of food and protection fate leads them to another goon. In return, Raghu has to barter away his unwillingness by turning himself as the goon's cohort; forced to succumb, he soon descends in to a world of power, money and drugs. His guns bestow on him power to keep off his enemies and the tainted money affords him the luxury of providing for his unwilling family, but in the bargain, gets hopelessly sunk in a tragic cul-de-sac where all his senses are firmly ruled by drugs and alcohol. Poignantly, after his final run-in with the law, he pleads his mother to shoot him down and free him from his dreadful state. The film ends with his mother obliging him. The scene, where he gives her the gun, joins his hands, imploring her to use it on him, is the darkest scene of the film.

Sanjay Dutt as 'Raghu Namdev' was terrific. As the young unemployed man spending his idle time in playful antics with his similarly placed friends and then the shocking realization of being sucked in the swamp of the underworld- Sanjay Dutt gave a rousing performance. The second-half where he has forgotten his days of wearing a 'vest'now struts around as a quintessential goon: in black 'pathani', gelled hair with a 'tilak' daubed on his forehead. The scene where he is gloating in his misdeeds by proudly brandishing a gun to his mother is scary; "*Dekh Ma isko boltey hain ghoda aur yeh trigger, isko kheecha to game khallas*" Lastly, his exhausted battle with his addictions and the fervent plea to his mother (Reema Lagoo) for setting him free – Sanjay Dutt breathed life in to a rather demanding role.

After missing it for 'Naam', 'Saajan' and 'Khalnayak', he finally bagged his first award in the Best Actor category'. Ironically, the man who had initiated the crippling textile strikes Dr Datta Samant, met his end by being gunned down in Mumbai's suburb.

The ripples of change were echoing. The Nineties had consigned to dust many contenders. The millennium was changing the way India shaped up. Jobs, an elusive necessity, were galloping towards her shores. After the dot -com burst, the road opened to globally promoted call centres mushrooming in many cities. Youngsters were lapped up giving a boost to the economy. The use of the English language gave the country an edge over her other Asian neighbours. More and more global software companies began outsourcing from India that led to more jobs and a distinct rise in the standard of living. Changing habits in turn led to changes in way films were being watched. The first distinct change to cater to this new lifestyle, appeared on the skyline of Mumbai where India's first Mall came up: Near Haji Ali Cross in Mumbai and not far from the visage of the Haji Ali dargah, the mall was aptly called as 'Crossroads'. With a dazzling array of shops, a string of movie screens which we now know as a 'Multiplex' and a huge food court, it was a revolutionary change in movie viewing. The stink of urinals, oily peanuts and hard-backed chairs would now give way to airconditioned complexes, couch-like seats, carpeted aisles and cheesy popcorns. At a price of course!

As those screens in multiplexes crackled with the moving images of the Khans, Amitabh Bachchan was facing the prospect of all out bankruptcy. Realizing that every penny earned would go a long way in entangling himself from the 'ABCL' mess, he decided to meet his old friend Yash Chopra. In his own words he confessed 'I walked across to Yash Chopra's house and requested him for work". Yash Chopra was too happy to help out his old friend. Incidentally, his son Aditya Chopra was casting for his new film 'Mohabattein' for which he had signed Shah Ruk Khan and Aishwarya Rai. He was also scouting for some one aged with a larger image to fit in to the shoes of an opposing protagonist. Amitabh fitted the role of 'Narayan Shanker' which was pitted against Shah Ruk's 'Raj Aryan'. Lavishly mounted as discernible in all Yash Raj films, 'Mohabattein' was a hit. It not only brought a fresh elixir in to Amitabh's life, also brought him back from his self imposed retirement.

But the biggest slice of opportunity that brought him succour came from an unlikely quarter. With the BJP ruled NDA government agreeing to open up DTH, Rupert Murdock owned StarTV decided to remake one of their marquee programme 'How To be a Millionaire' in to Hindi. As a part of their well thought out strategy of storming Indian homes, having Amitabh Bachchan as the anchor was in line with their thinking. An unheard of sum was offered which, if taken, could take care of most of his dues, save his home and bring him out of the woods. Wisely he agreed and the rest as they say is history. 'Kaun Bangea Crorepati' kept him busy, dissipated his debts and resurrected his charisma. The King was back in form.

In another related development, Jeetendra (Ravi Kapoor), phased out star of the 80's introduced his daughter Ekta Kapoor as an entrepreneur. She formed 'Balaji Telefilms'. In a short span Jeetendra's daughter would become the biggest authority in making content for television.

The Millenium was also weeding out dead wood and purging Bollywood of some long time jostlers. The tyranny of all formulas is a terrible thing; Like Mithun's formulaic films churning out trash, Govinda's excessive screeching of 'Number Ones' made by his piped piper David Dhawan: Beti No 1, Aunty No 1, and several more like 'Hadh Kar di Aapne', 'Jis Desh Mein Ganga Rehta Hain', and 'Joru Ka Ghulam'.

A decade and a half ago, when he debuted with the hit 'Ilzaam' he was wise enough to know that dance moves could never add longevity to his career. He found an answer much later when he discovered his knack for comedy by teaming up with David Dhawan. But now, the 'Govinda' brand of comedy failed to tickle the audience any more. Bobby Deol after 'Gupt' and 'Soldier' failed to sustain sinking deeper with 'Badal' and 'Bichoo'. So Did Sunil Shetty and Akshay Kumar. Aamir Khan too was left with a bloody nose when the big budget 'Mela' made by Dharmesh Darshan never lived to see beyond a couple of weeks. Salman Khan was hoping to recoup big time from films that were unfortunately low on quality: 'Har Dil Jo Pyar Karega', 'Kahin Pyar Na Ho Jayey'. They slowed him and Rani Mukherjee down for she was the single common factor in all the above flops of Bobby, Govinda & Salman.

In a strange twist of a familial tale, Aamir Khan's cousin Mansoor Khan, made a film called 'Josh' with Shah Ruk Khan. 'Josh' also had Aishwarya Rai, Sharad Kapoor, Chandrachur Singh. It also smelt of scenes from an English film called 'Westside Story'. While he had based 'JJWS' in the hill station of Kodaikanal, 'Josh' had the backdrop of sunny Goa. But it had neither the creative upsurge seen in his 'QSQT' nor the racy charm of 'JJWS'. 'Josh' met a terrible fate and wiped out almost everybody associated with it; Sharad Kapoor, a Mahesh Bhatt discovery who had banked a lot on 'Josh' went in to permanent obsolescence; the hero Chandrachur Singh who was originally Gulzar's discovery, vaporized; maker Mansoor Khan went off in to a permanent Sabbatical to open a cottage cheese farm, never to attempt film making again.

That left Shah Ruk Khan the main hero of 'Josh'. He was not a 'No 1' for nothing. Since the time he debuted as a second lead in 'Deewana' eight years back, he had treaded every step tactfully, leading him towards the throne. The title 'Super Star' was passé, Shah Ruk Khan was now known as the 'Baadshah' of Bollywood. The failure of 'Josh', and the average response to his 'Phir Bhi Dil Hai Hindustani' did not singe a single hair on his head.

The Greek God

"Mera Naam Karega Roshan, jag mein mera raaj dulara"--a song from the seventies.

If these events proved that Shah Ruk Khan was now the anointed one, then not very far from his sea-facing mansion; perhaps a few suburbs away, a film maker was grooming his son to be a bigger 'Baadshah'.

By sending him to acting schools, dancing classes and making him sweat out at the gym, film maker Rakesh Roshan seemed to be leaving no stone unturned. Voices abounded of a star in the making. Blessed with light amber eyes, naturally sculpted features indeed made him resemble one of those 'Gods of Greece'- Hrithik Roshan his son was being groomed for a job that was naturally cut out for him.

'Kaho Na Pyar hai' was a scrupulously polished film that a father could ever create for his son. It was an exemplary standard of a film made for one's protégé, discovery or muse. This film was not only a super hit but also turned on its head the science of launching one's progeny in to filmdom. Hritik Roshan serenaded into filmdom as the first 'Cool Dude' of the Millenium. A six feet physique studded with rippling muscles and a sculpted face Hrithik, in the looks department, passed his first test with flying colours. Next came the fights where his stunts and tall frame proved effective; in the dance department his relaxed, swaying moves peppered with leaps complemented the slow and gentle rendering of '*Ek pal ka jeena*' sung by Lucky Ali (son of actor Mehmood). In the acting department he proved to be versatile enough to shoulder the double roles of the distinctly different characters: Raj and Rohit.

None of the film houses, nor their patriarchs ever made their offspring hone their skills, before allowing them to leapfrog; All beliefs were etched on the pillar of lineage and leaned against the only wall: nepotism. The assumption of merely wearing the template of their famous surname was, as erroneously thought, a more than enough stripe to be worn in the quest for stardom. At best they would earn big bucks, worst scenario earn lacs: Atul Agnihotri a one time star aspirant in the nineties who also starred in A-List films like 'Aatish', 'Naaraz', 'Yeshwant' had candidly revealed rather tellingly that "rather than sweating it out in a 9-5 job for a few thousands, acting is a better option."

While Rakesh Roshan was toasting the success of his son's rightfully earned poster boy status, Amitabh Bachchan was celebrating his new found survival. The success of 'KBC' and Aditya Chopra's 'Mohabattein' had saved him. His son Abhishek had also completed his education in the USA and had returned back. It was largely felt that he was being honed to be at the helm of affairs at ABCL. Later there was a strong speculation of hush-hush plans afoot to launch him in the title role of 'Emperor Bahadur Shah Zafar' in J.P.Dutta's proposed opus 'Aakhri Mughal'. This kind of grapevine wafting in the wind made people swell in anticipation of watching Bachchan's son sprout wings. Expectations started rising. For now, there was a distinct veil of secrecy in the media as to the young junior's movements, appearances and exposure. Naturally the heightened curiosity was because of a high pedigreed, star aspirant being prepared for a yet to be announced project. His demeanour and rare public appearances, donning shiny sherwanis, sporting a thick mane of hair matched with a deep black stubble, indeed such signs pointedly matched to his rumoured launch as the 'Aakhri Mughal'.

Sadly, for reasons never known, J.P.Dutta's prestigious project which was never formally announced, remained a stillborn. He now replaced it with a script titled 'Refugee'.Nonetheless, 'Refugee' was big in terms of casting. It was now official that 'Refugee' would be the Junior Bachchan's debut and would have Kareena Kapoor, the second grand daughter of Raj Kapoor, as his heroine. The 'Rann of Kutch' was chosen as its backdrop. With his fondness for searching beauty in blandness, J.P.Dutta's camera man had his task cut out. The desert sands worn out by the might of the sun, in his past films like 'Ghulami' and 'Border', was now replaced by the never ending miles of salty clay and mud banks dotted with thorny bushes.

For the masses, 'Refugee' appeared as an art film set on a lavish commercial scale. Abhishek Bachchan, Kareena Kapoor, the entire cast of Kulbhushan Kharbanda, Ashish Vidyarthi, Jackie Shroff, Sunil Shetty, Anupam Kher. Helped by enchanting music by Anu Malik and lyrics by Javed Akhtar; his pen had enthralled listeners three years back in 'Border'.

Abhishek's debut film was appreciated but it failed to breach any records. Its money quotient remained true to its title; that of a 'refugee'!

The confused audience and the trade were in the midst of a long debate on whether Bachchan junior had it in him or not. As they were still trying to decipher and still undecided on their verdict on him, Abhishek Bachchan was handicapped again, by a quick-fire second release that left him gasping for breath. A disaster called 'Tera Jadoo Chal Gaya' in the form of his second film, released within a few weeks after the release of 'Refugee' harmed his equity. It also reflected his illustrious father's unplanned ways and lack of thought in planning his son's career. This became more telling in an Industry where he had been a Numero Uno for several years; well aware of the nitty gritties, the dos & donts. The failure of 'Tera Jadoo Chal Gaya' was a body blow which broke the young man's back. Even before a crisis management strategy could be taken up, along came another thunderous flop called 'Dhai Akshar Prem Ke' which had Aishwarya Rai alongside him.

The newest star son on the rise, Hrithik Roshan had producers eating out of his hand. The superlative box office success of 'Kaho Na Pyar Hai' rewrote the rules of rearing a superstar. So naturally, this young man was being wooed by several A-listed film makers. Prominent were Vidhu Vnod Chopra for 'Mission Kashmir' opposite Preity Zinta and Sunjay Dutt (Preity Zinta after her debut in 'Dil Se' had started giving tough competition to the established duo of Rani Mukherjee, Kareena Kapoor and the newly sprouted Ameesha Patel.) Subhash Ghai for 'Yaadein' opposite Kareena Kapoor,

Yash Chopra for 'Mujhse Dosti Karoge' opposite both Rani Mukherjee and Kareena Kapoor. There was the 'retail king' Kishore Biyani's foray in to film production where Hrithik's lead was played by Esha Deol- the daughter of Dharmendra-Hema Malini. There was also Rajshri Productions' 'Main Prem Ki Diwani Hoon'and Dharma Production's 'Kabhi Khushi Kabhi Gham'.

This young man who had everything on his side; admirable looks that epitomized suaveness, killer-packs, graceful dancer and the success of his film still warmly perched on his head appeared to be infallible. Therefore it became a matter of great intrigue when every film of his started toppling.

Like the proverbial domino effect, the failure of Hritik Roshan's films also hit his heroines where Rani Mukherjee and Kareena Kapoor too had to bear the brunt. It also gave a body blow to film makers like Subhash Ghai and Sooraj Barjatya. To the befuddlement of all this 'Greek God' seemed to be skidding towards a calamitous 'Greek tragedy'.

Being Cool

"Aaj Pooja, kal koi dooja"-Akash

The change in societal perceptions happened sooner with the advent of the millennium. Poverty and unemployment which had reached critical mass in the late seventies had actually started dimming in the nineties. The opening of the economy happened in 1991 when, the then Prime Minister Narasimha Rao under the tutelage of his finance minister Manmohan Singh, overnight, devalued the rupee against the dollar. This brought in dollops of FDI in to the opportunity starved country. The strategy worked and a decade later the country was on fast mode; steady income was changing the mindset as a result of which the youth were breaching a new level.

One of the first to showcase this social change was Farhan Akhtar's 'Dil Chahta Hai'.

Javed Akhtar launched his son Farhan, as a director in this path breaking film which gave a new impetus. The story was as fresh as the new millennium under which the youth of the country were basking. In the midst of all the opportunities in a country now surging ahead economically, Farhan's story skillfully merged the age old factors of friendship, love and commitment.

'Dil Chahta Hain' was a story of three friends: Aakash (Aamir Khan), Sameer (Saif Ali Khan) and Sidharth or 'Sid'(Akshaye Khanna), three urban guys playing three author backed roles. The backdrop is of a life in plenty and what actually troubles each of the protagonists is their individual take on love and commitment.

Akash feels love is 'silly', Sameer is confused but the allure of love makes him succumb at every step. Sid watches them with amusement but himself faces the heat when he falls in love with an attractive divorcee fifteen years his senior (the resurfacing of Dimple Kapadia in a rare role.) Ironically all the three in the course of leading their lives in the cool quotient of holidaying, partying, pursuing business and their hobbies, eventually discover love as an element which changes their lives. The film defined the onset of "being cool' where being committed and straddled with love was never a priority but in the end, the climax shatters this belief.

The song *"Koi Kahe Kehta Rahey '* sung by the three at a happening pub resonating with loud music and psychedelic lights, turned on it's head, the *'Papa Kehtey hain '* number which was picturised on one of them more than a decade ago.

Aamir Khan as 'Raj' the young collegian in 'Qayamat Se Qayamat Tak' extolled the virtues of his father and his intent in becoming worthy of him by either becoming an engineer or 'making a naam in business'. Thirteen years later the persona of 'Raj' had evolved for the better. He and his like minded friends in 'Dil Chahta Hain', do not believe in shedding tears on split bonds. They instead "pride on the sparks in their eyes where victory or defeat no longer has any meaning". *'Hum hain naye andaz kyon ho purana"* -we are the new so why should we bask in the old: these lyrics were a precursor to the 'New India'.

The act of zooming off on a sudden holiday to Goa; (Akash announces it in the middle of the night to his friends to "pack and leave"); the three driving away in a top less Mercedes stood out as the New India's iconic scene of freedom and adventure. Just as Ooty epitomized the nineties with its glades and tea plantations, Goa became an emblem of the millenium. The three staring at the sea from the top of 'Fort Chapora', unwittingly, inspired the country to draw out their back packs and travel to Goa. The state of Goa has perhaps never been more immortalized than this one scene from 'Dil Chahta Hai'. Sartorially, the gelled hair look started appearing. Musically, Shanker-Ehsan –Loy too gave their best, and of course that thousand watt smile by Preity Zinta- all added to this exuberance called 'Dil Chahta Hai'.

The success of 'Dil Chahta Hai ' gave the industry an avant garde prodigal called Farhan Akhtar and the echoes of this hit breathed a new life in to the careers of the three: Aamir Khan, Saif Ali Khan and Akshaye Khanna.

Of the three, Aamir Khan realized the far reaching effects of fringe elements in film making: the power of a script if well written, the music when it is topical and, the imagination of a laterally thinking director. In a way he could perhaps realize how Rajesh Khanna had benefitted from this: when the script, music, sets, locales, art direction were more focussed on their task than merely trying to harvest the box office appeal of one lone star. In addition, Aamir Khan for the first time meddled with his appearance; on the advice of Farhan Akhtar he had grown a little goatee below his lower lip, presumably to lend a touch of yuppiness to the persona of 'Aakash'. For Aamir Khan 'Dil Chahta Hai' was a watershed event. At the ripe age of 35 he woke up to the fact that his oscillation of fortunes could be arrested by having a third eye inside his mind that would focus on these other aspects and gain to stand a fool proof chance at the Box office.

His 'Lagaan' too became a landmark success and went off to become India's entry to the Oscars. Sitting pretty on the twin hits of 'Dil Chahta Hai' and 'Lagaan' Aamir Khan could now lay siege to Shah Rukh's throne.

It is also worth mentioning that, the day 'Lagaan' released, Anil Sharma- a defunct director from the eighties created box office history. The film was 'Gadar' which starred Sunny Deol & Amisha Patel with Amrish Puri. Said to have been based on one of those several tales thrown up by the 1947 partition, 'Gadar' struck all with awe. It proved to be Sunny Deol's biggest hits which overshadowed his 1990 film'Ghayal'. Interestingly, both 'Lagaan' & 'Gadar' clashed on a same Friday, yet both turned hits. 'Lagaan' was a more prized film in terms of being laterally different. Both the stories narrated was based on pre-independence, but 'Gadar' had more of jingoism wrapped around it and budget wise 'Gadar 'seemed to have spent a way larger sum than 'Lagaan'.

However, even though 'Gadar' made more money it was 'Lagaan' which won critical acclaim and walked away with all the awards. It swept the Filmfare awards in almost all categories:best film-best actor-best director-best lyrics-best story-best music. It even went off to celebrate its grand finale in Hollywood where it tragically missed the Oscar.

While the makers of 'Lagan' and 'Gadar', films based on pre-independence events, were savouring its dividends, down south Kamalahasan released his bilingual 'Hey Ram' which was based on an event just after Independence: the assassination of the 'Mahatma'.

Written produced and directed by Kamalahasan, it was a big budget movie that starred Shah Ruk Khan, Rani Mukherjee, Hema Malini, Vasundhara Das, Naseeruddin Shah and Kamalahasan as the leading man. 'Hey Ram' was well researched. Even though the title arched eyebrows, the events shown were stark facts. More heinous were those blood curdling riots that rocked Calcutta on the eve of Partition. This had happened due to a clarion call given by Muhammad Ali Jinnah which was notoriously named as 'Direct Action'. The film though made as an emblem for peace, love and brother hood, yet, was based on circumstances pointing to the failure of Gandhi in arresting the barbaric turn of events. 'Hey Ram' was embellished with decent performances, and its sets and music were true to that period. Especially the explosive performances by Saketh Ram (Kamalahasan) and Aparna (Rani) his wife. The eroticism between the two is crackling. Perhaps the only factors which went against its box office performance was the casting of Shah Ruk Khan in a stellar role (not as a hero) and Kamalahasan's zero box office value in the hindi belt.While the people gave a thumbs up to the jingoistic 'Gadar' and a thumbs down to the somber 'Hey Ram', one pair of film makers were playing out a rescue act.

If at one time there were Stars on whom film makers piggy backed to success, it was the other way round also. Teams like Abbas-Mustan ensured the survival of careers. Not only theirs but also certain actors languishing on the brink of obsolesence.

In 2001, Akshay Kumar & Bobby Deol got a fresh vial of elixir in the form of a thriller called 'Ajnabee'directed by the duo. Though a crime thriller, it was ostensibly based on millennial theme parties where grape vines whispered about the existence of taboo events like'wife-swapping'. Of course, there was no such thing and actually turned out an element of suspense thrown in to hoodwink the audience! The film was lavishly produced by the Jain Brothers with Akshay Kumar in a sort of negatively shaded role with Kareena Kapoor and newbie Bipasha Basu oozing oodles of sex appeal. Kareena Kapoor was already one rung higher with the unexplained success of a film called 'Mujhe Kuch Kehna Hain' that had Jeetendra's son Tushar Kapoor in the lead.

Salman Khan's ranking further dipped with an outrageous film called "Chori Chori Chupke Chupke'.

He also, inadvertently, affected the careers of his co-stars Preity Zinta and Rani Mukherjee. They were also hit by body blows due to the shocking flops by the blue-eyed boy Hrithik Roshan. But as they say 'Fortune favours the brave'; these pretty ladies were buoyed from an unexpected source; the rise of Saif Ali Khan.

In the arena of film making, Subhash Ghai, the self proclaimed 'Showman' hit few notches lower due to the debacle of 'Yaadein', another ex-performer N.Chandra after the sinking of 'Beqabu' plopped himself ashore with a comedy film called 'Style'. A low budget film with rank newcomers; Sharman Joshi and Reema Sen (Moon Moon Sen's daughter)

Raj Kumar Santoshi tried furthering his 'Damini' act by once again making a woman oriented film called 'Lajja'. It had Manish Koirala & Jackie shroff. With a title similar to a book by Taslima Nasreen which proved very controversial (and still is) and pre –reviews promising a film as shattering as expected, 'Lajja' failed to impress. The average performance of '1942-A love Story' and the flop of 'Lajja' pushed away the stardom of Manisha Koirala. She would now be lost in hubris of alcohol and obsolescence.

While Amitabh Bachchan achieved nothing by playing twin personalities in 'Aks' directed by a new director called Rakesh Omprakash Mehra, his son, again bit the dust in 'Bas Itna Sa Khwab Hai'.

In this morass of mediocre offerings by A-listers, the coast was clear for Karan Johar to hit bull's eye with his 'Mother of all multistarrers'. The film was 'Kabhi Khushi Kabhi Gam'.

Dharma Production's successful scion and the industry's much loved director released his second film, a magnum opus which had the veritable who's-who of the Industry.

It starred Amitabh and real life wife Jaya Bhaduri. The last time they acted together was a decade ago in the written off 'Silsila'. It also starred the reigning pair of Shah Rukh - Kajol; also had Hrithik Roshan & Kareena Kapoor with Rani Mukherjee thrown in as a special appearance. Remaining stellars shared by veterans like Farida Jalal, Alok Nath, Johnny Lever, Sushma Seth,Simone Singh and actress from the 50's, Shashikala. For the technical departments he hired the best: costume by Manish Malhotra, Rocky S and Sabrina Khan; makeup by Mickey Contractor; sets by Sharmishta Roy. The lyrics were penned by two and for its music he brought in three music directors and a fourth for the background score! Noted film critic Khalid Mohamed remarked "this film was a complete Banquet".

In terms of casting it paled in to insignificance all its predecessors. Its opulence went over the top to set new benchmarks of extravagance. A huge mansion nestled inside a coniferous forest in England, is to be believed, as the 'Raichand'residence in Delhi. In this 'Delhi mansion', Mr Raichand (Amitabh) is a rich business man who commutes in choppers, sips exquisite wines from narrow flute glasses while reclining on a deep couch beside a huge fireplace. For him opulence lies in overkill, like the daily morning 'puja' held by his wife that resembles a crowded wedding 'mandap', or his birthday celebrations graced by the hobnobbing rich, where shapely blonde woman shake their legs, or whether it is about spending'some millions' in buying an expensive chopper for his 'adopted' son Rahul(Shahrukh). When that son falls in love with a girl from a 'mohalla' of the 'hoi polloi'- hell breaks loose. Ties are severed, tears flow and the son leaves home in 'ramayan' style. The director's motive behind showing such symbols of opulence was to dwarf the wealth of Raichand under Rahul's act of abdication; for the audience, leaving choppers, luxury mansions and throwing away his right of inheritance made Rahul exemplary. But that didn't mean the audience is herded in to the 'mohalla' which triggered the abdication. The opulence is slightly toned down where the story moves away from huge mansions and shifts its focus to London where they live in duplex villas, visit 'rockaholic pubs',chill around in Hayabusas and Ferraris, where the younger brother Rohan(Hrithik) perseveres in bringing them together and also falls in love with 'Poo' (Kareena Kapoor)his 'babhi's sister.

While this film won five Filmfare awards that included Jaya Bachchan winning one in best supporting category, her son, Abhishek Bachchan was further tarred by the flop of 'Haan Maine Pyar kiya Hai'.

While Karan Johar was flying high the emblem of Dharma Productions, a group of makers were planning films on a chapter from pre-independence glory. It was about the Iconic revolutionary, Bhagat Singh. News soon spread about three films being a biopic on the same martyr. One was 'Shaheed-e-Azam' which had a new actor called Sonu Sood playing the role of Bhagat Singh. Coincidentally, another film based on the same topic was started by Rajkumar Santoshi who cast Ajay Devgan as Bhagat Singh. Funnily, this also made the Deol family start a film called '1931 Shaheed' where they cast their younger scion Bobby Deol as Bhagat Singh. Thus began a race where both films huffed and puffed towards the finishing line. The race became sensationalised and brought out their acrimony in to the open. Both released on the same day and as a result 'both the Bhagat's cannibalized each other'. While Santoshi's 'Legend of Bhagat Singh' was appreciated, Dharmendra's film which was meant to be a 'coup d'etat' turned out to be a 'coup de grace'! Both, Devgan and Raj Kumar Santoshi won a National Award for their efforts.

Similarly, an 'ephipanic' moment hovered over Anupam Kher. He tried a personal makeover by turning director in a film titled 'Om –Jai-Jagdish'. This was an interesting title taken from the opening lines of a very popular hymn. Rich business man turned producer called Vashu Bhagnani who had earlier produced the super-hit 'Coolie No.1' decided to back him and to steer it well, helmed in Anil Kapoor-Abhishek Bachchan-Fardeen Khan. But this 'heavenly title' failed to please the Gods and that put paid to Anupam Kher's directorial aspirations.

As Fridays came and went, it catapulted some unlikely actors and sometimes passed away without making any judgement. Epoch changes too were taking place where leading contenders for the throne were also setting up their own production houses.

Since the beginning, actors did dabble in production by starting their own banners: Dev Anand (Navketan), Manoj Kumar (VIP Films), Shashi Kapoor (Prithvi Pictures), Shatrughan Sinha (Ramayan Chitra), Rakesh Roshan (Filmkraft) Dharmendra (Vijayta Films),Jeetendra (Balaji Pictures). While Raj Kapoor of R.K.Films owned his own studio, some like Dilip Kumar (Citizen Films) or Rajesh Khanna merely invested and their banners had a short life. Many from yore burnt their fingers and even rendered penniless. Today's times had become more inherently insured.

Aamir Khan set up 'Aamir Khan Productions that produced 'Lagaan' and now Shah Ruk Khan set up 'Dreamz Unlimited' partnering with Juhi Chawla and her millionaire husband Jai Mehta. Shah Ruk Khan who by now had earned the moniker of 'Baadshah', came out with a historical film based on a page from India's ancient history. He tried making a film on 'Emperor Ashok' and the attempt was titled 'Asoka '. The film was directed by veteran cinematographer Santosh Sivan who was famed for filming Mani Rathnam's films like 'Iruvar' and 'Roja'. In Hindi film world he gained acclaim by earning the Filmfare award for filming Bobby Deol's debut film 'Barsaat'. As a cinematographer in 'Asoka, he certainly outdid himself but the script failed him. The major flaw was it's inability in portraying the emperor the way he should have been. The great emperor had gained a supreme position in history by his legendary exploits and who towered in history textbooks and the nation's Constitution where the greatest symbols of his legacy lie embedded (The Asok Chakra and the Four-headed lion). In hindsight it also appeared a case of miscasting where Shah Ruk Khan just could not match up to the great Emperor's stature.

The tepid response to 'Asoka' put paid to Santosh Sivan's directorial career, similarly his peer Ram Gopal Verma's

'Mast' (a story dear to his heart) also failed. So Verma decided to revert on his take on the Underworld- once again!

This time it was a film called 'Company' which clearly alluded to the exploits of fugitive don, Dawood Ibrahim. 'Company' traced the events leading to Dawood's rise and his supposed fallout with his one time key partner 'Chotta Rajan'. With a chilled out coolness displayed by Ajay Devgan, the thumping chases and see-saw moments all the way from Mumbai to Africa and on to Malaysia and the numbers *'Sab Ganda hai par Dhanda hai yeh"* and " *Bach Ke tu Rehna'* sung with an R.D.Burman fervor- all adding to it's tempo.

With 'Company''s success the industry got another star-son: Vivek Oberoi, erstwhile character actor Suresh Oberoi's son. Young Vivek was anything but rooky. With his mean boy looks, silken hair, piercing eyes, Vivek stood eyeball to eyeball against Ajay Devgan. To the great delight of Vivek, the success of 'Company' was soon followed up with YRF film 'Saathiya' where he starred opposite A-lister heroine Rani Mukherjee. Then followed 'hara-kiri'! Or was it mismanagement and over-confidence? That question never found an answer but what actually emerged was bright star Vivek Oberoi had started waning. He got stuck in subsequent Ram Gopal Verma projects like 'Road' which scuttled his promising career. His situation got further exacerbated when he crossed swords with Salman Khan over an alleged dispute concerning his then girlfriend.

Salman Khan was stuck in a whirlwind of disgusting films; mostly insipid love triangles starring Rani & Preity Zinta where the 2nd biggest Khan of the Industry was reduced to biting dust every Friday. Ridiculous films made seemingly without any motive like 'Chal Mere Bhai', 'Tumko Na Bhool Payenge', 'Kahin Pyar na ho Jaaye,' 'Chori Chori Chupke Chupke', 'Hum Tumhare Hain Sanam'--each outdoing the other in mediocrity. Clawing away every Friday and after entertaining a generation with unforgettable Blockbusters, he watched with disbelief the others racing ahead of him. It was a trying moment for this man who also had to go through the ignominy of putting up a regular appearance at Mumbai's Bandra Police station for allegedly being in the know, of tainted finance used for a film called 'Chori Chori Chupke Chupke'.

Xerox

"Kaun kambakht bardasht karne ke liye peeta hain."--Devdas-2

While the 'Second Khan' was battling on various fronts, the 'Third Khan' was getting ready to unveil the biggest extravaganza of his career. A remake of Bimal Roy's 1954 black and white classic 'Devdas', this one was produced by Bharat Shah, a prosperous diamantire and directed by Sanjay Leela Bhansali.

Brought out almost half a century after Bimal Roy's classic, he was able to maintain the poignance but went overboard in depicting the period. Since the time the novel was written more than a century ago, the word 'Devdas' remains a metaphor for people weighed down by a broken heart; A normal,well to do man when cloaked with a four week stubble and swept under a melancholic look, would inevitably be met with a barb that would read some thing like this:

"Kya Devdas banke aaya hai !!" (why have you come like a 'devdas'?)

The barb was loaded. It meant the man is battling depression, and on the path to be a sure loser. When a generation sighted that proverbial protagonist in Bhansali's film, they sat up and watched!

The remake remained true to its original. But he did take liberty in bending it by bringing together the two characters: 'Parvathi' and 'Chandramukhi'. Sarat Chandra Chatterjee the original writer kept them afar, while Bimal Roy had brought them fleetingly close in a background song sequence, in what appeared to be an exchange of a mere glance between the two. Bhansali took this liberty to perhaps enable him to insert a long song and dance extravaganza that seemed to put forth their personal links thru *dola re dola*. Indeed, Madhuri Dixit former 'numero uno' and Aishwarya Rai a strong contender, dancing together in front of the idol of goddess 'Durga' augmented Bhansali's larger designs.

But movie buffs would find it impossible not to compare it with the 1954 classic; just as one searches for cinematic similarity or artistic poaching between 'Deewar' and 'Ganga Jamuna'; or the merits in comparing the biggest hit 'Sholay' with it's failed parallel 'Shaan'.

For a Bimal Roy loyalist, Bhansali's 'Devdas' was a 'mere colour xerox'. Compared to Bhansali's presentation, Bimal Roy's film appeared too frugal but truthful. Those were days of the black and white era. Five decades of change had now ushered in modern techniques like cinemascope, SFX, Dolby-contributing to bring alive the scale imagined by Bhansali whereas Bimal Roy's 'Devdas', being true to its times, lacked the outrageously garish sets and costumes that resembled more of a Tsar's palace than the residence of an affluent zamindar from 19th century British-India.

Shah Ruk Khan was 'Devdas', the broken-hearted man who does not hit back by eloping nor harbors any designs of conquering 'Paro'; strangely, he finds triumph in consuming alcohol to throttle her memories. His friend 'Chunilal' (Jackie Shroff a poor patch if compared to Motilal) ushers him in to the world of nautch girl 'Chandramukhi' (Madhuri Dixit).

The choreography by Birju Maharaj, was another major highlight. It not only complemented the extra mile travelled by Bhansali but also showcased Madhuri Dixit's stature of having rightfully been a worthy successor to Sridevi. As 'Chandramukhi,' she certainly towered over Aishwarya Rai's 'Paro'.

Bimal Roy's version was soaked with an authentic Bengali feel, especially its music. More than two songs were based on the 'baul' form of music whose influence is still widespread in Bengal. Moreover, it was bejeweled with the likes of Dilip Kumar, Vyjayantimala, Suchitra Sen and Motilal who were arguably some of the first legionnaires of bollywood. While Bansali retained the symbols of Bengali marriagehood and a spattering of few bengali words, he did away with the 'bauls' and brought in Ismail Darbar's music based more on Hindustani classical. The differences even though clinical, both the versions succeeded in crying out his agony; A battle between the love and egos of the two tragic lovers, indeed, the tale of 'Devdas' epitomized the triumph of Sorrow.

Yet again Shah Ruk Khan won the aisles, and the awards; the others were still a distance away. There was the 1st Khan gingerly walking on a parapet. There were Akshay Kumar

& Sunjay Dutt, still able to hang around. Saif Ali Khan too was breathing after the appreciation in 'Dil Chahta hai'. But for Salman this was entirely his worst possible period. For quite some time bad films starring the once upon a time blue eyed boy, were being unfailingly torn apart, by critics and audience alike. His last major hit was Sanjay Bhansali's 'Hum Dil De Chuke Sanam'. Those days, his drunken escapades too had started appearing in leading papers. As a result, one dark night, on September 28th, 2002, Salman Khan, was alleged to have rashly driven down his SUV over a pavement, and himself- in to a cul-de-sac; he allegedly ran over three pavement dwellers. Flattened under a heap of flops, Salman Khan was in limbo. In such terrible times, 'Tere Naam' a Satish Kaushik directed film brought in rays of hope.

The film narrated the pain of a young man called 'Radhey'. Due to stark circumstances which run out of control, his beloved is married off by her brother to another man while Radhey is beaten up badly and later finds himself in a mental asylum.

Being a deeply emotional film, Salman Khan appeared miscast, but his true to life performance made the average cinegoer empathetic towards 'Radhey' (and towards Salman Khan) for a similar turmoil going on in his off screen- life. The empathy which was shown in the incarceration of Sunjay Dutt, that very element was working towards the emotional upheavals of the 2nd Khan. In one stroke 'Tere Naam', which was a remake of the tamil super hit "Sethu", erased both: the shoddy memory of his recent flops and the emotional quakes in his life.

With the second Khan finally heaving some sighs of relief, the next year saw the underworld expert (Ram Gopal) slipping away, eroding his equity in films like 'Darna Mana Hai'.

Abhishek Bachchan continued to get more trashed in films like "Kuch Na Kaho' and 'Mumbai Se Aaya Mera Dost'. Suraj Barjatya, the film maker with promise, was proving to be a flash in the pan. His big budget 'Main Prem Ki Deewani Hoon' with Hrithik Roshan-Abhishek Bachchan-Kareena Kapoor just disappeared. Hrithik Roshan too would have vanished after this flop if not for a reprieve from his father Rakesh Roshan. His film 'Koi Mil Gaya' was based on borrowed inspiration from the world wide classic made by Steven Spielberg during the eighties: ET- 'The Extra Terrestrial'. Rakesh Roshan the crafty film maker, deftly weaved an interesting story around this idea that showed Hrithik as a special child (Rohit Mehra) who gains immense physical prowess after coming in to contact with an alien who has lost its way in to Earth.

After a long time a Sci-fi film (after the long forgotten 'Mr X in Bombay') delighted the audience. For Rakesh Roshan 'Koi Mil Gaya' was more than just a feather on his cap; through this film, a father rescued his son from oblivion.

While a father kept his promise, another son failed to follow through on his debut success. Farhan Akhtar's second film 'Lakshya' based on a young boy's lack of focus in life proved to be a downright bad film.

Amitabh Bachchan, now in his successful new innings in both, the Big screen and small, climbed one more notch higher with the success of Ravi Chopra's 'Baghbaan'. Playing a couple on the verge of retirement, Amitabh & Hema Malini struck the right chord. As parents with limited financial reserves and practically no other options, 'Baghban' narrated the sad truth of society that we live in; where well-to-do children, if given a choice, would not mind keeping them a distance away. The success of 'Baghbaan' rekindled the name of 'B.R.Films'. Owned by B.R.Chopra who was the man behind many memorable hits of the nineteen-fifties and sixties 'Kanoon', Naya Daur', Waqt' 'Hamraz' and the popular television serial 'Mahabharath' of the eighties.

With the success of 'Aitraaz' Akshay Kumar remained eligible for the hunt. But of all the hunters, the 3rd Khan clearly had an edge. Not just as a Star but as a business man too. He soon demerged his production house 'Dreamz unlimited' and set up a bigger entity calling it 'Red Chillies Entertainment. It's first creation was 'Main Hoon Na' with Farah Khan, a renowned choreographer now donning the director's hat. The freshness in the film was perhaps for the first time, Shah Ruk Khan playing a character in his 30's as 'Ram Sharma', a captain in the Indian army. He works alongside his father 'Shekhar Sharma' (Naseeruddin Shah) who is a brigadier in the same regiment. In a skirmish with 'Raghavan' (Sunil Shetty) a terrorist, 'Shekhar' is mortally wounded and reveals in his dying gasps to 'Ram' that he has a step brother living far off in the hills. So in order to straighten out the past deeds of his father, 'Ram' sets about in visiting the college where his half-brother 'Lucky' (Zayed Khan) is studying. He enrolls as a student in the same college so as to monitor 'Raghavan's' nexus with guerilla elements and be in close proximity to

'Lucky'. Ostensibly, it is also meant to help him complete the formality of passing out as a graduate since this certificate had eluded him. Since his mindset is still from the early 'Nineties,' this throws up comic interludes and run-ins in the form of his sartorial sense; of wearing bell bottoms and rooting for songs from the 'seventies'.

Farah Khan's agility in maintaining twin roles of choreographer and director were seamless. The film resembled the trajectory of a Rakesh Roshan film wherin, every scene was inserted with a great deal of thought behind it. Anu Malik's music, the exuberance of Sushmita Sen as 'Chandni' the chemistry teacher (who catches the fancy of Ram), the debut villainy of Sunil Shetty as 'Ragavan', all added up to churn 'Main Hoon Na' in to a major hit.

Dr Bhai

"Life mein jab time kam rehta hai to double jeene ka"-Murli Sharma aka 'Munna Bhai'.

This one was from a director no one had heard of. His name was Raj Kumar Hirani, who regularly dabbled in making Ad films. Teaming up with Vidhu Vinod Chopra, Hirani came out with the mother of modern day comedies called 'Munna Bhai MBBS'.

From the maker who had taglined one of his earlier film 'Parinda' as the 'most violent film ever made', this was an unlikely subject. Through 'MunnaBhaiMBBS 'he added a fresh layer to the repertoire of Sunjay Dutt who had just been vindicated as an actor of substance in the dark classic,'Vaastav'. However, this new Bhai called 'Munna' turned the Bhai from 'Vaastav' on his head.

A well known goon (addressed as 'MunnaBhai') who had years ago left his village and sworn to his parents that he would become a doctor, instead, turns in to Mumbai's quintessential 'tapori'(goon). Back home, his parents believe that their son indeed has turned in to a certified doctor so decide to pay him a visit.The aftermath that follows, with the 'Bhai' and his gang hastily giving his 'basti' (slum) a transformation of a believable 'health-Care ' centre with all of them masquerading as 'ward-boys'and 'compounders' with

'Munna' himself strutting around with a stethoscope dangling around his neck- convinces his parents fully that their son is indeed a doctor. But a sudden missive by Dr Asthana, the dean (Boman Irani) exposes him and this triggers an audacious story where 'Munna' through various ingenuities, actually enrolls himself in to Asthana's Medical college as a bona fide student. Assisted by 'Circuit' (Arshad Warsi) his man Friday he drives the dean up a wall by foiling all his plans to get him rusticated. Redefining 'bhaigiri' he endears himself to everyone with his "Jaadu ki jhappi". Through his 'mumbai styled' rhetorics and highly believable situations, he claws in through the loop holes in the system, making this illiterate but intelligent 'wannabe doc' build up an emotional bond with patients downed with afflictions, such as the blocked-out 'Anand bhai',the terminally ill 'Zaheer' and the severely famished parsi 'pappa'. Jabbing every one's conscience with his quick-witted repartees he ends up taming the Dean.

The success of 'Munnabhai MBBS' brought not only instant fame to Rajkumar Hirani it also fortified the 'Vinod Chopra' banner or 'VC films'. For Sunjay Dutt it was an even sweeter event; after being in existence as an action hero, he won the Filmfare award in the category of 'Comic role'. However, even though it was a bigger hit than Shah Ruk's 'Main Hoon Na', two main factors prevented him to lay claim to the throne: His on going case under TADA and his age. The TADA case chewed away his golden years and spat it away in the form of a five year jail term at the Yerawada jail. But as 'Munnabhai' Sunjay Dutt remains timeless.

Very soon one more 'Khan' rose to be a contender, the unlikely Saif Ali khan. 'Hum Tum' was produced by the YRF banner and directed by former television anchor and host Kunal Kohli. 'Borrowing inspiration from the english hit 'When Harry met Sally' Saif & Rani Mukherjee were ideally cast. As the tongue-in-cheeked 'Karan', Saif had already showed his penchant for comedy three years ago in 'Dil Chahta hai'. He had also added a negative role to his repertoire in the Sriram Raghavan directed 'Ek Haseena Thi' as the two tongued despicable lover. The film had no 'hero' and its spotlight was on the cat and mouse game between the victim, Sarika (Urmila Matondkar) and Karan(Saif) who played a full-blooded villain; He kills for money and fakes love for money. But the success of 'Hum Tum' meant much more since it was his first Solo-hero hit. In an industry where you are known by how big was your last film this was an epoch in Saif Ali Khan's career. He could now firmly saddle himself in the league of A-listers. His success also meant succor to talented leading ladies like Rani Mukherjee and Preity Zinta who suffered because of Salman Khan's debacles.

Though his act as 'Karan' was entertaining, his winning the coveted national award for it, sounded of nepotism. Incidentally, his mother was chairperson of the censor board those days.

Soon came another English film, worth copying by, who else but none other than the banner of Mahesh Bhatt. This time he teamed up with Anurag Basu who by now, had the experience of a veteran by directing popular T.V serials like 'Tara' and the never ending 'Kyonki Saas bhi Kabhi Bahu Thi.

The concoction this time was called 'Murder' which was very much based on the English film 'Unfaithful'. The film was a big success; chiefly due to Anu Malik's catchy music and the liberal skin show by its leading lady Malika Sherawat. 'Murder' put it's hero Emran Hashmi (Bhatts' nephew) astride a stable path as his earlier 'Footpath' had shown him the door. Post 'Murder' Hashmi also earned a sobriquet of 'serial kisser'. As far as Malika Sherawat was concerned, if the 1986 'Tarzan' had thrown up Kimi Katkar as the 'sexy Jane', then 'Murder' gave the industry a sexy bimbo in Malika Sherawat.

Abhishek Bachchan maintained his continuum of a long bad run through unimaginative films like 'Kuch na Kaho' directed by an appreciated director like Raj Kanwar(he had directed Shah Ruk Khan's debut film) and 'Run' which was produced by 'potential spotter' Boney Kapoor. But Mani Rathnam's 'Yuva' which was a mini-multistarrer of that time having Abhishek-Ajay Devgan-Vivek Oberoi managed to garner some box office success. It even won him a FilmFare award in the 'Best supporting category'. But immediately after the good gained in the averagely successful 'Yuva', junior Bachchan was dealt a body blow by the Ram Gopal Verma directed 'Naach'. It was more of a vehicle designed to launch Varma's new muse: a young aspirant called Antara Mali where he throttled both of them. The ridiculous 'Naach' neutralized all the good that Abhishek achieved through 'Yuva'.

On the other hand his father was turning more ubiquitous than ever.

The show 'Kaun Banega Crorepati' on television had hooked families across and films like Govind Nihalani's 'Dev' and Raj Kumar Santoshi's 'Khakee' further fortified his stature. Practically every bill board in towns had his face with the unmissable 'goatee' endorsing a milieu of products; hair oils to Air Coolers, writing pens to wriggling noodles he was all over.

The YRF Factory

As a brand the name Yash Chopra was witnessing geometric growth. From his first 'Dhool Ka Phool' made in 1959 and in black and white, he had seen them all. By creating India's first true multistarrer in 'Waqt' and a decade later by directing the epics 'Deewar' and 'Trishul' where he, alongwith Salim-Javed, became synonymous with the success of Amitabh Bachchan. Over the past few decades, having watched fortunes grow and the pain of downsides left far behind, 'Yash Raj Films' by the millennium had turned in to a sort of 'Mecca' of bollywood. After the sweet success of 'Chandni' in 1989, he never again faced the barrage of failures which once upon a time had regularly lashed him. 'Lamhe' was the only exception (it did not make money but was creatively appreciated). 'Darr 'and 'Yeh Dillagi soared and of course then came the biggest: 'Dilwale Dulhaniya Le Jayenge'; Mohabattein' 'Dil To Pagal Hain' and 'Veer Zaara'added to the halo around YRF. Besides making films, the father-son duo soon brought in other verticals making it a complete production house. This vertical of overseeing the production of films, choosing ideas, selecting directors, auditioning new comers, were all supervised by the father-son duo. Whoever showed sparks of promise was immediately bank rolled. And they never stuck to their signature formulas of, say, a 'love story' or a 'drama'. YRF was open to any idea which could spell success.

'Dhoom' was exactly what the new 'YRF' now stood for; a new director in Sanjay Gadhvi, a hitherto untried multi-star cast of John Abraham, Abhishek Bachchan, Rimi Sen, Esha Deol and Uday Chopra; where Shah Rukh Khan was not mandatory.

After the success of 'Jism' actor John Abraham with his handsome looks and a formidable V-shaped physique had impressed the audience, richly earning him a lot of female fans. 'Dhoom' was all about bank heists occurring at various spots making the police huff and pant. The case is taken over by Cop Jai Dixit (Abhishek Bachchan). He tracks down the gang who have been committing this with continuous impenuity and zeroes in on Kabir (John Abraham) and his gang of four who disguise themselves as pizza delivery boys to shake chasing cops off their trail.

'Dhoom' was slickly made with an intense polish. It was pronounced a hit and added to John's star ratings. The film also vindicated the business acumen of a new Aditya Chopra, where he mulled extending the model with other stars but retaining the Abhishek-Uday pair. Something on the lines of successful Hollywood film series 'Mission Impossible'. But the 'Dhoom'series had an interesting twist; scripts would be having the main protagonist to have grey-shades and thus stand out to steal the thunder in the climax. In time to come the franchise would be kept as exclusive finished goods in YRF's factory where with slight recalibrations a new 'Dhoom' would roll out.

As John Abraham flashed his dimples, another handsome model turned actor was not able to reach the glory he deserved. His name was Arjun Rampal. A prime model; he was the brand ambassador of Dhirubhai Ambani's textile flagship brand called 'Vimal'. He too, on the lines of Hrithik Roshan had the perfect chiseled looks and physique. But all his good attributes stopped where they began and did not transform in to the charisma required.

Fast And Fade

The next two years threw up interesting films. Not a rash but like a magician's bagful of tricks; impressive historicals which gave you a peek in to the India of yore, a Shakespearean saga, a thriller based on an English copy book that took you on a dizzy ride, a successful franchise and joyful socials with a whiff of the soil that redeemed a superstar. A lukewarm copy of a terrific past some succeeded while a few spectacularly failed.

Ketan Mehta, the director and producer of 'Mirch Masala' fame and, 'Oh Darling Yeh Hai India' infamy, now released his latest-'Aar Paar'. In movie –making jargon it had what they call "masala' entertainment. It had Jackie Shroff as the 'hero' in the role of a 'crook', who believes his crooked ways are natural ways to accrue wealth. Paresh Rawal played the cop who is his 'bete noire' and Deepa Mehta played the 'femme fatale'. After being entrenched in off-beat films, 'Aar Paar' was Ketan's first foray in to mainstream but the film failed. The award winning director now set about with a team of investors for making a second foray. The subject chosen was on the colonial masters of 1857, whose quiet reverie was rudely jolted by an act of revolt by their own 'sepoy' called Mangal Pandey. Aamir Khan who evinced interest in this project was soon signed.

After the resounding success of 'Dil Chahta Hai', the 1st Khan had started weighing all pros and cons before affirming himself to new projects. In line with his proactive thinking he strived for authencity by drowning himself in the role. Therefore, to complete the look of a Brahmin soldier employed with the 'East India Company', Aamir Khan grew his hair shoulder length and started sporting a handle bar moustache. By being spotted all over the public domain in the same get up till it's shooting ended, Aamir Khan's look became a compelling publicity blitzkriek for 'Mangal Pandey- The Rising'. In a way 'Mangal Pandey' was a historical biopic and there were many such made earlier; The last known biopic known to the Hindi audience was on Bhagat Singh made by Raj Kumar Santoshi, prior to it was a muchdelayed 'Razia Sultana' by Kamal Amrohi, before that was 'Gandhi' made by Ben Kingsley and even before was the 1965 'Shaheed'. Travelling further back was 'Jhansi Ki Rani'and those 'Alexander –Porus' flicks made by the grand old man, Sohrab Modi. Closer in time, was Shah Ruk Khan's bastardized version on Emperor Ashoka.

The film's trailers and posters made people restless, after all 'Mangal Pandey' was the man who fired that 'first shot'. Aamir personally toured cities leading its campaign trail, and when it released, the opening scene in the credit titles tingled their excitement : a huge elephant ambling along on the banks of a river ghat and perched over it were three ballad singers, strumming their instruments, mouthing *Mangala Mangala* euologising an 'imminent awakening'.

Sadly, the excitement of the opening scene never traversed the whole length and what emerged was a disappointingly ordinary film. As the reels unspooled, people felt they were watching a run-down version of the 1981 'Kranti'.

As Aamir Khan and its maker were left pondering over the fate befalling their dream project, Amitabh Bachchan gave a knock out performance in Sanjay Leela Bhansali's 'Black'.

Post the success of 'Devdas', he was tall enough to dwarf bulwarks like Subhash Ghai, N.Chandra and even Yash Chopra.

Like Ghai- he focused on the script, like N.Chandra-on pathos and spread his sagas as wide as Yash Chopra, mounting them on lavish sets combing all over the minutiae of film making. After having himself firmly entrenched with the success of 'Hum Dil De Chuke Sanam' and 'Devdas', he now roped in 'Disney Pictures' as one of his producers. For costumes he hired fashion designer Sabyasachi Mukherjee, who with his out of the box collections had gained prominence at the 'Paris Fashion' and 'Lakme Fashion' week. Amitabh Bachchan played 'Debraj Sahay', the teacher of the little girl 'Michelle' who is blind and deaf. The heartbreak of her parents gradually takes the form of neglect for their daughter. This neglect turns her in to a persistingly obstinate and ill mannered child. But Sahay is of sterner stuff. He turns her around even at the cost of offending his employers. After weeks of turbulent sessions between the two, Sahay triumphs. The little Michelle is now a reformed girl and an earnest disciple. As years pass by, Michelle (Rani Mukherjee) grows up to be confident and never allows her twin handicaps to ever overcome her. As Sahay brings colour in to Michelle's dark world, he is slowly pulled in to another world of darkness when he is diagnosed with alzheimer's.

Amitabh & Rani complemented each other thoroughly. It rises higher due to other complementing factors; painstakingly created sets; innovative lightings and camera positions; high ceilings, stone walls and thick swathes of colours pushed every scene in to an old world charm right out off a Dickensian palette. A scene where the Town hall is criss crossed with houses and shops coloured in grey and charcoal, multitude of men walking in black, clasping black umbrellas, offer a metaphor to Michelle's world. The last scene brings out a lump from within when Sahay is spending his last phase of life battling alzheimers. His world is nothing but a blur and yet, peering through those dark clouds in his mind he manages to hoodwink the debilitating disease and recognize the soothing words of Michelle. 'Black' besides being a success also went on to bag more number of Filmfare awards than 'Dilwale Dulhaniya Le Jayenge'. However, just as he had derived success by xeroxing 'Devdas', so was 'Black', which is a complete photostat of an English film called 'The Miracle Worker'.

The abject folding up of 'Mangal Pandey' had dealt a body blow to brand 'Aamir Khan'; the one who was stepping ahead, yet treading carefully, was left stunned. The back to back successes of 'Dil Chahta Hai' and 'Lagaan' which had sprouted the new persona of a 'thinking' actor made the audience to think again ! Once again the focus was on his next move which was soon visible all over. He shaved off his handle –bar (carefully cultivated since a year) chopped off those long shoulder-length hairlocks and donned the avatar of a meterosexual for Rakesh Mehra's 'Rang de Basanti'.

Rakesh Mehra, for numerogical reasons was now writing his name in full form: Rakesh Omprakash Mehra.Even though his last release 'Aks' had tanked, he usually focussed hard on all departments of filmmaking. The story in which Amitabh played 'half- gentleman half-villain' due to the spirit of a slayed villain (Manoj Bajpai) possessing him, didn't impress the audience at all; but its negative result didn't deter Rakesh and he hung on.

'Rang De Basanti', begins with a few lines from the diary of a long dead Englishman who as a jailor in Colonial India, had supervised the hanging of three revolutionaries: Bhagat Singh-Rajguru-Sukhdev. The story was brilliantly anchored over the 1931 'Kakori Conspiracy' case and the five protagonists headed by Sidharth as 'Bhagat Singh and Karan', Kunal Kapoor as 'Ashfakul Khan and Aslam', Atul Kulkarni as 'Ram Prasad Bismil and Laxman' and Aamir Khan as 'Chandra Shekar Azad and Daljeet'. The story in a laterally innovative way blends the spirit and sacrifice of these immortal martyrs, with four youths from today's India, where the roles are cleverly interspersed in to double roles. The proceedings keep cutting back and forth: as episodes from the 'Kakori Conspiracy' and back to modern India. The four are shown as college students; studying is interspersed with bunking; hanging out is also interjected with beer-drinking escapades; harmless cuddle and an embrace also finds the true beat of love ! 'Rang De Basanti' was one of the biggest hit that year and it's biggest beneficiary was Aamir Khan. As they say, people have a short memory. The stink raised by 'Mangal Pandey' was blown off. His dream spell further took him on to another level where he turned director for a film made on dyslexic children.-'Tare Zameen Par'. But his success as a director lost some sheen when Amol Gupte, an ad film maker and original director of this film suddenly decided to abdicate mid-way.

Banners standing tall were YRF, Dharma Productios, Farhan Akhtar's Excel Ent,Sanjay Bhansali's 'SLB Films', Vidhu Vinod Chopra's VVC films, Rakesh Roshan's 'Filmkraft' Mahesh Bhatt's 'Vishesh films', and Sajid Nadiadwala's 'Nadiadwala Grandson'. Putting behind their founder's brutal murder, 'T-Series' bounced back.

The old guards like Subhash Ghai's 'Mukta Arts' were dissipating. The vintage ones like R.K.Films (Raj Kapoor) and Navketan(Dev Anand), MKD (Manmohan Desai) and PMP (Prakash Mehra Pictures) were grounded for lack of successors. Feroz Khan's F.K.Films could not sustain due to creative bankruptcy. These banners, who collectively at some time had been synonymous with the 'Housefull' boards put up during matinee shows, were now extinct. Rajshri Productions, the last word in family socials was suffering due to their unwillingness to hire from the outside. Their scion's record of two super hits swiftly followed by one average and two duds further slided its value. The 'Rajshri' team needs to change quickly. Their core ideas in making family socials is intact, they just need a fresh story teller.

Shah Ruk Khan's latest- 'Red Chillies Entertainment' had now turned in to a full-fledged production house. It had all the functioning departments in completing post-production works. Ambling away was Vishal Bharadwaj's banner- 'VB Pictures'. After having started his career as Gulzar's cinematographer in the film 'Maachis', he soon branched off as a film maker. His fodder for film making content came from Shakespearean tragedies. After the 'Macbeth' inspired 'Maqbool', he now chose 'Othello' as his next; a film called 'Omkara' based on the tragic black moor's unfortunate life. He chose Ajay Devgan as his 'Othello', Kareena Kapoor as the ill-fated 'Desdemona' Vivek Oberoi as the loyal savant 'Cassio',Bipasha Basu as the vixen 'Bianca', and Saif Ali Khan as the diabolic,'Iago'.

Post 1993 'Baazigar': playing a villain was no longer considered a risk, so long as the script was on his side. A continuous regimen at the gym had given him a perfect physique chiselled enough to shed his boyish looks. To cloak his 'playboy' image and also add a menacing look to his 'Iago', he made Saif Ali Khan shave off his head, put his casanova persona on a long pause and shoot non-stop. As the character called 'Langda Tyagi,' mouthing hindi cuss words, topped by a skull-cap hair cut and with an added feature in the form of a slight limp to his gait, ' Langda Tyagi' and his devilry, overshadowed the other males: The film went on to become a hit and made Saif Ali Khan - a hitherto 'limited actor', to bag the FilmFare award as the 'best villain'. 'Omkara's success cleared Saif Ali Khan's rise towards the throne; gloating from two back-to-back successes of 'Hum Tum' and 'Salaam

Namaste', with the latest 'Omkara', he appeared to be on course.

Senior Khan Aamir, topped up his big hit 'Rang De Basanti' with the YRF Produced "Fanaa' bringing him for the first time to be cast with his rival's heroine-Kajol. The film was interesting but the climax was hugely similar to an English thriller 'Eye of the Needle', written by Ken Follet. This fact robbed director Kunal Kohli's glory. 'Fanaa' did not mar Aamir's reputation nor dent the comeback by Kajol. In spite of its flaws it turned out a decent success. But YRF's next one was a money spinner which was the next version of Dhoom: 'Dhoom-2'.

With Aishwarya Rai and Hrithik Roshan, Bipasha Basu and Abhishek Bachchan, 'Dhoom-2'buzzed with excitement. The film went beyond the teaser trailers shown a week back and what unfolded was a mind blowing continuation of the 'Dhoom' spectacle. Flush with the success of 'Krish', Hrithik Roshan showered charisma and spunk which created a dizzying effect coupled with his terrific on screen chemistry with Aishwarya Rai; they looked made for each other. Dizzy locales of the Brazilian city Rio and kick-butting music made 'Dhoom-2' a terrific winner. As per figures available with BOTY, Dhoom-2 did an all india business worth 84 crores which was a landmark result. In a couple of years the prophetic benchmark for measuring success would soon change.

That year, Karan Johar in partnership with his pal Shah Ruk Khan and directed by his protégé Nikhil Advani, brought out 'Kal Ho Na Ho' a film based on much harnessed eternal elements of humanity, love and sacrifice topped with a terminal disease afflicting the hero. With reigning star Shah Ruk Khan as the terminally ill guy with beloved Preity Zinta & Saif Ali Khan 'Kal Ho Na Ho' was preordained to be a hit ! Soon Karan Johar, later that year, was seen attempting to break new ground by pulling out from 'under-the-carpet' taboo topic of extra-marital affairs. The film was 'Kabhi Alvida Na Kehna' and this film also signaled a changing phase in Indian society. In the new India the task of building careers and economic disparities between a man and woman were taking its toll, revealing deep rooted fissures. Relationships were either breaking down or being shoved under " an arrangement'. It spelt the end of popular delusions of 'pati-parmeshwar' and 'pati-vrata'; the fact that a married woman could sleep with another man-was now to be looked upon with empathy-not disdain.

True to his style, Karan brought in Amitabh Bachchan, Shah Ruk, Rani Mukherjee, Abhishek, Kiron Kher, Preity Zinta, and others, with the shooting done entirely in New York. While Karan was announcing the break up of the institution of marriage, another scion, Sooraj Barjatya was making yet another valiant attempt on the sanctity of marriage and called it 'Vivaah'. It kept alive its leading man Shahid Kapoor's and it's maker Sooraj Barjatya's search for that elusive hit, more pronounced. Shahid Kapur's senior Akshay Kumar, who a decade back was himself perched on a rocky boat had steadily swam across. His latest 'Bhool Bhulaiyaa' was a big hit. It was based on superstitions and split-personas and was a remake of a popular Tamil film where again, director Priyadarshan raked in the moolah.

But a remake that raised eyebrows was Farhan Akhtar recycling the 1977 hit 'Don'. It had Shah Ruk Khan essaying what Bachchan had done in his inimitable style. Shah Ruk made a brave attempt in playing both: the ruthless gangster and his simple look-alike which drew sniggers from the audience. This 'Don' could never transcend the magic of 1977, and its muted opening showed Shah Ruk Khan pleading people on television on the occasion of 'Eid' of 2011 to "go and watch his film". However, for all its shortcomings and average ratings and having a long list of loyalists, the film went on to do decent business.

In the midst of these big budget ups & downs came a simple story narrated superbly; the film was 'Khosla Ka Ghosla'. The word 'Ghosla' means a nest while, 'Khosla' was the name of this ubiquitous character you could bump in to while walking in the bylanes of Sadar Bazar or in any of those innumerable parks, neatly maintained by the Delhi Development Authorities.

By the middle of the millenium the effects of consumerism had firmly embedded itself in people's minds: In their thoughts, in their homes and their aspirations.

The national capital, especially, had become a city teeming with 'nouveau riche'. The accepted moral was means be damned; the end was important. What really counted was your duplex bungalow, your convertible and your daughter's destination wedding: How did one manage was not for asking.

To portray such a scenario, debut director Dibakar Bannerji, who was already established as a bonfide ad film maker, came out with 'Khosla Ka Ghosla'. The young director with his take on the social philosophy of the capital based it on characters, who represented the 'new' Delhi. With Anupam Kher(now quite aged) playing a retired government servant 'Kamal Khosla' who aspires to own a piece of land with his retirement benefits; he later realizes that he has been cheated by an unscrupulous real estate dealer Kishan Khurana (Boman Irani). The film ably narrated the aspirational yearnings of a middle class India where land is always looked upon as a safe investment that beats gold in the long run. And this is how most of the people encash this investment to fulfil their long term goals of education, marriage and retirement. The film also explores the under belly of the capital where sharks like 'Kishan Khurana's loud lifestyles is fed by ensnaring naïve prey like the 'Kamal Khosla's. 'Khosla Ka Ghosla turned out to be a good earner and also won a National Award. Its maker Dibakar Bannerjee certainly proved to be a new catalyst for the growth of emerging cinema. Two decades back such a film would be an open and shut case for being categorized under 'Art' cinema.

But in the world of entertainment, where Bollywood towered as the most affordable-the bulwark still had to lean upon Big banners and larger then life icons.

Once again Aamir Khan led the gravy train. The film was 'Ghajini'. It's original had infused great adrenaline in tamil films and it's hindi remake (incidentally by the same producer –director R.Muragadoss) created a bigger hysteria. For Aamir this was one more opportunity to express his acting skills by backing it up with formidable body language. The first was 'Dil Chahta hai' with his goatee; then came Mangal Pandey and his handle-bar followed by the young, clean-shaved look in 'Rang De Basanti'. For 'Ghajini' he sprang up to do the unimaginable; to develop an exemplary physique; complete with rippling biceps and six-packed abs. Toiling hard under a disciplined regime and an unrelenting focus helped him in reaching his goal in about six months. In continuation of the narrative of this film, he also underwent a 'closely-tonsured' hair cut which immediately became a cult fashion. The youngsters lined up at saloons offering the 'Ghajini cut':complete with fake scars on the temples. It's success, even though it was a remake, aided in raising the stature of the 'First Khan' bringing him tantalizingly close to the ranking of the 'Third Khan' who by now was the 'Numero Uno'.

Shah Ruk(the third) was not one to remain outwitted. Very soon he came up with not one but two block busters. The first was from his own banner 'Red Chillies 'where he hired acclaimed choreographer Farah Khan as it's captain. From the many aspirants for its leading lady, he chose a young model from the Kannada film industry called Deepika Padukone. The film was 'Om Shanti Om' whose content was loosely based on Subhash Ghai's 1981 'Karz' and its title, based on its marquee song. Shah Ruk too, on the lines of Aamir,chose to chisel his body by getting himself the fabled 'six-pack' which he gruellingly achieved at the ripe age of 43 years. The untethered success of 'Om Shanti Om' also gave a fillip to fading actors like Arjun Rampal who was in any case dangerously close to extinction. It also gave the industry two reasons to cheer: the rise of two woman- Farah Khan and the young lady Deepika Padukone. Farah Khan and her brother Sajid Khan were related to the Irani sisters; Honey & Daisy. This made them sort of cousins with Farhan Akhtar. As children they always had an even eye for a good film and as they grew they plunged headlong in to the film world; the sister became a choreographer and her brother, Sajid Khan, a television anchor.

The success of 'Om Shanti Om' also raised whispers about the need for the 'third Khan' to get a make over-a much needed change. Even his die-hard loyalists started examining this thought. They yearned for a change in his quotient. His entertainment company had risen to almost his stature. His newest acquisition – Kolkata Knight Riders or 'KKR', a cricket team from the IPL franchise, had a chief minister of a state rolling out the red carpet. But the murmurs for a change were turning in to a mighty roar. Mimicry artistes started building their own fortune by mimicking his acts and dialogue delivery. However, the snotty upstart turned all the naysayers on their heads when his next, a 'YRF' production, shut all in to a deafening silence. The film was 'Chak De'. Directed by Shimit Amin (ex -alumni from Ram Gopal Verma's production house) and scripted by Jaideep Sahni (of 'Khosla Ka Ghosla' & 'Bunty Babli' fame).

None of its ingredients could guarantee success-on paper at least. 'Chak De' was a sports film based on the least feted, yet ironically known, as the 'National Sports' of India called Hockey. It was more conspicuous because this was based on woman's hockey and a team comprising of sixteen rookie actresses. No leading lady.

The basic premise of 'Chak De' was about the harrowing experience of 'Kabir Khan' a hockey player who, in an Indo-Pak final match, concedes a goal and this outcome is held against him. Being a Muslim further exacerbates the opinion of his neighbours in the 'mohalla' where he lives. Shah Ruk Khan as 'Kabir Khan', the vilified muslim player, putting up a lonely battle in trying to vindicate himself by applying for the role of a coach in the Indian woman's team, on which no one is willing to lay their bets, gleamed brilliantly. It was a resurgence of a new kind bringing out the vintage charm of 1993 where he braved all odds and played a lateral character. In 'Chak De', he deglamourized himself completely of all his starry charisma: those trademark dialogue deliveries bringing in a consciously developed hush and quietish charm. 'Chak De' was a bullish hit and shut up all his detractors.

The 2nd Khan was down under. But off screen the man seemed to have tempered down. He was waking up to the fact that he was burning himself out, and all for the wrong reasons. However much he chastised his poor sense of judgement in choosing a project, and of all those adversarial events affecting his life, there was one that held him in good stead; his commitment in maintaining his physique and 'packs". *'Jab Mein commitment karta hoon tab apni ki bhi nahin soonta."*

This commitment came in good form in the Boney Kapoor produced and Prabhu Deva directed 'Wanted'. It brought an end to the incessant line up of flops and added a much needed silver lining to his quest in putting himself back in contention.

As Salman breathed in easy, his close friend, the adroitly accomplished Sanjay Leela Bhansali who epitomized films made up of lavish sets and reigning stars was in the process of mentoring two new ones. At the time of shooting 'Black' he was assisted by two star kids: Anil Kapoor's young daughter Sonam and Rishi Kapoor's son Ranbir. In the midst of creating the 'Black' masterpiece he was also impressed by the diligence of these two youngsters. This gave birth to his next 'Sawariya' that introduced Ranbir & Sonam to the world.

'Sawariya' was based on the Russian writer Fyodor Dostovensky's short story 'White Nights'.A young boy known as 'Sawariya' (Ranbir Kapoor) is in love with the shy Sakina (Sonam Kapoor). Bhansali let his imagination run wild in conceptualizing the sets, through his ingenuity in capturing the wintery coldness of those lands as in Dostoveski's story where inhabitants dwelled in houses made of stone blocks; tall narrow minarets overlooking white domes where scores of people in matching whites move in a graceful sway singing praise of the lord. His team literally recreated the sweeping landscapes and dark wintery nights from an imaginative period that appears fabled; tsarist, communist or Ottoman! He also cast his favourite Salman as 'Imaan', the man whom Sakina loves and Rani Mukherji as the narrator 'Gulabo', the prostitute with a golden heart.

In his debut, Ranbir Kapoor, the 4th generation scion of the Kapoor dynasty, was ironically not bankrolled by grand father Raj Kapoor's 'R.K.Productions. Even though 'Saawariya' proved to be a bumpy start, Ranbir Kapoor did leave an impression good enough for 'YRF' to sign him up for their next 'Bachna Ae Haseeno'. The title was a throwback to a song picturised about forty years ago on his famous father. His leading lady was the new lady, fresh from her success in 'Om Shanti Om': Deepika Padukone.

But the biggest heavy weight film loaded with stars, oomph, glamour, innumerable twists and precipitious turns in its script, exotic locations and high octane edge-of-the seat-suspense was 'Race.' Slick direction by the 'Twin'-Tyrewala brothers of 'Baazigar' fame, star names like Saif Ali, Bipasha Basu, Akshaye Khanna, Anil Kapoor, Katrina Kaif, Sameera Reddy made this film set screens on fire. Its success promptly hoisted Saif Ali Khan on fast track mode. 'Race' was a film, filled to its brim with steep twists and treacherous curves. The cloak and dagger games between the brothers Ranvir (Saif) and Rajiv(Akshaye Khanna) are straight out of a Ludlum thriller. With Anil Kapoor chipping in with his funny 'Hercule Poirot' act and Bipasha Basu and Katrina Kaif as the two 'femme fatales', the film was impregnated to be a heady cocktail of success.

Another contender, Hrithik Roshan, tightened his grip by the success of Ashutosh Gowariker's 'Jodha Akbar'. Its success was preceded by a good amount of trepidation because, a historical in today's time to see light of the day was seen as futile. The last known film based on a chapter from history was Shah Ruk Khan's dismal 'Asoka'. In fact when Gowariker started this project there was no benchmark to compare with. At best it could perhaps be lauded as a prequel to K.Asif's magnum opus 'Mughal-E-Azam'.

"Yeh hamara desh hain. Hum ispe loot ka zakhm nahin lagne denge"
--Jalaluddin Akbar

The film begins with the kingdom of Rajasthan being an epicenter of a mughal thrust to bring the entire clan under one ruler: the Emperor at Delhi. It is the rise of a prince returning back from exile helped largely by his ambitious uncle, the ruthless Behram Khan.This in effect is the core theme from where emerges the love between two most unexpected persons. On the backdrop of Akbar's battles to lay claim to the throne of Delhi, is woven, the sudden matrimonial alliance between 'Jodha' a Hindu princess and 'Jalaluddin Akbar', a Mughal prince. It will be inappropriate to call it a romance as it can wrongly conjure up images of a love story between a beautiful princess and a young prince. On the contrary, love blossoms long after they are pronounced man and wife.

Why and how, does a Mughal prince marry a Hindu princess belonging to a princely Rajput clan is what this celluloid tale is all about.

Ashutosh Gowariker narrates a story rich in heritage with rare panache which was sorely missed in his last 'Swadesh'. Hrithik Roshan is a pleasant surprise with an unexpectedly towering performance as the young 'Akbar'. Gowariker skillfully crafts the two units: the Hindu Rajput characters of Rajkumari Jodha, her father Jaymal the king of Amer

(Kulbhushan Kharbanda), her cousin SujaMal (Sonu Sood) willing to align with any one who can help him in regaining the Throne of Amer and the numerous motley kings of a balkanized 'Rajputana'. On the opposite side are the Mughals: 'Jalal' the prince who is later known as Akbar, 'Maham Anga' the ambitious 'dai'(nanny) who lays seeds of distrust on the path of 'Jodha'and 'Akbar', and 'Hamida Begum' as the Emperor's mother (a surprising cameo by Mrs. Shatrughan Sinha)

A few other characters who perk up the narration: a talkative eunuch giggling loudly at the prospect of a 'temple' being erected in the mughal courtyard; Akbar's childhood guardian, 'Behram Khan' who believes in decapitating the enemy after every conquest; Ataga Khan(Raza Murad) his revenue minister who has an empathetic approach to Jalal's mission in being just & impartial to all

Rewinding 'Jodha-Akbar':

- The ferocious battle of Panipat culminating in the beheading of the Hindu King Hemu by Bahram Khan

- Jalal's first meeting with Jodha (a resplendent Aishwarya Rai) patiently hearing out her conditions of erecting a temple inside the mughal premises: from a seething fury of an impending affront to an empathy towards her helplessness, Hrithik was brilliant.

- Jalal's 'Nikaah' with the reluctant Jodha and then followed by a Hindu marriage. Observe her quivering palm when kept on his.

- Jodha's torment on seeing herself as being palmed off for the sake of warding military threats to her father's kingdom. Being offered a vial of poison is the "only way out" suggested by her mother.

- Jalal holding court in the 'diwane-khas' and the notes of the 'man-mohana'a hindu hymn are within ear-shot distance of the Mughal noblemen. Those few seconds, an emperor and his dilemma as a consort are shown as entwined together.

- Jalal's fury raining down on Adam Khan, Maham Anga's son. He orders him to be thrown off the parapet twice; the first when he wants him killed and the second when he wants him pronounced dead. Later, his tear filled huddle with Maham Anga on why he had to carry out this exemplary punishment.

- Jalal being wonderstruck and tongue tied on being conferred the title of 'Akbar' by his subjects.The Sufi song sequence with each performer mouthing the song perfectly with coordinated movements in geometric precision, climaxing with Jalal going in to a trance-like- state with slow encircling steps.

- Jalal's mute embarrassing moment when he is unable to read what Jodha has written for him as he is an illiterate.

- His tactful skill in suppressing the ire of the 'mullahs' by saying he was not an Afghan marauder out to plunder the country. He was here to stay, rule and continue the lineage of the Mughals. Perhaps, the fact that his Emperor father Humayun was sent into exile weighed heavily on him.

- The final battle between Jalal and his brother-in-law with both their armies, daggers drawn waiting for the final signal to charge.

- Jalal grappling with a rogue elephant single handedly with his sinews well toned.

Cinematically, there was only 'Mughal-e-Azam' that came close to perfection in narrating Mughal history and facets associated with it. 'Jodha Akbar' could be a close second. While 'Mughal-e-Azam' was more about Akbar the Emperor and father of a young prince with romantic leanings, "Jodha-Akbar" shows the young Akbar returning back from exile and trying hard to recapture the glory of the 'Mughals. Looking into the future, he saw the need of winning the unconditional support of the warrior clans of Rajputana by being tolerant towards the religious sentiments of the vast hindoos. He envisaged that his supremacy over 'Hindustan' could not be kept leashed by military supremacy alone. Honour and loyalty too were important factors to be conquered. He not only used his cannons and cavalry but also exercised the power of love and bonding. And what better way than to enter into a matrimonial alliance with a princess of Rajputana, a kingdom that had always been a scourge for the mughals!

'Jodha-Akbar's success also provided food for thought to many film makers who would in coming years base more such projects on historical biopics.After this success the banner 'Gowariker Films' became as respected as it's owner.

With Shah Ruk Khan riding high on 'Chak de' and 'Rab Ne Bana Di Jodi', his closest rival Aamir could not be far behind. He again meddled with his physique where he shed the bulky frame gained for 'Ghajini' to play the role of a college student. He soared higher with that year's biggest hit called '3 Idiots'

"Life is a Race, if you do not run fast you will be a broken 'andaa'-
Professor Sahasrabuddhe

Post millenium, the quest for a life of plenty has become the goal of urban India. Where an entire generation prefers to watch their wards galloping towards a distant mirage for there dwells a bagful of materialistic goodies. Education has become a path to reach those goodies because, appreciative looks, party line whispers are generally about the haves and the have-nots. The end is what matters, damn the means!

The film questions the way education is imparted in an Engineering College (which ostensibly resembles the IIT). Where students have shed their inner aspirations, obeyed the dictum of their parents and enrolled themselves into this 'factory' that churns out robotic engineers onto society. Mr Sahasrabuddhe the principal (Boman Irani) rules with an iron hand and resembles a bureaucrat from the 'License-Raj' era. For Sahasrabuddhe, books are sacrosanct, the theories and definitions in them unquestionable. In his book of rules "life is a race" for students the moment they emerge from their mother's womb. His philosophical advice to them is to emulate the cuckoo who nudges out eggs from another's nest to give a head start to its own breed. His favourite amongst all is a student called 'Chaturlingam' who resembles geeks of today; who mugs his lessons during exams but actually absorbs nothing in terms of learning.

In such an environment enter the '3 Idiots': Ranchod Das Janjhad or 'Rancho (Aamir Khan), Farhan Qureshi (Madhavan) and Raghu (Sharman joshi). Of the three, Rancho is the leader while the other two have sort of lionized him due to his tact ways in bailing himself (and them) out of hopeless situations. By his way of handling the bureaucratic principal or by giving back to his seniors in their own coin when being ragged, Rancho sends all into a buzz. When he takes on the teachers head-on and starts questioning their methods the principal gets piqued and starts pouring fire & brimstone on Rancho and the other two 'idiots'. But Rancho shrugs off his threats and does his own things. He tickles people with his witty repartees, sets off questioning debates, mentors his co-idiots by shaking them by their collars convincing them to follow their hearts; Mentor ho to Aisa ! He finally brings the mighty Principal on his knees by not only topping the grades coveted by Chaturlingam but also gives invaluable aid during an untimely labor condition of his daughter (perhaps the only time where the movie ran a serious risk of being written-off).

Director Raju Hirani's strong script based on a Chetan Bhagat novel gave a contemporary edge to today's times. Aamir Khan, buoyed by an author backed role like Rancho, and aided by witty dialogues and hilarious narrations, was bound to do well.

Madhavan & Sharman as his co-idiots were adequate while Kareena added that mandatory glamour quotient. But it was

Boman Irani as the lisping Principal Sahasrabuddhe who almost stole the show from Aamir. His body language and his sartorial style gave the audience an insight of his mind. His reluctant expression of accepting Rancho as the numero uno student vindicated his acting skills. '3 Idiots' brought Aamir Khan shoulder to shoulder with Shah Ruk Khan. The industry now had two superstars.

While these two Khans were revelling in their hour of glory, Salman Khan had barely pulled himself out of his earlier morass when his next film 'Veer' was released. A period drama and supposedly, a remake of an old Hollywood classic called 'Taras Bulba' where Yul Brynner had played the lead.

'Veer' flopped. Even though it appeared to have been labored hard by it's director Anil Sharma, the film was a visible piece of unwanted relic. It pulled down Salman from the spot where he had clawed back with 'Wanted'.

Success in films remained varied, and these clearly could not throw up a perfect recipe. Be it a thriller (Race), Campus Drama (3 idiots) or a well researched and perfectly mounted historical (Jodha-Akbar). The presence of action oriented films appeared to have been sidelined. The era of films garnished with 'police-politico' nexus was becoming passé. But in the middle of 2010 this gospel was shattered when Salman Khan's home production 'Dabangg' released.

Hundred Crores

"Hum yahan key Robinhood hain"-- Chulbul Pandey

A decade of intelligentsia and thoughtful films; of Shakespearean tragedies and foreign localed love packs filled to their brim, in the midst of these dream catchers, a little known director called Abhinav Kashyap laid out a script from the hinterland of Uttar Pradesh. It smelt of Vishal Bhardwaj's mofussil towns minus the heavy-handedness; it had Ram Gopal Varma's underworld minus its dark and sleazy underbelly; a Mahesh Manjrekar styled story but minus its impetuous flare-ups and tearful sagas. An oft repeated tale of crime and punishment, this film was 'fearlessly' titled 'Dabangg'. Salman the 2nd Khan struck gold.

Being his home production its success made it sweeter. As 'Chulbul Pandey', Salman brought back action in its original glory. No blood, no gory images; the perfect fisticuffs and bang-bang ! Kashyap knew that a crisp fresh look would be the key factor in ensuring its success. The first to be discarded were the denims and T-shirts in all forms; sporting a moustache, wearing cotton trousers with shirt neatly tucked in and his famed torso concealed, Salman Khan breathed life in to this new messiah called 'Chulbul Pandey '. A bigger highlight were the cutting edge dialogues uttered 'Uttar

Pradesh' style; where sarcasm and a philosophical overtone went hand-in-hand.

"hum tum mein itna chhed karenge key confuse ho jaaoge ki saans kahan se ley aur paadey kahan sey"

"Abhi tak sabko nehlaya hain, ab sabko dhounga" (until now had given you all a bath-now am goin to wash you)

Another highpoint was an item number where Malaika Arora sizzled in her figure, just as she had done back then in 1998 atop the train chugging in the Shah Ruk Khan starrer 'Dil Se'. The crackling number *'Munni Badnaam hui'* where she cavorts with both, Salman and Sonu Sood, instigated people in multiplexes to let down their guard, stand up and jiggle unabashedly on the aisles. But the biggest figure dwarfing all was seen even before the end of week one: an hitherto unattained revenue of 100 crores in the history of Bollywood! Tsunami 'Dabangg' catapulted Salman Khan from a new darling (after Wanted) in to a prized possession. He now stood eyeball to eyeball with the other two Khans: Aamir & Shahrukh. Collectively they were now known as 'The Khans': an exclusive sobriquet that spelt triumph, glory and power.

Since that summer of 2010, Salman Khan the 'enfant terrible' has never looked back. The success of 'Dabangg' changed many lives; foremost being Salman and his family. After a long spell of uncertainty, destiny smiled! Being a bachelor and with a lull in his link-ups made all his fans curious about other members in his family; his brothers; their wives; their kids.It was as if his entire clan was now gold-wrapped.

The 4th Khan-Saif Ali, faltered in his subsequent releases; 'Race-2', 'Bullet Raja'. But the one that almost handed him a 'pink-slip' was YRF's 'Tashan'. Made with a great deal of fanfare in which, Anil Kapoor was roped in to play a villain for the first time; Akshay Kumar completing the multi star look and Kareena Kapoor adding real-life romance to the proceedings by sizzling within a bikini in her just acquired 'Size zero'. Yet- the film flopped. But Akshay Kumar absorbed this shock by the twin shields of 'Singh Is King' and 'Rowdy Rathore'. Saif Ali Khan finally put himself out of contention when his own production called 'Agent Vinod', directed by the much feted Sriram Raghavan flopped so badly that it skinned off Saif's star status and flung him out of the race.

Anil Kapoor spread his wings further, towards the West, by bagging an English film called 'A Slumdog Millionaire'. To his pleasant surprise, he found himself to have been a part of an Oscar winning team ! But his erstwhile colleague from the late eighties Jackie Shroff was relegated to an occasional villain's role or the brand ambassador of some obscure product on t.v. The handsome man was now saddled with a perennially puffy face, making him a pale shadow of his heyday, when he was not only a 'dashing lady-killer' but also that rare outsider to debut in this industry.

Speaking about 'Outsider' the same history was being recreated by Aditya Chopra. In line with his company's business model of introducing new actors, he brought in a young man called Ranveer Singh. Tall, decently built, average looks but extremely talented, this man had no familial ties with the industry. The result was 'Band-Baaja-Baraat', starring

Ranveer Singh and Anushka Sharma. The film surprised the audience with its simplicity, truthfulness and upheld the ubiquitous search for excellence and financial independence in mofussil towns; With the 'start-up' culture spreading amongst the youth this film's quick success reflected the aspirations of a quintessential Delhi girl'Shruti Kakkar' & her boy friend 'Bittoo Sharma'. The twosome: Anushka and Ranveer, were under the stipulated three film contract with YRF, therefore the super success of 'Band Baaja Baraat' ensured that the remaining two films would roll out in quick succession enabling the two to spread their wings fly higher.

With this new boy and girl firmly seated in their saddles, the time had come for a courageous lady, who had tethered the entire womankind of India to her soap operas, to now bankroll a film for the theatres. That film was called 'Dirty Picture'. The lady was Ekta Kapoor (Jeetendra's daughter) and the main protagonist was played by Vidya Balan, who incidentally, was a by- product of her earlier television serials.

In 'Dirty Picture' Ekta Kapoor takes you to the world of the 80's; where sex has always been a taboo topic laid bare open only behind closed doors; with conventional, morality bound straps, stretching taut over society; a world which was more regressive than today's permissive times. In such a choked world of socio -economic barriers, the males are either sexually starved or sexually ignorant. Where the three letter word was not an antidote but stamped as "Dirty". In such a world, 'Reshma' forays into the Madras film industry to find herself granting instant gratification to such males and lustfully christened as 'Silk'.

Vidya Balan as 'Reshma' (alias Silk), played the protagonist, which was said to be based on the life of well known starlet 'Silk Smitha'. Making her mark as a vamp Silk turned the concept of a heroine on its head. For distributors, the necessity of finding eternal box office value, hit the right spot when they discover that the serpentine queues outside theaters screening films starring jaded, ageing superstars, were actually a repeat audience who were interested in watching only 'Silk'. With her wailing moans and voluptuously fleshy body, grimacing to heavy dance steps pulverized the front benchers swaying to her movements. Bathed under a dewy sweat, these multitudes of men fantasized 'Silk'. She whets their appetite to break open wonderland, sorely missed in their conjugal world and soon she becomes a 'one-stop' shop for entertainment- Story- hero - heroine be damned!

'Silk' laps up the frenzy and she bares her heart out to strangers, puffs her way to glory and sashays down the ramp of success. Just as her rise is meteoric, her descent downhill is equally fast. She now yearns for true love but bitter truth gnaws away at her when she is jilted by her amorous lovers because she cannot be the 'good' girl to show off to mother, or wife.

Somewhere in between 'Reshma's' heavy moans and tart-like makeup, the movie gets caught in the standstill of monotony and be dismissed as yet another ordinary remake of a starlet. It rises again in the latter parts when she spirals downhill, to be sucked under a vice like grip of alcohol & nicotine. The smooth exterior of 'Silk' is ripped apart to reveal a lonely heart now devoid of any desires. Her last ditch attempts to make a comeback pushes the poor girl further into penury & oblivion. Her verbal duels and angst ridden dialogues with 'Abraham'(Imraan Hashmi) her staunchest foe, bring out the humane side of Reshma. She & her could –not-care-less attitude to 'Abraham's' somber questions are like flint stones out to set each other on fire.

Naseeruddinn Shah was an apt choice to be cast as 'Surya', an ageing superstar who inadvertently helps 'Reshma' usher in the 'Silk revolution'. He also extracts his pound of flesh in having amorous liaisons with her. The music is set to the nineteen-eighties' vigorously paced 'disco' times; one of them is a throwback to songs from the film 'Himmatwala'.

'Dirty Picture' stunned and surprised many. Mid-sized stars played life sized roles, so for its makers it was a money-spinner of another kind. Vidya Balan, hitherto small in stature, had recently crept in to our minds as the demure 'Parineeta' in Vidhu Vinod Chopra's remake of the 1955 film. She went to anchor herself in 'Munna Bhai lage Raho' which again was by the same maker. Vidya Balan until now a quiet romantic foil in her films dazzled all akin to what actress Rekha used to. In a film that boasted of male credentials like Naseeruddin Shah, Imran Hashmi and Tushaar Kapoor, with 'Dabangg' having recently captured the imagination of distributors and the audience alike, the success of 'Dirty Picture' was more pointed due to its ability in collecting almost the same money as 'Dabangg'.

She rose even higher with another one called 'Kahaani'.

Teen Sey Chhey

"Woh ek Kahani thi- Inspector Satyoki Sinha

Directed by Sujoy Ghosh, a name not known in the realm of hindi films, 'Kahani' became a standout example of a film shot as an art film amalgamating in to a massive commercial success.

An unknown, heavily pregnant woman from London, lands at the Netaji Subhash Bose international airport, Kolkata in search of her missing husband. He was last known to have come on an assignment to Kolkata. Now, he has become incommunicado with her and the rest of the world. The distraught wife lands in a city where she knows no one, has no friends, no place to stay and no leads. But how she alone and determinedly decides to venture into her own investigative journey to know the fate of her husband is what this film is about.

She has to face reluctant policemen, unwilling neighbors, rude government officials and blank leads. Fighting off all the negative factors she tries hard to connect with strangers. She realizes that in a man's world her tenacity is her biggest weapon. The poignancy of her grief can be felt when after another day of slow progress she can let loose her grief, only during nightfall, in the little room of her lodge where unobserved, she can cry copiously.

Vidya Balan as the protagonist 'Vidya Bagchi' (pronounced as Bidya in the Kolkata parlance) had a rather difficult role to enact. Not only did she have to shoulder a film sans a mainstream hero but she also had to conceal her sex appeal, which was one of the main stays in her last 'The Dirty Picture'; yet, both grossed 100 crores.

Director Sujoy Ghosh with his own screenplay & story sets you on a remarkable journey through the city. Questions lingering in the woman's mind also become a metaphor for the city's constant struggle in finding a place of calm, for searching truth in the maze of uncertainties. The screenplay befriends the viewers with Kolkata, where the jostling of daily commuters, the chores of the countless people and how they labour to move the wheels of this city. But in the midst of daily prattle there are other murky factors lurking in the dark, trailing her, waiting for an opportune moment to wipe out the truth. All these events, give a gritty look to the investigations by the lonely lady who is fearlessly trying to look beyond the murkiness.'Walk Alone' a poem written by Tagore tempers her steely resolve in moving ahead (Amitabh Bachchan's brilliant rendering is like the metaphor of your own inner voice singing aloud)

Amongst all the innocence & uncertainties arrives the festival of 'Durga Puja'. Like the first light of dawn that extinguishes the night; where the Goddess dispels fears, ushers in happiness and brings forth justice. In a chilling twist towards the end, she interlopes on the visage of the goddess 'Durga'. What happened in the end is not meant to be revealed here but what stood out was the fearless persona of 'Vidya Bagchi' enacted excellently by Vidya Balan.

With Bollywood being harnessed by the new generation woman, one more shone out loud and bright. A young girl called Kangna Ranaut. Coming from the interiors of Haryana she in fact ran the risk of almost getting excommunicated. She landed in Mumbai and very soon, after dabbling in photo shoots and few modeling assignments, she was noticed in Anurag Basu's 'Life in a Metro'. This led her to be cast as one of three protagonists in Madhur Bhandarkar's film called 'Fashion' which was based on the behind-the-scene going-ons of the fashion industry. In the midst of Priyanka Chopra, and the likes of Mughda Godse, Kitu Gidwani, Suchitra Pillai- she stood out as the bold 'Shonali' who succumbs to drugs and an abusive boyfriend. Kangna Ranaut broke the ceiling by bagging a National Award in the 'best supporting actress ' category. With another successful film called 'Tanu weds Manu' in between, she quickly replaced Vidya Balan whose fall was as swift as her rise. After promising to engulf us with more surprises Vidya Balan instead, buried herself and us all under terrible films like 'Shaadi Ke Side Effects' opposite Farhan Akhtar, 'Ghanchakkar' opposite Imran Hashmi and 'Hamari Adhoori Kahani' touted as a 'Mahesh Bhatt special'. But with Fridays packed with unpredictability, even Kangna Ranaut's rise got check mated by the startling yet deserving success of Mahesh Bhatt's daughter Alia. After debuting in Karan Johar's 'Student of the Year,' she cast all asunder with Imtiaz Ali's 'Highway.

What really stood tall with its tale of zestful, modern times was Zoya Akhtar's (writer Javed Akhtar's daughter) debut film as director in a film called 'Zindagi Na Milegi Dobara'.

"Dilon mein tum apni betaabiyaan leke chal rahe ho to zinda ho tum'-Imraan

Three strapping young dudes, get one big reason to come together, as one of them, Kabir(Abhay Deol) has decided to get married. Even though he is a trifle unsure about his decision nonetheless he wants to celebrate a memorable 'bachelor party' by taking his two buddies on a long sojourn to Spain. Imran (Farhan Akhtar) is a copywriter at work in Delhi but poet at heart while Arjun (Hrithik) is a glum faced stock broker from London whose prime goal in life is to anchor an "early retirement' plan, even if that means to set a trade off by metamarphosing into a 'dull jack '.

These are the hard shells where these three have crawled into and as the trip to Spain unfolds the script rolls out the various demons the trio attempt to cast away and shun their false exteriors.Their journey across the length and breadth of Spain is beautifully spelt on film. Their inner renaissance of following their hearts is brought out by their metaphoric attempts in hair raising sports like scuba diving or leaping mid air from an airplane to fall like a stone till the last second when parachutes open up.

This 'joie de vivre' contained a bagful of lessons with well etched roles. Hrithik Roshan as the hardnosed business broker with a condescending attitude towards love and anything mushy, Farhan Akhtar as the easy going bloke but a trifle reserved and Abhay Deol as the main protagonist who orchestrates the whole trip. Their friendship is a refection of today's times; those familiar phone calls; those drinking sessions that appear topical. Katrina Kaif as the love interest 'Laila' looks good and so are her attempts in drawing the banker into her pangs of love. Their travels, on a vintage Chevrolet car gave you that old feel from Zoya Akhtar brother's 'Dil Chahta Hai'. Naseeruddin Shah in a small role looked sick, old and very lost in Spain but the film landed Zoya smoothly in to bollywood.

Salman Khan by now had become the by-word for attaining the magical 100 crores. His latest film called 'Ready' – an ordinary one, in no time breezed that figure. But it was'Bajrangi Bhaijaan' which proved his success was no fluke.

With an armour of 100 crores wrapped around and wearing the crown of one of the biggest non-profit NGO called 'Being Human', people examined their new 'Bhaijaan' with greater interest.

He played 'Bajrangi' , an academically disinclined man from Haryana who has no goal in life. He is happy with his simple needs and has implicit faith in his 'only God', the mace wielding 'Hanuman'. Fed up of his 'zero' results, his father a professional wrestler sends him to Delhi to assist his old friend.

But Bajrangi get's more than he can handle; The pretty daughter(Kareena Kapoor) of his new master falls in love with him and a little mute girl Shahida, who is actually lost, crosses his path. Bajrangi is shy and for him 'Brahmacharya' is the foremost of all. (You can watch his hesitation in rolling up his sleeves to flaunt the rippling muscles beneath them, even when goaded by the beautiful Kareena)

Shahida , the mute girl, lives in an extremely beautiful green valley beside a foaming river, whistling waterfalls and chirping birds. Her father tends to sheep while her mother looks after their little wooden hut. But there is a hiccup; her home is located in an area called 'Azaad Kasmir' on her side and despised as POK ('Pakistan-occupied-Kashmir') the opposite side. Bajrangi faces a daunting task now of watching the little girl being either cast off by the do-gooders of society in to the bazaars of vice or, rescuing her to reunite with her unseen parents in a hostile country. It is a difficult decision for the 'goalless bajrangi' but the simpleton obeys his inner voice. With his belief in 'Bajrangbali' his only strength, the man goes forth on a long and arduous journey fraught with risks. Carrying the little Shahida, Bajrangi with his few belongings sets out on his mission.'Bajrangi Bhaijaan' reintroduced Salman Khan in a new avatar. It discarded all that was symbolic in Salman's films earlier. Kabir Khan the director, sent his famed torso to 'sleep' mode and concealed his fabled biceps inside loose khadi shirts. It was not about riding his physique nor about gaining brownie points in drumming beats of Indo-Pak jingoism. Bajrangi-Bhaijaan was a simple tale of a tough man staying true to his heart.

The demographic scenario in the country was changing. To the envy of the world, India's population was the youngest. In line with the emerging changes, start-ups with a larger tilt of obeying one's heart began witnessing a surge in myriad business ideas throwing up several young poster boys, invading Indian corporates and the bourses.Most of them invented some form of convenience for customers by creating app-based technologies by burning their midnight oil inside some garage or an attic. Few of them also tossed away their well-paying jobs to find their true calling in music. 'Rock-On' was based on one such aspiration.

Directed by a failed actor called Abhishek Kapoor, the film starred Farhan Akhtar, Arjun Rampal, Purab Kohli and Luke Kenny. They play five close friends who pursue their heart's desire of making it big in the world of music while at the same time struggle to meet their regular expenses. Desperate in their quest for a viable break, they are literally forced to swallow their pride by editing away their own compositions and make way for lyrics that is not in sync with their heart. That is when, Joe (Arjun Rampal), explodes physically on the producer and when Aditya (Farhan) tells him to stifle his fury Joe punches him back. Some more harsh words and fistcuffs shatter their dreams and tears apart their friendship. Years pass and the four are shown existing in a humdrum way-where music has no place. The narration cuts back to the present, where the four: 'Kedar' the drummer (Purab Kohli) is managing his father's shop.'Aditya' the lead singer (Farhan Akhtar) is an investment banker 'Joe Mascarenhas' lead guitarist(Arjun Rampal) is now assisting his wife in her fishing business, while Rob (Luke Kenny) makes ends meet by composing jingles for advertisements.

The four are reunited chiefly due to the efforts by Aditya's wife Sakshi (Prachi Desai) who discovers that her husband's true love lay in music.

The throbbing success of 'Rock On' had a total Farhan Akhtar flavor. As an actor he was not only one of the four protagonists but also the film's producer and even sang for himself.. Even though directed by a rookie called Abhishek Kapoor, 'Rock On' appeared thematically a close cousin of Farhan Akhtar's directorial debut 'Dil Chahta Hai'. While

'Dil Chahta Hai' was more about the pangs of friendship sans any goal, 'Rock On' was about friendship gone sour because of a goal. That singular act when Joe (Arjun Rampal) boxes the producer is where the point tips the cross-over act. Aditya (Farhan) is already weighed down by an albatross of having swallowed humble pie when he diluted original terms in the contract, but while he and his friends agree to it as a necessary evil, it proves to be unacceptable for Joe. And that's when the chasm appears.

The success of 'Rock-On' made Farhan Akhtar, perhaps, the first successful director to also emerge as a serious contender for the actor's throne. From 'Dil Chahta Hai', to 'Rock On' and 'Zindagi na Milegi Dobara' he was proving to be excellent in any hat that he wore: director, actor, singer. Trust him to break fresh ground which he did immediately with Rakesh Om Praksh Mehra's biopic on Milkha Singh-'The Flying Sikh'. This one did not feed upon his directorial skills or his vocals. Rakesh Mehra was clear of what he expected Farhan to do: to run and get fit for the role of India's most famed sprinter.

It would be an understatement to say that for the role of Milkha he took to it much as a fish takes to water. After several weeks of gruelling schedules at the gym he acquired that fitness what Rakesh had in mind. Weeks of running marathons helped develop that lean hungry look of a man, willing to run miles so as to 'binge on milk'- " *doodh milega yaar* "felt actually real. The rigorous discipline and his yearning to break free of the partition pangs made the viewers empathise with the young Milkha and when he outraced the Pakistani athlete in the climax, people erupted with joy. That epoch moment, when Pakistan's Prime Minister non-grudgingly calls him the 'flying sikh' was potrayed diligently. Even though the film had actress Sonam Kapoor playing his love interest, however, the focus was more about the horrors of partition that had become deeply embedded in the boy's mind and how he overcomes all to emerge as the famed runner. 'Bhag-Milkha-Bhag' smoothened out the dent on Rakesh Mehra's track record caused by 'Delhi-6'and Farhan Akhtar was now on a new plane that directly put him in to confrontation with the other contenders. But soon to the disappointment of many, films like 'Wazir', 'Rockon2', 'Lucknow Central' and the recent 'Sky is Pink' has blown away his chances.

'Wazir' was made by Vidhu Chopra and its failure did rock Farhan's cart. But Amitabh shrugged it off with the success of 'Pink', a hard hitting film on the issues of womanhood. The basic premise was whether woman should have the choice in what they wear, what they drink who they sleep with ? Is sex a man's right or a woman's prerogative? Should men respect their affirmations or should they just toss out when she refuses? The old had to be rewritten; from girls remaining coy in their salwar-kameez to the shedding of virginity was factored beneath metaphors of thunder, lightning if it was a 'NO' or a pair of flowers nestling each other under a hovering bee if a 'YES'. But that was four decades ago. Those days only vamps smoked and drank and only villains filled up their 'Vat-69' while the 'Good fellow' devoured 'gaajar-ka-halwa'. The three girls in 'Pink'who agree to party with three guys are hauled up in jail and land in court just because they said 'no'. As their lawyer Deepak Sehgal who is old, retired and a bit whimsical in his mind, Amitabh was brilliant. In far off times Amitabh fought with his fists to gain justice and today the old man as Deepak Sehgal uses his baritone and knowledge of the law. He stares at Minal Arora, the victim, and asks her point blank:"Are you a virgin'? The court is stunned. He stuns them again by saying: " when did you lose it?", " were you paid"? Minal is shaken but stifles her hiccups and reveals truthfully that she is not and she had liked someone long back and it was mutual. This is the moment of epiphany that Sehgal wants to show the judge, that by merely indulging in an act long ago in no way stigmatizes a woman nor diminishes her self respect- a 'No' means no. The film rightfully won a 'National award'.

In the case of the Kapoor grandson, Ranbir once again got besmirched in consecutive big-budget flops. They were the ones that held promise of crowning this scion of the first family. But reality proved to be something else. The rising glory of 'Yeh Jawani Hai Dewani ' also gave rise to equally huge surge of expectations. Soon enough some really big films looked forward to by the masses were released. They were 'Roy', produced by the T-Series Banner and 'Bombay Velvet' made by the dark specialist called Anurag Kashyap. The biggest USP of 'Bombay Velvet' was Karan Johar playing the villain's part. However, 'Bombay Velvet' proved to be an insult to film making; People fled out of theaters with splitting head aches, cursing their fate. No body had a clue as to what this film was about!

The next film called 'Roy' sank without a trace and another one called 'Besharam' sank with a lot of pre-release hullabaloo;

'Besharam' to the disbelief of all was the second offering from the director's baton of Abhinav Kashyap who had directed 'Dabangg. However for reasons unknown Abhinav split from the 'Dabangg' franchise and set forth in another direction. The result was a shoddy produce that shocked all. Abhinav since then is not seen around and it took a couple of years for Ranbir to stand up and walk. He was lucky to to be rescued by Vinod Chopra-Rajkumar combo who took him in the title role of 'Sanju'. With a business of more than 300 crores Ranbir not only saved himself but also came to eye level with another contender- Ranvir Singh who had just grown several feet taller from the twin successes of Sanjay Leela Bhansali's 'Bajirao-Mastani' and the rajasthani saga 'Padmavat'.

Medieval Rajasthan is imbued with many tales of chivalry and valour. Where men and women, wear martyrdom as a badge of honour. Facts which have over a period of centuries acquired legendary hues. 'Padmavat' is one such historical fact.

Bhansali's film not only narrates 'Padmavati's' short life but also enumerates the way of life during those times and dissects the characters of the two men directly linked to her name; her husband Rana Rawal who ruled Chittor and Alauddin Khilji who ruled Delhi.

<u>The Story</u>

Alauddin was the nephew of Sultan Jalaluddin Khilji who ruled Delhi. This ambitious man bides his time and thru crafty means married the Sultan's daughter Mehrunissa and soon, with gold looted from the Deccan kingdom he bought off the Sultanate and assassinates his father in law. Alauddin is now the new Sultan of the Delhi Sultanate and has everything he wished to possess; the most of Northern India under his command, immense wealth, and a large harem. But a challenge soon emerges in the form of a disgruntled sorcerer-cum-priest from the Court of Chittor who has an axe to grind by exacting revenge on the Rana and his beautiful wife Padmavati. His instigation works well enough to spur the sultan in invading Chittor. The army of Rana Rawal Singh is no match to the superior army and weapons of the Sultan. Forced in to a cul-de-sac, the Rana and his army ride out to fight their last battle while their wives led by Padmavati embrace death by committing 'jauhar'.

The Film

Deepika Padukone as Rani Padmavati exudes Royal charm. As the young princess from the land of Singala she is quite comfortable as the agile warrior princess wielding a bow and sufficiently demure as the girl in love with the young prince who has come to her father's kingdom in search of some rare pearls. Her quick transformation as the Queen of Chittor is grandly portrayed in the richly choreographed 'Ghoomar' song. Her moment of triumph, though, comes in the climax when to the beats of cymbals, chanting of shlokas, looking ethereal in a blood red ghagra she walks head held high holding the print of her husband's palm on a shroud, as she fearlessly enters the blazing pyre.

Shahid Kapur's perfectly sculpted body cloaked in exquisite tunics, strong arm clasping a broad hilted sword indeed completed the regal persona of the 'Rana'...as the stern, yet soft spoken Rana Rawal Singh he underplays his role, yet stands out when he proclaims aloud the necessitates of rajput valour and grabs your ears thru dialogues such as these:

"He, who impales worries on the tip of his sword...is a Rajput"

"He, who is beheaded yet goads his torso to battle...is a Rajput"

But it is Ranveer Singh as 'Alauddin' who is in top form as the maniacal, barbaric Sultan. Led by the director he is greatly aided by the entire back end; the dialogues, the make -up, choreography, script writer, action and the director. For a villain, he receives an apt makeover thru a get up that consists of shoulder length hair, unkempt beard and tell-tale scars on his face that gives out a repulsive feel.

Here the director swings a loop. The supposed 'villain' is not only given equally powerful dialogues but also makes him appear in almost the entire screen play. He woos a princess, loots gold, ravishes women with devilish glee and chomps like a glutton on heaps of meat. He burns historical parchments, tries his hand in composing some self-serving verses and then, sets his sights on the fabled queen of Chittor. Ranveer Singh as 'Alauddin' acts like the Devil, frowns like a tyrant, fights like a lion, sways like a dervish and dances like a blood thirsty wolf, in a song filled with Arabic words with emphasis on the word '*Habibi*' which means love and '*Khalbali*' which means disturbance or anarchy. This song-dance actually revealed a restless spirit residing within 'Alauddin' as he grapples with the responsibilities of a ruler, unbridled greed, fighting off conspiracies and searching for love that is proving elusive. The director also delves in to a humane side when 'Alauddin' considers himself to be 'unlucky in love'. He asks his confidant "whether his palm has the lines of love '. So did he want to ravish Padmavati like he did to innumerable women or he wanted to make her his queen ? The title 'Padmavat' perhaps, is a misnomer; it should have been 'Alauddin"

Scenes worth Rewinding:

- The question and answer session where the Queen intelligently replies to questions by the priest.

- The 'Ghoomar' song inside the Chittor fort with ghagras of many patched colours twirl in rhythmic synchronization to the old ballad. A thousand or more lamps glowing bright from every corner of the fort, you are almost transported to that Era.

- The battle scene between Alauddin's forces and the Mongols. From the gigantic clouds of dust rising under galloping hooves, Alauddin rides out with the chieftain's head impaled on his spear.

- The induction of Malik Kafur as Alauddin's slave. He proves his unquestionable loyalty by swiftly killing his new master's opponents and moves up the scale in palace intrigue by becoming his confidant. Malik who is an eunuch secretly nurses an attraction for his master but he knows that his handicap can never help him gain coital alignment. This fact is clearly brought out in the song '*Bin te dil Miseriya...*" While his master makes love to a woman from the harem, Malik faithfully draws a curtain but his face wears a longing look betraying his desires!

- When the Chittor fort trembles under the advancing army of Alauddin, rattling mirrors inside Padmavati's chambers setting in to motion battle stations all over the fortress.

- During peace overtures which lead to a symbolic lunch inside the fort, Alauddin quickly scans every inch of the walls around hoping to catch a glimpse of the beautiful Queen. Emboldened by the courtesy shown by his host he makes the cardinal mistake of enquiring about her to be rudely shaken apart by the unsheathing of several swords pointing his neck.

- After the gruelling duel with Alauddin, the Rana is almost getting the better of his opponent when a hail of arrows pierce his back. With life ebbing away, he still wears his rajput badge of honour by attempting several thrusts to strike down his foe

- Alauddin standing on the desert plains below the fort as his massive army with giant catapults wait behind for his signal. Like a besotted puppy he keeps waiting expectantly for Padmavati to emerge from the fort. As the truth dawns in the futility of his patience, he whispers reluctantly: "Yalgaar Ho !"

'Sanju' and 'Padmavat' collectively raked in revenues of more than 600 crores, which is almost five percent of total revenues from the industry. The sheer weight of these figures catapults the two young men, after the three Khans, in to the league of final contenders for the throne of Bollywood.

The sixth, Akshay Kumar, whose rise to fame on a platter full of 'Khiladi' prefixed films by sheer dint and hardwork and on the virtue of remaining bankable, stands strong as one of the six contenders. His background of being a martial arts exponent and his off-screen image of being a teetotaller and a fitness freak has greatly contributed in retaining his sheen. Interestingly, by putting a stop to any further milking of the 'khiladi' moniker and delving majorly in to socially relevant issues thru films like 'Padman', and 'Toilet:Ek Prem Katha' winning him many plaudits proves that he has some more aces to show.

The supremacy of the 'Three Khans' still runs deep. The first, with the 400 crore'Dangal' has been able to lock himself for posterity. The second, after his spit-fire success a decade ago has gone beyond 'Dabangg'; Besides being an extremely fruitful franchise he has proved to be a sort of Midas in churning out 100 plus crore nuggets in the form of 'Sultan', the 'Tiger' series and even the insipid 'Tubelight'.

The third Khan has been seesawing; almost derailed by 'Chennai Express', blown off with 'Harry Meets Sejal' but bounced back with 'Raees'. Nonetheless his stardom is strong enough to withstand a few flops.

Epilogue

"Kal khel mein hum ho na ho gardish mein taarey rahengey sadaa, bhoologe tum bhoolenge woh, par hum tumhare rahenge sadaa"---Raju the Joker.

The world is everchanging; so is the world of films.

From the Three Greats only Dilip Kumar is around. Raj Kapoor, the eternal shoulder for the underdogs passed away in 1987; while accepting the 'Dadasaheb Phalke' award he collapsed on stage to never come back. Dev Anand passed away in 2011 at the ripe old age of 87. His banner 'Navketan' is lying inactive and his son Suneil is perhaps not interested in reviving it.

The senior Kapoors have all passed away. Shammi Kapoor the 'Yahoo' man retired at a ripe old age and spent his later years as the 'Chairman of the Internet Association'. He passed away in 2011 when he had just turned 80. His children remain outside filmdom. Shashi Kapoor passed away in 2017 of old age. His children Kunal, Karan and Sanjana are no longer active in the industry. The sons of Raj Kapoor: Randhir and Rajeev are retired, while Rishi rightfully enjoys a great second innings.

'Bimal Roy Pictures' seem to have been inactive since the time of its founder's demise. He is survived by his son Joy

Bimal Roy and two daughters. They are not involved in film making.

The other great banner B.R.Films, which gave us the first multistarrer is inactive and Ravi Chopra is rarely heard of. After giving a line up of big budget failures and failing to enter the 100 crore club, former 'Showman' Subhash Ghai seems to have more or less retired; he is currently busy managing 'Whispering Woods', an acting school which he opened a decade ago. Director N.Chandra who brought forth the angst of Mumbai's suburbs, is no longer heard of and is perhaps enjoying his retirement. Old money- bag producers Mushir and Riaz are also not to be heard of. Big Banners of yore like Manmohan Desai's 'MKD Films' who gave us great films on brotherhood, and Prakash Mehra's 'PMP' productions, the fountain head of the 'angry' sagas and Feroz Khan's 'FK International' which personified 'Style', have wound up with the passing away of their creators. 'Trimurti Films' whose logo, represented the triumvirate of the cosmic world- the pantheon of Brahma-Vishnu-Mahesh had at one time been an of emblem of 'Big' films. However their urge to remain big seems to have dimmed in today's times. 'Nasir Husaain Productions', a banner synonymous with great musicals also seems to have shut shop.

Yash Chopra, the original dream-maker, passed away in 2012 while his son Aditya is actively operating the YRF empire. His brother Uday is also known to be a producer of English films.

Superstar Rajesh Khanna passed away in 2012 and his iconic bungalow 'Aashirwad' was sold off by his family. Nargis

Dutt, passed away in 1980 and two and half decades later her husband Sunil Dutt. Their son Sanjay completed the price of his blunder and today is very much active in the industry. Dharmendra our very own 'Samson' is hale and hearty. He spends time mostly at his farmhouse in Lonavala, near Mumbai and regales people with interesting couplets. Vinod Khanna recently passed away while Shatrughan Sinha launched his autobiography, dabbles in politics but continues to remain disgruntled. Tallest of them all, Amitabh Bachchan, who is still very involved and revered, just bagged a well-deserved 'Dadasaheb Phalke'award.

Mahesh Bhatt is still at the forefront and so is his banner, 'Vishesh Films'. We hope he can rekindle old sparks and one day give us something as memorable as 'Saaransh'.

Karan Johar's 'Dharma Productions' is currently one of the biggest banners in the country. His forte lies in introducing promising artistes and bankrolling potent scripts with talented directors.

Javed Akhtar is very much up and about. He still regales us all by writing lyrics and poems for himself and his children's productions. Salim Khan his erstwhile partner has truly retired. As any doting father he is perhaps seated on an armchair in his sea-facing apartment, savouring the success of his son.

'Rajshri Productions' still hope that their scion will one day pull out a hat-trick. 'Prem Ratan Dhan Payo' his film with Salman Khan, was a hit and made good money but that was primarily because of Salman's charisma; it lacked the epic qualities of the films that made Sooraj Barjatya. We hope he will one day regain his magic and, like me, many millions too look forward to that moment.

Rakesh Roshan and his banner 'FilmKraft' is still active, however, unlike YRF it mostly prefers to make films with Hrithik Roshan as their lead star. Sometimes I do wonder, what if Rakesh Roshan had directed Amitabh Bachchan in a spit-fire commercial film?

Jeetendra, now recalled as 'Natyasamrat' by netizens, is retired but ventures out as usual, in a dapper way. His banner 'Balaji Pictures' is active and managed by his son and daughter.

Mithun Chakraborty former 'Disco King' occasionally appears as a judge in some 'dance' based reality shows. In today's times, blogs know him as 'Prabhuji'.

Ashutosh Gowariker, the maker who reintroduced India to the concept of historicals and showed us pages from history is currently immersed in some new projects. History, particularly of India, is filled with countless names of kings and queens, poets and saints. Her pot of parables and legends is filled across to its brim. Hopefully, through him, and Sanjay Bhansali we shall get a peek in to more of them soon

Historicals is not every one's cup of tea and their prohibitive budgets deter players. The preferred landscapes in today's offerings are mostly based as social dramas coming out of mofussil towns with characters mouthing spit-fire dialogues whose pace takes time to set in. Music too has mostly been relegated to post climactic moments when the mandatory titles roll out.

Franchisees continue to rake in money and many banners own a successful one; 'Housefull' belongs to the Nadiadwala Banner; 'Dhoom' and the 'Tiger series'belongs to YRF, 'Golmaal' belongs to Rohit Shetty, 'Dabangg' belongs to Salman Khan Productions.

The future of 'Bollywood' continues to shimmer. As per an earlier article in the 'Economic Times' this fact is highlighted with glowing figures which is mentioned verbatim:

Revenues from the Hindi film industry are likely to cross 19,300 crore and the current estimated size; as of 2016 is 15,500 crore. Box office collections in India that are estimated at over 11,500 crore are likely to cross 14200 crore mark by 2017 and will account for about 74% of the majority of Bollywood revenues" said the joint study conducted by Assocham and Deloitte. The industry's overseas box office collections are likely to cross 1300 crore from current size of 1100 crore,it said. Rising demand for movies on TV along wth growing penetration of smartphones across the country will spur growth in cable and satellite rights. Online and digital aggregation revenues are likely to grow at a compounded annual growth rate of about 15%.The study noted that the home video industry will further shrink at a CAGR of 10% due to increasing piracy and growing popularity of digital platforms. "Home video has lost share to video on demand (VoD) through direct to home (DTH) operators and over the top(OTT) platforms,"the study added. Noting that the regional movies are gaining popularity in India and abroad, it said that cinema in southern India especially Tamil and Telugu may soon dethrone Bollywood from the top spot which accounts for 43% share in terms of box office collections by language. Large national producers plan to spend 20% of their annual budgets on regional cinema.

Couple of years back, the three Khans crossed fifty. Three decades ago, or slightly more, since they debuted, they have been in the thick of many planes; the highs of several hits; lows of shocking flops; of walking down paths of an unsure future and also fighting off the efforts of several colleagues, to emerge triumphant.

Nevertheless, in a couple of years, on one of those 'Friday', this supremacy might just melt away. The invincible Aamir did face rough weather in 'Thugs of Hindustan'. Shah Ruk's latest 'Fan' and 'Zero'is also a case in point; as 'Gaurav' the prosthetics enabled character, it failed to endear. Salman's orbit of success too has been hit by 'high on revenues-low- on-quality' fare like 'Race3' and 'Bharat'. Can his banner'Salman Khan Productions' look beyond relatives and become a powerhouse vertical remains to be seen.

Many makers over the years, have mulled the idea of bringing the 'Three Khans' together. Such a gigantic thought has indeed lost its moment. The stature of the Three, in last few years, has grown to an immeasureable height; with each of them being followed by 40 million fans on 'Twitter' they have travelled beyond all realms. In today's times, where casting the three would not only be financially prohibitive, even conjuring up a two hundred and thirty minutes of extravaganza that can give justice to the three can remain a vexing issue.

The recent successes of actors Ayushmann Khurana and Rajkumar Rao,Varun Dhawan and Tiger Shroff, may be ringing in the end of 'superstardom'.

Fridays will continue to come, and many more will continue to walk in to its embrace, but the old days of a singular force straddling the landscape, leading us all towards a 'housefull' board is perhaps a thing of the past.

Acknowledgement & Sources

- 'Trash lovers Paradise': fb page

- Rediff.com

- 'The Hindu' October 2016: 'Chupke Chupke'

- 'Filmfare'

- 'Screen'; 1981, 1989

- 'Forty Retakes': by Avijit Ghosh

- 'Written by Salim-Javed': Diptakriti Chaudhary

- Cine Blitz

- Stardust

- Movie

- 'Lehren'